Trans Biblical

"These essays offer a balm for troubled times through their oh-so-human efforts to make meaning anew, today, in relation to ancient sacred texts. In placing fraught contemporary questions of transness and gender squarely within traditions of scriptural hermeneutics, they reach below the superficial present to touch something profound in the depths that desperately needs to be surfaced in the here and now."

—Susan Stryker, author of *Transgender History*, coeditor of *The Transgender Studies Reader* volumes, and founding coeditor of *TSQ: Transgender Studies Quarterly*

"*Trans Biblical* is an essential collection that zooms both out and in, highlighting trans forms of analysis and action that can connect us, as well as forms of identity that make us unique. The contributors move boldly beyond passages and interpretations that have become staples in the genre, and I found myself pulled into new waters, buoyed by curiosity, wonder, and the sensation of being seen. I can't wait to have this book on my shelf."

—Austen Hartke, author of *Transforming: The Bible and the Lives of Transgender Christians* and founder of Transmission Ministry Collective

"Joseph A. Marchal, Melissa Harl Sellew, and Katy E. Valentine have compiled an impressive work on biblical interpretation from trans perspectives and experiences that are not limited to trans persons. The contributions move beyond the theoretical to the practical and pedagogical, covering texts from the Hebrew Bible, New Testament, rabbinic literature, and early Christian writings. Among the chapters are an excellent overview of the intersection of trans history and biblical interpretation and a reconsideration of the trans-cis binary and the trans*ness of John's Jesus using an African communal hermeneutic. The volume is fresh, engaging, and insightful. Explicit and implicit pedagogies are among the book's strongest features."

—Wil Gafney, author of *Womanist Midrash*, vols. 1 and 2, and Right Rev. Sam B. Hulsey Professor of Hebrew Bible, Brite Divinity School

"*Trans Biblical* gathers a remarkable collection of reflections, provocations, and interventions in biblical, religious, and gender, feminist, queer, and sexuality studies that together invite new ways of thinking and speaking about bodies, Scriptures, transformations, and historical as well as interpretive significance. Ambitious in theoretical and historical scope, the volume moves from the Hebrew Bible and the New Testament to rabbinic and early Christian literatures, addressing pedagogy, epistemology, (in)visibility, and corporeal change. Accessible, decisive, and nuanced, this book provides readers with urgently required words and concepts as together we face 'the biblical' in all its horror and potential."

—Jennifer Wright Knust, Professor of Religious Studies, Duke University

"*Trans Biblical* is a landmark publication—a timely arrival amid the current flux of toxic debate, embattled positions, and violence. Always compelling, occasionally haunting, often surprising, the insights of its impressive contributors demonstrate the continued relevance of ancient texts for trans identities, bodies, histories, and culture."

—Deryn Guest, Senior Lecturer in Biblical Hermeneutics,
University of Birmingham

"Wide-ranging and comprehensive, *Trans Biblical* offers not just a window onto but an inviting doorway into the robust and sophisticated state of trans biblical studies, with contributions from many of the foremost scholars in this increasingly well-established field. This collection is a superb resource for anyone seeking a more informed perspective on transness in the Bible than what is generally on offer in contemporary politics and popular media."

—Melissa M. Wilcox, Professor and Holstein Family and Community Chair,
Department for the Study of Religion, University of California, Riverside

"This exciting volume opens up a number of new paths in biblical scholarship. By highlighting the perspectives of trans people, the importance of gender variation, and insights from trans studies, the authors expand our understanding of both biblical texts and biblical interpretation. The diverse, innovative essays collected here will become necessary reference points for anyone working on gender in biblical studies."

—Ken Stone, Distinguished Service Professor and Professor of Bible,
Culture, and Hermeneutics, Chicago Theological Seminary

"*Trans Biblical* is not only groundbreaking but also important work that has potential to disrupt identitarian logics that have undergirded much of the queer scholarship in the study of theology and ethics. This book serves scholars and practitioners with insightful essays that will advance queer and trans scholarship in the study of religion, along with theology, biblical studies, and ethics. Embodying a somatic hermeneutical lens is at the core of *Trans Biblical*. I highly recommend it!"

—Roberto Che Espinoza, founder, Our Collective Becoming,
and Visiting Professor, Duke University Divinity School

Trans Biblical

New Approaches to Interpretation and Embodiment in Scripture

Edited by Joseph A. Marchal,
Melissa Harl Sellew, and Katy E. Valentine

© 2025 Westminster John Knox Press

First Edition
Published by Westminster John Knox Press
Louisville, Kentucky

25 26 27 28 29 30 31 32 33 34—10 9 8 7 6 5 4 3 2 1

All rights reserved. No part of this book may be reproduced or transmitted in any form or by any means, electronic or mechanical, including photocopying, recording, or by any information storage or retrieval system, without permission in writing from the publisher. For information, address Westminster John Knox Press, 100 Witherspoon Street, Louisville, Kentucky 40202-1396. Or contact us online at www.wjkbooks.com.

Unless otherwise indicated, Scripture quotations are from the *New Revised Standard Version, Updated Edition,* copyright © 2021 National Council of Churches of Christ in the United States of America. Used by permission. All rights reserved worldwide. Scripture quotations marked JPS are from *The TANAKH: The New JPS Translation according to the Traditional Hebrew Text.* Copyright 1985 by the Jewish Publication Society. Used by permission. Scripture quotations marked NIV are from the Holy Bible, New International Version. Copyright © 1973, 1978, 1984, 2011 by Biblica, Inc.® Used by permission. All rights reserved worldwide. Scripture quotations marked NRSV are from the New Revised Standard Version of the Bible, copyright © 1989 by the Division of Christian Education of the National Council of the Churches of Christ in the U.S.A. Used by permission.

Parts of chapter 1 are adapted from chapter 2 of Max K. Strassfeld, *Trans Talmud: Androgynes and Eunuchs in Rabbinic Literature* (Oakland: University of California Press, 2022), used by permission of the University of California Press, and from "Translating the Human: The *Androginos* in Tosefta Bikurim," in *TSQ: Transgender Studies Quarterly* vol. 3, nos. 3–4 (2016): 587–604. Copyright 2016, Duke University Press. All rights reserved. Republished by permission of the copyright holder and the publisher. www.dukeupress.edu.

Book design by Sharon Adams
Cover design by Kevin van der Leek

Library of Congress Cataloging-in-Publication Data

Names: Marchal, Joseph A., editor. | Sellew, Melissa Harl, editor. | Valentine, Katy E., editor.
Title: Trans biblical : new approaches to interpretation and embodiment in scripture / edited by Joseph A. Marchal, Melissa Harl Sellew, and Katy E. Valentine.
Description: First edition. | Louisville, Kentucky : Westminster John Knox Press, [2025] | Includes bibliographical references and indexes. | Summary: "Provides exciting new scholarly work in trans biblical interpretation to help us better understand our Bibles, our bodies, and one another in a fraught and fractious world"-- Provided by publisher.
Identifiers: LCCN 2025001918 (print) | LCCN 2025001919 (ebook) | ISBN 9780664268893 (paperback) | ISBN 9781646984176 (ebook)
Subjects: LCSH: Bible--Transgender interpretations.
Classification: LCC BS511.3 .T75 2025 (print) | LCC BS511.3 (ebook) | DDC 220.086/7--dc23/eng/20250221
LC record available at https://lccn.loc.gov/2025001918
LC ebook record available at https://lccn.loc.gov/2025001919

Most Westminster John Knox Press books are available at special quantity discounts when purchased in bulk by corporations, organizations, and special-interest groups. For more information, please email SpecialSales@wjkbooks.com.

Contents

Acknowledgments — vii

Abbreviations — xi

Introduction: Variations on Interpretation and Embodiment: Contextualizing Trans Approaches to Scriptures — 1
Joseph A. Marchal with Melissa Harl Sellew and Katy E. Valentine

1. Androgynes, Hybrid Animals, and the Project of Trans History — 31
   Max K. Strassfeld

2. Beyond the Trans/Cis Binary: An Experience-Centered Approach to Teaching and Practicing Trans Hermeneutics — 47
   Joy Ladin

3. Jael's Gender-Ambiguous Motherhood — 65
   Aysha Winstanley Musa

4. "Why Do You Transgress?": Nonbinary Biblical Readings of Mordecai and Beyond — 83
   Esther Brownsmith

5. Walking While Trans on the Jericho Road — 99
   Justin Sabia-Tanis

6. Putting the "Trans" in Transfiguration in Mark 9:1–9 — 117
   Katy E. Valentine

7. Grace, Truth, and Danger: Toward an Africana Queer Trans-Figuration of John 1:14 — 135
   Minenhle Nomalungelo Khumalo and Eric A. Thomas

8. Trans Historiography and the Problem of Anachronism: 151
Eunuchs and Other Non-men in Matthew 19:1–15 and
1 Corinthians 6–7
Rebecca Wiegel

9. This Is My Glorified Body: Pauline Transitions 167
Jaeda C. Calaway

10. Captive Genders, Fugitive Flesh, and Biblical Epistles: 185
Trans Approaches to Ancient Apostles and Assemblies
in the Afterlives of Enslavement and Imprisonment
Joseph A. Marchal

11. Considering the Body with the Gospel of Thomas 203
Melissa Harl Sellew

12. Achilles Breaks Gender: Tertullian's Trans Monster 219
Making in *De Pallio*
Ky Merkley

Bibliography 237

Index of Scripture and Other Ancient Sources 261

Index of Subjects 267

Acknowledgments

Many trans and gender nonconforming people's lives, and indeed many experiences of gender variation, move along timelines that might seem atypical or unconventional to many others. Such descriptions might, in turn, also resonate with the various twists and turns that finally bring this work on trans biblical interpretation into production, and into your hands or devices. These experiences are only complicated, multiplied, or simply compounded by the differential impacts of social, political, and health crises, like COVID, among other persistent pandemics, and all of their associated apocalypses. Likewise, as with many projects that straddle the times before, during, and "after" the COVID pandemic, this project is long-simmering, but we hope now well-seasoned, particularly given so many of the unanticipated delays caused by the various professional and personal challenges faced by nearly every one of the editors and contributors to this volume in this longer-than-expected interim.

This volume draws upon and selects from an increasing, critical mass of scholars interacting with trans studies within (or adjacent to) biblical studies. This attention reflects the work of a growing, but still relatively small, set of trans and gender nonconforming scholars attending and presenting at conferences like the annual meetings of the Society of Biblical Literature. A majority of its essays grow out of two separate yet dynamic annual meeting sessions, sponsored by the LGBTI/Queer Hermeneutics and Gender, Sexuality, and the Bible sections, both of which were lively and well attended. The first was a special session on "The Present and Future of Trans Hermeneutics"—little did we know then how far and how much we were speculating upon multiple futures (of our pasts and presents)! This first session and a specially dedicated follow-up session included several colleagues who presented, presided, responded, or otherwise supported this ongoing project but ultimately could not contribute to this current volume, including incredible scholars like Jo Henderson-Merrygold, Gwynn Kessler, Abby Kulisz, and Josie Wenig. We are thrilled that Jo has completed her dissertation and has revised it for publication since then (for more on her work, see our introduction as well as the essays by Ladin and Brownsmith). Beyond these participants, we also want to thank the colleagues from the SBL committees that sponsored and promoted these sessions, including Rhiannon Graybill, Jimmy

Hoke, Teresa Hornsby, Lynn Huber, Laurel Koepf, Jennifer L. Koosed, Peter Mena, Taylor Petrey, Erin Runions, David Tabb Stewart, and Caryn Tamber-Rosenau, not to mention the many colleagues who attended or engaged any of the presenters within and beyond these sessions, in the hallways, receptions, and curbsides of the conferences, and multiple other sites after, and those who recommended equally fabulous contributors beyond these events. We are thrilled and humbled to bring together what we believe to be the first edited collection of its kind within biblical studies, showcasing a significant number of trans and gender nonconforming scholars.

Among the coeditors, J Marchal would like to acknowledge multiple sources of support and inspiration for the work on their individual essay and the collection as a whole, only some of which they can explicitly name. Given the duration of the development of this project, the research and writing, revisions and elaborations, edits and collaborations were all made possible, in part, by the generous support of the Louisville Institute's Sabbatical Grant for Researchers program (even as any views, findings, conclusions, or recommendations expressed in this project do not necessarily represent those of the Louisville Institute). Many of the details and overarching aims of the introduction and my "Captive Genders" essay were first presented to a special joint session of the Minoritized Criticism and Biblical Interpretation and Racism, Pedagogy, and Biblical Studies sections (at SBL several years ago), and then a special session of the annual Queer and Trans Studies in Religion conference at the University of California Riverside (among other audiences). My own troubled and fluctuating, variable and often vexing sense of my gender is hardly apocryphal, yet neither is it entirely canonical. It is for this and so many other reasons that I remain immensely indebted, in too many ways to name, to my beleaguered and beloved friends, students, collaborators, and other colleagues, who have recurrently, patiently shown me the way.

Melissa Harl Sellew is grateful in the first instance for the many ways in which students, colleagues, family, and friends have responded to her experience of emerging in our professional world in my trans female identity. The invitation from J and Katy to join that first SBL panel on trans hermeneutics offered me my first opportunity to reread the Gospel of Thomas through the lens(es) of gender variance. Planning this volume and bringing it into print was hampered—as so very many projects were—by the shutdown of libraries and loss of personal connection by the arrival of the pandemic and its unanticipated effects, but during all that our contributors waited with patience as we pushed on. Interest and support from faculty members and graduate students at the University of Minnesota as well as the United Theological Seminary of the Twin Cities (where I have taught as a part-time adjunct) have been a true inspiration, along with dear friends at First Congregational Church of Minnesota, UCC. Most meaningful of all has been the constant support and encouragement of my spouse.

Katy E. Valentine thanks her generous spouse who believes in and supports this research and publication. While working on this project, life rolled along in strange, wonderful, and sometimes challenging ways, as it does. Between the beginning conversation with J of "what would a volume maybe look like?" until now, I had an international move, built a coaching practice, and also had a midlife realization that I have ADHD; my coeditors J and Melissa have been more than generous as I've learned to juggle and manage symptoms. Many kudos to Stonewall Alliance Center in Chico, CA, which provides critical services to the wider community and where I spent many fulfilling volunteer hours with heartfelt conversations with members of the trans community. Generous trans people (and a few fierce cis parents) gave their time and stories to me in a series of interviews in 2018–19, and these interviews inspired my contribution on the Transfiguration to this volume. To these and other trans persons who deeply value their relationship to the Divine as living embodiments of the Creator, I offer deep gratitude and acknowledgment with the hopes that this volume reflects a bit of your story and spirit.

The entire editorial team thanks Duke University Press and the University of California Press for permission to publish a revised and reworked version of previous publications by our wonderful colleague Max Strassfeld.

We have been honored and blessed to work with Julie Mullins, who immediately understood what a volume like this could be. Julie's unflagging efforts, in the midst of so many transitions, has been in turn matched by the entire team at Westminster John Knox Press, including José Santana, Julie Tonini, Daniel Braden, Ann DeVilbiss, and Jen Weers, who have capably and graciously delivered us through the final stages and into production. We all hope that this book reaches the audiences we have been anticipating together.

Yet, again and again, we return in gratitude for the early confidence, continued faith, and patient labors of all the contributors to this collection. Getting your work, individually and collectively, into the hands and before the eyes and ears of more people—many of whom could desperately use this work and your many insights and interventions—has been the animating and continuously motivating motor of this project, through the many trials and troubles of these times.

As we have collaborated with each other and so many other folks over these last few years, multiple sensations have stoked this work, from anticipation to anxiety, anger, and excitement. One growing sense among these is that, for many of us doing this work, we are enraged and threatened by resurgent waves of anti-trans animus and action, and often haunted by those we have lost, both proximately and more distantly. In many ways trans biblical interpretation can't *not* be haunted by what has come before. And, still, it is also bracingly, exuberantly true that gender variations are as ancient and as vibrant as the multiple traditions engaged in this volume. It is our sincere hope that this collection is one unique, possibly even powerful, testament to the persistence of gender variation and the still manifest potentials of trans interpretations of biblical materials. Our own modest dedication, then, is to those waiting for or already doing such interpretation, and the untold numbers who still need trans biblical interpretations.

Abbreviations

Hebrew Bible

Gen	Genesis
Exod	Exodus
Num	Numbers
Deut	Deuteronomy
Josh	Joshua
Judg	Judges
1 Sam	1 Samuel
2 Sam	2 Samuel
2 Kgs	2 Kings
1 Chr	1 Chronicles
Esth	Esther
Ps	Psalm
Isa	Isaiah
Jer	Jeremiah
Ezek	Ezekiel
Dan	Daniel

New Testament

Matt	Matthew
Rom	Romans
1 Cor	1 Corinthians
2 Cor	2 Corinthians
Gal	Galatians
Eph	Ephesians
Phil	Philippians
Col	Colossians
1 Thess	1 Thessalonians
2 Thess	2 Thessalonians
1 Tim	1 Timothy
2 Tim	2 Timothy
Phlm	Philemon
Heb	Hebrews
Jas	James
Rev	Revelation

OT Pseudepigrapha

2 Bar	2 Baruch
Jub	Jubilees

Other Ancient Sources

Achill.	Statius, *Achilleid*
Aen.	Virgil, *Aeneid*
Apol.	Tertullian, *Apologeticus*
Mart. Ascen. Isa.	*Martyrdom and Ascension of Isaiah*
b.	Babylonian Talmud
Ber.	Berakhot
Cels.	Origen, *Against Celsus*
Comm. Matt.	Origen, *Commentarium in evangelium Matthaei*
Contr.	Senecna, *Controversia*
Deipn.	Athenaeus, *Deipnosophistae*
Diogn.	*Epistle of Diognetus*
Ep.	Basil, *Epistle*
Ep.	Pliny, *Epistulae*
Epid.	Hippocrates, Epidemics
'Erub.	Eruvin
Gaius	Philo, *On the Embassy to Gaius*
Gos. Thom.	Gospel of Thomas
Hist.	Apollodorus, *Fragmenta Historica*
Ketub.	Ketubbot
LXX	Septuagint
m.	Mishnah
Metam.	Ovid, *Metamorphoses*
Mo'ed Qaṭ	Mo'ed Qatan
Mor.	Plutarch, *Moralia*
Moses	Philo, *On the Life of Moses*
Or. Graec.	Tatian, *Oratio ad Graecos*
Pall.	Tertullian, *De pallio*
Para.	Plutarch, *Parallel Lives*
Pesiq. Rab. Kah.	Pesiqta of Rab Kahana
Phil.	Cicero, *Orationes philippicae*
Protr.	Clement of Alexandria, *Exhortation to the Greeks*
Sacrifices	Philo, *On the Sacrifices of Cain and Abel*
SHA *Hadr.*	Scriptores Historiae Augustae *Hadrian*
Spec. Laws	Philo, *On the Special Laws*
t.	Tosefta
T.Ab	Testament of Abraham
T.Sol	Testament of Solomon

Secondary Sources

ANF	*Ante-Nicene Fathers*
BAR	*Biblical Archaeology Review*
BibInt	*Biblical Interpretation*
BSOAS	*Bulletin of the School of Oriental and Asian Studies*
BTB	*Biblical Theology Bulletin*
CBQ	*Catholic Biblical Quarterly*
CP	*Classical Philology*

ExpTim	*Expository Times*
GLQ	*GLQ: A Journal of Lesbian and Gay Studies*
HeyJ	*Heythrop Journal*
HS	*Hebrew Studies*
JAAR	*Journal of the American Academy of Religion*
JBL	*Journal of Biblical Literature*
JBQ	*Jewish Bible Quarterly*
JECS	*Journal of Early Christian Studies*
JFSR	*Journal of Feminist Studies in Religion*
JIBS	*Journal of Interdisciplinary Biblical Studies*
JNES	*Journal of Near Eastern Studies*
JSNT	*Journal for the Study of the New Testament*
JSOT	*Journal for the Study of the Old Testament*
JTS	*Journal of Theological Studies*
JTSA	*Journal of Theology for Southern Africa*
KJV	King James Version
NTS	*New Testament Studies*
Neot	*Neotestamentica*
SPhilo	*Studia philonica*
SPhiloA	The *Studia Philonica Annual*
SR	*Studies in Religion*
StPatr	*Studia patristica*
TSQ	*TSQ: Transgender Studies Quarterly*
VC	*Vigiliae Christianae*
WZKM	*Wiener Zeitschrift für die Kunde des Morgenlandes*

Introduction

Variations on Interpretation and Embodiment

Contextualizing Trans Approaches to Scriptures

JOSEPH A. MARCHAL

WITH MELISSA HARL SELLEW AND KATY E. VALENTINE

Gender variation is as ancient as stories about creation.

That such a statement is simultaneously obvious to some and controversial to others is one very clear sign of why we need trans biblical interpretation, now more than ever.

People are increasingly enlisting appeals to "the biblical" (texts or histories or sometimes just vague impressions) to discuss trans people and practices of gender variation and nonconformity. On the one hand, some more liberal groups have hailed the increased social and political visibility of (a few) trans and gender nonconforming people, claiming the arrival of a trans tipping point or marking trans rights and representation as the leading edge, or "what's next," in a sequence of civil rights fights. On the other hand, this moment of visibility—marked with certain kinds of progress, acceptance, and inclusion—is also matched with ongoing and even increasing violence against trans and gender nonconforming people, most especially trans women of color. The years in which we have been researching, writing, and editing the essays for this collection (the late 2010s and early 2020s) have been marked by persistent, resurgent violence against trans and gender nonconforming people. Not so coincidentally in this same short period, reactionary and regressive forces have directed a concerted, rapid-fire effort to pass hundreds of laws targeting especially trans and gender nonconforming young people, stoking in them panic and fear.

These conditions alone are enough to explain why biblical studies needs more sustained engagement with trans studies, even before we notice that many of these phobic and violent efforts appeal to biblical or historical claims. Indeed, a number of the essays in our collection explicitly take on such oppressive efforts, starting with our opening essay by Max K. Strassfeld. The Christian right is increasingly using trans people, especially young people, as targets in longer-standing fights over supposed family values. Too many groups refer to notions of divine creation or biblical times in efforts to construct gender identities as binarily distinct and complementary and to stabilize their (twenty-first-century) notions of sex, gender, and embodiment. In short, there is a fierce urgency for this collection and the development of trans biblical interpretation to create and support better, more sustained, and more informed engagements of biblical texts and traditions.

This collection provides an abundance of attention to precisely these matters, demonstrating the relevance and importance of trans approaches to scriptures, not only about creation, but about a range of biblical figures and events, parables and passages, practices and processes. By necessity this involves deeper and more reflexive attention to *our* practices and processes as biblical readers, receivers, and interpreters—how we cite, narrate, or explain biblical texts and traditions. Such attention and reflection are all the more crucial given the contexts in which we are currently laboring and living (if we're lucky).

This volume comes out of this urgent moment by drawing on and selecting from an increasing, critical mass of scholars interacting with trans studies. This attention reflects the work of a growing, if still relatively small, set of trans and gender nonconforming scholars attending and presenting at SBL meetings. Trans hermeneutics is now entering a key phase, with several vital questions animating its current growth.

- How are trans hermeneutics evolving as an independent and intersectional lens for interpreting biblical texts and traditions?
- How do interpreters navigate the relationships between gender variation in the ancient west Asian and Greco-Roman contexts and current-day variation and gender nonconformity?
- What makes a biblical reading trans, or a trans reading biblical, for that matter?

The contributors to this collection address these key questions from a variety of angles, shaping a number of approaches and emphases, appealing to different conversation partners and communities of accountability, and ranging widely across and past the edges of biblical traditions. They provide compelling new ways of engaging the stories of survival and solidarity, the forms of proclamation, incarnation, and transfiguration, and the impact of laws and letters we find in biblical texts and traditions. Their approaches converse with, draw upon, and intersect with feminist, queer, antiracist, posthumanist, or abolitionist approaches. The scholars assembled here move in varied gender constellations, including trans, nonbinary, gender nonconforming, and cisgender, among other gender identities. Together, these essays take readers from Genesis, through the Gospels and epistles, and into rabbinic and early Christian scriptural engagement.

TERMS AND INITIAL TRAJECTORIES WITHIN TRANS STUDIES

Trans people are not a particularly "new" phenomenon, and trans movements have been happening for much longer than you may have heard.

Just as the scholarship gathered in this book begins from different starting points, experiences, assumptions, and approaches, there is no one simple starting point for describing the emergence of trans studies, and the movements that led to it. Indeed, historically, the terms used for people and practices of gender variation have been regular subjects of both critique and comfort. The historian Susan Stryker has explained about her preferred use of transgender to describe gender variance and/or gender atypicality for the past and the present: "There is no way of using the word that doesn't offend some people by including them where they don't want to be included or excluding them from where they do want to be included."[1] Likewise, the authors and editors of *Trans Biblical* do not imagine that our own approaches to this subject will be perfect or complete. Yet, we do hope that our contributions can help to shift the terms of conversation and play a role in improving the debilitating conditions still faced by far too many trans, nonbinary, and gender nonconforming people so that, in turn, these approaches and results can also become the objects of justified critique and improvement. Justin Sabia-Tanis's essay in our collection particularly emphasizes the goal of justice: the purpose of trans hermeneutics is to liberate humanity from the tyranny of oppressive gender norms. Still, many trans scholars and activists working today are justifiably suspicious about claims of improvement, progress, or advancement. Our collection aims to add to such critical assessment. Terminologically, we do not believe that we have "progressed" from speaking about or as transsexuals, to transgender, to trans (or trans*) individuals, especially as a number of people use one or more of these descriptors for themselves, their lives, or their politics. (See especially Rebecca Wiegel's essay in our volume for a sharp discussion of the divides between transgender and transsexual narratives.) In a wider sense, we also refuse the framing of trans as part of a sequence. A rise in trans politics, progress, or even just survival is not "what's next," either politically, or socially, or historically, particularly as trans movements have been intertwined with and within others, including those focused on sexual, gender, racial, and economic justice.

1. Susan Stryker, *Transgender History* (Berkeley, CA: Seal Press, 2008), 24.

Nevertheless, one common narrative is that transgender studies coalesced early in the 1990s, inspired and informed by the approaches taken in touchstone works like Sandy Stone's essay "The *Empire* Strikes Back" (1991), Leslie Feinberg's pamphlet *Transgender Liberation* (1992), the performance art eventually gathered in Kate Bornstein's *Gender Outlaw* (1994), and historical interventions like Susan Stryker's article "My Words to Victor Frankenstein above the Village of Chamounix" (1994), among others.[2] In overlapping circles both academic and activist, these works encourage trans people to resist the silencing and stigmatization in how they have been treated medically and socially, to organize alliances among all people marginalized by or from current norms of gendered embodiment, and to likewise think more capaciously about histories of gender and embodiment, as well as our relations to these histories. Several of the essays in our collection focus on such broader alliances and more capacious models of gender, particularly those by Esther Brownsmith, Minenhle Nomalungelo Khumalo and Eric A. Thomas, and Joseph Marchal. Those key interventions from the 1990s, of course, have roots that extend much further historically. The term transgender, for instance, was coined in the 1980s, in some places to distinguish some people and practices from others, such as transsexual and transvestite, but in other places to gather any people who would use these terms under a broader umbrella for action as much as affiliation.[3] Further, such modes of identification and struggle had been practiced for decades before these terms were created and circulated.

Trans movements are interconnected with other parallel and overlapping struggles, and it is important to note trans contributions in the larger umbrella of queer struggles while also pointing out where trans movements stood apart. The ongoing efforts of trans people to grapple with dynamics of passing or closeting and resist stigma and silence point to the historic affinity between trans and queer movements. In advocacy and in the academy, queer and trans movements are in close, often overlapping, if still also fraught relations to each other. Of course, transsexuals were long part of what was once called gay liberation, so much so that our current patron saints of queer rights are the trans women who were at the forefront of the Stonewall uprising of 1969, Sylvia Rivera and Marsha P. Johnson.[4] Yet, this modern-day mythologizing has the potential to obscure both historical and ethical visions. A focus on heroic or exceptional individuals,

---

2. Sandy Stone, "The *Empire* Strikes Back: A Posttranssexual Manifesto," in *Body Guards: The Cultural Politics of Gender Ambiguity*, ed. Julia Epstein and Kristina Straub (New York: Routledge, 1991), 280–304; Leslie Feinberg, *Transgender Liberation: An Idea Whose Time Has Come* (1992), subsequently expanded to Feinberg, *Trans Liberation: Beyond Pink or Blue* (Boston: Beacon, 1998); Kate Bornstein, *Gender Outlaw: On Men, Women, and the Rest of Us* (New York: Routledge, 1994); and Stryker, "My Words to Victor Frankenstein above the Village of Chamounix: Performing Transgender Rage," *GLQ* 1:3 (1994): 237–54.

3. For a brief if helpful historical overview, see Stryker, "(De)Subjugated Knowledges: An Introduction to Transgender Studies," in *The Transgender Studies Reader*, ed. Stryker and Stephen Whittle (New York: Routledge, 2006), 1–17.

4. On the key role of religion in Rivera and Johnson's lives and politics, see Ahmad Greene-Hayes, "Street Evangelists and Transgender Saints: Sylvia Rivera, Marsha P. Johnson, and the Reli-

for instance, runs the risk of ignoring their place within collectives and movements. Johnson and Rivera founded Street Transvestite Action Revolutionaries (STAR) specifically to support and work within community, most especially younger people living on the streets. These Black and Puerto Rican trans women focused on the people most precariously situated at the intersections of multiple vectors of oppression (decades before the more recent mainstream recognition of intersectionality), grounded in their experience and expertise within multiple struggles, including civil rights, women's liberation, and antiwar movements. Trans and, or, even *as* queer critique and struggle, then, might better be conceptualized as multidimensional. Trans efforts are neither separate from, nor in a sequence "after" other, interrelated movements against gender, sexual, racial, and economic injustice.

Events like Stonewall were themselves far from spontaneous exceptions but part of longer-term, multipronged, and overlapping movements. Protest and resistance against police repression and harassment, for instance, had been happening since the late 1950s, at late-night coffeehouses and cafeterias in cities like Los Angeles, Philadelphia, and San Francisco.[5] Further still, we can reflect critically upon how the rising prominence and social authority of science and medicine in the nineteenth century brought the medicalized treatment of trans people for more than a century, with both enabling and constraining impacts. Scientific authorities focused their efforts by simultaneously insisting on a stable sex binary and, in turn, diagnosing and treating people who clearly troubled, fell out of, or crossed that binary they were working so hard to construct, including people with intersex conditions.[6] The rise of fascism in twentieth century Europe disrupted and ultimately targeted the treatment of, research about, and community building around trans people—possibly the most famous photo of Nazis burning books is from their 1933 destruction of the Institute for Sexual Science run by Magnus Hirschfeld in Berlin. This longer history should give many more people in the present pause, particularly those stoking panic and fear.

These longer histories of gender variation and movement are affected not only by European fascist forces but also by anti-Black racism and white supremacy in the United States. Indeed, C. Riley Snorton has provided an alternative, critical genealogy for the modern form of trans studies in which neither gender nor race are fixed or stable in the recent *Black on Both Sides: A Racial History of Trans Identity*. Rather, Snorton's project involves "tracing the circulation of 'black' and 'trans' as they are brought into the same frame by the various ways they have been constituted as fungible, thingified, and interchangeable, particularly within the logics of transatlantic exchange."[7] In identifying multiple intersections between

---

gions of the Afro-Americas," *QTR: A Journal of Trans and Queer Studies in Religion* 1:1 (2024): 32–52.

    5. See Stryker, *Transgender History*, 59–75.

    6. On the medicalized history of intersex treatments, see Alice Domurat Dreger, *Hermaphrodites and the Medical Invention of Sex* (Cambridge, MA: Harvard University Press, 1998).

    7. C. Riley Snorton, *Black on Both Sides: A Racial History of Trans Identity* (Minneapolis: University of Minnesota Press, 2017), 6. For the colonizing forms trans misogyny takes from the

transness and Blackness back through the nineteenth century, Snorton demonstrates how the fungibility of captive flesh (for instance, the objectification and exchange of enslaved people) historically made possible the modern production of gender as mutable and rearrangeable. This included both the ways enslavers used enslaved people, and the embodied and "cross-gendered" forms of resistance enslaved people took. Thus, grappling with the twists and turns of racism and enslavement is also crucial for a more capacious understanding of trans, in the past and the present. Critical reflections on racisms foreground the potential disciplinary effects of trans in more specific ways, particularly given the greater surveillance, incarceration, precarity, and debility of trans women of color.[8] The essays in our collection by Khumalo and Thomas, Marchal, and Melissa Harl Sellew build upon Snorton's project and these specific effects along different trajectories.

THE BIBLICAL IN TRANS STUDIES: APPROACHING THE PAST

Trans people have been engaging biblical materials for longer than you might think, too! The following engagements inform the essays in our collection and the approaches we hope will develop as a result.

Many corners of trans studies have shown a pointed interest in the ancient and even the biblical, especially among the historically inclined. Stephen Whittle's foreword to the landmark *Transgender Studies Reader* confidently notes: "we can determine that trans people have always existed."[9] Though it might be difficult to ascertain this bold claim of trans timelessness, it is easier to notice the appearance of ancient figures, including those from both Jewish and Christian scriptural traditions, in key works for transgender studies from before it was consolidated as a field, as well as their recurrence in many recent projects. These fleeting forms of biblical citation and figuration should help us further specify how to build more reflexive forms of biblical interpretation with or as trans studies now.

Like Whittle's foreword, Sandy Stone's 1991 manifesto points back to ancient sources like Sardanapalus and Philo of Judea before describing her essay's focus on "morality tales and origin myths."[10] Stone critically reflects on

---

nineteenth century forward, see also Jules Gill-Peterson, *A Short History of Trans Misogyny* (London: Verso, 2024).

8. See Dean Spade, *Normal Life: Administrative Violence, Critical Trans Politics, and the Limits of Law* (Durham, NC: Duke University Press, 2015); Snorton and Jin Haritaworn, "Trans Necropolitics: A Transnational Reflection on Violence, Death, and the Trans of Color Afterlife," in *The Transgender Studies Reader 2*, ed. Stryker and Aren Z. Aizura (New York: Routledge, 2013), 66–76; and Jasbir K. Puar, "Bodies with New Organs: Becoming Trans, Becoming Disabled," *Social Text* 33:3 (2015): 45–73.

9. Whittle, "Foreword," in *The Transgender Studies Reader*, ed. Stryker and Whittle, xiii.

10. Stone, "The *Empire* Strikes Back," 282, 284.

both medicalized protocols and the earliest transsexual autobiographies and, at one point, compares their narratives to a biblical practice of baptism, the "putting on" Christ found in Paul's letters, "what the New Testament calls *endeuein* [*sic*], or the putting on of the god, inserting the physical body within a shell of cultural signification."[11] Stone's aim here is to resist the canonization of certain dominant diagnostic narratives about transsexuals, frequently imagined as a citation of the scripturally created order. The specter of biblical bodies sticks particularly to naturalizing claims that collect around bodies across time. Stone's original essay even appeared in a collection that began with the gender ambiguities and transformations of ancient Christian women,[12] an important topic that Sellew's essay revisits in our collection.

Stone's essay is hardly the only one to highlight such ancient bodies. As Stryker asserts in her introduction to *The Transgender Studies Reader*, "attending to what we would now call transgender phenomena has been a preoccupation of Western culture since Greek and Roman antiquity."[13] Indeed, Stryker's own earlier (if not exactly ancient) pathbreaking 1994 essay (noted above) highlighted and then performed the transformative potential of the monstrous by first recalling that "monster" relates back to the Latin for a warning or divine portent (*monstrum*). She elaborates that, for people in the ancient world: "Monsters, like angels, functioned as messengers and heralds of the extraordinary. They served to announce impending revelation, saying, in effect, 'Pay attention; something of profound importance is happening.'"[14] Stryker alludes to "the ancients" in a familiar biblical idiom, of the prophetic and the revelatory—as Jaeda C. Calaway's essay in our collection also addresses. Stryker's article is an extended, if occasionally ambivalent, reclamation of the monstrosity attributed to trans bodies, beginning with this appeal to biblical announcements from ancient messengers. This is of course a clever challenge in response to (ostensibly radical) feminist theologian Mary Daly's characterization of trans women as monstrous invaders.[15]

While Stryker appeals to ancient religious figures to think through trans-ness across time, her main aims are political and her primary methods are historical. Over the course of her work, she complicates trans approaches beyond the search for points of identification and renarrates a much longer heritage. This renarration requires attention to many kinds of gender variation, though characterizing them all as transgender is both promising and perilous. On the one

11. Stone, 289.
12. Elizabeth A. Castelli, "'I Will Make Mary Male': Pieties of the Body and Gender Transformation of Christian Women in Late Antiquity," in *Body Guards*, ed. Epstein and Straub, 29–49.
13. Stryker, "(De)Subjugated Knowledges," 13.
14. Stryker, "My Words to Victor Frankenstein," 240.
15. Mary Daly, *Gyn/Ecology: The Metaethics of Radical Feminism* (Boston: Beacon, 1978), 69–72. For brief but helpful discussions of Daly and her student Janice Raymond in relation to trans, feminist, and transfeminist approaches to religious and theological studies, see Max Strassfeld, "Transing Religious Studies," *JFSR* 34:1 (2018): 37–53; and Cameron Partridge, "'Scotch-Taped Together': Anti-'Androgyny' Rhetoric, Transmisogyny, and the Transing of Religious Studies," *JFSR* 34:1 (2018): 68–75.

hand, Stryker is not terribly concerned about the anachronistic use of terms like queer and transgender, as long as they do helpful descriptive work in highlighting oppression or the crossing of gender boundaries.[16] On the other hand, by the time she introduces the second *Transgender Studies Reader* with Aren Z. Aizura, they stress that transgender studies will need to question "why we persist in the presentist fallacy of ontologizing a current framework and imposing it on the strangeness of the past."[17] Brownsmith's essay in our collection similarly reflects upon the tension between presentist and historicist goals.

Stryker and Aizura contextualize an entire section of historically oriented essays with a mixture of confidence and hesitation as "excavating pasts that certainly contained gender-variant cultural practices, without necessarily imposing the name 'transgender' on those historical moments."[18] In this section, for instance, premodern archaeologist Mary Weismantel disputes that such an approach forces a more recent category onto ancient remains. Rather, transgender studies' finer sensitivity to the potential complexity and variety of gender and embodiment means that it is *even more suited* to explain ancient phenomena. For Weismantel, a transgender kind of archaeology does not aim "to re-populate the ancient past with modern trans men and trans women," but "to replace the narrow, reductive gaze of previous researchers with a more supple, subtler appreciation of cultural variation."[19] By the time Stryker is introducing the very first issue of *TSQ: Transgender Studies Quarterly* with Paisley Currah, they explain the methodological possibilities for historical issues, asserting: "Transgender can, for example, be a useful neologism for interrogating the past" in part because it "facilitates a deeply historical analysis of the utter contingency and fraught conditions of intelligibility of all embodied subjectivity. It can be used to pose new comparative questions about gender difference over geographic space as well as over historical time."[20] Anachronism remains only a problem for identity, but not history, as long as transgender makes room for an approach that accounts for difference through contingency and comparison. Essays like Wiegel's and Ky Merkley's in our collection likewise deploy trans less as an identity category than as an analytic category.

The focus on these kinds of contingencies and comparisons complicates how we approach embodied figures, including in ancient times and places, biblical or otherwise. Stryker's ambivalent reclamation of monstrosity, for instance, requires wrestling with stigma without being determined by it. There might, for instance, be flashes of recognition when Stryker riffs off of the aforementioned ancient monsters, characterizing fabulous creatures like angels and declaring

16. Stryker, *Transgender History*, 23–24.
17. Stryker and Aren Z. Aizura, "Introduction: Transgender Studies 2.0," in *The Transgender Studies Reader 2*, ed. Stryker and Aizura (New York: Routledge, 2013), 6
18. Stryker and Aizura, "Introduction," 11.
19. Mary Weismantel, "Towards a Transgender Archaeology: A Queer Rampage through Prehistory," in *The Transgender Studies Reader 2*, ed. Stryker and Aizura, 321.
20. Stryker and Paisley Currah, "Introduction," *TSQ* 1:1–2 (2014): 1–18, 8.

"I whose flesh has become an assemblage of incongruous parts."[21] By risking stigma and abjection, the monster reconfigures the meaning of bodies and their assemblages. For Stryker the monster and/as the trans body moves us in directions prophetic, even apocalyptic, as "a revelation of the constructedness of the natural order."[22]

There are of course risks to such an approach to or as the monstrous, even as it could signal an alternative, even revelatory angle on the bodies that have been stitched together by various practices of scriptural citation. Still, as in Strassfeld's essay in our collection, we wonder about the costs of focusing on subversion and hesitate to reduce the options to those surrounding the abject and the monstrous. Indeed, before Stryker's words to Victor Frankenstein, Stone had already worried about the canonization of another constrained set of options for narrating the meaning of bodies. These narrations often require silence, as the preferred medicalized prescription for passing as cis while trans is to not speak of being trans. Of course, Stone notes, "it is difficult to generate a counterdiscourse if one is programmed to disappear."[23] In the face of the legitimizing trajectories that stress homogeneity for the permissible performance of gender, Stone begins to trace and revalorize "the bumptious appearance of heteroglossic origin accounts."[24] Stone's manifesto ventures its own daring suggestion, renarrating, even rewriting trans, not as a category for classifying people, "but rather as a *genre*—a set of embodied texts whose potential for *productive* disruption of structured sexualities and spectra of desire has yet to be explored."[25] This genre, as a larger repertoire, better reflects the ambiguities and polyvocalities of how bodies manifest.

These emphases also move us increasingly toward trans as a verb rather than a noun. This movement is not meant to minimize the significant political, social, material, and even religious value of identifying as trans, transgender, and/or transsexual for many. Yet, scholars (including Joy Ladin in our collection) have increasingly queried in what ways identifying only *certain* people or practices as transitive, intermediate, variant, or crossing falsely stabilizes terms (like trans *and* cis, but not only), as if everyone or everything else is intransitive, firm, fixed, and clear.[26] Such queries indicate that it might also be meaningful to think of trans-*ing* itself as an action or approach.[27] Stryker, Currah, and Lisa Moore suggest this now-influential formulation of "transing" as:

21. Stryker, "My Words to Victor Frankenstein," 240.
22. Stryker, 250.
23. Stone, "The *Empire* Strikes Back," 295.
24. Stone, 294.
25. Stone, 296.
26. See Finn Enke, "The Education of Little Cis: Cisgender and the Discipline of Opposing Bodies," in *Transfeminist Perspectives: In and beyond Transgender and Gender Studies*, ed. Enke (Philadelphia: Temple University Press, 2012), 60–77.
27. This approach of course also resonates with the interrogation of "queer" as a term of identification and the suggestion to use it verbally and contingently, without particular, proper objects (see, for instance Judith Butler, "Against Proper Objects," *differences* 6:2–3 (1994): 1–26). For two, brief considerations of the fraught relations between queer and trans, see Stryker, "The Transgender

a practice that assembles gender into contingent structures of association with other attributes of bodily being, and that allows for their reassembly. Transing can function as a disciplinary tool when the stigma associated with the lack or loss of gender status threatens social unintelligibility, coercive normalization, or even bodily extermination. It can also function as an escape vector, line of flight, or pathway toward liberation.[28]

This definition stresses how transing is an activity that we can observe and trace, but it also sounds and feels like something that interpreters can *do*, much as Strassfeld's essay in our collection highlights. Transing also underscores the potential for both disciplinary and liberatory effects.

The cyclical coincidence of violence and visibility for trans folks requires a different kind of approach for the field and for the transitivity people consider within it, as scholars like Snorton stress, and as the essays by Marchal and Khumalo and Thomas in our collection also address. For Snorton and Marquis Bey, trans evokes the potential for fugitivity—flight from racially dehumanizing conditions.[29] Scholars moving along such transitive or fugitive lines within trans studies also often turn back to the biblical. This is evident even in Jack Halberstam's brief, if characteristically jokey, discussions of Jesus figures, first in a Gospel encounter with the plural "legion," and then in the farcical Jesus movie, *The Life of Brian*.[30] More fugitively, though, the biblical shapes Eric Stanley's *Atmospheres of Violence*, which begins and ends with Sylvia Rivera and Marsha P. Johnson's description of the Hudson River as the River Jordan, a "(non)space where they would transition together, out of the bondage of a life circumscribed by imminent risk and into the promise of an elsewhere."[31]

Both Snorton and Stanley also imagine the end of the world, though Stanley more consistently so. Stanley, for instance, features a graffito from the 2020 Minneapolis uprisings (after the police slaying of George Floyd) that announced "another end of the world is possible."[32] In the opening he gestures to a world yet to come,[33] but in closing he returns to the realized eschatology he also sounded in *Captive Genders*: "not only that we need another world but that it's already here."[34] Snorton closes with a similar summoning of a future imperfect temporality in which Black and/as trans lives will have mattered. While this

---

Issue: An Introduction," *GLQ* 4:2 (1998): 145–58; and "Transgender Studies: Queer Theory's Evil Twin," *GLQ* 10:2 (2004): 212–15.

28. Stryker, Currah, and Lisa Jean Moore, "Introduction: Trans-, Trans, or Transgender?" *Women's Studies Quarterly* 36:3–4 (2008): 11–22, 13.

29. Marquis Bey, *Black Trans Feminism* (Durham, NC: Duke University Press, 2022), 66.

30. Jack Halberstam, *Trans*: A Quick and Quirky Account of Gender Variability* (Oakland: University of California Press, 2018), 11, 14–20.

31. Eric A. Stanley, *Atmospheres of Violence: Structuring Antagonism and the Trans/Queer Ungovernable* (Durham, NC: Duke University Press, 2021), 2; cf. 20, 123.

32. Stanley, *Atmospheres of Violence*, 83, 84; cf. 91, 114.

33. Stanley, *Atmospheres of Violence*, xiv, 27.

34. Stanley, *Atmospheres of Violence*, 113. Such spatial efforts against captivity strike a familiar temporal chord of anticipation, or what religious and biblical scholars might call a realized eschatology: "To this end, the time of abolition is both yet to come and already here" (Stanley, "Fugitive Flesh: Gender Self-Determination, Queer Abolition, and Trans Resistance," in Stanley and Nat

would effectively end the world (as we know it), Snorton almost shrugs, "but worlds end all the time ... 'it's after the end of the world.' Even so and as yet, there is still life."[35]

In these works, the biblical functions spatially and temporally, but also figuratively and fugitively. Snorton recognizes how the biblical can reinforce stigmatizing and racializing rhetorics, as when he notes gynecological references to the punishments in Gen 3:16 as symptomatic of (enslaved subjects') suffering and (white legal, cultural, and medical) dominion.[36] Furthermore, in multiple echoes of the Johannine incarnation (1:1, 14, 15), the "word made flesh" accounts for claims about flesh maintaining racially enslaving regimes.[37] Khumalo and Thomas return to this "transing of the Word to flesh" in the prologue of John in our collection. As both Snorton and Bey highlight, CeCe McDonald more recently also wrote toward freedom in her own letters from prison, referencing multiple biblical texts, while signifying upon the prison letters of both Paul and Martin Luther King Jr.[38] Marchal's essay in our collection further reflects on letter-writing to and within prison systems in relation to both ancient and present-day conditions. While Bey notes the potentially constraining divine decree of texts like Deut 22:5, they also shift the attention from Jesus's incarnation or resurrection to his "trans/figuration," as does Katy E. Valentine in her essay in our collection.[39] The transfiguration is reconfigured as an example of transitive fugitivity, not to elevate or idealize Jesus, but to feel for a mode of becoming otherwise. Jesus's body works for Bey as both transforming and not conforming (see Mark 9:2 and Rom 12:2), a poetic template of all bodies' intensifying capacities.[40] Further, Dean Spade highlights how trans and abolitionist advocates describe the logic of criminalization and incarceration on the evocatively biblical terms of exile.[41] Abolitionists reframe our focus to counter how the prison-industrial complex removes people from society and directs our attention away from the conditions these people face in prisons by adopting a "no exile" principle, insisting instead for education and connection, community and solidarity. Such a principle is crucial within trans advocacy since trans women, and especially trans women of color, are disproportionately targeted by policing and incarceration.[42]

Smith, *Captive Genders: Trans Embodiment and the Prison Industrial Complex*, expanded second edition (Chico, CA: AK Press, 2015), 14).

35. Snorton, *Black on Both Sides*, 198.
36. Snorton, 17–18.
37. Snorton, 31, 33, and especially 52.
38. CeCe McDonald, "'Go beyond Our Natural Selves': The Prison Letters of CeCe McDonald," ed. Omise'eke Natasha Tinsley, *TSQ* 4:2 (2017): 243, 247, 264.
39. As Bey notes briefly in the introduction and then at greater frequency in Bey, *Black Trans Feminism*, 18, 88–112.
40. Bey, *Black Trans Feminism*, 91–93.
41. See Bey, 118–22; Spade, *Normal Life*, 116, 135, and 137.
42. See Stanley and Smith, eds., *Captive Genders*; Spade, *Normal Life*; Toshio Meronek and Miss Major Griffin-Gracy, *Miss Major Speaks: Conversations with a Black Trans Revolutionary* (London: Verso, 2023).

Thus, trans scholars and/as activists care about and cite a range of biblical materials, alternately recognizing, reclaiming, or just trying to negotiate them. In following the biblical around trans approaches in the past and the present, we also note their intersections or simply alignment with race critical, queer, feminist, or abolitionist ideas and efforts. Biblical interpreters would be wise to attend to and draw upon the multiple, interlocking dimensions of trans studies in our approaches, even as we might insist that biblical texts and traditions require more sustained attention.

As biblical scholars tend to do, many of these resources from trans studies focus on historical or temporal processes, an emphasis that persists in several more recent efforts to think trans historically in pre-modern contexts, and particularly in essays by Strassfeld, Brownsmith, and Wiegel in our collection.[43] This makes some sense as the word trans resonates not only spatially, but also historically, connoting the crossing of time. Such connotations could boost our confidence about trans existence across time (and space), as reflected in the recurrent tactic among trans activists and writers like Kate Bornstein and Leslie Feinberg to claim past ancestors as a buoy for trans identification, legitimacy, and solidarity.[44] These people are often described strategically, if also still colloquially and a bit cheekily, as "trancestors," and the essays in our collection by Sabia-Tanis, Valentine, and Khumalo and Thomas explicitly appeal to biblical examples of such ancestors.

Thus, we emphasize, with the coeditors of *Trans Historical: Gender Plurality before the Modern*, that transgender people and practices are not "new."[45] Indeed, Greta LaFleur, Masha Raskolnikov, and Anna Kłosowska reject the "knee-jerk historicism" employed by some historians of gender and sexuality who insist that the past is so different that we apparently cannot use concepts like transgender (or homosexuality, or even sexuality).[46] While trans approaches to temporality and history should be comparative in noting differences, they can also be connective in finding "touches across time" between those marginalized in the past and in the present.[47] Calaway's essay in our collection in particular

---

43. Beyond the works discussed below, see also the following special issues: Leah DeVun and Zeb Tortorici, "Trans*historicities," *TSQ* 5:4 (2018); M. W. Bychowski and Dorothy Kim, "Visions of Medieval Trans Feminism," *Medieval Feminist Forum* 55:1 (2019); and Simone Chess, Colby Gordon, and Will Fisher, "Early Modern Trans Studies," *Journal for Early Modern Cultural Studies* 19:4 (2019).

44. Bornstein, *Gender Outlaw*; Feinberg, *Transgender Warriors: Making History from Joan of Arc to RuPaul* (Boston: Beacon, 1996).

45. Strassfeld's essay in our collection also counters this framing of trans as a "new" issue, specifically pointing to Gill-Peterson, *Histories of the Transgender Child* (Minneapolis: University of Minnesota Press, 2018).

46. Greta LaFleur, Masha Raskolnikov, and Anna Kłosowska, "Introduction: The Benefits of Being Trans Historical," *Trans Historical: Gender Plurality before the Modern* (Ithaca, NY: Cornell University Press, 2021), 9. For a similar critique of altericism, see Leah DeVun and Zeb Tortorici, "Trans, Time, and History," *TSQ* 5:4 (2018): 520.

47. See the argument in DeVun and Tortorici, "Trans," 520, building upon the conceptualization of such touches from Carolyn Dinshaw, *Getting Medieval: Sexualities and Communities, Pre- and Postmodern* (Durham, NC: Duke University Press, 1999), among others. For further reflections

resonates with such a conceptualization, reaching for a specifically transgender touch across time within what she describes as the "curvy time" of trans temporalities. These points of resonance matter because, as LaFleur, Raskolnikov, and Kłosowska stress about a number of pre-modern settings, transgender and gender-nonconforming people keep showing up, including in narratives about gender confirmation or transition. An openness to the differences of the past can help us meaningfully trace the place of outliers: "wherever and whenever structures of meaning existed for making sense of gendered experience, we will find people who were, in whatever way, outliers to those structures."[48] While this kind of history exposes the precarity or fragility of binary understandings of gender, it also shows the variety, heterogeneity, even abundance of gender across time and space.

Further, as Alicia Spencer-Hall and Blake Gutt stress in *Trans and Genderqueer Subjects in Medieval Hagiography*, non-normative gender is very often intertwined with religion in the texts and traditions of the past. This history demonstrates that trans or genderqueer subjects need not be posed as "against" or "outside" of religion (let alone Christianity!), as so many phobic forces might be claiming in the present. No doubt the concepts of gender in the medieval period are different from those in the modern period, yet transgender approaches can pay attention to gender norms and their transgressions in both periods.[49] Such transgressions in the past can challenge those who deploy biblical interpretation in marginalizing and stigmatizing directions in the present. Indeed, feminist scholars of medieval materials have long recognized the charged eroticism and gender transgression in interpretations of the Song of Songs, as well as the gender fluidity of Jesus.[50]

More recently, Leah DeVun has shown how "Christ is the ultimate nonbinary figure" in some of these late antique and medieval contexts.[51] In doing so, they (like several authors in our collection) use transgender, intersex, and nonbinary as analytical, not identitarian terms for premodern people and practices of gender crossing.[52] While at times DeVun characterizes the early Christian period in too optimistic a fashion as "embracing" nonbinary as an ideal, overall they seem right to note the enduring appeal of such figurations, given the alternating turns away and back to them in key moments of reflection on central

on queer temporalities in relation to biblical and theological studies, with some reference to trans temporalities, see Kent L. Brintnall, Joseph A. Marchal, Stephen D. Moore, eds, *Sexual Disorientations: Queer Temporalities, Affects, Theologies* (New York: Fordham University Press, 2017); and Marchal, *Appalling Bodies: Queer Figures before and after Paul's Letters* (New York: Oxford University Press, 2020).

48. LaFleur, Raskolnikov, and Kłosowska, "Introduction," 9.

49. Alicia Spencer-Hall and Blake Gutt, "Introduction," in *Trans and Genderqueer Subjects in Medieval Hagiography* (Amsterdam: Amsterdam University Press, 2021), 14.

50. Exemplary in this regard is Caroline Walker Bynum, *Jesus as Mother: Studies in the Spirituality of the High Middle Ages* (Berkeley: University of California Press, 1982).

51. Leah DeVun, *The Shape of Sex: Nonbinary Gender from Genesis to the Renaissance* (New York: Columbia University Press, 2021), 186.

52. DeVun, *The Shape*, 9–10; cf. 159–60.

Christian concepts, such as creation and incarnation, paradise and apocalypse. The essays by Strassfeld, Brownsmith, and Calaway in our collection converse with DeVun's work while turning to still other moments in biblical texts and traditions.

These historical approaches are slightly different than the identification of trancestors found in many circles and several essays here. But in recognizing outliers to structures, or transgressions of norms, this mode of historiography names, in part, an attraction to the past, the hope in engaging an archive. It often feels like a matter of survival, as Hil Malatino highlights: "When the milieu you inhabit feels hostile, it's deeply comforting to turn to text and image from another time."[53] To ask historically about trans is to dwell in a complicated affective terrain. Indeed, this terrain might reflect just how social gender is, how much recognition requires our supplication to others, as both Malatino and Merkley highlight. Historically, then, here is both an irreducible difference and a desire to do justice to the gorgeous messiness of memory, to attempt a kind of responsibility in "transtemporal solidarity," in spite of the confines of our language systems. As Malatino notes: "We are related to these subjects in some way, yes, but it is not an inheritance, not a lineage. These people are not our 'trancestors'. . . but they are nevertheless deeply implicated in our current conditions of possibility."[54]

Another way of putting it is: we cannot quite let go of these histories of gender variation.

TRANS IN BIBLICAL INTERPRETATION: HISTORIES OF APPROACH

The biblical shows up in a wide variety of ways in trans studies, providing leads for or reflecting resonances within trans approaches to biblical interpretation.

When turning to more focused examples of biblical interpretation, we likewise find that trans approaches have taken a number of forms from the start. To be sure, transgender interpretation often finds a home at first within queer hermeneutics, particularly in collections like *Take Back the Word* (2000); and then *Bible Trouble* (2011), and *Bodies on the Verge* (2019).[55] Key contributions from the first of these volumes demonstrate different strategies for exploring how trans biblical interpretation could operate. Justin Tanis's essay in *Take Back the Word*, for instance, rereads the encounter between Jesus and the Canaan-

---

53. Hil Malatino, *Trans Care* (Minneapolis: University of Minnesota Press, 2020), 51. For more on the affects of trans scholarship, see also Malatino, *Side Affects: On Being Trans and Feeling Bad* (Minneapolis: University of Minnesota Press, 2022).

54. Malatino, *Trans Care*, 59.

55. Robert E. Goss and Mona West, ed. *Take Back the Word: A Queer Reading of the Bible* (Cleveland: Pilgrim Press, 2000); Teresa J. Hornsby and Ken Stone, ed. *Bible Trouble: Queer Reading at the Boundaries of Biblical Scholarship* (Atlanta: SBL Press, 2011); Marchal, *Bodies on the Verge: Queering Pauline Epistles* (Atlanta: SBL Press, 2019).

ite woman (in Matt 15:21–28) from his perspective as a trans man in a way that encourages trust in the abundance that can be found in the God of the Gospels.[56] In the face of transphobia within and beyond the gay and lesbian community, Tanis presents Jesus as transformed by a mother's advocacy for her daughter's health, a messianic figure that suggests that we too should be transformed to advocate for each other. In this early essay, as well as in Sabia-Tanis's and Valentine's essays in our collection, trans interpretation has played a vital theological, even pastoral role.

Victoria Kolakowski, however, selects a potentially more complicated text in her essay in *Take Back the Word*, the death of Jezebel at the hands of eunuchs (in 2 Kgs 9), in order to offer a more ambivalent and reflexive intervention into the attractions and dangers of assimilation for transgender people.[57] On the one hand, Kolakowski qualifies lesbian and gay interpreters' previous reclamation of biblical eunuchs, pointing out that these figures might better fit in an argument for transgender inclusion.[58] On the other hand, the eunuch characters who follow the murderous instructions of Jehu could hardly be recuperated as exemplary points of identification or reclamation, particularly if their actions reinforce an ancient patriarchal structure or their comparatively "active" roles diminish a less manly tyrant. Eunuchs remain key figures to revisit and reconsider in trans approaches, as reflected in the essays by Brownsmith, Sabia-Tanis, and most especially Wiegel in our collection.

While not claiming to present a specifically transgender reading, a third essay from Ken Stone in *Take Back the Word* makes relevant contributions to such modes by queerly troubling the creation accounts of Genesis 1–3.[59] In conversation with previous feminist readings of the first human as androgynous, Stone shows how neither of these creation accounts line up with more recent expectations about binary gender.[60] Like Kolakowski, though, Stone does not insist that this makes it a "positive" text, but he does undermine homophobic and coincidentally transphobic citations by demonstrating how much Genesis is an unstable, even incoherent foundation for such claims. In just one early collection of queer readings, then, we find different potential strategies for trans biblical interpretation, situated ambivalently among (other) feminist and queer interpreters.

These early readings also highlight the role of specific figures of ancient gender variation, namely androgynes and eunuchs, who will remain central

56. Justin Tanis, "Eating from the Crumbs That Fall from the Table: Trusting the Abundance of God," in Goss and West, *Take Back the Word*, 43–54.
57. Victoria S. Kolakowski, "Throwing a Party: Patriarchy, Gender, and the Death of Jezebel," in Goss and West, *Take Back the Word*, 103–14.
58. Kolakowski, "Throwing a Party," 109; building off her previous essay, Kolakowski, "The Concubine and the Eunuch: Queering Up the Breeder's Bible," in *Our Families, Our Values: Snapshots of Queer Kinship*, ed. Goss and Amy A. S. Strongheart (New York: Harrington Park Press, 1997), 35–49.
59. Ken Stone, "The Garden of Eden and the Heterosexual Contract," in Goss and West, *Take Back the Word*, 57–70.
60. See especially Phyllis Trible, *God and the Rhetoric of Sexuality* (Philadelphia: Fortress, 1978).

in the longer treatments of biblical texts found within more theological and pastoral resources. Creative interpretations have been offered in theological work adjacent to biblical studies. Virginia Mollenkott, for instance, counters conservative and fundamentalist arguments from the (so-called) order of creation by also narrating how much the gender of the first human *and the deity* in Genesis do not conform to binary gender constructs.[61] After all, if both male and female are made "in the image of" the God in Gen 1:26–27, then this deity is also androgynous. Such an image corresponds with an increasingly popular declaration among (somewhat) progressive theists that "God is nonbinary!" Mollenkott counts the use of maternal "labor pains" to describe Jesus or Paul (in John 16:21–22 and Gal 4:19) and women putting on the presumably male body of Christ in baptism (Gal 3:26–28; Eph 5:30) as examples of transgender imagery in the New Testament.[62] She also identifies the role of the eunuchs of Matthew 19 and Acts 8 as demonstrating a biblical acceptance of transgender and transsexual people. Building off the arguments of Leslie Feinberg, Mollenkott even counters a text that attempts to exclude people with genital alterations (in Deut 23:1) with the blessings promised to eunuchs in Isa 56:3–5.[63] Indeed, Mollenkott frequently interacts with the work of both Leslie Feinberg and Kate Bornstein, noting the key role of Feinberg's *Stone Butch Blues* as a catalyst in the process of recognizing her own transgender identity.[64]

Tanis's book-length treatment of transgender theology and ministry, *Trans-Gendered: Theology, Ministry, and Communities of Faith*, also offers extended reflections upon the relevance of Christian scriptures for gender variance, asserting that these exclude transgender people only when they have been misinterpreted.[65] In conversation with Mollenkott and Kolakowski, Tanis examines the androgynous creation accounts of Genesis and focuses on a number of passages with eunuchs, arguing that "eunuchs are the closest biblical analogy we have to transgendered people."[66] He dismisses the Deuteronomy texts prohibiting "cross-dressing" and genital alteration (22:5 and 23:1) by noting that modern-day (mostly Christian) communities do not follow any of the surrounding prohibitions and opting to focus on more inclusive passages, like the baptism of the Ethiopian eunuch (Acts 8). Tanis enthusiastically concludes: "To me, seeing the record of our ancestors there at all, is affirming and amazing, but we are there."[67] Thus, Tanis and Mollenkott continue an advocacy-oriented process of taking

61. Virginia Ramey Mollenkott, *Omnigender: A Trans-religious Approach* (Cleveland: Pilgrim Press, 2001), 84–93.
62. Mollenkott, *Omnigender*, 110–14.
63. Mollenkott, 108, 118–21; see also Feinberg, Transgender Warriors, 50–51.
64. Mollenkott, viii–ix. For further context, see also David E. Weekley, "Across Generations: Becoming Grateful Allies: An Interview with Dr. Virginia Ramey Mollenkott," *JFSR* 34:1 (2018): 28–36.
65. Tanis, *Trans-Gendered: Theology, Ministry, and Communities of Faith* (Cleveland: Pilgrim Press, 2003), 55; later revised with an updated title *Trans-Gender: Theology, Ministry, and Communities of Faith* (Eugene, OR: Wipf and Stock, 2018).
66. Tanis, *Trans-Gendered*, 69.
67. Tanis, 84.

back these texts, developing an affirmative kind of reading from their social locations as transgender Christians.

These early readings of trans identities in conversation with Scripture also slightly preceded and overlapped with Christian faith communities who were grappling, often for the first time, with gender identity in the early 2000s. These writers began to provide resources to fill this gap in moderate and progressive communities to understand gender identity in conversation with Scripture. Many resources offered by faith communities revolved around care and understanding, and a few offered biblical assistance in video, sermon, pamphlet, and Bible study form. These encompass a wide variety of authors, both lay and clergy, sometimes referencing emerging trans scholarship but often offering their own nascent interpretations while Christian theology and biblical studies lagged in developing a trans hermeneutic.

Conferences evolved into publications that attempted to offer more systematic biblical interpretations. In 2004, Leanne McCall Tigert and Maren C. Tirabassi published *Transgendering Faith*, which offers a Bible study on nine passages, including a mixture of ones that explicitly address gender and ones that do not. Several questions follow each passage, which invite participants to consider bodily changes, family dynamics, and occasionally transgender experiences in light of the selected passages; the study does not offer critical resources or interpretations of the passages.[68] Notably, scholars and clergy contributed to an innovative Bible study published by the Human Rights Campaign, *Out in Scripture*, announced in 2006.[69] This lectionary-based Bible Study represents progressive Christian traditions and includes some openly trans writers and scholars known in queer interpretive circles with modest attention to trans experiences.

A mixture of resources from both trans people of faith and allies began to emerge in the 2010s. *This Is My Body: Hearing the Theology of Transgender Christians*, for instance, features personal essays drawn largely from the Sibyls, a spiritual group in the UK for trans people and allies, with sporadic biblical engagement.[70] As a trans activist in the Lutheran tradition, Austen Hartke provides more substantial biblical engagement from a trans lens in *Transforming*. There he reflects not only on name changes in the Bible, but on accounts of Joseph's coat and Deborah as being nonnormative in the ancient world and thus similar to trans believers today.[71] Another pastoral resource created by Chris Dowd and Christina Beardsley, with contributions from Tanis, was rooted in

68. Leanne McCall Tigert and Maren C. Tirabassi, ed., *Transgendering Faith: Identity, Sexuality, and Spirituality* (Cleveland: Pilgrim Press, 2004), 152–57.
69. Publication dates are not available on the individual Bible studies; see https://www.hrc.org/resources/out-in-scripture (accessed August 15, 2023).
70. Christina Beardsley and Michelle O'Brien, ed., *This Is My Body: Hearing the Theology of Transgender Christians* (London: Darton, Longman & Todd, 2016).
71. Austen Hartke, *Transforming: The Bible and the Lives of Transgender Christians* (Louisville, KY: Westminster John Knox Press, 2018; updated edition 2023).

a participant study and includes a helpful chapter on the Bible.[72] Alongside positive trans readings of texts such as Gen 1:26–27, they include less frequently examined passages such as Rom 5:12–17 as an example of trans acceptance rooted in the union with Christ.

Faith community resources for Christians have been somewhat limited in their biblical interpretations because few biblical scholars were publishing about transgender people and their concerns until well after 2010. These resources engaged with scholarship at varying levels, offering at times innovative readings of the Bible rooted in firsthand experiences and deep allyship. These publications show verve for making strides with very little material from the guild. Interestingly, though, the faith-based resources also looked strongly to theological writings that engaged trans identities well before most biblical scholars, appealing to Susannah Cornwall, Marcella Althaus-Reid, Lisa Isherwood, Vanessa Sheridan, Mollenkott, and Tanis.[73]

In the same time period, though, Jewish scholars and activists were producing significant work around the roles of eunuchs and androgynes in relation to passages in Bereshit (Genesis) and beyond. Sarra Lev's dissertation, for instance, examined gender crossing in tannaitic literature, focusing especially on how eunuchs were seen as transgressing sex/gender categories by moving from male to female or non-gendered categories.[74] Rabbinic materials discuss eunuchs and androgynes, and often pair the latter with *tumtumim*, people who lack an identifiable sex (possibly because a flap of skin obscures their genitalia). For the rabbis, both divine and human bodies were notably malleable, reflecting more thoroughly than the creation narratives on not only the androgynous image for God and the first human, but also the traditions about Abraham and Sarah as *tumtumim*.[75] Indeed, Elliot Kukla, the first openly trans person ordained as a Reform rabbi, identified with the *tumtum* in his master's thesis on ancient Jewish gender multiplicity, arguing: "These texts indicate an opening toward *infinite* locations for belonging that are still authentically connected to our histories and communities."[76] Continuing his work as a nonbinary and disabled rabbi with the online resource TransTorah, Kukla also helped to popularize the strategic

---

72. Chris Dowd and Christina Beardsley, *Transfaith: A Transgender Pastoral Resource* (London: Darton, Longman & Todd, 2018).

73. Marcella Althaus-Reid, *Indecent Theology: Theological Perversions in Sex, Gender and Politics* (New York: Routledge, 2000); Althaus-Reid and Lisa Isherwood, eds., *The Sexual Theologian: Essays on Sex, God and Politics* (London: T&T Clark, 2004); Mollenkott, *Omnigender*; Mollenkott and Vanessa Sheridan, *Transgender Journeys* (Cleveland: Pilgrim Press, 2003); Tanis, *Trans-Gendered*.

74. Sarra Lev, "Genital Trouble: On the Innovations of Tannaitic Thought Regarding Damaging Genitals and Eunuchs" (PhD dissertation, New York University, 2004); see also now Lev, *And the Sages Did Not Know: Early Rabbinic Approaches to Intersex* (Philadelphia: University of Pennsylvania Press, 2024).

75. See the discussions in Sally Gross, "Intersexuality and Scripture," *Theology and Sexuality* 11 (1999): 65–74; and Gwynn Kessler, "Bodies in Motion: Preliminary Notes on Queer Theory and Rabbinic Literature," in *Mapping Gender in Ancient Religious Discourse*, ed. Todd Penner and Caroline Vander Stichele (Leiden: Brill, 2007), 389–409.

76. Elliot Kukla, "A Created Being of Its Own" (master's thesis, Hebrew Union College, 2006), 58. See also the discussion of Kukla and the earlier zine by Micah Bazant (in 1999) that reclaimed

shorthand "there are six genders in ancient Judaism"—namely: female, male, *tumtum*, *androginos* (a person with both male and female characteristics), *saris* (a person who was castrated or born without a penis or reproductive capability), and *aylonit* (a female eunuch, or a female who does not develop reproductive capability).

As more trans, genderqueer, and nonbinary Jews were participating and increasingly leading within a wide spectrum of denominational settings, they pointed to a range of texts and traditions, profoundly undermining the persistently regressive or reactionary reading of Genesis that sanctifies only a heteronormative view of binary gender, as well as the frankly colonizing claims to speak of a univocal and timeless "Judeo-Christian" position that marginalizes and vilifies trans and gender nonconforming people. To be sure, though there are manifest differences between Jewish and Christian histories and practices, indispensable works like Max K. Strassfeld's *Trans Talmud* and DeVun's *Shape of Sex* thoroughly attest to the lengthy and considerable histories of attention to gender variation within Jewish and then Christian traditions of scriptural interpretation and engagement, respectively.

By the second and third decade of the "new" century, trans approaches to these scriptures were taking a number of forms and are still growing, though not quite (yet) to the infinite possibilities Kukla imagined. These contributions from rabbinic and other forms of biblical studies developed in part by drawing upon resources from both feminist and queer hermeneutics. Indeed, even a quick survey of some of the key works by Deryn Guest, one of the most prominent biblical scholars applying trans approaches, suffices as another gauge of the intertwined relations among these lenses. Guest's first major book elaborated a lesbian-feminist hermeneutics through the application of four principles: resistance, rupturing, reclamation, and reengagement.[77] Brownsmith's essay in our collection adapts these principles and, as we have already seen, many trans interpreters have reclaimed and reengaged biblical texts in this way, though perhaps without as much resistance to the silencing and erasure Guest's work identifies.

From within this principle of resistance, Guest's hermeneutic of heterosuspicion builds upon and specifies the sort of hermeneutic of suspicion elaborated by feminist biblical scholars like Elisabeth Schüssler Fiorenza.[78] In recent years, Jo Henderson-Merrygold critically engaged this hermeneutical proposal of Guest's to emphasize the need to treat cisnormativity with suspicion, thus coining a hermeneutic of cis-picion.[79] Henderson-Merrygold argues that we should be suspicious of a presumed binary and what variations of gender this presumption

---

the *timtum* as genderqueer in Strassfeld, *Trans Talmud: Androgynes and Eunuchs in Rabbinic Literature* (Oakland: University of California Press, 2022), 195–200.

77. Deryn Guest, *When Deborah Met Jael: Lesbian Biblical Hermeneutics* (London: SCM Press, 2005).

78. See Guest, *When Deborah*, 123–24; engaging works as early as Elisabeth Schüssler Fiorenza's *Bread Not Stone: The Challenge of Feminist Biblical Interpretation* (Edinburgh: T&T Clark, 1984).

79. Jo Henderson-Merrygold, "Gendering Sarai: Reading beyond Cisnormativity in Genesis 11:29–12:20 and 20:1–18," *Open Theology* 6:1 (2020): 496–509.

covers up in our interpretations of biblical texts, specifically in the ancestral narratives that feature Sarah and Esau.[80] Other figures from these narratives in Genesis have been recurrent figures of identification for trans readings, most especially Joseph, particularly considering the garment given by Jacob, the coat of many colors (of KJV and musical fame), is more likely a long robe with sleeves (Gen 37:3, 23, 31–34), the same kind worn by David's daughter Tamar (2 Sam 13:18–19). Though scholars interested in homoerotic dynamics, like Ted Jennings, helped to point out Joseph's (so-called) transgendering garment,[81] queer and trans performance artists and interpreters like Peterson Toscano and J. Mase III put this biblical knowledge into wider circulation through more popularizing presentations of Jo's or Josephine's "princess dress."[82]

To continue the survey of Guest's developing hermeneutical approaches, in later works they explicitly begin drawing upon transgender studies alongside feminist and queer theories to refine their approaches. For instance, though approaching Judges 4–5 with an explicitly lesbian lens in their "From Gender Reversal to Genderfuck" essay from *Bible Trouble*, Guest also engages Halberstam's work on female masculinity to note the various overlaps and tensions between butch lesbian, transgender, and transsexual circles.[83] One result is that Guest highlights at several turns how Jael's genderqueer presentation in this fraught biblical text looks differently to transsexual, transgender, or genderqueer readers, potentially as feminist readers. Likewise, in the longer work *Beyond Feminist Biblical Studies*, Guest suggests that interpreters practice genderqueer criticism, a feminist form of biblical scholarship more thoroughly informed by queer theories, critical studies of masculinities, and the constructedness of gender overall.

To Guest, one important difference for this type of feminist or gender studies approach is finding common cause with the trans activism of Sandy Stone and Kate Bornstein in order to resist and subvert the gender binary.[84] With greater attention to practices that trouble this binary, scholars like Aysha Winstanley Musa have also returned to some of the same texts that animated Guest's work, including the account of Jael in Judges. In both her dissertation and her essay in our collection, Musa approaches Jael from a nonbinary perspective, asserting

80. Henderson-Merrygold, *Introducing a Hermeneutics of Cispicion: Reading Sarah and Esau's Gender (Failures) beyond Cisnormativity* (London: T&T Clark, 2024).

81. Theodore W. Jennings Jr., *Jacob's Wound: Homoerotic Narrative in the Literature of Ancient Israel* (New York: Continuum, 2005), 177–96.

82. Though they adapt their depiction of this trans biblical character to the performance context, representative examples of their work include: Peterson Toscano, "Joseph and the Amazing Gender Non-Conforming Bible Story" from his solo performance "Transfigurations: Transgressing Gender in the Bible" (Pendle Hill, 2017), DVD, and https://www.youtube.com/watch?v=gkikBKW8vmQ; and J Mase III, "Josephine": Reconciling My Queer Faith, Huffington Post, October 4, 2013, http://www.huffingtonpost.com/j-mase-iii/josephine-reconciling-my-queer-faith_b_4014580.html.

83. Guest, "From Gender Reversal to Genderfuck: Reading Jael through a Lesbian Lens," in Hornsby and Stone, *Bible Trouble*, 9–43; Halberstam, *Female Masculinity* (Durham, NC: Duke University Press, 1998).

84. Guest, *Beyond Feminist Biblical Studies* (Sheffield: Sheffield Phoenix Press, 2012), 71–75.

that Jael is best described not as a woman, but as a gender ambiguous character, performing roles that have been constructed as feminine as well as those constructed as masculine.[85] In her essay in our collection, Musa shows how Jael's gender ambiguity is particularly evident through their performance of motherhood (in contrast to the frameworks reflected by Deborah and Sisera's mother).

One of the reasons we focus so much attention on the trajectories of Guest's work is that Guest and Teresa Hornsby were the first biblical scholars to coauthor a book on transgender biblical interpretation, *Transgender, Intersex, and Biblical Interpretation*. The gender binary remains the object of critique and resistance in this relatively brief yet potent book, as is evident from Hornsby's first contribution, pointedly titled: "Gender Dualism, or the Big Lie." Here, Hornsby asserts: "Even if we know nothing else about gender, its construct, and its ubiquitous presence, we can *look around* and *know* that it is simply not true that there are only two, opposing genders."[86] After briefly surveying some of Mollenkott's and Tanis's approaches to trans interpretation, Hornsby returns with Kolakowski to the ambivalent recognition that biblical texts and traditions can be made to support either the oppression or liberation of trans people. Given this challenging observation, Guest's attention to method in the two middle chapters of their and Hornsby's volume is especially valuable in venturing a way forward. As in their previous hermeneutical reflections, Guest articulates four elements to describe the transgender gaze: 1.) locating this gaze "in trans experience," 2.) exposing the constructedness of gender, 3.) confronting "heteronormativity with alternative visions of gender," and 4.) requiring "political and religious engagement, challenging the (negative) effects of biblical interpretation for trans people."[87] As with many interpreters past and present (within and beyond our collection), Guest names the ultimate goal of addressing and improving the conditions of trans people today. As Ladin, Calaway, and Sellew do in our collection, Guest also employs autobiographical reflections, specifically to locate themselves and to explicate their understanding of a trans reading approach. For instance, Guest points, like Mollenkott, to Feinberg's *Stone Butch Blues* as influential for their own identity.[88] Yet, Guest also returns to concepts and conversation partners from their own previous work, including Halberstam's transgender look, Stone's manifesto against invisibility, and Bornstein's challenge to gender categorization, in order to look more carefully at what makes a transgender gaze. (The essays by Calaway and Valentine in our collection draw upon some of these same interlocutors, most notably Halberstam and Feinberg, respectively.)

---

85. Aysha Winstanley Musa, "Jael's Gender Ambiguity in Judges 4 and 5" (PhD thesis, University of Sheffield, 2020).

86. Hornsby, "Gender Dualism, or the Big Lie," in Guest and Hornsby, *Transgender, Intersex, and Biblical Interpretation* (Atlanta: SBL Press, 2016), 16.

87. Guest, "Modeling the Transgender Gaze," in Guest and Hornsby, *Transgender, Intersex, and Biblical Interpretation*, 50–51.

88. Guest, 45.

Guest revisits these interlocutors and influences particularly to think through and potentially model how a transgender gaze, outlined in the four elements above, relates to trans experiences. Both in their essays in our collection and previous works, Ladin, Sabia-Tanis, and Sellew similarly each draw upon experience, at times in distinctive directions. Sabia-Tanis, for instance, stresses a grounding in the lived experiences of transgender people as the first presupposition for trans theology and hermeneutics. This means that trans interpretation can do more than look for biblical figures who can function as trancestors. It can read other passages not (as) explicitly related to gender—like the parable of the good Samaritan—through the lens of transgender experience. In her essay in our collection as well as her exemplary article reading the Gospel of Thomas through a trans lens, Sellew reflects upon how her place as a woman of transgender experience shapes a reader-centered approach.[89] Beyond *Thomas'* reconfiguration of the doubled creation narratives of Genesis, Sellew highlights how this noncanonical Gospel's focus on finding your true identity is particularly relevant for trans or gender nonconforming readers.

Such readers might also resonate with teachings that bodies can misrepresent our actual identities, providing opportunities to queer the gender of Jesus, as Valentine and Khumalo and Thomas also do in their essays in our collection. In her own essay in our collection, Ladin revisits her remarkable *Soul of the Stranger* with the explicit aim of clarifying how she defines trans hermeneutics in relation to experience. To Ladin, a "trans experience" is any experience in which someone notes a slippage between themselves and the identity-defining roles and categories they have been assigned. If one but learns to pay attention, then, anyone can look for mismatches or conflicts between their sense of themselves and the gender roles and categories others expect from them. For Ladin, this approach has the salutary ability to apply to our readings of biblical texts, while also undermining how the trans / cis binary oversimplifies and erases how variations and changeability are a part of any category. Ladin's framework un-queers trans and nonbinary identities.

Ladin's conceptualization, then, highlights that not all trans approaches to interpretation center around disruptive or subversive effects. Strassfeld's essay in our collection, as well as his larger, landmark work *Trans Talmud*, also worries about the cost of reading the appearance of the androgyne in rabbinic applications of scriptures as primarily subversive, particularly if these materials put them in a precarious position. As a result, both Ladin's and Strassfeld's approaches in part center around categorizations and expectations of the human. Ladin, after all, underscores how, since no human always fits within their assigned roles or categories, all people have trans experiences. Further, Ladin's goal for anyone engaging trans hermeneutics is not that we find the same trans experiences in the bible, but that we shift our assumptions about humans. Strassfeld underscores

---

89. Melissa Harl Sellew, "Reading the *Gospel of Thomas* from Here: A Trans-Centred Hermeneutic," *JIBS* 1:2 (Spring 2020): 61–96.

how rabbinic materials are deeply invested in related questions when they ask in what ways could gender variant people like androgynes or eunuchs fit within ritual or legal obligations; or in other words, in what ways are they (like other) humans? On the one hand, this creates space in the tradition, as when the androgyne is described as "a unique creation." On the other hand, their position in creation is acknowledged, their humanity is legible, only when this tradition is considering the case of their injury or death.

In this moment Strassfeld recognizes a resonance, from the work of Alexander Weheliye, with how racialization has historically functioned in the genres of the human, a category built on hierarchies, exclusions, and their violences.[90] Trans interpretation then can move in posthumanist and Black feminist directions,[91] as when Strassfeld reconsiders androgynes and eunuchs, not by way of an analogy to Black people and the histories of racism, but in learning to suspect an offer of access to a category like human on the basis of such critical reflections on these histories. Finding "us" in a sacred tradition is powerful, but Strassfeld questions on what terms and within what histories of categorization are "we" included? Along a similar trajectory Merkley's essay in our collection pointedly proposes to not treat trans as yet another category for humans, but to use trans as a mode for examining how and what categorization does.

Trans forms or figures within biblical interpretation then should not be located solely within queer hermeneutics. Sellew's specifically reader-centered approach also points us in other directions, particularly when she grounds her approach as "reading from this place," building on the monumental work of Fernando F. Segovia and Mary Ann Tolbert on social location.[92] If we bother to look, we can see how trans people or practices have peeked in occasionally within other works or collections focused with less explicitly trans specific emphases, including within ethnically and racially minoritized hermeneutics. Michael Joseph Brown's examination of African American biblical hermeneutics, for instance, concludes with an extended meditation on the experiences of two Black trans women.[93] Brown proposes that these women's experiences matter for womanist and other Afrocentric approaches, not because they are respectable representatives, but because they are among the most marginalized. Brown underscores how one of these women "recognizes that the oppression she encounters is multiple and simultaneous," exemplifying how critical reflections on positionality can move us toward an intersectional analysis.[94] The inclusion

---

90. Alexander Weheliye, *Habeas Viscus: Racializing Assemblages, Biopolitics, and Black Feminist Theories of the Human* (Durham, NC: Duke University Press, 2014).

91. For a reconsideration of rabbinic treatments of human and non-human animals, in light of queer theory, trans theory, and disability studies along posthumanist trajectories, see Rafael Rachel Neis, *When a Human Gives Birth to a Raven: Rabbis and the Reproduction of Species* (Oakland: University of California Press, 2023).

92. Sellew, "Reading," 63–64; Fernando F. Segovia and Mary Ann Tolbert, eds., *Reading from This Place: Social Location and Biblical Interpretation*, 2 vols. (Minneapolis: Fortress, 1995).

93. Michael Joseph Brown, *Blackening of the Bible: The Aims of African American Biblical Scholarship* (Harrisburg, PA: Trinity Press International, 2004), 175–83.

94. Brown, *Blackening*, 181.

of their perspectives in such reflections runs the risk of tokenization or fetishization but, as Khumalo and Thomas also note in closing their essay in our collection, Brown candidly acknowledges: "If, however, the possibility of the actual inclusion of such a hermeneutical perspective rests entirely on the presence of these individuals in the guild, then their voices may never be heard."[95]

A similar spirit likely animates Tat-siong Benny Liew's reconsideration of the Gospel of John for minority biblical criticism in the light of what Liew calls "transgendering" dynamics. Like Strassfeld often does, Liew opens by reflecting on the longer histories of racist policing of bathrooms to underscore the intersectional convergences of race, gender, and sexuality.[96] Liew, as well as Khumalo and Thomas in our collection, reconsider, with many Johannine scholars, the intriguing gender dynamics of a Jesus who is described as both a female *Sophia* and a male *Logos*. When Liew reads this Gospel for multiple, racially or sexually coded signs (like clothing, categories, and crossing), then he recognizes this Jesus as a cross-dressing and border-crossing drag king trickster. Though Liew locates himself in his essay as a trickster like this elusive Jesus, at one point he explains that his approach "hopes to give recognition and life to those who desire to live otherwise gendered or transgendered lives."[97] These select examples of minoritized forms of biblical criticism engaging trans materials underscore how trans approaches have not been as racially attuned as they could be, a significant problem that some of the essays in our collection, particularly those by Strassfeld, Sabia-Tanis, Khumalo and Thomas, and Marchal, hope to address.

TOWARD TRANS BIBLICAL VARIATIONS OF INTERPRETATION

Our collection represents a historic effort to expand and elaborate upon the sometimes-disparate trajectories of trans biblical interpretation, intensifying and enlarging the set of biblical texts and interpretive approaches, relevant histories and theories, conversation partners and force multipliers in order to question, qualify, challenge, and ultimately alter the conditions of our time and place. Even when parts of our collection might seem to be narrowing or squeezing so as to contract the focus, they often move alternately, accordion-like, to open our paths for exploring trans elements in biblical texts and traditions. For instance, while Ladin shifts our focus to the many kinds of trans experiences of mismatch between expectation and reality that *anyone* can have, Wiegel makes a strong case for specifying a single criterion for historically identifying a trans person

---

95. Brown, *Blackening*, 178.
96. Tat-siong Benny Liew, "Queering Closets and Perverting Desires: Cross-Examining John's Engendering and Transgendering Word across Different Worlds," in *They Were All Together in One Place?: Toward Minority Biblical Criticism*, ed. Randall C. Bailey, Tat-siong Benny Liew, and Fernando F. Segovia (Atlanta: SBL Press, 2009), 251–52.
97. Liew, "Queering," 267, 261.

in the pre-modern past. Like others, Wiegel critiques scholarly approaches that have over-identified trans as another disruptive version of queer and highlights the variability in gender categories in different cultures, both historically and geographically. This variability is not particularly a problem for doing trans historiography for Wiegel, if we do not expect people in the past to imitate our present-day categories. In fact, this helps Wiegel to arrive at her argument that "a trans person is someone who seeks or desires to transition from one category of sexed or gendered intelligibility (telling an intelligible story with their body) to another category of sexed or gendered intelligibility, or someone who seeks or desires to transition from intelligibility to unintelligibility because of the inadequacy of their culture's categories for them." Wiegel then applies this narrow definition to see which people might fit it in biblical texts, starting with Jesus's vexing saying about "eunuchs for the kingdom of heaven" in Matt 19:12. Yet, even in this most rigorous contraction, Wiegel also shows how this concise definition can shift our attention away from expected texts in previous searches for trancestors toward wider sets of texts, including those that involve movements that do not at first appear to be analogous to transgender narratives, as in the emphasis on virginity over marriage in texts like 1 Corinthians 6–7.

Thus, in its range of approaches to trans interpretation, *Trans Biblical* does not ignore the texts about eunuchs, androgynes, or clothing long held as important for trans approaches to biblical traditions. The two essays that bookend the collection—by Strassfeld and Merkley—provide some of the most helpful engagements of androgynes in Genesis 1 and clothing prohibitions in Deuteronomy 22, precisely through their treatment of distinctly Jewish and Christian traditions of interpretation, among the rabbis and early church fathers, respectively. Strassfeld's essay strategically juxtaposes the rabbinic treatment of androgynes with the very different contemporary legal context in which trans people are (recurrently) targeted in the present-day United States.[98] The rabbinic approach to androgynes and hybrid animals stems from a rather different, if also rather *religious* reading of creation from the one promoted by the brand of evangelical Christian theology that animates so much anti-trans animus in more recent years. While neither Strassfeld's exploration of Genesis 1 nor Merkley's of Deuteronomy 22 (and investigation of Tertullian's interpretation of gendered clothing choices) find the most affirmative views in either of these traditions, they demonstrate how resources from trans studies can redirect our focus with these ancient texts and challenge the lingering influence of normalizing and naturalizing categories.

After Strassfeld's opening essay, the next three expand the array of biblical texts and characters from the Hebrew Bible treated within trans interpretation. Ladin, for instance, applies her capacious delineation of trans experience beyond the creation narratives toward the ancestral cycles in Genesis. Ladin argues that

---

98. For other anachronistic juxtapositions in relation to trans people and practices, see Marchal, "The Corinthian Women Prophets and Trans Activism: Rethinking Canonical Gender Claims," in Hornsby and Stone, *Bible Trouble*, 223–46; and Marchal, *Appalling Bodies*, especially 30–67.

Jacob's resistance to his birth assignment (as the second-born son) is a meaningful example for trans hermeneutics, not because this made him transgender, but because this resistance is akin to how trans or nonbinary people refuse or challenge their birth assignments. The next two essays, by Musa and Brownsmith, approach two other biblical characters as nonbinary: Jael in Judges and Mordecai in Esther. Musa employs a genderqueer methodology to specifically disrupt the binary framework most readers bring to biblical texts and traditions. For Musa, even interpreters who argue that Jael performs a kind of gender reversal unwittingly reinforce this binary, and thus miss how Jael performs motherhood in a gender ambiguous manner—in a nonbinary way. Brownsmith likewise sees a nonbinary Mordecai resisting a gender binary in Esther, a characterization that helps us to recognize multiple genders, even as we cannot naively map our current versions of gender on ancient texts. Brownsmith feels the pull between two different horizons: a presentist context in which the Bible is read as scripture that speaks to the lives of present-day people (why many *care* about these texts), and a historicist context that scholars can bring to read a biblical text (information many might *need* in order to understand these texts) as a product of a specific time, reflecting the worldview of very distant people.[99] The chapters in *Trans Biblical* alternately, if still recurrently, work toward both of these ends.

Our collection turns then to a number of essays on the Gospels and letters of the New Testament. Indeed, *Trans Biblical* intentionally provides more attention to these texts from the distinctly Christian canons of scriptures, for two reasons. The first is that both Jewish studies and Jewish devotional communities of practice are relatively "further ahead" than their larger Christian counterparts in considering trans people and practices of the past and the present. The second reason, though, is the more potent: some of the loudest transphobic forces in the present day come from those who claim to be Christian—followers of a Savior and his scriptures. Many people need to understand these particular biblical texts and traditions differently and better.

The next three essays by Sabia-Tanis, Valentine, and Khumalo and Thomas focus primarily upon prominent portions of the canonical Gospels: the parable of the good Samaritan (in Luke), the transfiguration (in Mark), and the incarnation of the Word (in the prologue to John). Sabia-Tanis adeptly transposes the beloved Samaritan parable into our present context by placing transgender people at the center, not the margins, of teachings by Jesus. Placing different figures within the parable in a trans social location shifts our perspective. The disproportionate violence against trans people, especially trans women of color, could suggest an analogy to the person who was robbed, assaulted, and abandoned, yet Sabia-Tanis primarily reads the Samaritan as trans to convey a lesson about our neighborly obligations as exemplified by those who have been excluded and despised.

---

99. For an important intervention into doing trans history, discussing gender as a hyperobject in order to address similar concerns, see Ky Merkley, "Writing Trans Histories with an Ethics of Care, While Reading Gender in Imperial Roman Literature," *Gender and History* 36:1 (2024): 14–31.

While Sabia-Tanis writes as a trans theologian, the next two essays foreground the importance of allies with trans people contributing to broader efforts to change biblical interpretations of Jesus. Prompted by insights from trans Christians, Valentine explores the transfiguration of Jesus in Mark 9:1–9 as a positive example of a gender transformation in the Gospels. Building upon the interests of her interviewees and their positive attachments to this account,[100] Valentine surveys bodily changes in the ancient world, including the metamorphoses of gods, humans, and animals, to help contextualize the femme form Jesus takes on the mountain alongside the gender-queer ancestors Moses and Elijah. Khumalo and Thomas likewise advance an understanding of Jesus as a proto-ancestor in Africana interpretation, for readers in critical empathy and responsive ally relationships with transgender people, particularly given Jesus's incarnation in the flesh. They highlight the bodily incarnation of *Logos* in the prologue of John as a figural representation of trans* experience, a transitive figuration that is recurrently misrecognized and "deadnamed" by other traditions that demand suffering and death.

The next three essays move the collection into an engagement with the Pauline epistles, but not before Wiegel's essay revisits the eunuchs of Matthew 19 alongside the valorization of sexual renunciation in 1 Corinthians 6–7. Here Wiegel boldly advances a single criterion in looking for trans people in the premodern past, focused upon an act of transition, as mentioned above, "from one sexed or gendered intelligibility" to another, or a desire for it. These two texts are alike, not because the latter shows that the former is "really" about celibacy, but because both advocate crossing categories and thus transgressing gender boundaries. In contrast to the prevailing androcentrism in early Christianities, Wiegel's interpretation of these practices opens up a possible valorization of the female and feminine as something worth transitioning *into* and not merely *away from*.

Calaway's essay seeks a transgender touch across time with transformed bodies later in 1 Corinthians, particularly the glorified, resurrection bodies in 1 Corinthians 15. This metamorphosis provides an opportune theme for pursuing a hermeneutics of resonance and dissonance. Paul's ongoing androcentrism strikes a dissonant chord for Calaway as a trans woman, yet this cannot block out the description of bodies in transition that resonates, a rise from flesh into a glorious sparkling. Marchal similarly moves the focus from the individual person of Paul to other figures like Hagar, Onesimus, and Epaphroditus (in Galatians, Philemon, and Philippians) as potential examples of captive genders and fugitive flesh negotiating greater precarity and proximity to death. Informed by efforts at the intersections of critical race, trans, and abolitionist practices to specifically address the diminished life chances disproportionately faced by trans people, Marchal highlights how the roles of (formerly) incarcerated trans women and their networks of support and solidarity today can creatively reposition biblical

---

100. See also Katy E. Valentine, "Examining Scripture in Light of Trans Women's Voices," in *The Oxford Handbook of Feminist Approaches to the Hebrew Bible*, ed. Susanne Scholz (Oxford: Oxford University Press, 2020), 508–23.

practices of letter-writing, circulation, and assembly within longer histories of imprisonment and enslavement.

Our final two essays explore beyond the biblical canons, interpreting and engaging the Gospel of Thomas and Tertullian and, in turn, reflecting upon other, canonized texts. Indeed, as Sellew and Merkley highlight, both *Thomas* and Tertullian's *De pallio* reflect an anxiety over and/or the diminishment of the exterior. Sellew contrasts the Gospel of Thomas's approach to renewal and transformation as possible in the here and now to the anxious apocalypticism evident in Paul's letters. In the Gospel's emphasis on an introspective process of salvation focused on one's inner, less visible self, Sellew finds strong resonances with trans people's experience, especially processes of self-understanding, self-acceptance, and public assertion of our true gendered selves. Such potentially validating resonances, then, are tied to the dissonance between an inner self-understanding and others' claims on the basis of one's external, bodily self. Merkley similarly zeroes in on other moments of contestation, namely the meaning of clothing in early Christian negotiations of scripture within Roman norms of masculinity. Tertullian's approach to Deut 22:5 differs from Clement of Alexandria's by emphasizing Achilles as a monstrous example of gender crossing, an argument with chilling continuities with recent claims that trans people are deceptive or threatening. Yet, Tertullian's manifest efforts to construct this boogeyman demonstrate how long gender has been a multicultural site of contestation, given the ancient presence of gender nonconforming people, even in these early Christian debates. The mere presence of this contestation allows for more inclusive and gender expansive readings within the Christianity of today.

Thus, the experience, effort, and expertise assembled by the scholars in this collection provide a series of distinctive and important interventions within both biblical studies and trans studies. The present and future of more just arrangements of gender and embodiment require a greater reckoning with the past and a new kind of attention to the many kinds of gender variation. Biblical scholars, of course, bring a crucial, multifaceted expertise—in the ancient west Asian and Greco-Roman contexts and the select texts that were later canonized religiously and culturally—to trans studies and praxis. An approach attuned by, with, or simply as trans studies, in turn, calibrates the study of biblical texts and traditions with a finer sensitivity to the potential complexity and variety of gender and embodiment. Trans kinds of biblical scholarship, or biblical kinds of trans scholarship, are uniquely positioned, and potentially *even more suited* to address both ancient people and practices and current deliberations and developments. This combination, of trans and biblical, facilitates new comparative, interdisciplinary, and intersectional questions about differences in gender and embodiment—historically, geographically, linguistically, socially, politically, and theologically. Thus, this *Trans Biblical* collection equips its readers to grapple with stigma, ridicule, anxiety, and violence, without being determined by them, moving the variations on interpretation and embodiment in dynamic, reflexive, and capacious directions.

We hope that this introduction serves to situate the contributions of *Trans Biblical* within longer streams of scholarship and advocacy, within, beside, or beyond biblical studies. In presenting some key voices and movements within both trans studies and biblical studies, we entertain no pretensions at absolute comprehension of a complex and still growing series of convergences where trans and biblical might still feed into each other. Thankfully the following essays themselves return to these convergences and can point readers to even more resources and conversation partners. When and where we engage with trans theories and movements, we believe this collection acts as a helpful entrée for biblical interpreters to make new, more creative, reflexive, and accountable connections to influential texts and traditions. For those already familiar with some of the prior trans identifications with biblical figures or texts, this volume encourages us to think more broadly about forms of gender variation and in wider sets of texts besides those that focus on androgynes or eunuchs. Of course, it is extremely valuable to see gender variance in the biblical materials themselves. Gender variation *is* as ancient as stories about creation! *And* stories about resistance, and escape, and resurrection, and transfiguration, and incarnation, and on and on. Biblical texts and traditions are more capacious and variable than most expect, often disrupting present-day assumptions of a gender binary. *Trans Biblical* sharpens our awareness of what is "in" these texts and builds up our capacities for what can be done "with" our encounter with/in biblical texts and traditions.

In short, the work of these scholars meets an important, even urgent need by providing a range of entry points and approaches to biblical texts and traditions in a contextually and theoretically nuanced fashion. It is past time to engage these variations on trans and biblical.

Chapter 1

Androgynes, Hybrid Animals, and the Project of Trans History

MAX K. STRASSFELD

In 2018, a memo from the US Department of Health and Human Services was leaked to the *New York Times*. The memo offered a definition of sex: "Sex means a person's status as male or female based on immutable biological traits identifiable by or before birth."[1] As the *Times* reported, this definition would eradicate federal recognitions of trans people who have gone through bureaucratic processes to change their legal status. While nothing in the memo references religion directly, journalists traced the language back to its Christian evangelical roots.[2] The category of sex is currently at the heart of legal and policy wrangling over trans embodiment.[3] In this chapter, I will practice deliberate anachronism

---

1. See Erica Green, Katie Benner, and Robert Pear, "'Transgender' Could Be Defined Out of Existence under Trump Administration," *New York Times*, October 2018. https://nyti.ms/2R9W1jB.
2. In the popular press, *Mother Jones* has reported on the connection between the anti-trans bills and evangelical Christian theology. See Samantha Michaels, "We Tracked Down the Lawyers behind the Recent Wave of Anti-Trans Bathroom Bills," *Mother Jones*, April 25, 2016, https://www.motherjones.com/politics/2016/04/alliance-defending-freedom-lobbies-anti-lgbt-bathroom-bills/. The reporters argue that the language found in the memo originates with the Alliance Defending Freedom (ADF), a Christian legal organization.
3. On this question, see Paisley Currah, *Sex Is as Sex Does: Governing Transgender Identity* (New York: New York University Press, 2022).

by weaving together a rabbinic tradition about an androgyne with contemporary legal battles. In doing so, I illuminate what is at stake in these divergent struggles over the definition of sex and gender in law.

In my book *Trans Talmud: Androgynes and Eunuchs in Rabbinic Literature*, I explore various nonbinary rabbinic categories. I argue that the rabbis simultaneously use these figures to extend their regulation of sex, gender, and embodiment, even as they paradoxically carve nonbinary space into the tradition.[4] I use the term "transing" (as a verb) to describe my method of interpretation.[5] Drawing on the work of trans studies theorists and historians, I argue for a reading strategy that attends to the materiality of sex and gender and the concurrent costs of regulation.[6]

With the term "transing," I also raise the question of what it means to read historical sources through a specifically trans lens. I am skeptical as to whether the tools developed to study histories of sexuality are sufficient to address the study of androgynes and eunuchs in antiquity. Throughout this chapter, I pose a broader question: How might our reading practices need to be shaped by the specificities of the bodily regulation and surveillance of intersex and trans people?[7]

The most central early rabbinic source on the androgyne is found in tractate Bikkurim.[8] In this source, the rabbis debate the extent to which law can

---

4. What follows is a revised version of an argument that appears in different forms elsewhere, including the second chapter of my book, Max K. Strassfeld, *Trans Talmud: Androgynes and Eunuchs in Rabbinic Literature* (Oakland: University of California Press, 2022), and an earlier article under the title "Translating the Human: The *Androginos* in Tosefta Bikkurim" in *TSQ* 3:3–4 (2016): 587–604. I am grateful to Rafe Neis and the fellows of the Frankel Institute for their response to an early draft of the chapter, and the reviewers for subsequent comments.

5. I do not originate the use of transing as a verb; it was first used by Joanne Meyerowitz in a talk and then elaborated on in a special issue of *Women's Studies Quarterly*. Joanne Meyerowitz, "A New History of Gender," in *Trans/Forming Knowledge*, University of Chicago (February 2006); Susan Stryker, Paisley Currah, and Lisa Jean Moore, "Introduction," *Women's Studies Quarterly* 36:3–4 (Fall/Winter 2008): 11–22.

6. Eva Hayward, "More Lessons from a Starfish: Prefixial Flesh and Transspeciated Selves," *Women's Studies Quarterly* 36: 3/4 (2008): 64–85; Joseph A. Marchal, *Appalling Bodies: Queer Figures before and after Paul's Letters* (Oxford: Oxford University Press, 2020); Jules Gill-Peterson, *Histories of the Transgender Child* (Minneapolis: University of Minnesota Press, 2018); C. Riley Snorton, *Black on Both Sides: A Racial History of Trans Identity* (Minneapolis: University of Minnesota Press, 2017); Leah DeVun, *The Shape of Sex: Nonbinary Gender from Genesis to the Renaissance* (New York: Columbia University Press, 2021); Susan Stryker, "The Transgender Issue: An Introduction," *GLQ* 4:2 (1998): 145–58; Stryker, "My Words to Victor Frankenstein above the Village of Chamounix: Performing Transgender Rage," *GLQ* 1:3 (1994): 237–54.

7. In this chapter I primarily address anti-trans law in the contemporary U.S. context; there is much more that could be said about the way the term transgender is being used globally to collapse specific cultural and religious configurations of sex and gender, and the specific impacts on the Global South. See, for example, the themed issue of *Transgender Studies Quarterly*: Aren Z. Aizura, Trystan Cotton, Carsten/La Gata, Carla Balzer, Marcia Ochoa, and Salvador Vidal-Ortiz, eds, "Decolonizing the Transgender Imaginary," Special Issue *TSQ* 1:3 (2014): 303–465.

8. Gwynn Kessler has persuasively argued that this text has been overemphasized in the scholarship. I certainly agree with her conclusion that more attention needs to be paid to the ways the *androginos* and *tumtum* are invoked more broadly in the literature. See Gwynn Kessler, "Rabbinic Gender: Beyond Male and Female," in *A Companion to Late Ancient Jews and Judaism: Third Century BCE to Seventh Century CE*, ed. Naomi Koltun-Fromm and Kessler (Hoboken, NJ: Wiley & Sons, 2020), 353–70.

incorporate mixed bodies, both animal and human. The rabbis simultaneously determine whether androgynes can be included in different ritual and legal obligations, as they assert that the androgyne is part of the order of creation.

In rabbinic literature there are two terms for androgynes that are commonly used and neither type of androgyne is found in the Hebrew Bible. The first term, *androginos*, is a compound of the Greek words for "man" (*anēr*) and "woman" (*gynē*). The rabbinic text I analyze here suggests that the *androginos* has dual genitalia. This androgyne appears more frequently in the halakhic materials—what are conventionally translated as "legal" discussions.

In the early rabbinic source I address in this chapter, the androgyne is paired with a hybrid animal, who is a mix of a domesticated and wild animal, called the *koy*.[9] To understand the androgyne in Bikkurim, we first need to unpack the connection between animality and gender.

THE KOY: ANIMALITY AND HYBRIDITY

The origin of the *koy* is not entirely clear; the term is not found biblically.[10] Moreover, the rabbis debate the definition of the *koy*—while some rabbinic traditions seem to classify the *koy* as a mix of any wild and domesticated species, others define it more precisely. One opinion in the Talmud, for example, argues that the *koy* is a crossbreed specifically between a goat and a stag.[11]

The rabbinic traditions about the androgyne and the hybrid animal are organized in a similar format; both take the form of a list. The hybrid animal list is separated into subsections, and each is introduced by a question: How is the hybrid animal like a wild animal? How is the hybrid animal like a domesticated animal? Under each of those headings comes a list of laws that describe how the hybrid animal functions legally within these categories. So, for example, the *koy* functions as a wild animal in the way in which it is slaughtered for consumption.

The structure of the list is designed to work through all the ways in which the hybrid animal fits into the established dichotomy of wild and domesticated animals. However, when the list proposes that the hybrid animal is like both

---

9. In the longer version of this chapter, I explore the different versions of the androgyne list that circulate, and the scholarly debate over whether this text properly is in the Mishnah or the Tosefta. I remain agnostic on the question of which composition the androgyne list belongs to. There I argue that one version of the text preserves the original arrangement of the pairing of the androgyne and *koy*, while the other version of the text helps explain why these lists are found in tractate Bikkurim altogether. The version usually attached to the Mishnah locates the androgyne within a chapter discussing various objects that cross established dichotomies.

10. While the words for wild and domesticated animals appear in the Bible, there is no biblical word *koy* that refers to a hybrid animal. The Septuagint translates the "*'ako*" in Deut 14:5 as *tragelaphos*. On the connection of the *koy* to the *tragelaphos* see Judith Romney Wegner, "Tragelaphos Revisited: The Anomaly of Women in the Mishnah," *Judaism* 37:2 (1988): 160–72.

11. See b. Ḥullin 79b–80a. This disagreement over the definition of the *koy* is carried into the commentators. See, for example, Maimonides, who argues that they could not decide whether the *koy* is a kind of wild or domesticated animal: Maimonides, Mishneh Torah, hilkhot n'zirut, 2:10. Tosafot, on the other hand, points to a contradiction between b. Keritot 21a and b. Ḥullin 79b–80a.

wild and domesticated animals in some respects, it suggests that there are some qualities common to all kinds of animals. In other words, the category of being "like both wild and domesticated" implies that there is a concept of animality that supersedes other taxonomical distinctions.

Beth Berkowitz, in her monograph *Animals and Animality in the Babylonian Talmud*, argues that in the Talmud, animals both have selves and are used to negotiate the boundaries between the rabbinic self and its various "others" (pagan, Samaritan, nonrabbinic, etc.). The Talmud reinforces a dichotomy between humans and animals, and it describes animals as property, props, and sources of domestic labor (although some humans are described in these terms as well). At the same time, she notes that the sources almost systematically undermine those very distinctions.[12]

Divisions between wild and domesticated animals are not self-evident, although some of the distinctions in rabbinic law are inherited from biblical texts. The boundaries between domestic and wild animals are occasionally contested; there are rabbinic debates about whether certain animals (e.g., dogs) are considered wild or domesticated.[13] Given Berkowitz's conclusions, it should not be surprising to us that these taxonomies tend to situate animals in relation to human needs. A taxonomy of wild and domesticated in relation to the *koy* similarly centers human perspectives by dividing animals into those that are considered a part of the household and those that are not. This distinction spatially maps animality based on human kinship structures. Moreover, the category of the domesticated animal implies human ownership of the animal's "domesticated" labor.

Situating animals as property in relation to human households can also be a gendered, and at times racialized, enterprise. The most famous rabbinic source on the establishment of the household comes from the first chapter of Mishnah Kiddushin, over which much feminist ink has been spilled.[14] This chapter establishes the figure of the rabbinic householder and describes how he acquires his property. It is no accident that the opening of the tractate on marriage laws succinctly lays out the method for acquiring wives, slaves, and animals. Taken together, the acquisition of the three "objects" establishes an androcentric household based in property relations and the subjugation of certain classes of beings. The category of domestication, therefore, is simultaneously a mode of acquisition and both gendered and sexualized. The figure of the hybrid animal

---

12. Beth Berkowitz, *Animals and Animality in the Babylonian Talmud* (Cambridge: Cambridge University Press, 2018). On the categories of human/animal in the context of generation and reproduction, see Rafael Rachel Neis, *When a Human Gives Birth to a Raven: Rabbis and the Reproduction of Species* (Oakland: University of California Press, 2023). On bestiality, see also Mira Wasserman, *Jews, Gentiles, and Other Animals: The Talmud after the Humanities* (Philadelphia: University of Pennsylvania Press, 2017), 73–119.

13. See, for example, m. Kil'ayim 8:6, where the rabbis disagree about whether the dog belongs in the category of wild or domestic.

14. See Gail Labovitz, who situates these discussions in her book, Labovitz, *Marriage and Metaphor: Constructions of Gender in Rabbinic Literature* (Lanham, MD: Lexington Books, 2009).

perches on precisely these interstices. The *koy* becomes a site to contemplate animality and processes of domestication.

"LIKE NEITHER": ANDROGYNES AND HYBRID ANIMALS

In this section, I will examine the parallel androgyne list and the debate over the legal status of the androgyne in gendered law. I will argue that the androgyne has a paradoxical effect: they undermine dichotomous gender in the law and, at the same time, solidify gender as an ontological category in law.

The most famous tradition about the androgyne begins with a thesis statement that mirrors the *koy* list:

> [In the case of the] androgyne: there are ways in which they are like men, there are ways in which they are like women, there are ways in which they are like both men and women, and there are ways in which they are not like men or women (t. Bikkurim 2:3).[15]

This topic statement signals that what follows will be a list. In many respects this list is a classic example of the genre of early rabbinic lists, although in some respects it diverges from that form.[16] The traditions found within this list are also dispersed throughout the corpus in their topical legal contexts. The legal traditions follow the structure of the introductory sentence and are arranged in four sections to demonstrate how the androgyne functions in four different ways—that is, like men, like women, like both, and like neither.

The androgyne functions as a man, for example, in that he becomes impure through seminal emissions, just as men do. Similarly, the androgyne must "marry rather than be married," as men must. This can be interpreted to mean that they may initiate a marriage contract with a woman (as men do) but may not be married (a phrase that is grammatically in the passive), as women are to

15. Hebrew grammar uses masculine language for the androgyne. Because of the androcentric conventions of Hebrew, it is difficult to know how to weigh that fact. In the past I have translated this text using "ze/hir," primarily because the cognitive dissonance (particularly for those unfamiliar with gender-neutral pronouns) was helpful in disrupting any easy translation. In doing so I was drawing on the work of early trans activists who were playing with translation and this text—primarily Reuben Zellman and Elliot Kukla. Drawing on my translations, Moshe Halbertal uses ze and hir in his recent translation and reading of this source as well. See Moshe Halbertal, *The Birth of Doubt: Confronting Uncertainty in Early Rabbinic Literature*, trans. Elli Fischer (Providence, RI: Brown Judaic Studies, 2020), 171–203.

Currently, in my corners of the trans community, it is more common to encounter the singular "they" than ze/hir. Any perceived awkwardness in the singular "they" should, I hope, help to signal the awkwardness of discussing nonbinary embodiment in English. The drawback of translating the androgyne's gender as "they" is that it papers over the androcentrism of using male grammar as the default. Each solution is decidedly less than perfect.

16. Classically, the topic sentence would include the number of clauses to follow in order to aid memorization, although this is not the only list in the tannaitic corpus where the numbering is absent. For a recent dissertation on the genre of the list in the Mishnah, see Roy Shasha, "The Forms and Functions of Lists in the Mishnah" (PhD dissertation, University of Manchester, 2006).

a man. It would be difficult to formulate a more concise distillation of rabbinic androcentrism than that six-word sentence.[17]

The list continues to spell out the ways in which the androgyne is like a woman: like a woman, she becomes impure through menstruation, and like a woman she is disqualified from serving as a legal witness.[18] Both the obligations and the exemptions that pertain to women are applied to the androgyne. In this way, some of the legal exclusions that the androgyne faces are based not on their status as an androgyne but on their status as potentially female. A law stating that women and androgynes may not serve as legal witnesses only needs to be formulated when another group (men) can fulfill this role. The androgyne is therefore like women in that their legal subjectivity is curtailed.

The first half of the list may seem to be a prosaic discussion of the status of the androgyne in relation to specific laws, but at the same time the list incorporates the androgyne into the law, thereby conferring legitimacy on them. If the ideal legal subject for the rabbis is the one with the most obligations, then when the sages compare the androgyne to both men and women, they demonstrate the ways in which the androgyne has legal obligations (as well as restrictions).[19] There may be some practical difficulties in the enactment of these restrictions; for example, according to the laws of seclusion (*yiḥud*), the androgyne is not permitted to be alone with either men or women—but there is an effort to establish the androgyne as a legal subject.

The third category appears to take the inclusion of the androgyne one step further. When the list asks how the androgyne is like both women and men, it suggests that there are laws that are not contingent on gender. So, for example:

> [How is the] androgyne like both men and women? [The person who injures the androgyne] is liable for injuring [the androgyne] as if [they had injured] either a man or a woman, the intentional murder of the androgyne [incurs the capital punishment] of decapitation [in the same way it would if a man or a woman was murdered]. . . .

If the androgyne is injured, their injury is treated like the injury of either a man or a woman. Their murder is treated in exactly the same way as the murder of

---

17. On this passage see Sarra Lev, "Defying the Binary? The Androgynous in Tosefta Bikkurim," in *Annual Meeting of the Association for Jewish Studies* (Washington, DC, 2011); Charlotte Fonrobert, "Regulating the Human Body: Rabbinic Legal Discourse and the Making of Jewish Gender," in *The Cambridge Companion to the Talmud and Rabbinic Literature*, ed. Fonrobert and Martin Jaffee (Cambridge: Cambridge University Press, 2007), 270–94.

18. Just as men become impure through "white" (seminal emissions), women become impure through "red" (menstrual blood). This constructs male and female bodies as analogous to one another. On the language in this section, see Y. N. Epstein, who argues that the specific formulation of obligation is only used when comparing a matter that is unclear to a matter that is clear and agreed on. See Yakov N. Epstein, *M'vo'ot l'Sifrut haTanaim: Mishnah, Tosefta, u'midrashei halachah* (Jerusalem: Magnes, 1957), 220.

19. Feminist scholars have demonstrated that being exempted from legal obligation is a detriment in the rabbinic system of law. See, for example, Rachel Biale, *Women and Jewish Law: The Essential Texts, Their History, and Their Relevance for Today* (New York: Schocken, 1984), 10–44.

a man or a woman; if it was a deliberate and premeditated murder, then the punishment is decapitation, one of the two crimes for which this is mandated.[20]

The text continues to generate several more ways in which the androgyne functions as both men and women do; however, it is worth dwelling briefly on this category itself. If the overall goal of the list has been to understand androgynes within the context of gendered law, why include a section on androgynes in ungendered law? Is there an actual question as to whether the androgyne's death should be treated like any other human death? This section seems, on the face of it, utterly unnecessary. It appears to exist solely to challenge binary gender in law.

There is a similar problem with the category of "both" on the hybrid animal list. For example, the hybrid animal is like both wild and domesticated animals in that one cannot consume its limbs while it is still alive. This law, which originates in the Bible, applies to all animals. Given that, one might question why it is necessary to state this prohibition in relation to the hybrid animal. Just as the murder of an androgyne seems to obviously be murder, is not the torture of an animal still obviously torture?

Ironically, this statement about protecting an animal from torture also highlights the many other kinds of licit violence that structure the hybrid animal list. The list addresses a host of legal issues, including the covering of the hybrid animal's (spilled) blood, the rules of its slaughter, and which sections of the animal's body may and may not be consumed. While the specter of violence is present in both the androgyne and the hybrid animal list, violence in relation to the hybrid animal is mostly sanctioned. Only suffering that is unnecessary for the human use of the animal is disallowed. Animality, broadly speaking, incurs vulnerability to sacrifice, consumption, and forced labor.

In the case of the androgyne, the redundancy of being like "both" men and women also asks us to think about the gendered effects of this category. If being "both" creates a list of laws that transcend gender, then perhaps this allows a concept of humanness, independent of gender, to emerge. It is tempting to conceptualize these statements, particularly the ones touching on such topics as injury and murder, as recognizing the "human rights" of the androgyne.[21] Perhaps, then, suffering transcends the gender binary.

In his monograph *Habeus Viscus*, Alexander Weheliye explores the constitution of the category of the human through the lens of Black feminist thought. He writes the following about human rights laws: "Frequently, suffering becomes the defining feature of those subjects excluded from the law . . . due to the political violence inflicted upon them, even as it, paradoxically, grants them

---

20. For the rabbinic assignments of punishment, see Devora Steinmetz, *Punishment and Freedom: The Rabbinic Construction of Criminal Law* (Philadelphia: University of Pennsylvania Press, 2008).

21. Charlotte Fonrobert makes the point that this category establishes the androgyne as human in Fonrobert, "The Semiotics of the Sexed Body in Early Halakhic Discourse," in *Closed and Open: Readings of Rabbinic Texts*, ed. M.A. Kraus (Piscataway, NJ: Gorgias Press, 2006), 69–96.

access to inclusion and equality."[22] Weheliye critiques a frame that adjudicates access to human rights through a comparison of suffering to evaluate whose suffering requires recognition. In this analysis, humanity is bought at the cost of violence. At the same time, this access to the category does not trouble the basic (racist and sexist) terms of the human; the human is built on a foundation of anti-Blackness.

The concept of rights-based legal thinking is not the primary framework of rabbinic discourse. The focus of these legal traditions is on the obligation of the person who harms the androgyne, not on the rights of the androgyne per se, for example.[23] However, it is worth noting that the androgyne functions legally as a human uniquely through their injury or death. For those clauses, it is through suffering that the androgyne becomes a legible human under the law. Similarly, the hybrid animal becomes an animal through the statement that torture is not allowable. Acknowledging the category of the animal means recognizing the pain of animals. Becoming human, as well, may come both posthumously and as the result of violence.

My intention here is not to analogize the androgyne and anti-Blackness but rather to learn from Black feminist theory in order to interrogate the mechanisms of imagining the category of the human. Despite the fact that the injury of the androgyne would seem to pose a concept of "universal" human rights that transcends binary gender, this category of "both" is still framed through the poles of gender dichotomy. To belong, the androgyne must be like men and women. The gendered terms of the human are not fundamentally challenged by the inclusion of the androgyne.

The final section of the androgyne list details the ways in which the androgyne is not like either men or women. For example, if someone makes a vow that they will undertake certain restrictions if the androgyne is neither a man nor a woman, the vow is valid.[24] This, too, appears as a parallel clause in the hybrid animal list. The vow is not a statement of self-identification: a non-androgyne is making the vow over the androgyne or the hybrid animal. In other words, a third party who makes a truth claim about the androgyne's or *koy*'s hybrid status is deemed to have made a valid statement. This puts the androgyne into a passive role shared with the *koy*. At the same time, however, it also crucially suggests that inclusion in the category of human or animal does not depend on

---

22. Alexander Weheliye, *Habeas Viscus: Racializing Assemblages, Biopolitics, and Black Feminist Theories of the Human* (Durham, NC: Duke University Press, 2014), 75–76.

23. For a discussion of the frame of "rights" and how it plays out in relation to transgender communities, see Paisley Currah, Richard Juang, and Shannon Price Minter, eds., *Transgender Rights* (Minneapolis: University of Minnesota Press, 2006).

24. Although I am translating using the Vienna manuscript, I chose examples that appear in both versions of the list. See Lieberman's commentary: Saul Lieberman, *Tosefta Kifshuta* (New York: Jewish Theological Seminary Press, 2007), 835. The law about the *koy* and Nazirite vows can be found in m. Nazir 5:7. On the text of the *koy* Nazirite vow, see Zechariah Frankel, *Darchei HaMishnah: Chelek Rishon* (Leipzig: Sumptibus Henrici Hunger, 1859), 253. On the androgyne and Nazirite vows, see m. Nazir 2:7 and t. Nazir 3:19. For a discussion of the androgyne and vows, see Kessler, "Rabbinic Gender."

complete disambiguation. Even if binaries structure the majority of the list, for this moment of the list, binaries are discarded to explore how androgynes are not like either men or women. In the next section I will begin to explore some of these broader ontological questions about gender in law.

"A UNIQUE CREATION": THE ONTOLOGY OF GENDER IN RABBINIC LAW

If the strategy of the list in Bikkurim is generally to incorporate hybrid bodies into law, then the coda to the lists takes a decidedly different approach. There are parallel codas to the hybrid animal and androgyne list, and it is in the coda that we find the first attributed statement. For the androgyne list the coda reads: "Rabbi Yose disagrees:[25] The androgyne is a unique creation and the sages could not decide about them[26] whether he is a man or she is a woman . . ."[27] In other words, Rabbi Yose differs from the strategy of the list, which incorporates androgynes into a set of legal choices. As Rabbi Yose sees it, the sages would have had to designate the androgyne as either a man or a woman. As is made clear by the ways in which the androgyne is like both men and women, the sages did not assign them one legal gender. For Rabbi Yose, the implication of this "failure" is that the androgyne must be excluded; this final statement opposes the work of carefully fitting the androgyne into gendered laws.

And yet, paradoxically, while Rabbi Yose seeks to exclude the androgyne from the rabbinic enterprise, he also establishes a space for the androgyne as a "unique creation." Scholars and activists have read Rabbi Yose's refusal to assimilate the androgyne as carving a space for the existence of nonbinary people.[28] Rabbi Yose's rejection of the androgyne in law is also an acknowledgment that gender exceeds a binary. In that sense, Rabbi Yose, who has the final word, radically subverts binary gender.

I am not opposed to that interpretation of the coda, particularly when activists use it as an argument against contemporary transphobia within Judaism; I am not particularly interested in policing the meaning of this list. I do, however, worry about the cost of reading subversion here. To acknowledge the androgyne as unique but unassimilable into social structures (governed by law, custom, and

---

25. The Vienna printed edition and other manuscripts cite Rabbi Yose. In the Parma manuscript however, this statement is attributed to Rabbi Meir. The Parma manuscript for the *koy* list also lacks the final statement, so there is no comparable statement to assess attribution. I will use Rabbi Yose here, but I remain agnostic about the question of the proper attribution of this tradition. For further philological discussion of these sources, see the version of this chapter in my book.

26. I am translating this pronoun as "them" because this statement is a strikingly clear example of how grammar hinders the ability to express gendered indeterminacy in Hebrew, even when that indeterminacy is the subject of the discussion. If I were translating literally, it should be "him."

27. I am not treating here the ending of the coda which discusses the category of the *tumtum* (who seems to be liminally unsexed).

28. See Kessler, "Rabbinic Gender." Kessler also points out that Rabbi Yose's statement has staying power in rabbinic literature.

ritual) is to put them into a precarious social position indeed.[29] I have no wish to purchase subversion using androgynes as currency, even as I will argue that Rabbi Yose's statement implicitly understands the androgyne as a part of the order of creation. I shall explore the ways Rabbi Yose's statement implicitly cites the Genesis story shortly.

Even though most scholars interpret the list and the coda by Rabbi Yose as diametrically opposed, there is another way to understand the relationship between the two; read in a certain light, the list and the coda collude with each other.[30] It is true that the two approaches have very different effects for the androgyne. Still, both the list and Rabbi Yose mark gender as central to halakhah (conventionally translated as law). The framers of the list see gender as a crucial organizing principle for law and generally assimilate the androgyne into that structure. For Rabbi Yose, on the other hand, gender is so essential to the rabbinic legal project that the androgyne cannot fit within it.

The apparent challenge posed by the androgyne and *koy* obscures the reification of the categories of gender and domestication. The androgyne and hybrid animal are not disambiguated; on the contrary, they remain hybrid. Their incomplete exclusion from halakhah means that they will haunt rabbinic discussions for centuries to come. But they are domesticated. The cementing of ontologies of gender and domestication is one of the foundations for the regulation of women, androgynes, slaves, and animals in law. This tradition in Bikkurim, therefore, is not merely a reflection of the gendered nature of rabbinic law. Rather, it can be understood as a foundational moment in establishing gender as central to halakhah.

At the same time, the coda of the hybrid animal and androgyne lists connects both by calling them "unique creations,"[31] an uncommon phrase. This category of "unique creations" thus enacts a kind of union between androgynes and hybrid animals. This union between androgyne and *koy* papers over the violence that inheres in the animal list; it is a kind of limited connection between those who test the boundaries of taxonomy. Albeit unwittingly, Rabbi Yose has created potential allies in the androgyne and the *koy*.

This invocation of "creation" can be linked to both the creation story in Genesis and anti-trans law. In the next section, I will explore these two very divergent receptions of Genesis.

29. I am thinking in particular of some of the darker sides of monstrousness, such as the death of Filisa Vistima. See Stryker, "My Words to Victor Frankenstein."

30. Fonrobert sees them as opposed. In her brilliant reading, she argues that while the list may function as a project of inclusion, it is in fact a demonstration of the discursive strength and flexibility of law. See Fonrobert, "Gender Duality and Its Subversions in Rabbinic Law," in *Gender in Judaism and Islam: Common Lives, Uncommon Heritage*, ed. Firoozeh Kashani-Sabet and Beth Wenger (New York: New York University Press, 2014), 106–25.

31. It is true that the *koy* list in some recensions lacks the coda. The versions that do have it, however, suggest an implicit connection between the androgyne and the *koy*, an impression that is only strengthened by all the parallels between the lists.

THE GENESIS OF TRANSPHOBIA

Elsewhere I describe the widespread invocation of androgynes in creation stories that circulated in antiquity.[32] Creation stories remain surprisingly relevant in contemporary legal battles over trans embodiment as well. Legal advocacy groups turn to Genesis to frame their regulatory efforts. The Alliance Defending Freedom, a conservative evangelical legal group, has as one of its central doctrines the following statement: "We believe God creates each person with an immutable biological sex—male or female—that reflects the image and likeness of God."[33] This is a direct reference to Gen 1:27: "And God created [the] human in God's own image, in the image of God, God created him, male and female God created them." For the ADF, this verse refers to God's creation of biological (and immutable) sex.[34] In other words, for conservative Christian theologies, Genesis is frequently the proof text for the impossibility of sexed changes.

The formulation of the 2018 Health and Human Services memo (with which I began this chapter) is a variation of the language found in the so-called bathroom bills—bills that seek to regulate trans access to many public facilities. In this section I will read closely the language of one of these anti-trans laws from Mississippi, called the Religious Liberty Accommodations Act.[35] This law is just one of a slew of proposed bills that focus on bathrooms in the continuation of the history of white supremacist regulation of restrooms.[36] These anti-trans laws are intertwined with extralegal efforts to regulate trans embodiment, including the deadly pattern of violence directed primarily at Black trans women and trans people of color, as well as the array of "administrative violence" (as Dean Spade has termed it) that trans people experience routinely.[37]

---

32. Strassfeld, *Trans Talmud*, 33–54.

33. See Alliance Defending Freedom. "Alliance Defending Freedom Doctrinal Distinctives," https://www.adflegal.org/about-us/careers/statement-of-faith.

34. Why evangelicals are turning to Genesis in particular, as opposed, for example, to Deut 22:5 or the first chapter of Romans exceeds the scope of my discussion here. I suspect it is related to complementarian theologies. But it is not just the Alliance Defending Freedom that invokes Genesis. See also the position of Focus on the Family: Issue Analysts, "Transgenderism- Our Position," Focus on the Family, 2018, https://www.focusonthefamily.com/get-help/transgenderism-our-position/.

35. Gayle Salamon has crucially explored transphobia in her book in which she argues that Latisha King's gender expression is read as a provocation that justifies her murder. See Gayle Salamon, *The Life and Death of Latisha King: A Critical Phenomenology of Transphobia* (New York: New York University Press, 2018).

36. The tactic of referring to them as "bathroom" bills is designed to play off a long history of white supremacist regulation of bathrooms. Whether white supremacists were invoking the anti-Black specter of sexual predation or constructing certain racialized bodies as conduits of sexually transmitted infections, the contemporary regulation of public facilities along ableist, racialized, and gendered lines has a long history in the United States. Sheila Cavanagh argues that the whiteness of bathroom porcelain is significant, and renders a kind of white, able-bodied, straight space. See Sheila Cavanagh, "Gender, Sexuality, and Race in the Lacanian Mirror: Urinary Segregation and the Bodily Ego," in *Psychoanalytic Geographies*, ed. Paul Kingsbury and Steve Pile (New York: Routledge, 2014), 323–39.

37. Dean Spade, *Normal Life: Administrative Violence, Critical Trans Politics, and the Limits of Law* (Durham, NC: Duke University Press, 2015).

The text of the law purports to protect individuals and organizations that discriminate against queer and trans people on the basis of "sincerely held religious beliefs or moral convictions." The opening clauses define what specific religious beliefs are protected as state-sanctioned grounds for legal discrimination. The first two protected religious beliefs are:

1. Marriage is or should be recognized as the union of one man and one woman;
2. Sexual relations are properly reserved to such a marriage.

Within the context of this law, religious belief is defined as a conviction that marriage is necessarily both heterosexual and monogamous. The choice of the words "is or should be" in the first clause evokes a wish to reframe heterosexual marriage, even as the law protects a belief in that reframing. The gap between "is" and "should be" points to a gap between the ideal and reality.[38] Similarly, the language that sex should be "properly reserved" to marriage gestures toward a gap between this ideal and the fact that ("improper") sex outside of marriage is widely practiced.

In this section of the bill, in other words, religious beliefs are counterfactual. A different social order hovers just beneath the surface of (an imagined) secular societal reality. The counterfactual nature of these beliefs constitutes an implicit argument for their legal protection.[39] Presumably, if the framers of the bill felt that their world more closely resembled this religious social order, these beliefs would not require legal protections.

The third clause functions differently from the first two clauses on marriage and sex. It reads:

3. Male (man) or female (woman) refer to an individual's immutable biological sex as objectively determined by anatomy and genetics at time of birth.[40]

If marriage is the union between one man and one woman, only certain men and women qualify. The pairing between heterosexual monogamy and binary

---

38. Judge Carlton Reeves, in the preliminary injunction that initially blocked the law, reads it as a response to gay marriage victories in court. See *Barber v. Bryant*, 193 F. Supp. 3d 677 (S.D. Miss. 2016), reversed, 860 F.3d 345 (5th Cir. 2017).

39. I am arguing here that the (secular) social reality to which the bill responds is also imagined, a part of US white evangelical narratives of secular/sexual social decay. See, for example, Sara Moslener's work on the growth of the youth abstinence movement in the 1990s, which harnessed white supremacist (and anti-Black) sentiment to fund Republican/Christian abstinence-only education (Moslener, *Virgin Nation: Sexual Purity and American Adolescence* [Oxford: Oxford University Press, 2015], 109–30). This entire line of argumentation is also greatly influenced by the analysis in Ann Pellegrini and Janet Jakobsen, *Love the Sin: Sexual Regulation and the Limits of Religious Tolerance* (Boston: Beacon Press, 2004).

40. The resonance of this language with the definition of sex proposed in the 2018 memo from the US Department of Health and Human Services is obvious. This language comes almost directly from a proposed school policy on bathrooms that the Alliance Defending Freedom (ADF) sent to school boards across the country. See Michaels, "We Tracked Down the Lawyers."

gender is not accidental. In the service of heterosexuality, the regulation of sexuality and gender identity must go hand in hand.

The third clause asserts that both sex and gender identity are assigned at birth. Let us pass over the assumed notion that anatomy and genetics always align, a point many intersex activists would take issue with.[41] The language of biology and genetic testing also introduces the question of science and medicine into a law designed to protect and define religious belief. Medicine and religion collude to determine the immutable truth of sex at birth.[42] When the law entwines the scientific and the theological, it conspires to naturalize a divinely ordained gender binary. According to state law in Mississippi, science and religion do not believe in transsexuals.

I want to note the differences between the two sets of clauses. The state of Mississippi protects the belief that gay and nonmarital sex *should not* exist. At the same time, the state also affirms the conviction that transsexuals *do not* exist.[43] In this manner, imagining religious freedom impacts trans and queer people differently.

Trans studies theorist Eva Hayward takes up the question of gendered ontology. Citing the actress and activist Laverne Cox, Hayward notes the way trans women are commanded, "Don't exist." One way to combat the murderous imperative of this erasure might be to insist on the humanity of trans women of color. Drawing on Black feminist theory, Hayward rejects this strategy and argues that any attempt to revise the category of the human to include trans women is compromised. The category of the human itself is shaped by foundational anti-Black and misogynist logic and used to determine whose suffering is meaningful. Instead, she urges us to push against ontology itself: ontology is the ultimate architect of the mandate to trans women of color: "Don't exist."[44]

The gendered theology of the law in Mississippi (a mandate disguised as a belief) is the ontological scaffolding for the dictate to trans women: "Don't exist." In consequence, as the rest of the law goes on to describe, discrimination is transubstantiated. Refusing trans people services is the material instantiation of a protected religious belief that trans people cannot exist. This bill manifests a

---

41. For a discussion of the earlier tendency of the court to move away from a reliance on birth sex and chromosomes, see A. Sharpe, *Transgender Jurisprudence: Dysphoric Bodies of Law* (London: Routledge, 2002).

42. The connection among secularism, religious freedom, and sex/gender are the subjects of prolific scholarship. See, for example, Joan Wallach Scott, "Sexularism: On Secularism and Gender Equality," in *The Fantasy of Feminist History* (Durham, NC: Duke University Press, 2011), 91–116.

43. I am specifically discussing a contemporary US political context here. The relationship between science, trans sexual embodiment, law, and religion will look different in other times and places. For an excellent analysis of the contemporary Iranian context, see Afsaneh Najmabadi, *Professing Selves: Transsexuality and Same-Sex Desire in Contemporary Iran* (Durham, NC: Duke University Press, 2013).

44. Hayward, "Don't Exist," *TSQ* 4:2 (2017): 191–94. In the context of intersex studies, the mandate, "Don't exist," functions differently. Intersex activists resist the mythologization of their bodies, including in the persistence of the term "hermaphrodite" (an amalgam of Hermes and Aphrodite) as a tactic of writing intersex bodies out of existence. On this topic, see, for example, Thea Hillman, *Intersex (for Lack of a Better Word)* (San Francisco: Manic D Press, 2008).

religious belief in immutable sex, and it thereby closes the gap between religious ideals and gendered mores.

I want to return to these questions of the creation story and gender in the coda to the list in Tosefta Bikkurim—namely, the statement by Rabbi Yose that the androgyne is a "unique creation." Like Mississippi anti-trans law, this coda also contains an oblique reference to Genesis. The phrase "the androgyne is a unique being" uses a noun form of the verb "to create" found in the very first verse of the Hebrew Bible.[45] The citation of the word "create," coupled with the narratives that circulate widely throughout late antiquity about androgyne creations, brings to mind Genesis. This may be a direct reference to early rabbinic exegesis on the creation story, which argues that the original human was an androgyne.[46] Drawing on the exact same verse as the ADF, Gen 1:27, the rabbis understand that the first human was an androgyne. If this is indeed an oblique reference to Genesis, then although Rabbi Yose is ejecting the androgyne from law in the coda, he is also explicitly associating the androgyne with the order of creation. In other words, the androgyne is created by God. Whatever else Rabbi Yose's statement accomplishes, it is also a powerful theological assertion.[47]

I have argued that the list/coda is invested in domesticating the androgyne and the *koy*, and that it establishes gender as central to law. Still, unlike contemporary trans women of color, neither the androgyne nor the hybrid animal is

---

45. The phrase, a "unique creation," is rare in tannaitic literature. It occurs in this tradition and in t. Kil'ayim 1:9, where the rabbis discuss the status of several animals including the antelope from Deut 14:5. The root word for "creation" itself is not at all rare; we see that the word has the meaning of God's creations—as, for example, b. Ḥullin 127a. Even outside the context of an exegesis on Genesis, therefore, this word most often is associated with God's creation (although not always).

46. The rabbis comment on the fact that there are two creation narratives in the Hebrew Bible, and that these stories have discrepancies between them. Current source criticism would account for this textual conflict by arguing that the narratives reflect different source materials. The rabbis, however, explain that these are distinct stages of creation. In this reading, God originally created a single human with two faces and two sets of genitalia. The second stage of creation represents the splitting of this androgyne into two bodies. The rabbinic exegesis in the eighth chapter of Genesis Rabbah has parallels: see Leviticus Rabbah 14, b. Ber. 61a, b. Ketub. 8a, and b. 'Erub. 18a. See also Genesis Rabbah 1:26, which glosses a being with two sets of genitalia. For a recent discussion of the context of Genesis Rabbah within an increasingly Christianized Roman Palestine, see Sarit Katan Gribetz, David M. Grossberg, Martha Himmelfarb, and Peter Schäefer, eds, *Genesis Rabbah in Text and Context* (Tübingen: Mohr Siebeck, 2016). Daniel Boyarin describes the first-century philosopher Philo's version of the creation narrative, which is shaped by a Middle Platonic dualism. See Daniel Boyarin, *Carnal Israel: Reading Sex in Talmudic Culture* (Berkeley: University of California Press, 1993), 31–61; and "Gender," in *Critical Terms for Religious Studies*, ed. Mark Taylor (Chicago: University of Chicago Press, 1998), 117–36. Leah DeVun thinks that Philo is the bridge to early Christian ideas on the topic. See DeVun, *The Shape of Sex*, 16–40.

47. Similar formulations circulate in various traditions in late antiquity. For example, in the Apocryphon of John, the divine triad (mother-father-son) are all described in ways that bend simple gender assignment. Jonathan Cahana reads the Gnostic engagement with the symbolism of the androgyne as a subversion of Greco-Roman definitions of family. See Jonathan Cahana, "Gnostically Queer: Gender Trouble in Gnosticism," *BTB* 41:1 (2011): 24–35. On 1 Corinthians, see Marchal, *Appalling Bodies*, 30–68. For a trans reading of androgyne creation narratives and the Gospel of Thomas, see Melissa Harl Sellew, "Reading the *Gospel of Thomas* from Here: A Trans-Centred Hermeneutic," *JIBS* 1:2 (2020): 61–96.

told, "Don't exist."[48] While the Bikkurim source is certainly not utopian by any standards, it stands in marked contrast to contemporary receptions of Genesis. In the list and the coda, androgynes exist, even if there is a question about whether violence against them constitutes violence as it would against other human beings. Mississippi anti-trans law, in contrast, understands Genesis to be the origin story of a cisgendered ontology.

Historian Jules Gill-Peterson has argued that the way trans children have been figured as a "new" social problem not only ignores trans children in the history of the United States but also deprives trans children of a history that might work to empower them. The erasure of trans history, in this case, is not neutral; it is a deliberate forgetting in the service of subjecting trans children to medical authority. Similarly, as Iain Morland points out, the intent of intersex treatments is to efface the history of the intersex body. Morland argues that we need to rethink surgical practice, which has often been portrayed as cementing male or female sex. Instead, surgeons create an accepted version of the appearance of sexed congruity and work to erase the presurgical body. In that sense, surgery memorializes the contact of a body with someone who sought to erase it.[49] One might argue, then, that the "rediscovery" of intersex issues by the mainstream media every few years is predicated on the consistent forgetting of intersexuality. Like surgery, this manufactured "forgetting" is designed to suppress the possibility of intersex history.

The contemporary negation of trans and intersex existence means that trans and intersex historical projects are always caught up in ontological dilemmas. If, as Morland writes, genital surgeries both indicate the attempted erasure of intersex history, and also function as the marker of that history, then contemporary contests over intersex and trans embodiment are already embroiled in both history and ontology.[50] Trans history cannot fight the ontological battles of the present by itself, but the project of trans history is not divorced from this struggle. In this chapter, I have tried to address and attend to some of those specificities, both by rooting my analysis within the context of the study of androgynes in late antiquity, and by making explicit the connection to the contemporary ontologies of sex and gender that govern trans and intersex existence. In the face of such historical and contemporary suppressions, trans and intersex histories become all the more crucial.

48. See also texts like t. Ber. 6:3, which address the blessing recited over seeing an "unusual" creation. On this, see Julia Watts Belser, "Queering the Dissident Body: Race, Sex, and Disability in Rabbinic Blessings on Bodily Difference," in *Unsettling Science and Religion: Contributions and Questions from Queer Studies*, ed. Lisa Stenmark and Whitney Bauman (New York: Lexington Books, 2018).

49. Iain Morland, "Afterword: Genitals Are History," *Postmedieval* 9:2 (2018): 209–15.

50. It is for this reason that a history of sexuality approach, which has in the past been primarily organized around the dangers and possibilities of constructing a gay (and sometimes lesbian) past, will be insufficient to address these very specific ontological matters. While trans and intersex historical projects are not totally distinct from the field of history of sexuality, they are also not entirely contiguous with it either.

Chapter 2

Beyond the Trans/Cis Binary

An Experience-Centered Approach to Teaching and Practicing Trans Hermeneutics

JOY LADIN

How can people who do not identify as transgender or nonbinary learn to read the Bible from a trans perspective?

I was asked that question by a heterosexual, cisgender rabbi at a Jewish educators' discussion of my book, *The Soul of the Stranger: Reading God and Torah from a Transgender Perspective*. I was taken aback. I had been sure that the book made that clear—so sure that when I got back to my hotel room, I flipped through it, looking for the explanation I would have sworn I included. When I realized it was not there, I tried to quickly cobble together a handout for the next day's workshop. That is when I discovered that not only had I not explained my approach to trans hermeneutics in the book, but I had not defined my approach clearly enough to teach or even explain it to others.

Because it was framed as a pedagogical question, I set about trying to answer the rabbi's question through trial-and-error experimentation in classes and workshops I offered to a wide variety of groups—Jewish and non-Jewish, LGBTQ and cisnormative, religious and secular, students, educators and interested lay people. While some included participants with backgrounds in biblical, religious, and queer and gender studies, the classes, like the book they grew out of, were designed for non-specialists, and assumed no prior training in or experience with either the Bible or transgender perspectives.

Through these classes, I clarified, broadened, and simplified my approach, shifting from reading from a transgender perspective, which for me entails identifying parallels to transgender-specific experiences like gender transition in biblical texts, to reading from a *trans* perspective, by which I mean reading with awareness of and attention to the slippage between biblical characters and the roles and categories, including those not related to gender, with which they are identified. No human being perfectly or permanently fits our identifying roles and categories, and so that slippage—and the trans experiences that grow out of it—is a feature of all our lives, whether or not we identify as transgender.

As this approach to trans hermeneutics developed, I was also learning to teach others, including cisnormative people like the rabbi, to practice it themselves. But when I tried to put what I had learned in writing, I realized that the rabbi's question was not just pedagogical. Though the approach is simple (at least by comparison to academic approaches to trans hermeneutics), answering the rabbi's question required me to consider the role of the trans/cis binary in trans hermeneutics, to define my approach in relation to other trans hermeneutic approaches, and to articulate my approach's theological underpinnings. That is what I do in the first parts of this chapter, and, in the process, explain the concepts and terms that are central to my approach to trans hermeneutics. In the final sections, I offer a step-by-step explanation of how I teach this approach in workshops for nonspecialists.

THE TRANS/CIS BINARY

When the rabbi asked how he, as a heterosexual, cisgender rabbi, could learn to read the Bible from a transgender perspective, he did so diffidently, knowing that he was crossing one of the red lines in contemporary discourse about transgender issues: the absolute distinction between cisgender people, who embrace and identify with their assigned binary gender roles and expectations, and transgender people who reject, rebel against, and disidentify with the male or female identities we were assigned at birth. How *could* a cisgender person learn to read from a transgender perspective, when "cisgender" and "transgender" are binary opposites, mutually exclusive categories that mark transgender and cisgender lives, experiences, perspectives—and, by extension, ways of reading biblical texts—as inherently, inescapably different.

The trans/cis binary is a powerful conceptual and rhetorical framework that has become central to political, social, and academic efforts to center transgender and nonbinary lives, experiences, needs, feelings, and perspectives. The trans/cis binary elevates "transgender" from a marginal group defined by deviation from gender binary norms to a category that is conceptually equal to "cisgender," despite the comparatively small number of people who identify as transgender or nonbinary; it also demotes "cisgender," from a norm that erases or stigmatizes other gender identifications, to one of two equally possible relations to gender. Further, because binary categories are mutually exclusive and thus mutually defining, "cisgender," practically as well as conceptually, cannot be separated from "transgender," because "cisgender" is only a meaningful distinction when we acknowledge that some people do not identify with their assigned gender identities. It is hard to recognize the harmonious relation between sex, gender, communally assigned identity, and individual self-identification to which the term "cisgender" refers, except in contrast to the more complicated relations represented by the term "transgender." In other words, the trans/cis binary defines humanity in such a way that only by knowing what it means to be transgender can cisgender people know themselves.

But the benefits of the trans/cis binary come at a cost. Like any binary framework we use to think about what it means to be human, the trans/cis binary drastically oversimplifies, and thus misrepresents, humanity, erasing those, like nonbinary, intersex, and agender people, who do not identify with either category, or lumping them into the trans category in ways that make it hard to reckon with the ways they may differ from one another or from those who identify as transgender. Because binaries magnify similarities within and differences between categories, the trans/cis binary makes it hard to account for both variations within each category and things those assigned to opposite categories have in common, such as the fact that some non-trans people consciously reject or oppose traditional binary gender roles, while some trans people wholeheartedly embrace them. Moreover, because, like all binaries, the trans/cis binary encourages us to think of its categories as unchanging essences, it ignores and obscures the diversity, complexity, and changeability of individuals, who may, at one moment or another, fit in one, both, or neither category. As a result, the trans/cis binary is woefully inadequate for understanding even the transgender lives it is used to center and affirm.

THE TRANS/CIS BINARY IN TRANS HERMENEUTICS

When the trans/cis binary is invoked in trans hermeneutic work, it is often used to critique "cisnormativity"—the web of presumptions, traditions, institutionalized modes of interpretation, and so on, that make it common to read the Bible as a text that is only about and for those who fit binary gender norms. Cisnormativity not only makes it difficult to see or imagine transgender and nonbinary characters in the biblical texts; it also erases, or at least marginalizes, the concerns, perspectives, and insights of contemporary trans and nonbinary Bible readers.

Because the trans/cis binary demotes "cisgender" from a default assumption about humanity to one possible relation to gender, using it as a framework for examining traditional biblical interpretations helps trans hermeneutics practitioners expose cisnormativity as an interpretive choice rather than an inherent feature of biblical texts, highlight the ways that cisnormativity has shaped the way biblical characters and stories have been read, and frame readings that assume characters are cisgender as active erasure of other possibilities that should be considered.

For example, Jo Henderson-Merrygold argues that critiquing "cisnormativity" in biblical interpretation is an essential part of trans hermeneutics because "literary tradition has cisnormalised the texts, erasing indication of potential transness to ensure the characters we encounter *are* to all intent and purpose, cis."[1] As this argument suggests, trans/cis binary-based critiques of cisnormativity frame the absence of "transness" in biblical texts and interpretive traditions not as a sign that "transness" is not there, but as a sign that "cisnormalization" has erased it, because, the trans/cis binary holds, wherever cis is, trans must also in some way be. That is why Henderson-Merrygold and others put such emphasis on critiques of cisnormativity: because those critiques prompt us to read biblical texts and traditions through a trans/cis framework that assumes "transness" is always already there. From this perspective the paucity of trans characters in biblical and literary tradition reflects their active erasure ("cisnormalization") rather than their absence or, as gender binary traditionalists would insist, their impossibility. This in turn creates space to show how sparse biblical character sketches could be interpreted as signifying trans or nonbinary identities, as Henderson-Merrygold does in her "cispicious" reading of Sarah as "a trans matriarch."[2]

But as I suggested above, we cannot harness the power of the trans/cis binary without also taking on its limitations. For example, when we read biblical texts through a trans/cis framework, we read characters as either cisgender—as completely identifying with the gender roles they were assigned at birth—or as transgender, as completely disidentifying with those roles, without regard to the complexity of trans and nonbinary identities. Thus, when Henderson-Merrygold describes Sarah as "a trans matriarch," the trans/cis framework makes it easy for her to overlook what Sarah's relation to trans identity might have been, whether, for example, she hoped to pass as a cisgender woman or proudly embraced her "transness," and whether and how her relationship to female gender identification changed during her life.[3] The trans/cis framework obscures such questions

---

1. Jo Henderson-Merrygold, "Viewing Sarah Cispiciously: Cisnormalisation, and the Problem of Cisnormativity" (paper presented at the annual SBL meeting, Denver, CO, 19 November 2018), 2, http://dx.doi.org/10.17613/v38b-3w36. Henderson-Merrygold offers a detailed demonstration of what "cispicious" reading of Biblical characters means in "Gendering Sarai: Reading beyond Cisnormativity in Genesis 11:29–12:20 and 20:1–18," *Open Theology* 6:1 (September 2020): 496–509, https://doi.org/10.1515/opth-2020-0133.
2. Henderson-Merrygold, "Viewing Sarah Cispiciously," 9.
3. Perhaps in recognition of such problems, Henderson-Merrygold's "Gendering Sarai," a more nuanced reading of the same Biblical character, focuses not on a critique of cisnormativity, but on exploring the textual cues and interpretive processes through which readers develop ideas of her gender. By de-emphasizing the trans/cis binary, Henderson-Merrygold reduces the pressure to overread some aspects of the text and underread others in order to assign or see Sarah as either trans or cis, and

by prompting us to focus our trans hermeneutic attention on assigning biblical characters to one side of the binary or the other.

THE TROUBLE WITH READING GENDER IN BIBLICAL TEXTS

According to Jane Nichols and Rachel Stuart, the problems with trans/cis binary-based trans hermeneutic approaches (and, for that matter, with cisnormative approaches as well) are more fundamental than the simplifications inherent in binary thinking. Rather, they argue, the problem is that whenever we interpret biblical characters' gender (or even translate terms related to gender), we are projecting onto ancient texts anachronistic ideas that are foreign to and would not be recognized by members of the various cultures represented in them.[4] Once we read or translate Bible texts in terms of our assumptions about gender, whether because we read them cisnormatively, or through the trans/cis binary, or because we are simply trying to make sense of the gendered terms they use, we then see these texts as reflecting and confirming our assumptions. We see this circular interpretive process in both trans hermeneutic work, like Henderson-Merrygold's argument that we can see "transness" (a contemporary concept of recent vintage) in the portrayal of the biblical Sarah, and in cisnormative arguments that biblical texts portray and sacralize contemporary binary gender norms and roles. As Nichols and Stuart convincingly argue, biblical texts portray cultures so different from ours that we should be suspicious of any readings, trans hermeneutic or otherwise, that interpret characters' gender identities, roles, or even the basic categories, such as male and female, to which biblical pronouns, verb forms, nouns, and narratives seem to assign them.[5]

Though Nichols and Stuart do not address it, their critique implies an additional challenge to trans hermeneutic approaches like Henderson-Merrygold's that invoke the trans/cis binary to overcome erasure of transgender and nonbinary presence in biblical texts and traditions. Because transgender and nonbinary gender identities are not rooted in physical maleness or femaleness, are not assigned at birth, and are by definition outside established systems of gender, they can only be established by self-identification—that is, by individuals identifying themselves as transgender or nonbinary, regardless of the gender identities or roles to which they have been assigned. As a result, the trans/cis binary (and any gender system that includes self-identified identities) requires us not to gender others until and unless they explicitly gender themselves.

---

so is able to consider not only how Sarah might be read as a cis or trans woman, but suggest many ways the same textual cues allow Sarah to be gendered, such as the possibility (raised in midrashic tradition) of reading her as intersex, or seeing her more generally as "gender diverse."

4. Jane Nichols and Rachel Stuart, "Transgender: A Useful Category of Biblical Analysis?" *JIBS* 1:2 (Spring 2020): 1–24.

5. Nichols and Stuart, "Transgender," 6–7.

But I am not aware of any passages in which biblical characters self-identify in terms of gender, or in which the narration tells us how characters identify themselves. As a result, while we can guess whether biblical characters were trans or cis, gender diverse or gender normative, our conjectures can never be more than conjectures, speculative projections of anachronistic contemporary categories (which themselves are in a state of flux) onto sketchy descriptions that are always missing the information that, according to transgender theory and gender diversity practice, is the only way to know someone's gender: self-identification.[6]

But since no biblical character tells us how they identify in terms of gender, we cannot assign them to either side of the trans/cis binary without violating the principle which that binary is based upon: that gender is a matter of self-identification. Efforts to overcome cisnormativity in biblical tradition by reading transgender and nonbinary identities into the text paradoxically mirror the cisnormative practices of projecting anachronistic categories onto ancient texts and of treating gender as something that is assigned by others rather than determined by individuals themselves.[7]

TRANS HERMENEUTICS BEYOND THE TRANS/CIS BINARY

As Nichols and Stuart argue, in order to escape these problems, any approach to trans hermeneutic approaches needs to accept that though gender systems—that is, roles and categories that structure individuals' relations to one another and to larger social units—clearly play important parts in biblical characters' lives and stories, we cannot precisely determine what ancient gender categories and roles were.[8] Instead of focusing on the unknowable particulars of ancient gender systems, Nichols and Stuart argue that trans hermeneutics should focus

---

6. This is true even of Joseph, one of the most fully developed Biblical characters, one who even many rabbinic midrashim read as effeminate or gay, and who has more recently often been held up as an example of an explicitly queer, trans, or nonbinary Biblical character (depending on the agenda of the writer), based mostly on Joseph's father's gift to Joseph of the famous coat of many colors (Gen 37:3; see also the introduction to this collection). Since Joseph's response to the gift is not recorded, we do not know how, if at all, the gift might reflect Joseph's gender identification or sexuality.

7. Even though ascriptions of gender identity to Biblical characters violate the principle of self-identification that is foundational to trans and nonbinary identities, I am not suggesting that we should not "trans" or "queer" Biblical characters. As midrashic tradition, the ancient Jewish equivalent of Biblical fan fiction, shows, reimagining the Bible's sparsely portrayed characters by filling in the narrative silences that surround them has, for millennia, enabled readers in different ages and cultures to see these texts as speaking to their times and concerns. So as long as we remember and are clear that positing Sarah as a trans matriarch or Joseph as a crossdresser are midrashim—imaginative projections—this is an appropriate and deeply traditional way to respond to Biblical texts.

8. The question of what gender means becomes particularly complex in Biblical stories—and there are many—that feature characters such as Rebecca, Joseph, and Moses, who traverse multiple cultures.

on characters' relations to (and particularly rebellions against) what they call the "gendered categories" to which characters are assigned:[9]

> [The aim of a] transgender hermeneutic that resists both anachronism and the projection of colonial categories . . . . should not be to identify figures or narratives that are transgender according to our modern understanding of gender and transgender identity, but rather to highlight those that struggled against and navigated the gendered categories of their day in ways reminiscent of the ways that transgender people today struggle against and navigate gender. The goal of this hermeneutic is not to project transgender identity onto the text or upon biblical/historical figures, but instead to place transgender people in a long and storied tradition of category rebels and boundary crossers. . . . People have been transgressing social distinctions and obligations for just as long as societies have been producing them. It is this lineage that the transgender hermeneutic seeks to reclaim in the text, not transgender identity itself.[10]

In other words, Nichols and Stuart suggest that rather than trying to identify characters who might have been what we now call "transgender" or "nonbinary," as the trans/cis framework encourages us to do, trans hermeneutics should focus on characters who are described in ways that highlight the kinds of complex, conflicted relations between individuals and assigned roles and identities so that we see both contemporary transgender and nonbinary have existed "for just as long as societies have been producing them."

To demonstrate this trans hermeneutic approach, Nichols and Stuart turn to one of the most important and fully fleshed-out examples of gendered-category rebellion in the Bible: the story of Jacob's resistance to the subordinate second-born category he is assigned to by virtue of being born a moment after his twin, and his struggle to attain the status, or at least the privileges, of the gendered category *bekor*, or first-born son, assigned to his slightly older brother Esau (Gen 25:22–34; and 27:1–29). As Nichols and Stuart show, we do not have to fully understand what being a first-born son meant to Jacob, his family, or his culture in order to recognize that the text portrays it as an important—indeed, life- and destiny-defining—gendered category, or to examine Jacob's rebellion against the second-born category to which he is assigned and his efforts to "navigate" his way toward first-born status.[11]

As Nichols and Stuart note, I have also used this story to demonstrate an approach to trans hermeneutics, one that directly anticipates major features of

---

9. While their survey of gender theory is well worth reading in full, Nichols and Stuart offer a useful pocket definition of "gendered categories": "[W]e understand gendered categories to be (1) constitutive elements of social relationships serving to facilitate the organization and reproduction of the family and/or operative kinship structure through the production of difference; and (2) a primary way of signifying relationships of power" ("Transgender," 11).

10. Nichols and Stuart, 11.

11. For a summary of what the Jacob story, and other Biblical traditions and modern scholarship do and do not tell us about what it meant to be a first born, see Nichols and Stuart, 12–14.

theirs.¹² Like theirs, my approach involved treating aspects of contemporary transgender experience as examples that can help us recognize the often complex relations between biblical characters and the roles and categories to which they have been assigned. As theirs does, my reading portrayed Jacob's resistance to the second-born role he was assigned at birth as demanding trans hermeneutic interpretation, not because it suggests that he "was" transgender (it does not), but because his resistance is analogous to the resistance to birth assignment that is the basis of contemporary trans and nonbinary identities. In both our readings, the focus of hermeneutic interest is not Jacob's gender identity, but on the ways that he rebels against the place in the gender system he was born into.

In short, both Nichols and Stuart and I use the analogy between Jacob's and contemporary transgender people's resistance to the "gendered categories" we are assigned at birth to show how what I call "the lens of transgender experience" can help us understand biblical texts and characters without projecting contemporary ideas of gender and identity onto them.¹³ As Nichols and Stuart suggest, this lens is useful because, although it is anachronistic to read transgender experiences or identities into biblical narratives, human societies are partly organized by assigning individuals to "gendered categories" which, as we see in both Jacob's story and in trans and nonbinary lives, individuals may not fit, identify with, or accept. Trans and nonbinary lives offer striking contemporary examples of a phenomenon that is built into human nature and social organization: the slippage between individuals and the identity- and role-defining categories to which they are assigned.

But Nichols and Stuart find it difficult to recognize what our approaches have in common because, as their critique of it shows, my reading of the Jacob story is so entangled with references to my personal experiences as a transgender person—with what they call my "complicated affinity, as a transsexual woman, with Jacob"—that they are unable to discern in it "a transgender hermeneutic" that is distinct from (and independent of) my idiosyncratic transgender perspective.¹⁴ Though this reading of the Jacob story, and the readings that follow it, do demonstrate an approach to trans hermeneutics, as their critique shows, I do not clearly distinguish between that approach, and the way I personally read the Bible as a transgender person.

As the rabbi's question showed, Nichols and Stuart were not the only ones confused by how I presented my approach to trans hermeneutics—or, as I called

---

12. Joy Ladin, *The Soul of the Stranger: Reading God and Torah from a Transgender Perspective* (Waltham, MA: Brandeis University Press, 2019), 35–60.

13. More specifically, I use the lens of transsexual experience to understand Jacob's struggles, which, like those of transsexuals, grow out of his culture's insistence on assigning newborns to one of two mutually exclusive binary categories (determined by sex, in the case of transsexuals, and birth order, in the case of primogeniture) that are seen as determining the rest of their lives. In the Torah's account, the primogeniture binary is strikingly paralleled to the male/female binary by descriptions that assign the brothers opposite gendered traits—hairiness and hyper-masculinity in Esau and smoothness and female-associated domesticity in Jacob (Jacob is portrayed as close to his mother, cooking, and feeding his brother).

14. Nichols and Stuart, "Transgender," 14, 16.

it, "reading from a transgender perspective." But despite the confusion my description of "reading from a transgender perspective" in *The Soul of the Stranger* occasioned, it does identify the cornerstone of the approach to trans hermeneutics I have developed: the idea that the focus of trans hermeneutic attention should be what I call "trans experience," that is, moments in biblical texts when the slippage between identity-defining roles and categories and characters assigned to them plays a role in situations or stories.

Every transgender-specific experience (that is, experience specific to those who embrace a trans identity) is a trans experience, but most trans experiences are not transgender-specific. Though I note this distinction in *The Soul of the Stranger*, the sketchy definition of trans experiences I offer there does not clearly delineate the relation between the general category of trans experiences and the subcategory of transgender experiences. That is why Nichols and Stuart were confused: because I do not clearly distinguish reading from a *transgender* perspective—reading in light of transgender and nonbinary specific experiences, such as my "complicated affinity, as a transsexual woman, with Jacob"—with reading from a *trans* perspective, by which I mean reading with awareness of and attention to the slippage between biblical characters and the roles and categories, gender-related or otherwise, with which they are identified.

Though it is my life as a transgender person—a person who does not fit the "gendered categories" of my culture—that taught me to be keenly and often painfully aware of this slippage, no human being perfectly or permanently fits any of our identifying roles and categories, and so that slippage—and the trans experiences that grow out of it—is a feature of all our lives. This means that, to answer the rabbi's question that prompted me to develop this approach, because people on both sides of the trans/cis binary have trans experiences, cisgender people can learn to use their own trans experiences to read biblical texts from a trans perspective.

TRANS-EXPERIENCE-CENTERED APPROACHES TO TRANS HERMENEUTICS

While Nichols and Stuart and I adopt trans-experience-centered approaches to trans hermeneutics, our approaches differ significantly in terms of the scope of trans experiences they consider. Nichols and Stuart are concerned only with one family of trans experiences: those which relate to opposition or other kinds of resistance to "gendered categories," like Jacob's resistance to the category of second-born son. Their hermeneutic ambitions are equally specific: their approach, they suggest, will help "identify a strong tradition of [gendered] category rebels throughout the Bible who would not [otherwise] have been read together."[15]

Because Nichols and Stuart do not give other glimpses of their gendered-category-resistance-centered approach or the sort of category rebels it might

---

15. Nichols and Stuart, "Transgender," 22.

identify beyond the story of Jacob, it is hard to tell if they are only interested in characters like Jacob who directly rebel against gendered categories to which they themselves are assigned, or whether, to take a more ambiguous example from the same story, their approach would also include a character such as Rebekah, Jacob's mother, who subverts the family's patriarchal pecking order by helping her younger son steal her older son's blessing. But it is clear that their hermeneutic approach would not be interested in characters whose relations to gendered categories are something other than rebellion, such as Esau, who involuntarily endures the trans experience of losing first-born privileges, or Isaac, whose passionate gender conformism is reflected in his determination to give his blessing, and the relation to God that goes with it, to his first-born son as primogeniture demands.

Because Nichols and Stuart's approach focuses on gendered categories, it would also presumably exclude examining biblical characters' relations, rebellious and otherwise, to other kinds of identity-defining roles and categories that play a role in biblical narratives, such as Joseph's complex position after being elevated from an enslaved person imprisoned for attempted rape to Pharoah's second-in-command (Gen 41:9–52), a role that radically alters his identity (for example, he was given a new Egyptian name and an Egyptian wife) and places him in intersectionally complex positions, as when his subordinates refuse to sit at his table because Egyptians find Hebrews abhorrent, and, famously, when his brothers fail to recognize him and see him as an Egyptian rather than a Hebrew (42:6–8; and 43:30–32).

The trans-experience-focused hermeneutic approach I have developed has a much broader scope than that proposed by Nichols and Stuart, because it recognizes that any identity-defining roles or categories may give rise to trans experiences, such as those we see in Joseph's transitions from favorite child to enslaved person to prisoner to ruler. This approach attends not only to characters' rebellions against "gendered categories," but to the entire range of relations between biblical characters and any of the categories and roles, gendered or otherwise, to which they are assigned or with which they are identified. It sees potential hermeneutic interest in both characters who flourish outside established roles and categories like Sarah—whose childbirth in her nineties miraculously collapses the normally distinct categories of elderly woman and new mother (Gen 21:1–8)—and in those who, like Joseph in the role of Pharoah's second-in-command, flourish within them, understanding that even the most conformist relations entail (and may be understood as a response to) some degree of slippage between individual and identity-defining roles and categories. In this approach, hermeneutic interest depends not on the kind of role or category, or relation to them, but on whether the question of the individual's relation to a given identity-defining role or category matters in terms of how we interpret the character, story, or text.

The broad scope of my approach is designed to help those who use it become aware of trans experience in both biblical texts and their own lives. When we gain this awareness, we see that transgender and nonbinary lives and perspectives are not marginal to biblical tradition and interpretation, but a source of insight and firsthand expertise regarding the slippage between individuals and identity-defining roles and categories that plays an important part in many foundational biblical narratives and in every individual's life.

TEACHING OTHERS HOW TO READ THE BIBLE IN TERMS OF TRANS EXPERIENCE: A THREE-STEP APPROACH

When the rabbi asked me how a non-trans person could learn to read the Bible from a transgender perspective, he was asking two questions simultaneously: a theoretical question about how those on one side of the trans/cis binary could access the perspective of those on the other, and a practical question about teaching and learning. Thus far, I have focused on responding to the first question; here, I will respond to the second. I developed and tested the teaching strategies described below in workshops and seminars whose participants included trans, nonbinary, and non-trans people; students, professors, and non-academics; those who identify as religious and those who do not; Jews and non-Jews; clergy, religious educators, and those who had little familiarity with the Bible. I told each group that I was using our time together to learn how to teach trans hermeneutics (though I used the phrase "reading the Bible from a trans perspective"), and designed the sessions in ways that encouraged participants to share their own ideas and feedback.

My approach to teaching trans-experience-centered hermeneutics has three steps:

1. **Recognizing Trans Experience.** The first step is to help students think outside the trans/cis binary by teaching them to recognize, understand, and name trans experiences in their own lives—that is, times when they have been aware of the slippage between who they knew they were and the identity-defining roles and categories to which they were assigned.
2. **Focusing on the *Pshat* or "Plain Sense" of the Text.** The second step is to teach students to focus on a simplified version of what Jewish hermeneutic tradition calls the *pshat*, the plain sense of the text, a discipline that requires us to set aside, strip away, or suspend pre-existing ideas about what the Bible says (including assumptions about gender and normativity) and try to focus only on what the text does and does not say.
3. **Identifying and Interpreting Trans Experience in the Text.** The final step is to guide students through practice in reading biblical texts in light of trans experiences in their own lives, so that they read what characters do and say not as inevitable expressions of essential identities but as choices made by people who, like them, are never exactly what they are supposed to be.

TEACHING STUDENTS TO RECOGNIZE TRANS EXPERIENCE

When I began developing this pedagogical approach, I realized that rabbi's question had shown me where each class needed to start: by addressing anxieties fostered by the trans/cis binary that discourage us from recognizing what those on opposite sides have in common. To do that, I had to help students look at the trans/cis binary as an intellectual tool rather than a political or moral commitment, a tool suited for some tasks and not for others.

As I learned to explain the trans/cis binary to students, it became easier to understand and articulate the relation between what I now call trans and transgender-specific experience. That is the next step: to help students distinguish between transgender-specific experiences (experiences exclusive to those on the left-hand side of the trans/gender binary, such as gender transition) and the broader category of trans experiences (which anyone may and all of us do have), and to then identify what transgender-specific and trans experiences have in common: that they are both the products of the inherent mismatch between our messy, constantly changing selves and the categories and roles we rely on to identify ourselves and others.

When we focus on trans experiences, the difference between those on either side of the trans/cis binary becomes a matter of degree rather than kind. All human beings have trans experiences, including trans experiences related to gender, but for those who identify as transgender or nonbinary, the frequency, intensity, and importance of gender-related trans experiences is so great that they feel definitive of who we are (and of who we are not). For example, Jacob's high-stakes impersonation of his brother's hypermasculinity must have been an intense trans experience, but it was not a transgender experience: not only did it not lead him outside binary gender roles, it does not seem to have changed his relation to masculinity in any lasting way.

This framework enables students to distinguish trans experiences from the questions of identity they may or may not raise, and to see that whatever individuals make of them, these experiences are common to both trans and nontrans students. In other words, it un-queers trans and nonbinary identities, defining them not in opposition to some presumed normal, but as different ways of responding to the inevitable slippage between human beings and the identity-defining roles and categories to which we are assigned. This framing may feel like a loss to trans and nonbinary students who embrace the queerness typically associated with these identities, but in at least partial compensation, it also moves them from the margins of biblical interpretive tradition to the center, positioning them to be seen as experts in naming and navigating the trans experiences that are important features of biblical narratives and a definitive aspect of being human.

As I know from growing up in a binary-gender world that had no language to describe lives like mine, it can be hard to recognize, distinguish, reflect on, and even remember feelings and experiences for which there are no words. Recent decades have seen great expansion in the terms available for describing LGBTQ lives, and though pronouns and terms for specific identities get most of the attention, a rich informal vocabulary for transgender and nonbinary-specific experiences has also developed, much of which, I have found, can also be used more generally for trans experiences. For example, "passing" not only fits efforts to be seen as a gender other than the one assigned at birth, but it has long been used to describe Black people who live as white people.

I have compiled a list of these terms into a handout including brief definitions and, where I could think of them, quick biblical examples, designed to help students in trans hermeneutics seminars and workshops recognize, describe, and name trans experiences in their own lives. Reflecting the colloquial nature of this emerging language, many terms overlap, or address similar trans experiences from a different experiential or attitudinal angle; none grow out of or have been refined through systematic studies or theorization. My goal in presenting this list is not to ensure that everyone will use the same language for trans experience, but to help each student develop language for their own trans experiences, and thus come to see trans experience as a common aspect of their own and others' lives.

After discussing some of the terms on the list, I invite each student to find one that identifies a trans experience they have had, encouraging but not requiring them to focus on gender-related experiences since those are both familiar and, after the discussion of the trans/cis binary, at the forefront of our minds. In my limited experience—I have only taught one-off classes and seminars—this is a crucial moment in the workshop, the moment when students turn abstract theory into a means of understanding their lives. If it goes well, several students volunteer to name and describe their trans experiences, sometimes by using and sometimes by adapting terms and definitions on the list, and other students respond by embracing those descriptions ("yes, that's happened to me too"), modifying them to fit their own lives ("I know what you mean, but in my family, . . ."), or volunteering different trans experiences they have had.

For students who do not identify as transgender or nonbinary, this exercise can be a revelation. Even those who present as comfortably cisnormative find they can remember times when they have experienced a mismatch, slippage, or conflict between their sense of themselves and the gender roles and categories to which they were assigned. For example, many non-trans men, perhaps most, have experienced "gender failure," failure to live up to their families' ideas of what men are or should be, and so many can remember experiences akin to Jacob's when they tried to meet family expectations by passing as different kinds of men than they know themselves to be. Even students who identify as transgender or nonbinary and thus have worked to recognize trans experiences may find this exercise useful, as they may not be accustomed to naming trans experiences that are not related to gender, and may welcome expanding their vocabulary for those that are.

For all students, the point of this exercise is to shift their assumptions about human beings—and thus their readings of biblical characters—so that they are personally as well as theoretically attuned to the fact that people are always more than, and often conscious that they are other than, the roles they perform and the categories to which they are assigned. As they develop an awareness of trans experiences in their own lives, it is easier for students to read biblical texts with an eye to the slippage between individuals and identity-defining roles and categories, and the varieties of trans experience that may arise from it.

TEACHING STUDENTS TO FOCUS ON THE *PSHAT* (PLAIN MEANING)

Before learning to recognize and interpret trans experiences in biblical texts, students must learn to read biblical texts in a way that makes these experiences visible. That means learning to at least temporarily ignore interpretive traditions that not only tend to assume heteronormativity but which harmonize, smooth over, fill in, or otherwise obscure the gaps and contradictions in biblical texts that may signal slippage between characters and who they are supposed to be. It can be hard to approach biblical texts from outside the cloud of voices, interpretations, versions, and so on that has accumulated over the millennia and defamiliarize some of the most familiar stories in human history. But if we do not, we are likely to keep reading in terms of the assumptions and paradigms institutionalized in earlier readings and versions, and thus less likely to notice trans experiences that do not fit these assumptions and paradigms.

Jewish tradition has long recognized the importance of focusing on the text itself apart from interpretive filters, a kind of reading it calls *pshat*.[16] When we focus on the *pshat* of a biblical text and read it from previously marginalized, ignored, or suppressed perspectives, familiar stories and characters can look very different indeed. For example, as Phyllis Trible's *pshat*-focused "depatriarchalizing" rereadings of the stories of the creation of humanity show, reading this way can enable us to see that texts long interpreted as supporting traditional hierarchies and worldviews may, when those interpretive traditions are set aside, suggest very different and even directly contradictory meanings.[17]

---

16. Jewish hermeneutic tradition identifies the focusing on the *pshat* as the most basic of four ways of reading Biblical texts—or, in some versions, as the first and most readily apprehensible layer of meaning those texts. As scholars of Jewish interpretive tradition know, describing *pshat* as "the plain sense" is a drastic oversimplification, if not a complete misrepresentation, of a practice which traditionally requires grappling with complex questions of Hebrew grammar and syntax, scribal practices, idiomatic interpretation (what is the "plain sense" of a phrase that demands interpretation to be understood?), historical context, and, in the more modern versions, editing and transmission of Biblical texts. The form of *pshat* reading I describe in this essay is a nontechnical, simplified version.

17. See, for example, Phyllis Trible, "Depatriarchalizing in Biblical Interpretation," *JAAR* 41:1 (March 1973): 30–48; and Trible, "Eve and Adam: Genesis 2–3 Reread," in *Womanspirit Rising: A Feminist Reader in Religion*, ed. Carol P. Christ and Judith Plaskow (San Francisco: Harper, 1992), 74–83.

Of course, traditional commentaries and interpretations can also be productively reread from previously marginalized or excluded perspectives, as trans scholars, for example, have shown in drawing attention to *midrashim* (traditional rabbinic reimaginings of biblical texts) that challenge the assumption that Bible-based religious traditions are inherently invested in the idea that human beings can only be male or female (see, for instance, Strassfeld, in this collection). But we cannot fully develop, test, or establish hermeneutic approaches grounded in perspectives other than those that have traditionally been centered unless we also return, as much as possible, to the plain sense of biblical texts and read them anew.

Nichols and Stuart demonstrate the link between *pshat*-focused reading and trans hermeneutic interpretation when they lay the ground for their trans hermeneutic reading of Jacob as a "gendered-category rebel" with a detailed critique of interpretive practices that project ideas about gender onto biblical texts. By prompting us to see past these projections and the interpretive traditions that institutionalize them, they enable us to recognize the *pshat* of Jacob's relation to the "gendered category" of first-born son—that is, they enable us to focus on what the text does and does not say about this category, and thus to reinterpret the story from a trans hermeneutic perspective as Jacob's rebellion against the second-born category he was assigned at birth.[18]

The process of defining a *pshat* for trans hermeneutic examination is, in essence, quite simple. The first step, for novices as well as experts, is to clear away assumptions and interpretations about biblical texts so that we can recognize and reexamine what they do and do not say from a trans perspective. To define a *pshat* for trans hermeneutic purposes, we need to inventory what the text we plan to interpret does and does not specify about characters' relations to identity-defining roles and categories. Only when we have made such an inventory are we ready to recognize potential slippage between characters and those roles and categories and consider the possible trans experiences that could arise from it. So, though it goes against all my literary and poetic training, when I teach students to define the *pshat* of a biblical text, I direct their attention not to details of diction, grammar, or syntax, but to what Russian formalists in the early twentieth century called the "story-stuff": the materials—actions, dialogue, descriptions, scenes, events, and so on—which we synthesize into recognizable stories.

To help trans hermeneutics students collectively practice distinguishing the *pshat* of biblical texts from their own preconceptions and interpretations, I have developed the following exercise.

18. Henderson-Merrygold's essay "Gendering Sarai" offers a more detailed demonstration of the relation between *pshat* and trans hermeneutic reading, showing how little the text actually says about Sarah's gender, and inviting us to engage in new, trans hermeneutic interpretations of the cues it provides. When Sarah is introduced, Henderson-Merrygold points out, she "bears only her name, status as Abram's wife, and carries the portentous knowledge that she 'was barren; she had no child' (v. 30). No more is known of her at this introductory stage. Her silence and lack of initial context indicate ruptures in the anticipated reproductive continuity of the narrative and, as Jack Halberstam argues, create a space for queer and trans interpretation" (Henderson-Merrygold, "Gendering Sarai," 496–97).

1. Pick a widely known biblical story, one that is short enough to examine in detail but rich enough in character, situation, and identity-defining roles (such as "father" or "queen") or categories (such as "woman" or "Israelite") to make it relatively simple for students to put trans hermeneutic theory into practice. Tell students what story you have picked, and, before you hand out the text, ask each student to write a summary of the story as they remember or think of it. These summaries will reflect, and, in step 3, help students become aware of, the interpretive assumptions and traditions they have internalized.
2. Hand out a readable (that is, not archaic) and reliable translation of the biblical text and ask each student to read it and briefly summarize what it says about the story. Lead the group through a comparison of the text and two or three pre-text summaries. Then invite others to say how their pre-text summaries differ from the text and from the summaries examined by the group. As they do so, make a list of how student summaries differ from the text and from one another; conclude this step by sharing the list with the group. This will help students become attuned to the ways that individual interpretations and inherited versions tend to vary from the text.
3. Return to the original text and, as a group, make a list of the "story stuff" in it, that is, a list of what the text does and does not say about the story which, as they have just seen, is synthesized by different readers into somewhat different stories.
4. Prompt students to identify the "story-stuff" on the list that relates to characters and the roles or categories with which they are identified—that is, to identify the story-stuff that is relevant to the practice of trans-experience-centered hermeneutics.[19]

Teaching students to identify the story-stuff of biblical narratives prepares even those who are not trained in biblical or gender studies to engage in the radical rereading required by trans hermeneutics by enabling them to see exactly what the text does and does not say about characters' relations to identity-defining roles and categories, and so to recognize the potential slippage that is the focus of trans-experience-centered hermeneutics.

TEACHING STUDENTS TO DO TRANS-EXPERIENCE-CENTERED HERMENEUTICS

When students have practiced identifying trans experience as a common aspect of human lives that may occur whenever they or other individuals are identified in terms of roles and categories, and have collectively developed a *pshat* of a biblical text that includes either explicit trans experience (like the Jacob story) or

---

19. Because one exercise is not enough to teach students how to define a *pshat*, I reinforce the learning from the exercise by using the same text and *pshat* when we practice trans hermeneutic interpretation, and by referring back as often as appropriate to how the *pshat* we defined is like and unlike other versions and interpretations of the story. If we have time to work with more than one text, I lead students through the exercise each time we turn to a new passage. I always conclude this part of the workshop by reminding them that they can use this exercise to define *pshats* on their own, and that it is useful to do so whenever they work with Biblical texts, whether for trans hermeneutic or other purposes.

the potential for it, they are ready to learn how to do trans-experience-centered hermeneutics.

This form of trans hermeneutics begins where the *pshat*-preparation process ended: by making an inventory of how the text portrays each character's relations to the identity-defining roles and categories with which the text associates them. I prompt students to use this inventory to consider questions such as: What does the text explicitly say about these relations? What information does it omit? Are there indications as to whether characters embrace, resist, reject, or otherwise identify or disidentify with the roles and categories they are associated with? How clear, ambiguous, contradictory, or hazy are those indications? Where and how do our interpretations of each character's relations to identity-defining roles and categories matter—that is, where and how do our readings of these relations play a role in how we understand a character, utterance, action, event, scene, relationship, or larger story? (Though this last set of questions may not come up or be practical to address in introductory workshops, it is important to explain that one of the criteria for trans-experience-centered hermeneutics is that the possible interpretations of a character's relation to their identity-defining roles or categories must matter in terms of some larger reading; in other words, to be worthy of hermeneutic attention, that relation has to play a role in the story.)

Because these questions are at the heart of this trans hermeneutic approach, I lead students through them as a group. However, if time allows, I then engage students in the traditional Jewish practice called *chevruta* study.[20] I break them into pairs and ask them to discuss the text from the trans-experience-informed perspective afforded by the questions above, focusing on where they see slippage between character and identity-defining roles or categories, what possible trans experiences might arise from this slippage, and how different possibilities affect their understanding of the character and story. After a minimum of ten minutes (though, in my experience, students always want more time than that), we reconvene as a group, and each pair reports what they noticed when reading the passage for trans experiences. This exercise offers individuals practice in trans-experience-centered hermeneutics, helps them recognize a range of possible trans hermeneutic interpretations, and offers a glimpse of the ways our own experiences of slippage between our sense of ourselves and how we are identified can sensitize us to trans experiences in biblical texts. The exercise may also prompt students to offer new terms for trans experience that can be shared with future groups. Most importantly, this exercise helps students see how trans-experience-centered reading can open up new ways of reading familiar stories and characters. These insights are rewarding in themselves and also demonstrate the potential rewards, for trans and non-trans people alike, of reading biblical texts from a trans perspective.

20. The practice of *chevruta* study assumes that no two people will read the same biblical text the same way, and treats these differences as sources of insight, encouraging partners to engage in arguments intended not to establish which reading is right, but to help each person understand and be informed by how the other reads the text.

My goal in each workshop is to empower students to engage in trans-experience-centered hermeneutics whether or not they identify as transgender or nonbinary, or have special training in gender or transgender theory or in biblical studies. All they need is attention to the *pshat* of a given story or scene; awareness, grounded in their own trans experiences, that no one is only or always the roles and categories with which we are identified; and recognition of this slippage in the biblical texts that have long shaped understanding of humanity, God, and the relations between them.

Chapter 3

Jael's Gender-Ambiguous Motherhood

AYSHA WINSTANLEY MUSA

Building on my previous work where I put forward that Jael's gender is nonbinary,[1] I argue here that Jael's performances of motherhood rupture the cultural association between femininity and motherhood. I disrupt a binary framework of gender and employ a genderqueer methodology to argue that Jael performs motherhood in a gender ambiguous manner. I take as foundational Judith Butler's argument that gender is performative[2] and Deryn Guest's understanding that gender can shift and change.[3] Here I address a role that is socially constructed as feminine—motherhood—yet articulate an interpretation of Jael's motherhood as gender ambiguous. In doing so I contribute a unique reading of Jael as a biblical nonbinary mother during which I employ gender neutral pronouns to refer to Jael. My application of a queer methodology makes evident the instability of identities, in particular gender identities, especially that of the quintessential position of mother as a feminine role. Through exploring

---

1. Aysha W. Musa, "Jael Is Non-Binary; Jael Is Not a Woman," *JIBS* 1:2 (Spring 2020): 97–120.
2. Judith Butler, *Gender Trouble: Feminism and the Subversion of Identity* (London: Routledge, 1999), 78, 179.
3. Deryn Guest, *Beyond Feminist Biblical Studies* (Sheffield: Sheffield Phoenix Press, 2012), 21.

the narrative theme of motherhood and demonstrating Jael's gender ambiguous motherhood, this essay recognizes the complexity and diversity of ways in which motherhood can be performed—through feminine and masculine behaviors.

This essay addresses the verses that scholarship has primarily used to frame Jael as performing as a mother to Sisera, Judg 4:18–19 and 5:25:

> Jael came out to meet Sisera, and said to him, "Turn aside, my lord, turn aside to me; have no fear." So he turned aside to her into the tent, and she covered him with a rug. Then he said to her, "Please give me a little water to drink; for I am thirsty." So she opened a skin of milk and gave him a drink and covered him. (4:18–19, NRSV)

> He asked for water and she gave him milk,
> she brought him curds in a lordly bowl.
> (5:25, NRSV)

Jael performs false motherhood towards Sisera—feminine performances perceivable as motherly that result in Sisera's death. Jael's mother-like performances towards Sisera are a ruse, evident since Jael kills him. However, it is through these performances and the act of killing Sisera that Jael's role as symbolic mother to the children of Israel becomes evident.

Jael embodies masculine performances of motherhood—like Deborah's behaviors (4:4–6; 5:7)—and feminine performances of motherhood—like Sisera's mother's performances (5:28)—concurrently. Evident in the text are Deborah's masculine performances of motherhood, especially of initiating violence and taking on a leadership position, as well as Sisera's mother's feminine motherhood, through their separation from the battle and their exhibition of emotion.

Despite arguing that Jael performs gender ambiguously, I use the gendered term mother to refer to Jael's performances, rather than the gender-neutral term parent, for two reasons. The first is that Jael's performances can be understood as motherly but not as fatherly. Central expectations of fathers in the Hebrew Bible include circumcising their sons,[4] working outside of the home in the public sphere,[5] and leading the religious practices of the household.[6] Jael is not presented as taking on these fatherly roles. Referring to Jael as a parent would suggest that they perform according to the expectations of mothers and of fathers, but this is not the case. Jael's behaviors line up with expectations of mothers, despite my claim that these motherly behaviors are performed in a gender ambiguous

---

4. Daniel Block, "Marriage and Family in Ancient Israel," in *Marriage and Family in the Biblical World*, ed. Ken M. Campbell (Downers Grove, IL: InterVarsity Press, 2003), 47, 53; Andreas J. Kostenberger and David W. Jones, *God, Marriage, and Family: Rebuilding the Biblical Foundation* (Wheaton, IL: Crossway, 2004), 87–88.

5. Kelly J. Murphy, *Rewriting Masculinity: Gideon, Men, and Might* (Oxford: Oxford University Press, 2019), 19; Johanna Stiebert, *Fathers and Daughters in the Hebrew Bible* (Oxford: Oxford University Press, 2013), 6.

6. Block, "Marriage," 47, 53; Kostenberger and Jones, *God*, 87–88.

manner. My second reason for maintaining that Jael behaves as a mother rather than as a parent is due to the text presenting a theme of motherhood, not of parenthood. There are no characters indicated to be fathers in the text, and the figure who is commonly viewed as the father of the Israelites, YHWH, is largely absent from Judg 4 and 5. Thus, through naming Deborah as "a mother in Israel" (5:7) and including Sisera's mother (5:28), a theme of motherhood, not fatherhood or parenthood, runs through Jael's narrative. In addition, the structure of Judg 5, in particular, highlights the theme of motherhood; to begin, the text introduces Deborah, "a mother in Israel" (5:7), symbolically placing her as the mother of the national/ethnic Israelite community, and as the chapter ends Sisera's mother is introduced (5:28–31); Jael appears in the middle (5:24–27). Mothers appear at key junctures of the poetic account, emphasizing a theme of motherhood. Both named mothers exhibit a range of performances relating to motherhood: Deborah is protective and active in defending the children of Israel and Sisera's mother shows concern for her son whilst waiting and watching, eager for his return. Despite Jael not being labelled as a mother in the text, their behaviors are commonly interpreted as motherly in biblical scholarship.

The theme of motherhood and the frameworks of motherhood evident in Judg 4 and 5 are useful for understanding Jael's nonbinary gender, since it presents a set of feminine and masculine maternal behaviors against which Jael's performances can be examined. Deborah and Sisera's mother exhibit different forms of motherhood. Deborah as "a mother in Israel" (Judg 5:7) exhibits motherhood through behaviors constructed as masculine, namely through exerting power and authority and initiating violence. Deborah is an active mother who takes on a public role. Differently, Sisera's mother's motherhood is mostly evident through behaviors constructed as feminine, such as emotional distress, "she cried out," and concern for her son, "Why is the clatter of his chariot delayed?" (5:28, NIV). She is a passive mother; unlike Deborah, Sisera's mother waits to hear news of her son and takes no action. Both embodiments of motherhood are multifaceted and complex, in that they embody a range of elements relating to their roles as mothers, as will become clearer below.

Before contributing my own articulation of Jael's motherhood and shedding light on Jael's gender ambiguity, the role of mother and its construction as a feminine role is worth considering. This following section lays out the expectations of mothers in the Hebrew Bible and in doing so highlights how the gendered positions of woman, wife, and mother have many similarities due to their mutual grounding in binary femininity.

THE FEMININE ROLE OF MOTHER

The role of mother can be understood in two main ways: as a biological possibility for those sexed as female and as a gendered institution constructed as feminine.[7] It is motherhood as a feminized institution that is of interest here. Motherhood as a gendered role places behavioral expectations on women regarding their actions in relation to children.[8] Motherhood and mothering take many forms with ideologies relating to child-rearing, varying extensively historically and culturally. Performances of mothering, motherhood, or mother-like behavior can be considered feminine gender markers due to their grounding in ideals of femininity. However, all ideologies relating to mothering are constructions, with there being no natural reason for women to raise children in a particular way, or at all.[9]

The Hebrew Bible constructs motherhood as a feminine ideal and relates the role of mother to the expected role of women to be or become wives, who will be or become mothers. Performances constructed as relating to motherhood are largely the same behaviors expected of wives/women in relation to husbands/men. That women in the Hebrew Bible are or will become wives is highlighted through the Hebrew term *'ešet* being used interchangeably between woman and wife, as Hebrew has no specific word for wife.[10] This indicates that a distinction between women and wives is not deemed important in the Hebrew Bible; they are one and the same. Women are expected to become wives to men and mothers to the children of those men.

Pertinently, there is no instance in the Hebrew Bible where a woman is framed as not wanting children or refusing to care for their child.[11] Guest, supported by others such as Esther Fuchs and Tikva Frymer-Kensky, comments that the "rhetoric of [biblical] narratives encourages readers to associate women with an ardent desire for children."[12] Women as mothers are expected to set aside their own goals and interests in order to devote themselves entirely to their children. Biblical mothers' devotion to their children can be seen in various biblical narra-

7. Elizabeth A. Suter, Leah M. Seurer, Stephanie Webb, Brian Grewe Jr., and Jody Koenig Kellas, "Motherhood as Contested Ideological Terrain: Essentialist and Queer Discourses of Motherhood at Play in Female–female Co-mothers' Talk," *Communication Monographs* 82/4 (2015): 458–83, 464; Sharon Hays, *The Cultural Contradictions of Motherhood* (New Haven, CT: Yale University Press, 1996), 13.

8. Gerda Lerner, *The Creation of Patriarchy* (Oxford: Oxford University Press, 1986), 17; Terry Arendell, "Conceiving and Investigating Motherhood: The Decade's Scholarship," *Journal of Marriage and Family* 62/4 (2000): 1192.

9. Hays, *Cultural Contradictions of Motherhood*, 4.

10. While in Judg 4 and 5 (*'ešet*) is commonly translated as "wife," in Deut 21:10–11, Ruth 3:11 and 1 Sam 28:7, for example, the same term is translated as "woman." See also J. Cheryl Exum, "Shared Glory: Salomon de Bray's *Jael, Deborah and Barak*," in *Between the Text and the Canvas: The Bible and Art in Dialogue*, ed. Exum and Ela Nutu (Sheffield: Sheffield Phoenix Press, 2009), 32.

11. There are, however, a limited number of occurrences where men appear to show a lack of desire for children or at least a resistance to having a child: Onan "spilled his semen on the ground" rather than impregnate Tamar (Gen 38:10), David tries to pass his child off as Uriah's rather than his own (2 Sam 11). There are instances of childless women whose childlessness does not feature as the central point in their story like Esther.

12. Guest, *When Deborah Met Jael: Lesbian Biblical Hermeneutics* (London: SCM Press, 2005), 132; Esther Fuchs, "The Literary Characterization of Mothers and Sexual Politics in the Hebrew Bible," in *Feminist Perspectives on Biblical Scholarship*, ed. Adele Yarbro Collins (Chico, CA: Scholar Press, 1985), 133; Tikva Frymer-Kensky, *In the Wake of the Goddesses: Women, Culture and the Biblical Transformation of Pagan Myth* (New York: Free Press, 1992), 123.

tives which focus on the relationship between mother and child, usually mother and son (Gen 21:10; 2 Kgs 4:8–37). Surrogate mothers are also framed in the Hebrew Bible as fulfilling the role of motherhood through caring behavior that puts the child's needs first. Women who are not mothers are still framed as taking on the symbolic position of mother and enact mothering behaviors which are grounded in expectations of femininity (2 Sam 4; 2 Kgs 11).

Becoming a mother in the Hebrew Bible is constructed as the ultimate expression of femininity. Motherhood as an expected role of women/wives is pervasively normalized in the Hebrew Bible,[13] evident in the language used to label women who have not had children. The Hebrew Bible calls these women "barren"[14] (Gen 11:30, 25:21, Judg 13:3, Ps 111:9), indicating an absence or lack since they have not fulfilled the role that has been culturally ascribed to them.[15]

Childlessness in the Hebrew Bible is presented as "woman's greatest tragedy" whereas becoming a mother is considered a fulfillment of femininity, where the roles of woman, wife, and mother are largely amalgamated. The similarities between the expected behaviors of women, wives, and mothers leads to the frequent conflation of these feminized roles. Women, wives, and mothers are all expected to perform the feminine role of caring for others. Mothers are expected to physically and emotionally care for their children as women/wives are expected to care for men/husbands. At the center of each of these feminine roles is the expectation to provide care leading to their frequent conflation.[16] The behaviors associated with women, wives, and mothers are so similar that if an individual can be considered as one (as either woman, wife, or mother) then they are assumed to be or to become all. This is evident through the ongoing stereotyping of mothers as "what women *are*" and mothering as being "what women *do*,"[17] so much so that if a woman does not become wife and mother they are framed as deviant.[18] The similarities between these roles are so close that women, wives, and mothers offering food is a trope in the Hebrew Bible that links these feminine roles. Alice Bach comments that the presence of food can transform a woman into a "wifely character," since she perceives that "the

---

13. Susanne Scholz, *Introducing the Women's Hebrew Bible: Feminism, Gender Justice, and the Study of the Old Testament* (London: Bloomsbury, 2017); Fuchs, *Sexual Politics in the Biblical Narrative: Reading the Hebrew Bible as a Woman* (Sheffield: Sheffield Academic Press, 2000).

14. The term barren is the prevalent term used in biblical translations and is also used by many biblical scholars, despite this term being largely considered derogatory and even misogynistic since women are blamed for their own inability to produce children (Robin E. Jensen, "From Barren to Sterile: The Evolution of a Mixed Metaphor," *Rhetoric Society Quarterly* 45:1 [2015]: 27). For this reason, I use the term childlessness from here on.

15. Fuchs, "Literary," 130; Adrienne Rich, *Of Woman Born: Motherhood as Experience and Institution* (New York: W. W. Norton and Company, 1995), 29.

16. Frymer-Kensky, *In the Wake*, 139.

17. Gayle Letherby, "Mother or Not, Mother or What? Problems of Definition and Identity," *Women's Studies International Forum* 17:5 (1994): 525, (italics added); Rosemary Gillespie, "When No Means No: Disbelief, Disregard, and Deviance as Discourses of Voluntary Childlessness," *Women's Studies International Forum* 23:2 (2000): 225 (italics added).

18. Scholz, *Introducing the Women's Hebrew Bible*; Lerner, *Creation*, 17.

standard convention of a good woman [is that she is] soothing or nurturing a man with food."[19] Bach takes this further, commenting that feeding is related to femininity and carries connotations of "maternal" behavior.[20] Evidently, in the Hebrew Bible food and nourishment are related to women generally as well as more specifically—through their caring roles—to wives and mothers.

Another feminine expectation in the Hebrew Bible of women generally and mothers and wives more specifically is that they are largely expected to remain within their domestic space, with mothers in particular being expected to enact motherhood within feminine domesticity.[21] Victor Matthews and Don Benjamin note that a man was expected to provide a tent for each of his wives,[22] which suggests that the domestic space is not just women's space but also wives' space. The tent as a domestic space is a woman's/wife's space but also a mother's space. The matriarchs Sarah (Gen 18:10), Rebekah (Gen 24:67), Rachel (Gen 31:33), and Leah (Gen 31:33) are all mentioned in relation to their tents, the space in which each became a mother. The matriarchs live and spend the majority of their time in their tents: they birth the children of Israel in their tents; they raise said children in and around their tents. The domestic space relates to the conflated feminine roles of woman, wife, and mother, demonstrating how closely interwoven these feminine roles are. They are constructed in the same way, based on the same set of behaviors, and are largely interchangeable. This leads to women being assumed to be wives *and* mothers as well as mothers being assumed to be women *and* wives, when they may not be all. Caryn Tamber-Rosenau highlights "that even women's non-childbearing activities are framed in the language of reproductive futurism."[23]

Evidently, Jael exhibits a number of behaviors that are expected of women, wives, and mothers, including their offer of safety, care, nurture, nourishment, and reassurance towards Sisera (Judg 4:18–19, 5:25).

A FRAMEWORK OF MOTHERING

Jael's motherhood is embodied in ways that are similar and different to that of Deborah's and Sisera's mother's performances of motherhood. In studies of Jael, two patterns are apparent regarding comparisons between Jael, Deborah, and Sisera's mother. The first is that commentators almost unanimously compare

---

19. Alice Bach, *Women, Seduction, and Betrayal in Biblical Narrative* (Cambridge: Cambridge University Press, 1997), 176.
20. Bach, *Women*, 204.
21. Shira Weiss, *Ethical Ambiguity in the Hebrew Bible: Philosophical Analysis of Scriptural Narrative* (Cambridge: Cambridge University Press, 2018), 201.
22. Victor H. Matthews and Don C. Benjamin, *Social World of Ancient Israel 1250–587 BCE* (Peabody, MA: Hendrickson Publishers, 1993), 87.
23. Caryn Tamber-Rosenau, "The 'Mothers' Who Were Not: Motherhood Imagery and Childless Women Warriors in Early Jewish Literature," in *Mothers in the Jewish Cultural Imagination*, ed. Marjorie Lehman, Jane L. Kanarek, and Simon J. Bronner (Liverpool: The Littman Library of Jewish Civilization, 2017), 201.

and contrast Jael with Deborah and Sisera's mother as three women rather than as three mothers. Scholarship, first and foremost, perceives these characters as women;[24] their role as mothers is rarely treated as significant to their importance in the narrative. Jael's motherhood is eclipsed by their assigned role as a woman, which I interpret as merely one facet of their ambiguous gender. My own analysis of these three characters places significance on their role as mothers, rather than their attributions of womanhood. The second pattern is that Jael is most commonly compared to Deborah *or* compared to Sisera's mother, but not to both concurrently. Differently, I compare all three characters together to highlight that, as well as having similarities with both characters, Jael is the mediating mother who combines the two extremes of motherhood that Deborah and Sisera's mother exhibit. Deborah's motherhood presents as masculine, Sisera's mother's motherhood conforms to feminine expectations, and Jael's motherhood is concurrently more than one gender and is thus recognizable as nonbinary.

Biblical scholars frame Jael's motherhood as being performed solely through feminine behaviors, overlooking Jael's masculine performances of motherhood.[25] Consequently, Jael's femininity is given greater significance than their masculinity, erasing their exhibition of nonbinary motherhood and the masculine elements of their performances. Also, commentators place significance on Jael's, Deborah's, and Sisera's mother's femininity, rather than focusing on these character's roles as mothers—a significant role in Judg 4 and 5. The result of framing these characters primarily as women rather than as primarily mothers, coupled with placing greater significance on Jael's femininity over their masculinity, is that Jael's attributed femininity is perpetuated at the expense of their nonbinary gender. Those few studies that compare Jael as a mother rather than as a woman largely compare Jael to only one other mother, or compare Deborah and Sisera's mother as mothers, but do not include Jael in the comparison.[26] As such, an interpretation of Jael as a mother who concurrently exhibits Deborah's masculine motherhood *and* Sisera's mother's feminine motherhood is yet to be acknowledged. Considering Jael's motherhood concurrently with Deborah's and Sisera's mother's motherhood makes evident that motherhood can be performed through feminine and masculine behaviors and that Jael employs both gendered sets of motherly characteristics.

---

24. Athalya Brenner, "A Triangle and a Rhombus in Narrative Structure: A Proposed Integrative Reading of Judges 4 and 5," in *A Feminist Companion to Judges*, ed. Brenner (Sheffield: Sheffield Academic Press, 1993), 102; Fokkelien Van Dijk-Hemmes, "Mothers and a Mediator in the Song of Deborah" in Brenner, *A Feminist Companion to Judges*, 112–13.

25. Dijk-Hemmes, "Mothers," 112; Mieke Bal, *Death and Dissymmetry: The Politics of Coherence in the Book of Judges* (Chicago: University of Chicago Press, 1988), 213; Robert S. Kawashima, "From Song to Story: The Genesis of Narrative in Judges 4 and 5," *Prooftexts* 21:2 (2001): 159; Tamber-Rosenau, "The 'Mothers' Who Were Not," 194.

26. Exum, "Shared Glory," 33; Matthews and Benjamin, *Social World*, 94; James G. Williams, "Other Feminine Figures: The Multifaceted Israelite Feminine," in *Women Recounted: Narrative Thinking and the God of Israel*, ed. David M. Gunn (Sheffield: The Almond Press, 1982), 74; Lillian R. Klein, *The Triumph of Irony in the Book of Judges* (Sheffield: Sheffield Academic Press, 1988), 45.

Two notable exceptions to the patterns of scholarship I summarize include Judy Taubes Sterman's 2011 article on "Themes in the Deborah Narrative (Judges 4–5)"[27] and Freema Gottlieb's 1981 article titled "Three Mothers."[28] Both briefly address Jael as undertaking motherly behavior and Gottlieb specifically compares Jael, Deborah, and Sisera's mother as three mothers. Yet, Jael's motherhood remains binarized as feminine, with temporary gender shifts, rather than a recognition of gender ambiguity.

JAEL AS MOTHER TO THE CHILDREN OF ISRAEL

Scholarship rarely acknowledges Jael's masculine performances of motherhood. I argue that a shift in perspective is required: when interpreting Jael as mother to the children of Israel, Jael's performances of feminine motherhood on behalf of their children (for example consideration and selflessness) are evident alongside their performances of masculine motherhood, also undertaken on behalf of their children (behaviors such as controlling and killing). By committing the masculinized act of killing, Jael fulfills the feminized expectations of a mother to care for their children—to act selflessly and to ensure their children's health and wellbeing—whilst simultaneously performing as a warrior mother and caring mother by killing those who wish their children harm. As Jael's simultaneous caring for the children of Israel and killing of Sisera demonstrates, Jael's motherhood is performed gender ambiguously rather than purely through behaviors constructed as feminine.

My claim that Jael is recognizable as mother to the children of Israel is supported by Jael's lack of biological children, which can be considered an indicator that Jael should be understood as mother to the nation of Israel. Childlessness as suggesting symbolic motherhood is a motif that is commonly picked up on in studies on Judith and can be extended to Jael and even other characters that are childless, such as Deborah and Esther. In studies on Judith, it has been argued that it is her lack of children that makes her suitable to be understood as a mother of Israel. Erin K. Vearncombe highlights Judith's childlessness as well as her willingness to risk her reputation and put herself in danger for the good of the Israelite people.[29] She understands Judith as being in a position to risk herself because she does not have children that prevent her from dedicating herself to Israel as a mother. While Jael is not said to be a widow, unlike Judith, Jael is only ambiguously linked to a husband and acts without the oversight of any man, like Judith. Similarly, Jael "gave spiritual and political life" to their

27. Judy Taubes Sterman, "Themes in the Deborah Narrative (Judges 4–5)," *JBQ* 39:1 (2011): 15–24.

28. Freema Gottlieb, "Three Mothers," *Judaism: Periodicals Archive Online* 30:2 (1981): 194–203.

29. Erin K. Vearncombe, "Adorning the Protagonist: The Use of Dress in the Book of *Judith*," in *Dressing Judeans and Christians in Antiquity*, ed. Kristi Upson-Saia, Carly Daniel-Hughes, and Alicia J. Batten (Surrey: Ashgate, 2014), 117.

people.[30] By these criteria, then, both Jael and Deborah can be understood as a mother in Israel. Deborah, like Judith and Jael, has no children, is under the authority of no man, acts to save the Israelites, and is even labeled as a mother to the nation (Judg 5:7). Thus, I recognize Jael, alongside Judith and Deborah, as a symbolic mother to the children of Israel.

Parallels between Deborah's and Jael's forms of motherhood as well as between Jael's and Sisera's mother's are an important aspect of the narrative. This comparison, below, demonstrates that Jael's motherhood draws on the two existing frameworks of motherhood in the narrative in a way that combines feminine performances and masculine performances of motherhood, allowing Jael to be read as a nonbinary mother.

JAEL'S GENDER AMBIGUOUS MOTHERHOOD

Jael's performances of motherhood are a complex amalgamation of femininity and masculinity, drawing on the wider narrative theme through shared motherly qualities with the two named mothers in Judg 4 and 5. This section articulates my own claim that Jael embodies motherly behaviors toward Sisera in order to fulfill their role as symbolic mother to the children of Israel. Their performances of motherhood are embodied in a gender ambiguous manner with the best interest of the children of Israel being of foremost concern. Jael performs a variety of masculine acts and behaviors that can be interpreted as part of their motherly role, many of which draw from the masculine framework of motherhood exhibited by Deborah, "a mother in Israel" (Judg 5:7), including assertive and controlling behavior as well as acts of violence and engagement with warfare. Jael also behaves as a mother in a range of ways that have been constructed as feminine. Many of these, such as domesticity, physical separation from the battlefield, and emotional concern are also exhibited by Sisera's mother when "Out of the window she peered," and when she asked "Why is his chariot so long in coming?" (5:28, NRSV).

When Jael performs motherhood through masculine behaviors, commentators do not frame Jael as performing masculine motherhood or gender ambiguous motherhood but present Jael's masculinity as temporary performances of gender reversal. A close reading of the text, with motherhood as the focus, will make evident that Jael performs motherhood through concurrent masculine and feminine behaviors. When Jael performs in ways that are understood by scholarship as feminine—motherly behavior toward Sisera—their actions are simultaneously interpretable as masculine motherhood toward the children of Israel. For example, when caring for Sisera by alleviating his fears (feminine motherly behavior), Jael is luring him into a position of vulnerability so Jael can protect the children of Israel from this threat (masculine motherly behavior).

30. Vearncombe, "Adorning," 117.

AGENCY

Key aspects of the mothers' behavior in Judg 4 and 5 is their respective agency and passivity as mothers. These states of being have been binarized, with agency being constructed as masculine and passivity as feminine by gender scholars and biblical scholars alike.[31]

Roles in the public sphere are largely framed as masculine,[32] with women being framed as "passive carers" whose domain is the private sphere. Consequently, when characters who are expected to be passive demonstrate agency, they are framed as deviating from their assigned gendered role. Jael is one of those characters. Jael's motherhood is undertaken through a combination of passive and active behaviors that can be understood by drawing on the other two mothers' frameworks of motherly performances in Judg 4 and 5. Deborah is an active mother, Sisera's mother is a passive mother, and Jael embodies aspects of both frameworks of motherhood concurrently, gender ambiguously.

Jael behaves as an active mother to the children of Israel by initiating contact with the Israelites' enemy, Sisera, inviting him into their tent before he has the chance to approach or act himself. Jael employs initiative throughout their interaction:

> Jael came out to meet Sisera, and said to him, "Turn aside, my lord, turn aside to me; have no fear." So he turned aside to her into the tent, and she covered him with a rug. Then he said to her, "Please give me a little water to drink; for I am thirsty." So she opened a skin of milk and gave him a drink and covered him. (4:18–19, NRSV)

Jael demonstrates assertive behavior constructed as masculine. This masculine behavior is performed through mothering behavior of caring for Sisera. Jael is not only active in bringing Sisera into their tent but also takes initiative by switching a harmless drink for a soporific drink (4:19, 5:25),[33] taking an active role in ensuring Sisera is in a vulnerable position—sleepy, covered up, expecting protection (4:18–20). Jael's active behavior and initiative show Jael's willingness to be involved in the events—the war—that affect the children of Israel. It is through Jael's masculine agency and initiative that Jael is able to enact their motherhood by liberating the children of Israel from their Canaanite oppressors. Jael's active

---

31. Pierre Bourdieu, *Masculine Domination*, trans. Richard Nice (Stanford: Stanford University Press, 2001), 30; Ken Stone, "How a Woman Unmans a King: Gender Reversal and the Woman of Thebez in Judges 9," in *From the Margins 1: Women of the Hebrew Bible and Their Afterlives*, ed. Peter S. Hawkins and Lesleigh Cushing Stahlberg (Sheffield: Sheffield Phoenix Press, 2009), 79; Deborah F. Sawyer, "Gender Criticism: A New Discipline in Biblical Studies or Feminism in Disguise?," in *A Question of Sex? Gender and Difference in the Hebrew Bible and Beyond*, ed. Deborah W. Rooke (Sheffield: Sheffield Phoenix Press, 2007), 8.

32. Deborah F. Sawyer, *God, Gender, and the Bible* (London: Routledge, 2002), 66; Cheryl B. Anderson, *Women, Ideology, and Violence: Critical Theory and the Construction of Gender in the Book of the Covenant and the Deuteronomic Law* (London: T&T Clark, 2004), 92.

33. Klein, *Triumph*, 42.

and assertive behavior is an aspect of their motherhood that is paralleled by Deborah's motherhood. Deborah not only takes an active role in beginning the war but also leads it (5:12) as "Israel's chief military leader."[34] The masculinity of Jael's and Deborah's motherhood benefits the Israelite nation at Sisera's expense.

Sisera's mother, unlike Jael and Deborah, exhibits no active behavior, but rather is firmly presented in the literature as a passive mother, one who waits and watches:

> Out of the window she peered,
> the mother of Sisera gazed through the lattice:
> "Why is his chariot so long in coming?
> Why tarry the hoofbeats of his chariots?"
> (5:28, NRSV)

She has no active responsibility, political or otherwise, and does not act "in defence of her child"; in fact, she does not act at all.[35] She does not move from her window, not even to find out what has become of her child, thus adhering to feminine expectations of passivity. While Deborah and Jael, mothers of Israel, are active in securing their children's safety and wellbeing, Sisera's mother watches and waits, passively. The outcome for her child is markedly different than the outcome for the children of Israel, highlighting that Jael's and Deborah's active, masculine motherhood is not only beneficial but is a significant aspect of their success as mothers.

DOMESTIC SPACE

Jael's active motherhood and Sisera's mother's passive motherhood both take place within the domestic space (4:18, 5:24), a sphere that is related to women and mothers as their designated space in opposition to men's agency in the public domain.

A conflation of the woman's role and the mother's role often occurs in relation to this private space. As well as being constructed as a feminine space, the domestic space is commonly understood as the space in which mothers and children reside, as the place where children are raised by their mothers.[36] In part, this is because women have historically been tasked with caring for the home, the household; the care of children falls within this remit.[37] By depicting Jael within a space that has conventional ties to femininity and motherhood, Jael's

---

34. Susan Ackerman, *Warrior, Dancer, Seductress, Queen: Women in Judges and Biblical Israel* (New York: Doubleday, 1998), 31.

35. Don Seeman, "The Watcher at the Window: Cultural Poetics of a Biblical Motif," *Prooftexts* 24:1 (2004): 19.

36. Rich, *Woman*, 13; Weiss, *Ethical Ambiguity*, 201.

37. Johanna W. H. van Wijk-Bos, *Reformed and Feminist: A Challenge to the Church* (Louisville, KY: Westminster, John Knox Press, 1991), 75.

performances of femininity are conflated with performances of motherhood. Reading Jael as a feminine, domestic mother is possible and typical.

Jael's domestic space lends itself to images and interpretations of Jael as a mother in general, but more specifically as "a mother in Israel." The poem's reference to Jael as "most blessed" in relation to their position as a tent-dweller (5:24) highlights their location in a domestic space and has been understood by some scholars as a reference to the tent-dwelling matriarchs. This is stressed in Shira Weiss's comment that in the text Jael is being "praised among the matriarchs."[38] Thus, depicting Jael in a domestic space and referring to Jael as a tent-dweller creates an image of Jael as a mother, but not just any mother: "a mother in Israel"—like the matriarchs.

Associating Jael with the biblical matriarchs, as a mother to the children of Israel, establishes a parallel between Jael's motherhood and Deborah's motherhood. Deborah is also framed as a mother to the children of Israel, "a mother in Israel" (5:7). Deborah is understood in this way because she metaphorically rose up to protect the children of Israel from the Canaanite threat, as Jael does. Cheryl Exum states that "A mother in Israel is one who brings liberation from oppression, provides protection, and ensures the well-being and security of her people."[39] Both Jael and Deborah fulfill these expectations. Between Deborah and Jael, the Canaanite threat is eradicated because these mothers were willing to put themselves in harm's way for the benefit of Israel.

While Jael's location within the domestic space links Jael to Sisera's mother, it distances Jael from the masculine motherhood performed by Deborah. Unlike Jael and Sisera's mother, Deborah is presented as being outside, in the public arena, not within a private space or a domestic space: "She used to sit under the palm of Deborah between Ramah and Bethel in the hill country of Ephraim; and the Israelites came up to her for judgment" (4:5, NRSV). It is Jael's performance of motherhood within the confines of domesticity that highlights a difference between Jael's and Deborah's motherhood. This aspect of Jael's motherhood conforms to the feminine expectations of domesticity, whereas Deborah's public motherhood does not. Sisera's mother is described as being within the private, domestic space, looking through a latticed window (5:28). It is within this space that she is expected to remain and await the outcome of the war, performing her role of mother. Jael and Sisera's mother share this feminized facet of their motherhood, their restriction within the domestic, private sphere. It is, in part, this motherly space that allows Jael's performances of motherhood to benefit their symbolic children, the children of Israel. Sisera enters a woman's space, but also a mother's space. When Jael invites Sisera into their tent and reassures him that he should "have no fear," Jael acts as a warrior mother leading the enemy of their children into a trap. However, scholarship has largely viewed Jael as

---

38. Weiss, *Ethical Ambiguity*, 201.
39. Exum, "'Mother in Israel': A Familiar Figure Reconsidered," in *Feminist Interpretation of the Bible*, ed. Letty M. Russell (Philadelphia: Westminster Press, 1985), 85.

taking "a child into her home and car[ing] for him."[40] Sisera is not only drawn into the tent by the appearance of motherly concern but also as "a child seeking his mother's shelter."[41] Sisera cannot reach his own mother and her motherly, domestic space, and thus accepts Jael's false performance and tent as a substitute.

Sisera's death within a mother's domain allows for a number of conclusions and parallels to be drawn. Jael's killing of Sisera indicates that Jael is a symbolic mother to the children of Israel. Also, Jael's killing makes clear that although Jael remains within the domestic space, they still participate in the war as Deborah does. Both of these mothers of the Israelites act in defense of the children of Israel and both are willing to initiate motherly violence to do so. Jael's motherly behavior is performed in a gender ambiguous manner: care and kindness are interwoven with tactical maneuvering and violence.

Jael, as the mother of the children of Israel, offers the feminine mothering that Sisera's own mother has to offer within her mother's domestic space. However, Jael employs masculine behaviors of warfare and control, like Deborah, concurrently with feminine behaviors of motherly doting. Jael does this to dominate Sisera, not as a mother dominates a child, but as a warrior mother removes obstacles from the path of their children's wellbeing. It is within Jael's private space, the mothers' space, that Jael enacts emotional concern toward Sisera, leading him to believe he is in a place of maternal safety. Consequently, this domestic space, coupled with the emotional and maternal implications, allows Jael to bring safety to the children of Israel through gender ambiguous performances of motherhood.

EMOTIONAL CONCERN

Jael calls Sisera into their domestic space with an exhortation that suggests concern for Sisera's wellbeing: "Turn aside, my lord, turn aside to me; have no fear" (4:18). This apparent concern is in line with expectations of feminine, maternal behavior.[42] Danna Fewell and David Gunn suggest this indicates Jael's sympathy,[43] signaling that Sisera's emotions are important to Jael and that Jael wishes for Sisera to feel safe and secure. Sterman understands Jael's show of concern to soothe Sisera as a mother's words would be expected to do.[44] Demonstration of emotion and emotional concern for others has been commonly

---

40. Bal, *Death and Dissymmetry*, 213.
41. Jack M. Sasson, "'A Breeder of Two for Each Leader': On Mothers in Judges 4 and 5," in *A Critical Engagement: Essays on the Hebrew Bible in Honour of J. Cheryl Exum*, ed. David J. A. Clines and Ellen van Wolde (Sheffield: Sheffield Phoenix Press, 2011), 343.
42. Exum, "Whose Interests Are Being Served?," in *Judges and Method: New Approaches in Biblical Studies*, ed. Gale A. Yee (Minneapolis: Fortress Press, 2007), 72.
43. Danna Nolan Fewell and David M. Gunn, "Controlling Perspectives: Women, Men, and the Authority of Violence in Judges 4 & 5," *JAAR* 58:3 (1990): 392.
44. Sterman, "Themes," 21.

characterized as a feminine trait, and in relation to children as a motherly trait.[45] Jael's emotional concern for Sisera creates an image of Jael as mothering Sisera in conventional feminine ways. Adrien Janis Bledstein comments that Jael's actions and concerns "are aligned with the expected behavior of a woman as lover, adviser, mother and loyal servant."[46] Jael's performances, thus, can be perceived as an exhibition of the feminine ideal of a caring and considerate mother.

However, Jael's demonstration of emotional concern can also be understood as a masculine maneuver to gain control over Sisera and thus shows a simultaneous embodiment of femininity and masculinity. Jael's performance of emotional concern misleads Sisera: as Tammi Schneider notes, their reassurance of Sisera is employed in order to "lull Sisera into a false sense of security."[47] Jael's emotional concern forms a segue into physical demonstrations of concern, such as covering Sisera with a blanket (4:18), giving him a soporific drink (4:19), and allowing him to sleep (4:20–21). Such acts of concern, both emotional and physical, allow Jael to encourage Sisera to lie down and go to sleep. Jael's show of emotions leads Sisera to trust Jael and gives Jael the opportunity to take control of Sisera's actions. Jael wins Sisera's trust through mothering and, in doing so, Sisera becomes vulnerable to Jael, allowing Jael to "cleverly and powerfully [dispatch] him after making him feel that he had nothing to fear from her."[48] It is this vulnerability, achieved through Jael's apparent feminized motherly concern for Sisera's wellbeing, that allows Jael to take control of the interaction. It is Jael who decides whether Sisera will have sanctuary in their tent or not (4:18). It is also Jael who decides whether Sisera will live or die:

> He said to her, "Stand at the entrance of the tent, and if anybody comes and asks you, 'Is anyone here?' say, 'No.'" But Jael wife of Heber took a tent peg, and took a hammer in her hand, and went softly to him and drove the peg into his temple, until it went down into the ground—he was lying fast asleep from weariness—and he died. (4:20–21, NSRV)

Ultimately, Jael's show of motherly, emotional concern is concurrently a masculine maneuver of control that presents Jael with the opportunity to kill Sisera, again as a mother defending the children of Israel. When Jael performs feminine emotional concern and masculine domination, simultaneously, Jael embodies symbolic motherhood to the children of Israel in a gender ambiguous manner.

The emotional concern Jael exhibits, regardless of their motivation for doing so, allows parallels to be drawn between Jael's performances of motherhood and the two other mothers' performances of motherhood. Jael's concern, framed

---

45. Anderson, *Women*, 97.
46. Adrien Janis Bledstein, "Is Judges a Woman's Satire of Men Who Play God?," in Brenner, *A Feminist Companion to Judges*, 40.
47. Tammi J. Schneider, *Judges* (Collegeville, MN: Liturgical Press, 2000), 79.
48. Jo Ann Hackett, "In the Days of Jael: Reclaiming the History of Women in Ancient Israel," in *Immaculate and Powerful: The Female in Sacred Image and Social Reality*, ed. Clarissa W. Atkinson, Constance H. Buchanan, and Margaret R. Miles (Boston: Beacon Press, 1987), 357.

as feminine,[49] links Jael's mothering behavior to Sisera's mother's demonstration of motherhood, since both mothers show concern for Sisera's wellbeing. Sisera's mother is also emotional when considering her son: "Why is his chariot so long in coming? / Why tarry the hoofbeats of his chariots?" (5:28). She demonstrates emotion, voicing worry regarding her son, and shares her worries with the women around her. Jack M. Sasson has interpreted Sisera's mother's show of emotion as "tenderness."[50] This tenderness is similar to that embodied by Jael toward Sisera when Jael tells Sisera to take shelter and "have no fear" (4:18). Jael's emotion and tenderness draw from the feminine framework of motherhood demonstrated by Sisera's mother in Judg 4 and 5. Jael's assurance that Sisera should "have no fear" also establishes a parallel between Jael and Deborah's motherhood since this emotional exhortation can be understood as a call to war, as explained below. Thus, this phrase allows Jael's motherhood to be recognized as both feminine, through emotional concern, and masculine, through its connotations of warfare and violence.

VIOLENCE

Deborah does show concern for her children, the Israelites, but that concern is exhibited not through comforting behavior, as Jael does with Sisera, but through a call to war against those who threaten the Israelites: "She sent and summoned Barak son of Abinoam from Kedesh in Naphtali, and said to him, 'The LORD, the God of Israel, commands you, "Go, take position at Mount Tabor, bringing ten thousand from the tribe of Naphtali and the tribe of Zebulun"'" (4:6). Deborah's motherhood toward the children of Israel is largely masculine. This same masculine way of showing concern is evident in Jael's behavior. The phrase Jael uses when talking to Sisera, "have no fear" (4:18), suggests emotional concern but is also related to warfare in the Hebrew Bible. For example, this phrase's association with warfare is evident in Deuteronomy's rules of war that YHWH's warriors "shall not be afraid of them" (Deut 20:1, NRSV), soon after repeating: "Today you are drawing near to do battle, against your enemies. Do not lose heart, or be afraid, or panic, or be in dread of them" (20:3, NRSV). Similarly, YHWH reassures Joshua before he goes into battle, saying: "Do not be afraid of them, for tomorrow at this time I will hand over all of them, slain, to Israel" (Josh 11:6, NRSV). Mieke Bal understands "fear not" as a phrase that "belongs to the vocabulary of war," and Jael's use of this phrase as linking their character and their actions to the masculine domain of battle, violence, and killing.[51] Bal interprets Jael's phrase as an invitation to war, which is supported by its use elsewhere in the Hebrew Bible. Violence and killing are behaviors characterized as masculine and thus have been understood as contradictory to the feminized role

---

49. Anderson, *Women*, 97.
50. Sasson, "Breeder," 345.
51. Bal, *Death and Dissymmetry*, 212.

of motherhood. This is particularly evident from Colleen Conway's comment that Jael's killing is "a surprising act of violence from a female character against a male figure" as it goes against feminine gendered expectations.[52] This violence and killing, however, does not upset Jael's position as mother, as Jael commits violence in order to protect the children of Israel, and ensure their wellbeing.[53] Jael's act demonstrates their willingness to put the children of Israel's wellbeing above their own as expected of a mother.[54] Jael cares for the children of Israel by killing Sisera, concurrently showing feminine motherly care and concern as well as masculine motherly protection through the single act of killing.[55]

Employing language that has ties to violence and warfare, "have no fear" (Judg 4:18), brings to the fore similarities between Jael's motherhood and Deborah's motherhood. When Deborah calls herself "a mother in Israel," she does so in reference to her willingness and ability to enact violence:

> The peasantry prospered in Israel,
>   they grew fat on plunder,
> because you arose, Deborah,
>   arose as a mother in Israel.
> When new gods were chosen,
>   then war was in the gates.
> Was shield or spear to be seen
>   among forty thousand in Israel?
> My heart goes out to the commanders of Israel
>   who offered themselves willingly among the people.
> Bless the LORD.
>
> (5:7–9, NRSV)

As Fewell and Gunn point out, "Deborah is a bellicose mother."[56] Deborah's willingness and ability to instigate violence, violence that is considered to be in the Israelites' best interest, is a position that Jael also embodies. Jael performs as a warrior mother first through their "encouragement to battle"[57] through the phrase "fear not," and then by their maneuvering of Sisera into a child-like state of vulnerability to violently kill him.

Jael and Deborah are both mothers who initiate violence. Jael initiates violence when they went "softly to him [Sisera] and drove the peg into his temple" (Judg 4:21, NRSV), while Deborah initiates violence when she summons Barak and tells him to begin a war against the Canaanites: "'I will draw out Sisera, the general of Jabin's army, to meet you by the Wadi Kishon with his chariots and his troops; and I will give him into your hand'" (4:7, NRSV). Here, Deborah

---

52. Colleen M. Conway, *Sex and Slaughter in the Tent of Jael: A Cultural History of a Biblical Story* (Oxford: Oxford University Press, 2017), 7; Fewell and Gunn, *Gender, Power, and Promise: The Subject of the Bible's First Story* (Nashville: Abingdon Press, 1993), 126.
53. Fuchs, "Literary," 133; Bach, *Women*, 204.
54. Hays, *Cultural Contradictions*, 3; Matthews and Benjamin, *Social World*, 94.
55. Matthews and Benjamin, 94.
56. Fewell and Gunn, *Gender, Power, and Promise*, 125.
57. Bal, *Death and Dissymmetry*, 212.

begins the war by making known what is assumed to be communication from YHWH; a war is to be waged. Her role as a judge is to lead the war and as such, she "went with Barak to Kedesh" (4:9, NRSV), where the Canaanites are being led for a battle (4:7). Deborah calls for her children to engage in battle, marking her as a mother who is willing to invoke violence and warfare to free her children from Canaanite rule. Jael and Deborah, as mothers, enact a violent method of eliminating the threat to the children of Israel, unlike Sisera's mother, who merely awaits the outcome of the war, staying separate from it as women were expected to do.[58] In this way, Jael's performances of motherhood, like Deborah's, include masculinity as an integral aspect; they are both warrior mothers who act violently to protect their children, the children of Israel.

CONCLUSION

Recognizing Jael and their behaviors as feeding into the text's theme of motherhood addresses some aspects of ambiguity evident in Judg 4 and 5, in particular Jael's motivation for killing Sisera. As noted by Elie Assis, Jael's motivation is "not apparent in the story."[59] Although scholarship has widely picked up on Jael's mothering behavior, it has largely framed Jael as mother to Sisera rather than as mother to the children of Israel. Jael's killing of Sisera makes evident that Jael should be understood as performing only false motherhood towards Sisera. If one overlooks the importance of the theme of motherhood, Jael's motives remain a mystery. Jael's false mothering of Sisera, which results in his death, is explained by Jael's position as a mother to the children of Israel acting in defense of their children.

The theme of motherhood also explains why Deborah is referred to as "a mother in Israel" (5:7) and why Sisera's mother appears in the narrative (5:28). Deborah could have been labeled in a number of ways, as a judge or a leader more generally. Further, any Canaanite woman could have been depicted worrying about Sisera and his wellbeing, especially a wife. However, these characters are included and labeled as mothers. Their inclusion as mothers highlights the theme of motherhood in Judg 4 and 5 as well as allowing parallels to be drawn between the motherhood of Jael, Deborah, and Sisera's mother.[60] Rather than including three characters who are women, the text includes three characters who are mothers.

Despite studies of Jael widely framing them as behaving as a mother, the focus in scholarship is on Jael as mother to Sisera. This essay demonstrates that Jael embodies false motherhood toward Sisera and is more suitably recognized as performing true motherhood toward the children of Israel. Here, I have

---

58. Murphy, *Rewriting Masculinity*, 19.
59. Elie Assis, "'The Hand of a Woman': Deborah and Yael (Judges 4)," *Journal of Hebrew Scriptures* 5:19 (2005): 11.
60. Tamber-Rosenau, "Mothers," 195.

articulated that Jael's mothering shares commonalities with Sisera's mother's motherhood through emotional concern and their location within a private domestic sphere, as well as with Deborah's motherhood through engagement with warfare and violence on behalf of the children of Israel. Jael embodies some behaviors evident in the masculine framework of motherhood exhibited by Deborah whilst simultaneously embodying feminine behaviors that manifest in Sisera's mother's framework of motherhood. Consequently, Jael's performance as a mother in Israel is a gender ambiguous one, presenting Jael as a nonbinary mother to the children of Israel.

Chapter 4

"Why Do You Transgress?"[1]
Nonbinary Biblical Readings of Mordecai and Beyond

ESTHER BROWNSMITH

In his medieval commentary on Genesis, the great Jewish scholar David Kimḥi (Radak) discusses God's promise to Abraham: that he would make his descendants (literally his "seed," *zera*) as numerous as the dust of the earth (Gen 13:16). But, Radak says, even when Abraham complained that God had given him no seed (*zera*) in Gen 15:3, he did not think that God had deceived him. Why not? Perhaps, he suggests, Abraham thought that God had meant "seed" in the sense of "descendants of other family members." As evidence for this meaning, Radak brings up Esth 10:3, which says that Mordecai cared for "all his seed (*zera*)." To Radak, this verse is a key example of an instance where "seed" does not mean "progeny of a man."[2] Mordecai had "seed"—but no biological children. And in the summation of the successful life of a heroic Jewish protagonist, that fact is remarkable.

So who *was* Mordecai? My answer to that question stems from my work on queerness within the book of Esther, where I noticed that multiple authors have

---

1. Unless otherwise noted, all translations are my own. This title quotes from Esth 3:3, where the king's servants ask Mordecai, "Why do you transgress the king's commandment?" Cf. my conclusion for discussion.

2. Radak, *Radak on Genesis*, 15.3.1.

identified queer aspects of Mordecai's character[3]—not just in sexual orientation, but in Mordecai's gender identity. The word "nonbinary" is absent from these studies, which use language like "feminization" and "gender transgression," but the more that I researched, the more that "nonbinary" felt like the most appropriate term. (In this decision, I was also guided by my personal investment in the lives of many nonbinary friends.)

My first goal with this chapter is to construct a biblical hermeneutic that can open up the biblical text to nonbinary readers as something that does not, inherently and unrelentingly, enforce a binary notion of gender. My second is to make sense of the Hebrew Bible's depiction of Mordecai, in the context of the broader queerness and gender transgressiveness of the book of Esther. There is a certain inherent ideological tension in these goals, because they conflate a presentist interpretation of the Bible, in which the Bible is read as scripture that speaks to the lives of modern humans, with a historicist interpretation, in which the Bible is read as a historical document reflecting the worldview of very distant authors.[4] Yet I would contend that these interpretations, though in tension with each other, are not wholly independent. A historicist view provides the sturdy roots of historical details from which presentist views can grow and reach new heights of modern relevance; neither roots nor branches can flourish on their own.

My chapter thus has three components. In this first part, I relay my goals and briefly review the concept of nonbinary gender. In the second part, I survey existing attempts to locate nonbinary figures in the Bible, in order to see what strategies others have employed. Finally, I turn to the book of Esther and summarize the ways in which Mordecai's character resists a gender binary, reflecting on the implications and questions raised by that fact.

METHOD AND APPROACH

For scholars of the ancient world, there is a dichotomy that we take for granted: the dichotomy between the cleaned-up categories of religious texts and the messiness of real practice. From the archaeology of Jericho (whose famous walls likely

---

3. E.g. Randall Bailey ("'That's Why They Didn't Call the Book Hadassah!': The Interse(ct)/(x)ionality of Race/Ethnicity, Gender, and Sexuality in the Book of Esther," in *They Were All Together in One Place: Toward Minority Biblical Criticism*, ed. Randall C. Bailey, Tat-siong Benny Liew, and Fernando F. Segovia [Atlanta: SBL, 2009], 227–50), Timothy Beal (*The Book of Hiding: Gender, Ethnicity, Annihilation, and Esther* [London: Routledge, 1997]), and Gwynn Kessler ("Let's Cross That Body When We Get to It: Gender and Ethnicity in Rabbinic Literature," *JAAR* 73:2 [2005]: 329–59). In particular, see the first half of the "The Disidentification of Mordecai: A Drag Interpretation of Esther 8:15," by Katherine Gwyther and Jo Henderson-Merrygold (*HS* 63 [2022]: 119–41), which overlaps with my argument in its discussion of Mordecai as someone whose masculinity is "ambivalent" and "unstable." This chapter was largely written before I encountered Gwyther and Henderson-Merrygold's article, but our conclusions are complementary to each other.

4. For the terms "presentist" and "historicist," and more reflections on these tensions, cf. Sheldon Pollock, "Philology in Three Dimensions," *Postmedieval: A Journal of Medieval Cultural Studies* 5:4 (2014): 398–413.

did not tumble for the Israelites)[5] to the ongoing debate about Judean pillar figurines (which may document widespread non-Yahwistic religious practices),[6] it is clear that the Bible does not represent "the whole truth, and nothing but the truth" when it comes to ancient Israelite life. But even as intrepid academics have questioned many of the assumptions that came from taking the Bible at face value, they have rarely questioned the human gender binary. God, many feminist theologians say, is beyond gender; but it is only very recently that we have begun to imagine that humans could be as well.

In reality, biological science and sociology alike have shown that the idea of a gender binary is a gross oversimplification. An increasing number of people identify as neither male nor female, or as some combination of the two; they may call themselves agender, genderqueer, genderfluid, or other terms, but I refer to them in this paper by the umbrella category of "nonbinary." Identities beyond the gender binary are widespread in the modern world, and increasing numbers of archaeological studies, like a report on a Finnish grave that made recent news headlines,[7] acknowledge their presence in the past. The question is how we let that fact affect our understandings of the Bible and the world that produced it.

In the foundational work of lesbian biblical studies, *When Deborah Met Jael*, Deryn Guest proposes four guiding principles for a lesbian hermeneutic: resistance, rupture, reclamation, and reengagement. That is, a lesbian reading of the Bible should **resist** a heteronormative framework that renders lesbian connections invisible. It should **rupture** the binary boundaries of gender and sexuality. It should **reclaim** biblical passages using bold and creative appropriation. And it should constantly **reengage** with actual lesbians and current political issues, maintaining its own relevance. These four principles encompass a spectrum of hermeneutical approaches, ranging from re-engaging with classic text-critical scholarship through a hermeneutic of "hetero-suspicion" to exploring imaginative practices of midrashic creativity. In this chapter, I will be drawing from all four principles as they similarly apply to nonbinary readings.[8]

---

5. The modern archaeological consensus (contested by conservative scholars) is that Jericho was destroyed a couple of centuries before the biblical narrative of Joshua's conquest would have taken place, though its impressive ruins would have inspired tales about divine destruction. See Piotr Bienkowski, "Jericho Was Destroyed in the Middle Bronze Age, Not the Late Bronze Age," *BAR* 16 (1990): 45–49.

6. Scores of stylized female clay figurines have been found in archaeological excavations of ancient Israel. The interpretation of these figurines (as goddesses, icons, or even toys) remains the subject of debate, but at a minimum, most scholars connect them to popular female religious practices that received little (and largely negative) documentation within the Bible. For an overview of the evidence, see Erin Darby, *Interpreting Judean Pillar Figurines: Gender and Empire in Judean Apotropaic Ritual* (Tübingen: Mohr Siebeck, 2014).

7. Ulla Moilanen, Tuija Kirkinen, Nelli-Johanna Saari, Adam B. Rohrlach, Johannes Krause, Päivi Onkamo, and Elina Salmela. "A Woman with a Sword? Weapon Grave at Suontaka Vesitorninmäki, Finland," *European Journal of Archaeology* 25:1 (2022): 42–60.

8. Because of the impact of personal identity in this work, I should position myself. I come to this as someone who is cisgender, not nonbinary, although a number of nonbinary and trans friends are very dear to me. I am particularly grateful to those who offered comments on drafts of this paper;

My goal is not to prove that Mordecai was nonbinary, any more than Guest's work "proves" that biblical characters were lesbians; such a claim would anachronistically project modern frameworks of identity on a world that did not contain them. Rather, I am arguing that our models of gender have to be both *agile* and *capacious*. They need to recognize that the past, present, and future all include multiple masculinities and femininities and nonbinary genders, and that one era's identities cannot be mapped naively onto another's. Neither the Bible's gender categories nor our own are timeless, and the differences between them reveal the gaping cracks and chasms of gender constructs that are in constant flux and transformation. If our research can shatter the myth that biblical gender was binary and unchanging, then we can better resist modern efforts to "re"-impose gender ideologies that never truly existed.

Finally, I want to note three crucial, yet inadequately differentiated, categories: gender expansiveness, gender transgression, and nonbinary gender. In other words, if a character does something that troubles a straightforward gender identification, are they reflecting a more expansive view of their binary gender, are they transgressing temporarily outside their gender, or are they revealing a nonbinary gender? (For instance, the debate is still ongoing on whether biblical images of God acting as a midwife are indications of God's non-male gender.)[9] These categories are vital in the modern world, where some people engage in gender-transgressive acts while still identifying with a single binary gender, while others identify as nonbinary despite generally conforming outwardly to one gender. But they are particularly difficult to untease when working with the gender norms of the ancient world and the limitations of literary depictions. As my next section will show, a given character like Jael could be identified as gender-expansive, gender-transgressive, or nonbinary, depending on who is discussing them. In this particular paper, I choose the lens of nonbinary for two reasons. First, nonbinary as a gender identity is relatively new and under-discussed in scholarly literature, and this chapter is an effort to highlight its productivity. Second, in distinction with their unambiguous Jewishness, Mordecai's gender reads to me as deliberately ambiguous. Unlike how they perform their indomitably Jewish identity, Mordecai does not perform masculinity in an overt way. Rather, they seem to resist being pigeon-holed into either binary gender, modeling a reading of the text that recognizes people who are neither male nor female.

A NONBINARY SURVEY

In this section, I review the existing scholarship on nonbinary biblical figures, i.e. figures who are neither male nor female. But in my roughly chronological

---

any remaining problems are of course my own. I hope that my remarks will be seen as a contribution to the field that amplifies our desire to learn more from the lived experiences of our nonbinary colleagues, not an attempt to usurp their voices.

9. Cf. Hanne Løland Levinson, "Still Invisible after All These Years? Female God-Language in the Hebrew Bible: A Response to David J. A. Clines," *JBL* 141:2 (2022): 199–217 for a recent overview of the state of this debate.

survey, I will begin with the term "liminal" and the identification of "liminal figures." These days, the term "liminal" is not unproblematic;[10] nor does it overlap neatly with the term "nonbinary," given that it inherently depends upon a binary. To use colors as an analogy, if we consider a spectrum with red at one end and blue at the other, the purple zone in the center is liminal. But where do green and yellow fit into this picture? They are not liminal; they are nonbinary altogether, pointing to the artificially limited scope of our initial spectrum. Nonetheless, in earlier generations of scholarship that still presupposed binary gender, conversations about "liminal" figures were a way to approach characters who blurred the gender binary. One example is Gale Yee's article "By the Hand of a Woman," in which she argues that woman warriors like Deborah and Jael are liminal figures, "occupying a structurally anomalous position in the human domain, being neither completely male nor female but sharing features of both."[11] But despite this ontological statement of "being neither completely male nor female," Yee still uses female pronouns and refers to the characters as women. They are liminal, but ultimately they exist within a binary framework.

Almost two decades later, in 2011, Deryn Guest would take up the subject again in "From Gender Reversal to Genderfuck: Reading Jael through a Lesbian Lens." Guest points out the "long-standing reception history that has repeatedly reinforced a primary—essential—female identity for Jael as if this is the 'natural' state or the 'ground' from which Jael's performance deviates."[12] Noting Jael's masculine traits, which include a masculine name, the use of a masculine imperative verb directed at her, and her actions of penetrative violence, Guest argues that Jael disrupts the gender binary. "Jael is a figure who unsettles and destabilizes, whose performativity provides one of those unintelligible genders that give the lie to ideas of sex as abiding substance."[13] Guest is careful to note the various fractures and divergent identities within the apparently tidy "LGBT" acronym, noting that while this reading focuses on lesbian readers, "Genderqueer readers, especially perhaps those for whom the Bible remains a significant and/or sacred text, might find Jael's occupation of a not-man-not-woman ground not only of interest but a joyous and unexpected treasure."[14] Guest stops short of identifying Jael as nonbinary, but the chapter leaves little doubt that binary gender is inadequate as a way to account for Jael's depiction.

10. Cf. Caryn Tamber-Rosenau, *Women in Drag: Gender and Performance in the Hebrew Bible and Early Jewish Literature* (Piscataway, NJ: Gorgias Press, 2018), 23–26.

11. Gale A. Yee, "By the Hand of a Woman: The Metaphor of the Woman Warrior in Judges 4," *Semeia* 61 (1993): 125.

12. Deryn Guest, "From Gender Reversal to Genderfuck: Reading Jael through a Lesbian Lens," in *Bible Trouble: Queer Reading at the Boundaries of Biblical Scholarship*, ed. Teresa J. Hornsby and Ken Stone (Atlanta: SBL, 2010), 17.

13. Guest, "From Gender Reversal," 26.

14. Guest, 31. It is worth noting that, in an article dated five years later, Guest discusses their own ambiguous gender identity: "I have self-tagged as butch lesbian in most of my writing to date, but I have FTM affinity and regularly ponder surgery and transitioning" ("Modeling the Transgender Gaze: Performances of Masculinites in 2 Kings 9–10," in Hornsby and Guest, *Transgender, Intersex, and Biblical Interpretation* [Atlanta: SBL Press, 2016], 53). Thus, those "genderqueer readers" might eventually have included Guest themself.

In 2016, Rhiannon Graybill would similarly interrogate binary gender around Moses and find it lacking. Graybill notes "an assortment of textual evidence associating Moses's body with the female body," most especially in the scene when he veils himself, "an act ordinarily performed by women."[15] She positions this feminization within "an understanding of the prophetic body that encompasses femininity, disability, and other axes of identity, without, however, being bound to them."[16] However, rather than using terms like nonbinary, Graybill ultimately situates Moses within a "non-phallicized masculinity," a "queer masculinity."[17] Moses may be feminine, but he is never not essentially male. Nonetheless, Graybill's 2016 book represents an important effort to push back on the male/female binary as applied to biblical characters, and it has much to say when read through a nonbinary lens.

In 2020, Aysha W. Musa published "Jael Is Non-binary; Jael Is Not a Woman." Musa's article argues that Jael is characterized with both feminine and masculine gender markers, and that Jael should therefore be described as nonbinary or "gender ambiguous." Her argument draws upon previous generations of scholarship—most notably Deryn Guest—but it distinguishes itself by deliberately using "they/them" pronouns for Jael, rather than "she/her." Musa is clear that her goal is to change how we talk about Jael: "Jael ought not be identified as masculine or feminine, but as masculine *and* feminine."[18] Mustering much of the same evidence as prior scholars for Jael performing both feminine and masculine behavior, Musa also makes much of Jael's masculine name, arguing that the juxtaposition of masculine name and feminine label sets them up as nonbinary from the start. Musa's ultimate point is that scholarship has forced Jael into a binary gender, viewing their masculine aspects as an aberration instead of an equally important gender marker, and that the Bible's original portrayal is nonbinary at its core.

In the same year, Jo Henderson-Merrygold published "Gendering Sarai: Reading beyond Cisnormativity in Gen 11:29–12:20 and 20:1–18," which argues that Sarai can be read as something other than cis, with a "quirky, chimerical, ever-changing gender."[19] Henderson-Merrygold acknowledges that their reading is "intentionally whimsical and somewhat anachronistic in order to playfully challenge enduring preconceptions that lead to the cisgendering of biblical characters,"[20] but it is also based on an array of evidence: Sarai's abrupt introduction, her barrenness, and Abram's lack of concern about her having sex with other men—not to mention the historical interpretation of the rabbis,

---

15. Rhiannon Graybill, *Are We Not Men? Unstable Masculinity in the Hebrew Prophets* (New York: Oxford University Press, 2016), 36.
16. Graybill, *Are We Not Men?* 38.
17. Graybill, 45.
18. Aysha W. Musa, "Jael Is Non-Binary; Jael Is Not a Woman," *JIBS* 1:2 (2020): 99.
19. Jo Henderson-Merrygold, "Gendering Sarai: Reading beyond Cisnormativity in Genesis 11:29–12:20 and 20:1–18," Open Theology 6:1 (2020): 498.
20. Henderson-Merrygold, "Gendering Sarai," 507.

who called her either an *aylonit* or a *tumtum*, both intersex categories.[21] However, this nonbinary reading of Sarai fades in later biblical chapters, according to Henderson-Merrygold, where there is "an attempt to retcon Sarah in order to facilitate a cisnormalised reading."[22] Henderson-Merrygold calls their own approach a "cispicious scepticism," and it acts most strongly on Guest's second principle of "rupture": the goal is not to somehow prove that Sarai was not cisgender, but rather to break open the assumptions that lead readers to assume a binary gender in places where the Bible leaves enticing gaps instead of clear gendering.[23]

Then, in 2021, Nicholaus Pumphrey turned a nonbinary lens on the story of Joseph. Noting Joseph's "princess robe," his passivity and beauty, and his positioning in the role of a eunuch (as a servant who works alongside Potiphar's wife), Pumphrey concludes that "his gender expression is not binary."[24] Moreover, he argues that Joseph's nonbinary gender attributes are evidence against scholars' assumptions that biblical gender is strictly binary; rather, biblical gender resembles the more diverse gender roles evident in the broader ancient Near East. Pumphrey's argument bears a strong resemblance to Theodore Jennings' argument in *Jacob's Wound*, back in 2005, where Jennings amasses similar evidence to argue that "Joseph decidedly troubles the gender categories that circulate around the edges of his story."[25] However, where Jennings slots Joseph into the category of "somewhat transgendered,"[26] reflecting the available gender categories of sixteen years ago, Pumphrey confesses, "I do not have a name or fixed categorization to place upon Joseph's gender identity and gender performativity."[27] Taken as an umbrella category rather than an identity label, "nonbinary" seems like a reasonable start.

Finally, although it does not deal directly with the Hebrew Bible, I would be remiss not to mention Alicia Spencer-Hall and Blake Gutt's 2021 book, *Trans and Genderqueer Subjects in Medieval Hagiography*, which contains chapters filled with excellent examples of how to examine figures of the past through a nonbinary lens. Spencer-Hall and Gutt begin with an introduction that argues that "something more than tolerance of trans people's physical existence in the present is required. That something is full ideological existence—the ability to

---

21. B. Yevamot 64a–64b. Cf. Gwynn Kessler, "Perspectives on Rabbinic Constructions of Gendered Bodies," in *The Wiley Blackwell Companion to Religion and Materiality*, ed. Vasudha Narayanan (Hoboken, NJ: Wiley, 2020), 61–89, for more detailed discussion of these terms.

22. Henderson-Merrygold, "Gendering Sarai," 506.

23. Cf. also Henderson-Merrygold's chapter "Jacob: A (Drag) King amongst Patriarchs" (in *Women and Gender in the Bible: Texts, Intersections, Intertexts*, ed. Zanne Domoney-Lyttle and Sarah Nicholson [Sheffield: Sheffield Phoenix, 2021], 125–40), which is more focused on a trans than a nonbinary reading.

24. Nicholaus Pumphrey, "Unexpected Roles: Examining Ancient Gender Construction in the Joseph Narrative," in *Troubling Topics, Sacred Texts: Readings in Hebrew Bible, New Testament, and Qur'an*, ed. Roberta Sterman Sabbath (Berlin: De Gruyter, 2021), 90.

25. Theodore W. Jennings, *Jacob's Wound: Homoerotic Narrative in the Literature of Ancient Israel* (New York: Continuum, 2005), 190.

26. Jennings, *Jacob's Wound*, 193.

27. Pumphrey, "Unexpected Roles," 90.

imagine a transgender past, and a transgender future."[28] They later clarify that "We do not argue that 'transgender' is somehow an ahistorical or historically transcendent framework, but rather that the patterns of thought enabled by trans theory resonate with the content of the texts under consideration, animating the development of productive new readings."[29] I strongly agree with this perspective. The choice to approach gender as something beyond a binary, something fuzzy and fluid, is an approach that can benefit gendered interpretations of all times and places, whether or not their specific norms and categories of gender resemble our own.

Having concluded my literature survey, I will point out a few trends. First, the label of "nonbinary" is a new one, and the dearth of literature that draws upon it reflects that newness; only in the past couple of years have scholars begun to use it as a category of analysis, rather than relying on concepts like liminality and ambiguity to describe transgression of the gender binary. Second, with the notable exception of Musa, scholars have been reluctant to use pronouns other than those that the biblical text uses for characters, even when they argue for the characters' nonbinary identity. (In a blog post about "(Gender)queering Joseph," Danya Ruttenberg defends this approach, noting "the absence of any evidence, textual or otherwise, that Joseph would have used other pronouns" and calling him "a gender nonconforming person who uses he/him pronouns."[30]) While I understand that approach, I believe it minimizes the deep divide between the biblical world and our own. The Bible does not mention cats or the color yellow;[31] yet we now have the language to do so. In fact, we make a similar translational move when we use "it" to discuss biblical objects, instead of the binary "he/she" used by the Bible. "They" is the most common way to refer to someone nonbinary in modern English, so it is the pronoun I use in this chapter.

Third, most recent scholars are operating individually—for instance, discussions of Joseph do not mention Jael, and vice-versa—but they usually aim to make a broader point about binary and cis readings of the Bible, arguing that these readings are imposed by later readers, rather than reflecting an inherent biblical inflexibility about gender. All four of Guest's hermeneutical principles are evident in play, even as different authors take different approaches; some make the positivist claim that the text itself portrays a nonbinary character, while others turn their gaze on scholars and seek to unravel cisnormative reading strategies. To my knowledge, no one paper has gathered these disparate attempts into a single survey, which is part of why I have discussed them at such length. But this survey also serves as a necessary context for my own explorations,

---

28. Alicia Spencer-Hall and Blake Gutt, "Introduction," in *Trans and Genderqueer Subjects in Medieval Hagiography*, ed. Spencer-Hall and Gutt (Amsterdam: Amsterdam University Press, 2021), 11.
29. Spencer-Hall and Gutt, "Introduction," 14.
30. Danya Ruttenberg, "(Gender)Queering Joseph," *Life Is a Sacred Text*, 25 October 2021, https://lifeisasacredtext.substack.com/p/queering-joseph.
31. The root *yaraq* had a semantic range "which stretches from 'pale silvery' to 'green' and 'yellow'" (Athalya Brenner-Idan, *Colour Terms in the Old Testament* [Sheffield: JSOT Press, 1982], 100).

showing the strategies that others have employed in the search for nonbinary biblical representation.

MORDECAI AND THEIR GENDER

I now turn to my own analysis of a particular nonbinary character. Mordecai is, by some accounts, the hero of the book of Esther;[32] by all accounts, they play a significant role in the story, to the point where the brief final chapter of the book solely focuses on Mordecai, without a mention of Queen Esther. Their behavior—specifically, their unexplained refusal to bow down to Haman on multiple occasions—has elicited both praise and condemnation from scholars.[33] But what has received less attention is the extent to which Mordecai is a character whose gender traits dance between male, female, and neither. Indeed, from the first introduction of Mordecai, readers are already cued to view their gender as other than simply masculine, and their later appearances only further that impression.

The first major clue comes in our introduction to Mordecai's relationship with Esther. According to major translations, Mordecai "was foster father" to her (JPS); they "had brought [her] up" (NRSV). But the verb here (*aman*) is an unusual one; in the feminine, it means "to nurse," as in 2 Sam 4:4 and Ruth 4:16, and even in the masculine, it seems to have similar implications. For instance, we can examine Num 11:12 and Isa 49:23, where a nursing man is depicted as a counterfactual: Moses insists that his job is not to nurse the Israelites,[34] while Deutero-Isaiah promises that kings and queens will be humiliated before Israel, becoming their wet-nurses.[35] In short, by a plausible reading of the verb, Mordecai is acting as Esther's wet-nurse, and the rabbis picked up on exactly that implication:

> But did Mordechai feed and sustain? R. Yudan said, "One time he went to all the wet nurses but could not find one for Esther, and thus he nursed her." R. Berekiah and R. Abbahu in R. Eleazar's name said, "Milk came to him and he [himself] nursed her [always]." When R. Abbahu expounded

---

32. E.g. Michael V. Fox, *Character and Ideology in the Book of Esther*, 2nd ed. (Eugene, OR: Wipf and Stock Publishers, 2010), and Carey Moore, *Esther* (New Haven, CT: Yale University Press, 1974). Cf. the discussion of "Who Is the Protagonist of Esther?" in Jonathan Grossman, *Esther: The Outer Narrative and the Hidden Reading* (Winona Lake, IN: Eisenbrauns, 2011), 27–35.

33. Cf. Fox's discussion in *Character and Ideology*, 191–95. See also the lengthy discussion in Eliott Horowitz, "Mordecai's Reckless Refusal," in *Reckless Rites: Purim and the Legacy of Jewish Violence* (Princeton, NJ: Princeton University Press, 2006), 63–80, for an overview of historical reception of Mordecai's decision not to bow to Haman.

34. Cf. Graybill, *Are We Not Men?*, 33–34 for a broader discussion of the complex gender dynamics at play in this passage.

35. The only counterpoint is 2 Kgs 10:1, 5, in which Jehu seeks the loyalty of the *omnim* of Ahab, usually translated as "the guardians of the sons of Ahab." However, it could instead refer to the other meaning of the verb *aman* (to be faithful) and mean "those men faithful to Ahab."

this publicly, the congregation laughed. He said to them, "Is this not a mishnah? R. Simeon b. Eleazar said: The milk of a male is pure."[36]

As Gwynn Kessler notes, this passage "simultaneously subverts male gender boundaries but sustains gender binaries."[37] It imagines Mordecai as someone who does the traditionally female task of nursing a child, but it affirms that they are inherently male, hence a source of *pure* milk. In other words, "men can do that which women are supposed to do, perhaps even better."[38] Kessler's observation is an important reminder that a text can both queer its characters and reinforce binary norms. Nevertheless, I would argue that the Masoretic Text *is* queering Mordecai's gender here. Unlike Moses, Mordecai is a character whose pronouns are male but who does nurse a child.

Moreover, even if we follow mainstream translations and interpret *aman* in the cisnormative, neutral sense of raising a child, Mordecai is raising that child alone, without a mother or female caretaker in the picture—something literally unprecedented in the Hebrew Bible,[39] in contrast to several instances where a mother with a dead or nonexistent husband has children[40] and other instances where a wet nurse intervenes to protect and nurture her charge.[41] Mordecai occupies the social role of wet nurse and mother, whether or not they literally breastfeed their child.

Timothy Beal argues, along similar lines, that "Mordecai's own sexual identity is ambiguous, insofar as he is unmarried and has no children of his own—an uncommon position for a male subject in the Hebrew Bible."[42] This is hardly a common position for female biblical subjects, either, but Beal's point still stands: Mordecai's lack of wife and children mark them as queer, divergent from the masculine norm. Moreover, Beal brings up two additional points in his argument for the "feminization" of Mordecai, which I will address in turn: their narrative parallels with Vashti, and their close association with eunuchs and their liminal realm.

Two major refusals drive the plot of the book of Esther: Vashti's refusal to come before the king's banquet, and Mordecai's refusal to bow to Haman. As Beal observes, "the pattern of Mordecai's refusal, Haman's rage, and his return to happiness after legislating the exscription of all Jews, closely parallels the pattern of events

36. Genesis Rabbah 30:8, translation in Kessler, "Let's Cross That Body," 335.
37. Kessler, 335.
38. Kessler, 337.
39. The only rough parallel is Lot and his daughters (Genesis 19), but they were already sexually mature when they lost their mother.
40. Cf. Pharaoh's daughter, the wise woman of Tekoa, Hiram's mother, the widow of Zarephath, Jeroboam's mother, Micah's mother (Judg 17), etc., though it is unclear how old some of their children were when they became fatherless.
41. Cf. Claudia D. Bergmann, "Mothers of a Nation: How Motherhood and Religion Intermingle in the Hebrew Bible," *Open Theology* 6:1 (2020): 132–44, for a discussion of how wet nurses in the Bible are agents of resistance and protection, particularly in times of national crisis. Perhaps this motif is why the evocative verb of nursing is attributed to Mordecai.
42. Beal, *Book of Hiding*, 115.

involving Vashti and Ahasuerus in Esther."[43] The connections that Beal notes are both structural and semantic; for instance, "Mordecai's refusal fills Haman with 'rage' (*hemah*), the same rage that burned in Ahasuerus when he heard about Vashti's refusal."[44] The result is, in Beal's words, "a kind of 'feminization' of Mordecai and 'Judaization' of Vashti."[45] Boundaries become blurred when a foreign woman receives the same narrative treatment as a Jewish man.[46]

Beal also examines Mordecai's actions beyond opposing Haman, and he finds a similar nonbinary element (though he does not use the term) in Mordecai's association with the eunuchs. Mordecai clearly spends significant time around the eunuchs, enough to be aware when they are plotting against the king (Esth 2:22). Moreover, when Mordecai appears in the narrative, they appear in the same liminal spaces that the eunuchs occupy: the gate (Esth 3:2) and the entrance to the harem (Esth 2:11). The text thus encourages readers to think of Mordecai alongside the eunuchs: "Mordecai himself appears to have one foot on the threshold with Bigthan and Teresh and the other eunuchs, and one foot in the throne room with Esther."[47] Or, as Randall Bailey playfully puts it, "one has to wonder: Why is Mordecai hanging around with the eunuchs?"[48] It is worth noting that we cannot equate eunuchs with nonbinary people in an uncomplicated way; as has been argued by Omar N'Shea in recent years, eunuchs in Mesopotamia may have been viewed as fully male, their beardlessness a contrast with fatherhood rather than with masculinity.[49] Nevertheless, as I have argued elsewhere,[50] the eunuchs in the book of Esther play a liminal narrative role, serving as intermediaries who mediate both between palace and populace and between men and women.[51] Their association with the eunuchs therefore encourages us to view Mordecai as one who similarly evades simple binary categorization.

43. Beal, *Book of Hiding*, 47.
44. Beal, 55.
45. Beal, 47.
46. A side note that could easily be expanded into its own paper: there is a fascinating implication here when a feminist lens is combined intersectionally with a post-colonial lens. Namely, the book of Esther seems to be arguing that *gender is less important than subject-status within an empire*. Vashti and Mordecai both attempt to resist the power structures of their empire, and both of them are brutally punished for it with imperial decrees—even if Mordecai's punishment was, in the end, overturned. It matters not whether women exhibit feminist convictions or men hold fast to their ideals. If "God helps those who help themselves" (a common mindset for reading religion back into the book of Esther), then the approach to empire that God favors is one of power-gathering, outward obedience, and carefully timed appeal, as enacted by Esther—not the approach of brash resistance.
47. Beal, *Book of Hiding*, 115.
48. Bailey, "'That's Why,'" 243.
49. Omar N'Shea, "Royal Eunuchs and Elite Masculinity in the Neo-Assyrian Empire," *Near Eastern Archaeology* 79:3 (2016): 214–21.
50. Esther Brownsmith, "Love and Eunuchs: Esther and Ishtar as Queer Queens" (paper presented at SBL Annual Conference, San Antonio, November 2021).
51. Cf. Martti Heikki Nissinen, "Relative Masculinities in the Hebrew Bible/Old Testament," in *Being a Man: Negotiating Ancient Constructs of Masculinity*, ed. Ilona Zsolnay (London: Routledge, 2016), 228: "eunuchship appears as a status that, as I would argue, still *was* considered a kind of masculinity. However, eunuchs appear as queering figures who challenge stable gender identities and transgress fixed gender categories."

Unlike Bailey, who views Mordecai's homoerotic elements as a critique of assimilationist Jews like Mordecai, Beal views the text's genderqueerness in a more supportive light: "[Mordecai's] feminization in Esther is not intended as a cut-down; rather, it presents a solidarity of not-selves.[52] (Here "not-selves" is Beal's term for "the other," the "abject": the person who is fundamentally different from us—and yet often inextricably entangled with our identity.) I concur with Beal; Mordecai is depicted as a positive figure in the book of Esther, yet/ and they are also depicted as a genderqueer character. As someone who "nursed" Esther, consorted with eunuchs, positioned themself in thresholds, and mirrored Vashti's resistance, Mordecai exemplifies the way that the book of Esther deconstructs binaries of masculinity and femininity in its pursuit of a carnivalesque middle ground.

In fact, the biblical text may be leading up to this nonbinary identity from its very first mention of Mordecai as a member of the tribe of Benjamin—literally, the "son of the right hand." Ironically, this tribe is particularly associated with left-handedness, as seen in Judg 3:15, 20:16, and 1 Chr 11:2: the only places in the Bible where left-handedness is mentioned, and all of them associated with Benjamin. Geoffrey Miller[53] and Suzie Park have both suggested a link between queerness and the Benjaminites' left-handedness. In particular, Park connects femininity to the book of Judges' allusions to Saul:

> [G]endered connotations associated with left-handedness are also utilized to insult Saul's leadership abilities. As stated earlier, both narratives about the tribesmen of Saul in Judges subtly question the masculinity of the Benjaminites: [. . . T]he message seems to be that Saul, as a member of this effeminate, deviant, left-handed tribe, is not manly enough to be considered a true king.[54]

If these associations for Saul were in the mind of the author(s) of Judges, then they may well also apply to Mordecai. Indeed, most commentaries note the links between Mordecai and Saul[55]—not only are they from the same tribe, their great-grandfathers share a name—but they do not fully explore what the Saul connection might have connoted: an aura of femininity.[56]

---

52. Beal, *Book of Hiding*, 114.

53. Miller's study of "verbal feud" notes that "The claim that the Benjaminites were left-handed thus implicitly attributed impure features to them, including, very possibly, femininity and associated sexual deviance" (Geoffrey P. Miller, "Verbal Feud in the Hebrew Bible: Judges 3:12–30 and 19–21," *JNES* 55:2 [1996]: 113). He sees the theme as a taunt in Judg 19–20, but a counter-response in Judg 3, where the hero Ehud is left-handed. "The story [of Judges 3] thus contains a warning that anyone (Ephraimites included) who attributes homosexuality or other defects to the Benjaminites by virtue of their left-handedness risks experiencing the kind of retribution that a fierce, left-handed Benjaminite warrior is capable of exacting" ("Verbal Feud," 116). But the very presence of subversion indicates that there was something to subvert—namely, an existing association between Benjaminites, left-handedness, and femininity.

54. Park, "Left-Handed Benjaminites and the Shadow of Saul," *JBL* 134:4 (2015): 719.

55. E.g. Beal, *Book of Hiding*, 26; John Levenson, *Esther: A Commentary* (Louisville, KY: Westminster John Knox Press, 1997), 56–57.

56. A further queer connection may exist. One of the most prominent tales about Benjaminites in the Bible is Judg 19, the story of the "outrage at Gibeah," in which the town's Benjaminite inhab-

Finally, one key scene worthy of further scholarly examination is Esther 6, in which the king rewards Mordecai by parading them through town in royal robes. On its surface, this text might seem to reinforce Mordecai's masculinity as one who wields power and honor second only to the king. But on a closer look, the text uses several details of syntax to link Mordecai here with Queen Esther. The king describes Mordecai as the one whom the king "desires" to honor—the verb *ḥafaṣ*, whose only other appearance in Esther is in 2:14, when the king *desires* his favored concubines. Mordecai's horse wears a royal crown or turban, a *keter*, whose only other appearance in the book is on the heads of the queens, Vashti and Esther. Mordecai's robes are *levush malkhut*, "clothing of royalty," which evoke the same *malkhut* that Esther wore in 5:1. In short, using these cues of specialized vocabulary, the text may be dressing up Mordecai in the role of a queen at least as much as a noble man.

But why depict Mordecai's gender in this way? Although the queer, subversive nature of the book of Esther likely plays a role, Mordecai's nonbinary nature may also have an early precedent in Marduk, the Babylonian deity who was almost certainly their namesake.[57] In *Ludlul Bel Nemeqi*, a poetic text that addresses the problem of human suffering, the first forty verses describe Marduk in hymnic fashion. For one lengthy sequence, lines alternate between describing Marduk's wrath and his mercy—the latter sometimes using feminine terms.

> His heavy punishment is instantly terrible,
> (but then) he becomes merciful, and immediately turns motherly.
> He looks sharp and butts like a wild bull,
> But (then) like a mother cow he solicitously turns back.[58]

I am not arguing for a direct textual link between *Ludlul* and Esther, but if first-millennium Mesopotamian scribes[59] could imagine Marduk as both "terrible" and "motherly," both a "wild bull" and a "mother cow," then perhaps the

---

itants sought to gang-rape a male traveler and brutalized his female companion instead. The story has several links to the tale of Sodom and Gomorrah (cf. Stuart Lasine, "Guest and Host in Judges 19: Lot's Hospitality in an Inverted World," *JSOT* 9:29 [1984]: 37–59; and Susan Niditch, "The 'Sodomite' Theme in Judges 19–20: Family, Community, and Social Disintegration," *CBQ* 44:3 [1982]: 365–78), particularly around the mob seeking to rape a man. To be sure, there is substantial debate over when ancient interpreters focused on the homoerotic aspects of these stories; elsewhere in the Hebrew Bible, the crime of Sodom was linked to other sins, such as stinginess (cf. Ezek 16:49). But by the first century CE, the connection had been made; Philo overtly links the destruction of Sodom to "men who lusted after each other" (Philo, *On Abraham*, 135–137), as would countless commentators after him. It may be that the author of Esther, potentially writing as late as the first century BCE, would similarly have viewed Benjaminites as entwined with male-penetrative rape.

57. Scholars since the nineteenth century (e.g. P. Jensen, "Elamitische Eigennamen: Ein Beitrag zur Erklärung der elamitischen Inschriften," *WZKM* 6 [1892]: 47–70) have argued widely for the onomastic connection. Indeed, Marduk may be more than Mordecai's namesake; scholars like Adam Silverstein ("The Book of Esther and the *Enūma Elish*," *BSOAS* 69:2 (2006): 209–23) and myself have argued that Mordecai is based on him as a character.

58. *Ludlul* I.17–20, trans. Michela Piccin and Martin Worthington, "Schizophrenia and the Problem of Suffering in the Ludlul Hymn to Marduk," *RA* 109:1 (2015): 113–24. I am indebted to JoAnn Scurlock for pointing out this passage to me.

59. The text may have been composed in the second millennium BCE, but all our existing attestations are from the first millennium, when it was "well-known, widely-diffused, and highly valued"

biblical author was similarly inspired to create a character unbound by gender binaries.

FORWARD-LOOKING CONCLUSIONS

So what have I demonstrated in this chapter? I have *not* proven that Mordecai was nonbinary, because "nonbinary" is a modern category; even the later rabbinic multiplicities of gender were closer to what we would call intersex categories than the nonbinary gender that many people now identify as.[60] Moreover, my analysis so far has thus mainly reflected Guest's first two hermeneutical categories: it has resisted cisnormative interpretations that assumed Mordecai was uncomplicatedly male, and it has ruptured the binary assumptions that "male" and "female" are the only options for Mordecai. In my conclusion, I turn to Guest's final two categories of reclamation and reengagement.

What might it mean to reclaim Mordecai for a nonbinary audience? We can start by building an image of Mordecai's character outside a binary framework. They are stubborn, resisting both Haman and Esther when they tell them how to act. They are loyal to the state, informing on the eunuchs' plot against the king, and even more loyal to the Jewish people. They know when to nudge Esther into action and when to step back and let her act. They are quite concerned with clothing, from mourning rags to bright royal robes. They are beloved and respected by the Jewish community.

Notably, none of the traits I just mentioned are stereotypically gendered traits. Unlike so-called warrior women like Jael, who abound with both masculine and feminine markers, Mordecai's main masculine attribute is that the king assigns them a high rank that is not dependent on their spouse. Other than that, they are a caring, stubborn, fashionable, kind person: neither a father nor a mother but a cousin. It would be easy to tell imaginative stories about them, none of which relied upon their assigned gender, let alone their genital configuration. Indeed, despite the centrality of Queen Esther, the book of Esther ends with a glimpse of Cousin Mordecai "speaking healing to all their kin" (Esth 10:3).

I hope that someday, someone will creatively retell the story of Cousin Mordecai and reclaim it for nonbinary people. But in the meantime—and here I turn to the category of reengagement—it is vital that we recognize that the subversive, carnivalesque nature of the book of Esther extends to undermining gender binaries and transgressing gender norms, because it is vital that we affirm the scriptural precedent of gender transgression to modern nonbinary and otherwise gender-nonconforming people. In a 2020 article, Helana Darwin

---

(Amar Annus and Alan Lenzi, *Ludlul Bēl Nēmeqi: The Standard Babylonian Poem of the Righteous Sufferer* [Helsinki: Neo-Assyrian Text Corpus Project, 2010], ix).

60. Cf. Kessler, "Perspectives on Rabbinic Constructions," for an overview of these categories, and see Max K. Strassfeld, *Trans Talmud: Androgynes and Eunuchs in Rabbinic Literature* (Oakland: University of California Press, 2022), for an extensive and thoughtful discussion of these categories in light of modern gender theory.

found that nonbinary people encountered substantial obstacles "while navigating the religious gender binary," including ideological, liturgical, and ritual obstacles[61]—obstacles severe enough that of her twenty-nine nonbinary case subjects raised within Christianity, only three still identify as Christians.[62] In her presentation of "ideological obstacles," Darwin notes the importance of Gen 1:27, in which God creates humans as "male and female," for establishing a binary ideology that later religious traditions would only reify. Darwin did not note any biblical counter-traditions to this binary ideology.[63] She concluded that nonbinary people "have little recourse within these religious communities but to accept their gender's erasure or leave the religious community altogether, an impasse that presents a lose–lose scenario in either case."[64]

The recognition of stories like Mordecai (and Jael, and Joseph) within the Bible offers a third path: one in which nonbinary identities are not erased from religious traditions. I am not so naive as to think that Mordecai alone can influence conservative religious traditions to overcome their deeply ingrained cisheteronormativity. Nonetheless, for moderate and liberal churches that may already accept a variety of sexualities among their members, gender-transgressive biblical characters may provide a model for welcoming members of diverse genders as well. This real-world implication means that our scholarship does not take place in a void. Rather, to repeat the quote from Spencer-Hall and Gutt, this scholarship generates "the ability to imagine a transgender past, and a transgender future." Or, as DeVun eloquently puts it:

> Transgender history, then, allows us to foreground different kinds of gender-crossings from the past, making them legible and meaningful to readers now. Such histories can foster a sense of connection between gender-crossing individuals across time, and they can make the existence of such communities in the future more imaginable.[65]

In the third chapter of Esther, Mordecai refuses to bow down to Haman. In response, the king's servants ask them, "Why do you transgress (*avar*) the king's command?" (Esth 3:3). This Hebrew verb, *avar*, can mean "to disobey," but it can also mean "to pass over," "to overflow," "to ignore," "to move past": all of which could characterize Mordecai's attitude toward gender norms.

Notably, Mordecai never answers this question. Their motive for transgressing remains an object of speculation. What matters is not why Mordecai transgresses but the fact that Esther, and the author of her book, never question their right to do so.

---

61. Helana Darwin, "Navigating the Religious Gender Binary," *Sociology of Religion* 81:2 (2020): 192.
62. Darwin, "Navigating," 191.
63. Neither does Joy Ladin, who argues that "the Torah doesn't speak to the fact that there are people who are not simply male or female." (Joy Ladin, *The Soul of the Stranger: Reading God and Torah from a Transgender Perspective* [Waltham, MA: Brandeis University Press, 2019], 107)
64. Darwin, "Navigating," 195.
65. Leah DeVun, *The Shape of Sex: Nonbinary Gender from Genesis to the Renaissance* (New York: Columbia University Press, 2021), 9.

Chapter 5

Walking While Trans on the Jericho Road

JUSTIN SABIA-TANIS

After a long and troubling day, a man decided to walk home from work rather than take the bus; he thought it might clear his head. The route to his neighborhood ran through the financial district, which was utterly deserted this late in the evening. His mind elsewhere, his footsteps echoing off the empty buildings, he did not notice the group approaching him until it was too late to run. They descended on him, took his wallet and cell phone, beat him, and dragged his half-dead body into an alley, leaving him there. He spent the night in agonizing pain, drifting in and out of consciousness.

Early the next morning, a priest was walking that same route. He saw the man's huddled body and thought this was just another drunk passed out in the alley, so he crossed the street and continued on his way. Another passed by and, seeing the man, wondered whether this was a trap to lure her into a dangerous situation down that alley, and so, shuddering, went to the sidewalk on the other side and hurried on to her destination.

Finally, a tall woman walked down that street, her head held high, her gait stately and calm. She was on her way to work, but she heard a moan coming from the alley and glanced in to investigate. Looking more closely, she saw the blood on his head and the tears in his clothes. She leaned down and gently shook him. He startled awake—pulling back a little in fear. She was Black and he was white; she was transgender and he had never encountered someone like that in person before. But he shook his head to clear his prejudices—this was someone helping him and he hurt so much all over. "It's okay now," she said, "shhhh." And he promptly passed out.

When he came to, they were in the emergency room of a hospital. "No, no," he rasped, frantic, "I can't afford this. I don't have insurance. I gotta get out of here." "Don't worry," she said. "I'll pay the bill. Just rest until the doctor sees you." Sleep overtook him again. The doctor roused him in due course, examined him, sent him for tests, and then told him that he was lucky that more damage hadn't been done. But, the doctor cautioned, he'd had a bad blow to the head and suffered a concussion. He should stay with friends for the next few days to be sure he was okay. The doctor cautioned that he should return for medical care if his headache or nausea worsened or didn't go away, if he had seizures, or had difficulty waking, speaking, or walking. After the doctor told him he was ready to be discharged, the man looked at his rescuer. "I live alone. I just moved here. I don't know anyone. What should I do?"

"Don't worry about it, it's okay," she said again. "I've got to head out of town on business, but I've got good friends who will look after you. They run an Airbnb. We'll put you up there, that'll give them a little income, and they can take care of you. Give me a few minutes to make the arrangements and I'll meet you in the lobby." Sure enough, it all happened as she said. When they arrived, he was shown into a comfortable room. She said to her friends, "Look after him and when I get back, I will reimburse you for any extra expense you may have." They replied, "Anything for you, hon. We'll take good care of him." And they did.

In the parable of the Good Samaritan, Jesus asked, "Which of these do you think was a neighbor to the man who fell into the hands of robbers?" The expert in the law replied, "The one who had mercy on him." Jesus told him, "Go and do likewise." By responding to the question, "who is my neighbor?" with this familiar story of the Samaritan—the religiously and ethnically Other of his day—Jesus elucidates our shared responsibilities to one another and points to the despised Other as a spiritual exemplar. The Samaritan here embodies the core values of God's realm as taught by Jesus, despite the enmity with which Jesus's listeners would have viewed Samaritans.

It is important to recognize that this is a risky tactic on Jesus's part for several reasons. First, tensions between Jews and Samaritans were high during this period, with both sides having attacked the other's sites of worship in the recent past.[1] The Samaritans were not just the "other" but a group hated on both religious and ethnic grounds. Jesus and his followers had recently themselves been unwelcome in a Samaritan village, a story recorded in Luke 9:51–56. When Jesus sent messengers to the village to prepare a place for him, the people there refused

---

1. Greg W. Forbes, "The Good Samaritan (10.25–37)," in *The God of Old: The Role of the Lukan Parables in the Purpose of Luke's Gospel* (Sheffield: Sheffield Academic Press, 2000), 33.

to do so. The disciples James and John responded by asking Jesus if he wanted them to "command fire to come down from heaven and consume them?" but Jesus rebuked them and simply went on to another village (Luke 9:54–55). It is in this context that Greg Forbes notes, "Jesus demonstrates extreme courage in telling this story."[2]

It was not enough for Jesus to refuse to participate in this effort to annihilate the villagers or even to rebuke his followers for wanting to do so. Instead, he went on to tell a story in which someone from this same group of rejected and rejecting people figured as the embodiment of one of the two highest commandments of God—the love of neighbor. Thus, we should understand this story on at least two levels: both the teaching conveyed through the actual content of the story and Jesus's embodiment of his own understanding of neighborliness through the choice of characters with which he tells it. For Jesus, to be a neighbor is to be in relationship; it is an action, a verb, the showing of mercy, not a status or a condition between two people. Despite having been unable to stay in the Samaritan village, Jesus is a neighbor because he continues to see and affirm the humanity and goodness of the Samaritan people. He builds bridges and create relationships where they do not currently exist. The focus of neighborliness is to treat the Other with mercy, bringing about healing.

Therefore, we begin our trans reading of this passage logically, with a transgender woman as the Good Samaritan. Transgender people, despite increased visibility and a few high-profile celebrities, continue to face devastating levels of discrimination and violence. Over the past several years, an ever-escalating number of anti-LGBTQ bills have been introduced and passed in state legislatures,[3] with 66 bills proposed in 2020, 143 in 2021, 174 in 2022, and a staggering 589 in 2023. According to the American Civil Liberties Union, in the 2024 legislative session, 574 bills were introduced at the state level to limit transgender people's access to public accommodation, medical treatment, and identification that accurately reflects their gender, among others.[4] Many of these bills, including those signed into law in Florida, Arkansas, Tennessee, Texas, and Mississippi, specifically deny minors access to gender-specific medical treatment and participation in sports teams that match their gender identities. These actions constitute a systemic strategy to encode discrimination into the law; moreover, limiting access to appropriate medical treatment is decried by professional medical and psychological organizations and seen as directly threatening the life and health of young transgender people.[5] Through

---

2. Forbes, *The God of Old*, 65.

3. Daniel Trotta, "US Republican Transgender Laws Pile Up, Setting 2024 Battle Lines," *Reuters*, May 18, 2023, https://www.reuters.com/world/us/us-republican-transgender-laws-pile-up-setting-2024-battle-lines-2023-05-18/.

4. American Civil Liberties Union (ACLU), *Mapping Attacks on LGBTQ Rights in U.S. State Legislatures in 2024*, https://www.aclu.org/legislative-attacks-on-lgbtq-rights-2024, accessed March 1, 2024.

5. American Psychological Association, "Criminalizing Gender Affirmative Care with Minors: Suggested Talking Points with Resources to Oppose Transgender Exclusion Bills," 2023, https://www.apa.org/topics/lgbtq/gender-affirmative-care.

these laws, transgender people are denied access to public accommodations used freely by others; even the introduction of the bills legitimizes these efforts to limit transgender people's use of public space and to demean our community. Three-quarters of transgender and nonbinary youth already report regular bullying, segregation, and discrimination in school.[6] The concern is, of course, that legal sanction against nonbinary and transgender people only legitimizes this stigma.

In addition to the systematic exclusion of transgender people, discrimination and violence remain rampant. This is particularly true for transgender people of color, with Black and Latina transgender women facing a staggering rate of murder and assault,[7] and exponentially higher rates of discrimination in employment, housing, and other metrics of wellbeing.[8] The same dynamics of discrimination appear within religious communities as well. A 2015 study noted that, of their respondents who had ever been a part of a faith community, 19 percent had been rejected outright, with another 39 percent leaving the community due to fear of rejection.[9] All of these numbers were elevated in communities of color.

Thus, as a gay and transgender theologian, I believe we can make a strong, and painful, case for transgender people, particularly transgender women of color, as the despised Other in the eyes of American society, a parallel for the Samaritan whom Jesus employed to demonstrate the character and agency of the Neighbor. Both categories experience(d) alienation on religious, social, and political grounds, subjecting them to violence. Both were rejected from religious spaces and have subsequently rejected religious figures—in the case of the Samaritans, the unwillingness to welcome Jesus into the village; in the case of transgender people, along with lesbians, gay men, bisexuals and queers, a level of religious participation that is significantly lower than the general population[10] as a strategy to avoid discrimination and harm. In *Transgender Journeys*, Virginia Ramey Mollenkott and Vanessa Sheridan write,

6. Movement Advancement Project, GLSEN, National Center for Transgender Equality, and National Education Association, "Separation and Stigma: Transgender Youth & School Facilities" (2017), 3, https://www.glsen.org/sites/default/files/2019-11/Separation_and_Stigma_2017.pdf.

7. Jo Yurcaba, "As Anti-Trans Violence Surges, Advocates Demand Policy Reform," *NBC News*, March 11, 2021, https://www.nbcnews.com/feature/nbc-out/anti-trans-violence-surges-advocates-demand-policy-reform-n1260485.

8. Jaime Grant, Lisa Mottet, and Justin Tanis, "Injustice at Every Turn: A Report of the National Transgender Discrimination Survey" (Washington, DC: National Center for Transgender Equality and National Gay and Lesbian Task Force, 2011), https://transequality.org/issues/resources/national-transgender-discrimination-survey-full-report. S. E. James et al., "The Report of the 2015 U.S. Transgender Survey" (Washington, DC: National Center for Transgender Equality, 2016), http://www.transequality.org/sites/default/files/docs/usts/USTS%20Full%20Report%20-%20FINAL%201.6.17.pdf.

9. James et al., "Report," 77. It is noteworthy that the same survey found that 43 percent of those who left faith communities due to rejection were later able to find an affirming community, demonstrating the diversity of religious positions on the issue of gender identity.

10. Pew Research Center, "Religious Groups' Policies on Transgender Members Vary Widely," *Pew Research Center* (blog), https://www.pewresearch.org/fact-tank/2015/12/02/religious-groups-policies-on-transgender-members-vary-widely/.

At the time of Jesus' physical presence upon this earth, the Samaritan was the symbol of bigotry and prejudice for all observant Jews. Samaritans were loathed, despised, rejected, and considered unworthy of even breathing the air. Today, for folks with a traditionalist mind-set, transgender persons (along with lesbians, gays, and bisexuals) are filling that same symbolic role. We are considered "untouchables" and undesirables within traditional Christianity. We are the socioreligious pariahs of the twenty-first century. We are the new Samaritans.[11]

We can also note that Mollenkott used this passage from Luke eponymously for an extremely significant work in LGBTQ religious history. In 1978, Mollenkott and Letha Scanzoni published *Is the Homosexual My Neighbor: A Positive Christian Response*. The first edition began with the words, "The question that makes up the title of this work shouldn't be necessary." Indeed.

Let us pause for a moment to reflect on methodology before we return to examine more specifics of this parable. I come to this text as a pastor, educator, scholar, and activist, and as a white man who transitioned nearly thirty years ago, and now holds a tenure-track position at a Christian seminary. I have worked both within religious settings and in public policy advocacy for gender diverse communities and seen firsthand the devastation of the discrimination and violence visited upon our people. Six years ago, I was presenting at a conference for families with transgender and gender expansive children. At the end of the session, an older man stood up, holding a document I had cowritten, the results of a survey of more than 6,000 transgender people. In it, 41 percent of our respondents reported that they had attempted suicide at one point in their lives, compared with 4.6 percent of the general population.[12] The report included devastating levels of violence and discrimination against those outside of the gender binary, with levels of homelessness, substance abuse, and other signs of social stress high above those of the general population. The gentleman's voice shook as he said, "My granddaughter is eight years old and she's transgender. I love her." He waved the paper at me, pleading, "What can I do to prevent THIS? What can we do?"

This is our starting point—in my mind, trans hermeneutics is valuable to the degree that it helps this man and his granddaughter, and the millions like them. Our work must address the conditions that lead so many to feel that their lives are untenable or unworthy. Our work must address the factors that allow others to view transgender, nonbinary, or other gender different people as targets for violence, discrimination, prejudice, and rejection. Only if our work addresses the realities of their lives can we declare it good. I hold myself accountable to this man and his granddaughter. It is my hope to read and interpret the Bible in ways that helps that child and others like her lead fulfilling lives, free from discrimination and violence. For me, theology is valuable insofar as it strengthens human

---

11. Virginia Ramey Mollenkott and Vanessa Sheridan, *Transgender Journeys* (Eugene, OR: Wipf & Stock, 2010), 19.

12. Grant, Mottet, and Tanis, "Injustice at Every Turn," 2.

flourishing in connection with all that is holy. It must be relational, life-giving, and sustaining.

To speak accurately, helpfully, and honestly of trans theology, we must begin from a point that acknowledges the pains and losses we have experienced. To do otherwise erases the realities in which transgender and nonbinary people live our lives and risks developing a theology that glosses over these realities in favor of decency and conformity. Therefore, we must examine this text in light of the current and ongoing legislative and cultural attempts to drive transgender people from the public square, prevent children's access to appropriate medical care, and foster a climate in which violence and discrimination are condoned and even encouraged.

Let me suggest some presuppositions that I bring to this discussion. First, as I have stated, trans hermeneutics and theology must be grounded in the lived experiences of transgender people's real lives. We must be clear that this is not a trendy way to look at hermeneutics, not the latest fashion in religious studies, but a struggle for the very lives, wellbeing, dignity, and health of transgender, nonbinary, and other gender expansive people. The realities of these lives—our lives—must be centered in this mode of inquiry. Thus, we must read the story of the Samaritan looking for those who in a similar fashion are ostracized and hated.

Second, trans hermeneutics must include an acknowledgment and articulation of the devastating impacts of anti-transgender beliefs, attitudes, and practices, which are exacerbated and multiplied by racism, misogyny, nationalism, and other forms of oppression. This includes acknowledging the role of religious groups in general, and the Christian church in particular, in perpetrating this stigma. While expressing anti-transgender sentiments may win "amens" in some churches and votes in some elections, it is neither moral nor in keeping with Jesus's teachings about mercy to exploit the vulnerable for these purposes.

We create and articulate theology and employ hermeneutics in the face of staggeringly high levels of violence faced by young transgender women of color, the astronomical suicide attempt rate, and significantly increased incidences of poverty, homelessness, family rejection, and on and on. We are theologizing, we are analyzing, from the midst of a war zone, in which those outside of the gender binary are repeatedly targeted. Transgender and nonbinary people of color, those who are migrants and asylum seekers, and those who are young are especially vulnerable and in danger. Those of us who are Christian need to acknowledge the church's complicity in stoking this discrimination and its active role in the culture wars, which uses nonbinary and transgender people as pawns to stir up discomfort and dissent.

Third, justice must be centered as the goal of our efforts. As Sheridan and Mollenkott write,

> We must acknowledge that a spirituality rooted in liberation is always predicated upon the conviction that the systemically oppressive structure

of society and its institutions is always open to reconstruction in the service of greater justice. In a specifically transgender-based theology of liberation (or any other liberation theology, for that matter), proactively striving for positive social change is recognized as a necessary condition in order to foster liberation for everyone. Peacefully striving to eliminate oppression through positively transforming an unjust social structure is doing the work of creative justice.[13]

That is, that our work here is valuable only to the degree that it can further justice and enhance wellbeing. The saving of souls and the freeing of spirits are intrinsically bound with the safety and thriving of the body, particularly the gender expansive body. Transgender liberation will benefit all of humanity, freeing us from the gender-based strictures that harm, limit, and deny the full expression of our beings. Living into the full God-given potential of humanity means striving for wider and deeper freedom to be our authentic selves. When we seek justice for the most marginalized, we will discover it for all of us.

If these are the theological underpinnings of my argument, then what methodologies might we employ to achieve this vision? I would like to suggest two specific approaches to reading the Bible. The first methodology is to read the Bible prioritizing the stories of those who live between gender lines and/or rupture expected gender norms; this includes eunuchs, barren women, and women and men who act in gender atypical ways. The presence of those outside of the modern gender binary affirms for us that ancient peoples were well aware of gender variations, both those from birth and those as a result of human actions—as Jesus states in Matthew 19. We might then note that contemporary attempts to oversimplify the human community to two genders, based on birth genitalia, flies in the face of not only current medical science, but knowledge of gender that stretches back thousands of years.

Reading with an eye towards these "transcestors" yields some of the richest stories of inclusion in the Bible, such as Isaiah 56, in which faithful eunuchs are given an everlasting name, one better than sons and daughters, and Acts 8, in which the Ethiopian eunuch faces no barriers to baptism into the emerging Christian community. In both cases, the text points us to profound inclusion, and that the criterion for acceptance is faith. By uncovering and prioritizing eunuchs and other signs of gender diversity in the Bible, we challenge readers to consider the entirety of the biblical story, even when it seems out of step with what most readers have been told it says. Perhaps *especially* when it seems contrary to what most people have been taught about the Bible; as we will see, this seems to be one of Jesus's goals in the telling of the Good Samaritan story. This approach allows readers to gain courage for similarly breaking gendered lines and see themselves and their loved ones within the sacred text. We uncover the biblical complexity *and* God's desire for and affirmation of complexity.

---

13. Mollenkott and Sheridan, *Transgender Journeys*, 19–20.

When we look to the reality of gender diversity in the Bible, we can draw life-giving conclusions. If eunuchs were blessed then, those who are gender diverse can be blessed now. This identifies those outside of gender norms as having sacred purpose, sacred callings, sacred worth. In a society that devalues and dehumanizes transgender and nonbinary people, this is a radical statement. That means that the eight-year-old transgender girl who knows herself to be a girl can see herself within the sacred text. She is not the first of her kind, and she has a place in the holy story of God's people. If her parents, grandparents, teachers, doctors, and other adults around her can affirm this, they too will understand her sacred worth. They will know that while she may be unusual, she is simply part of the wonderous diversity that God intended for this earth. This is urgent for all of our children; but more so for those who are transgender, nonbinary, children of color, migrants, and other marginalized young people. Being seen as holy children of God is one strategy to resist devaluation in this society. Thus, to hear about "people like us," those who resemble our own selves and our lives, in the Bible and other sacred texts, could then be a right afforded to all listeners of the word, and not just a privilege for the majority. It is a reminder that all people are of holy worth and is thus a survival strategy. This process can also uncover nuance and possibility instead of a blanket rejection of the Other. In the course of this process, we might uncover that which is not-obvious. We might learn that, like trans people, there might be more to a text than the original reading, more than the obvious interpretation.

The second methodology I would suggest is the reading of biblical passages that are not specifically related to gender or gender identity through the lens of transgender experience, as we are doing in this chapter. The purpose of this is to consider how to apply formative biblical teachings to our understanding of gender identity.[14] For example, we might consider biblical stories with emotional content or outcomes that can be adapted to a transgender context, such as Joy Ladin's reading of the story of Jonah as a way to understand transgender people's impulse to flee from a transgender identity but then ultimately to come back around to address, accept, and embrace that identity. In my earlier writing, I told the story of the Canaanite woman who challenged Jesus that even the dogs eat the crumbs that fall from the table as a parallel to a mother who fiercely advocates for the wellbeing of her transgender child.[15] This biblical story does not address gender identity, but the two mothers share common strategies and passions when their children's needs for survival are not being met.

By turning to biblical passages that contain formative and key elements of faith and theology, we explicitly name that transgender people are a part of the

---

14. For additional examples, please see David E. Weekley, "Across Generations: Becoming Grateful Allies: An Interview with Virgina Ramey Mollenkott," *JFSR* 34:1 (2018): 34–35, https://doi.org/10.2979/jfemistudreli.34.1.06.

15. Tanis, "Eating the Crumbs That Fall from the Table: Trusting the Abundance of God," in *Take Back the Word: A Queer Reading of the Bible*, ed. Robert E. Goss and Mona West (Cleveland: Pilgrim Press, 2000), 43–54.

story of faith. For example, how do Jesus's teachings about the least of these—feeding the hungry or clothing the naked—address the highly disproportionate levels of poverty in the transgender community? The purpose of this hermeneutic is to position transgender people within a wider faith narrative and to point out that these seminal passages do not, in fact, limit these teachings to hetero- and gender-normative peoples but are meant to be universal. By considering these passages that speak to the heart of faith, we might notice two important things. First, that they do not differentiate based on gender identity or any other demographic characteristic. Second, they guide us in how to faithfully live in this world, which leads us to learn how to respond appropriately to other human beings, including those who are different because of their gender identity or any other demographic characteristic.

This process in one sense removes gender and gender identity from the equation, not to erase but to include. There can be power in pointing out what is not there—that these critical dictates of faith do not have a caveat to allow for the exclusion of some individuals; in fact, Jesus seems to take pains to point out that there is no such escape clause. Liberating theologies require us to pay attention to those who are most marginalized. As Venezuelan theologian Otto Maduro writes, speaking of liberation theology and sexuality,

> A humble and courageous theology, conscious of its own limitations and temptations, has the ethical duty to ask itself which are the aspects and new situations arising from our context that we may be forgetting; which experiences and which cries are we blind and deaf to; whom we are overlooking and who might be the possible victims of our particular viewpoints. For these reasons, I want to underline the need for a deep ethical and epistemological humility. We need to recognize the particularity, finitude, fallibility, and provisionality of our knowledge, and therefore the duty to revise, doubt, question, rethink and constantly criticize what we know, and how we use our knowledge in terms of other people's relationships. In other words, I am referring to the duty to patiently search and attentively listen to people who have different life experiences from ours, who hold other viewpoints and understandings of our reality; especially if we are dealing with people usually considered as irrelevant, absurd or disturbing. It is in the contrast that we shall be able to see the limitations, contradictions, mistakes, incoherencies and holes in our ways of grasping reality.[16]

As Maduro points out, we look to the margins for those who are excluded and may be victims of our own prejudices not simply because it is right to do so, but also because this consideration allows us to identify a greater and more accurate reality. Transgender people are often considered "irrelevant, absurd, or disturbing," and therefore provide a lens through which we can see the text, and its concomitant theology, more accurately. As modern readers seeking to draw closer to

---

16. Otto Maduro, "Once Again Liberating Theology? Towards a Latin American Liberation Theological Self-Criticism," in *Liberation Theology and Sexuality*, ed. Marcella Althaus-Reid (London: SCM Press, 2009), 29.

Jesus's meaning in telling this story, we will be most effective when we challenge ourselves by seeing those on the margins, and those groups of people most challenging to our understanding of the world, as central to this parable.

In our reading here of the Good Samaritan, I see the Samaritan, as a result of being a despised outsider to most of Jesus's listeners, as a transcestor because of the commonalities of their experiences of exclusion and as the objects of hatred. But even more compellingly, the Samaritan story is Jesus's way of illustrating the central tenets of faith to his Jewish audience and followers, and his subsequent Christian adherents. We can both see ourselves within the story and recognize that we, too, are heirs to the tradition and teaching about how to be a neighbor.

As multiple commentators have pointed out, attention to our spiritual inconsistencies and limitations seems to be a central aspect of the parables. Alyce McKenzie notes, "Jesus uses parables to subvert traditional wisdom and to point to a new, inbreaking reality, the kingdom of God. He places seemingly everyday stories next to this new reality, the reign or kingdom of God, and allows the connections and the disconnections between the two to spark in the hearer's mind."[17] By using the Samaritan to illustrate one of the two highest commandments of God, Jesus creates a conflict in the listeners' minds between what society believes about a group of people and the place of those people within the dominion of God. It is this profound contrast that offers us the opportunity to form a more true and complete understanding of God's valuation of humanity, one liberated from prejudice and judgment. As Robert Shore-Goss writes in his study of Luke in *The Queer Bible Commentary*, "Jesus is a boundary-breaker, transgressing the purity codes of fundamentalists and challenging the proto-heterosexual hegemony. He uses provocative riddles, parables and symbolic acts to challenge religious normativities."[18] We are *supposed* to have our world views upended by hearing the parables; it is one of their key attributes.

Therefore, seeing the Good Samaritan as a transgender woman of color is highly appropriate and helpful to us as people of faith and scholars because—in a transphobic and racist world—she offers the starkest contrast between the sanctified (and often sanctimonious) image of the religiously and socially acceptable "good," "normal" person and the vision of God's realm that Jesus paints for us. It is precisely that gap between "conventional wisdom" and the wisdom of Jesus's teachings that he is asking us to consider and overcome. The shock and disconnection between today's realities of violence, discrimination, and rejection, and God's loving acceptance is the point of the story. As Maduro states, we have a "duty to revise, doubt, question, rethink and constantly criticize what we know, and how we use our knowledge."[19] Jesus uses the contrast here to prompt us to do this. Brian Stiller writes, "In his parables, Jesus allowed no one

---

17. Alyce M. McKenzie, *The Parables for Today* (Louisville, KY: Westminster John Knox Press, 2007), 9–10.

18. Robert E. Goss, "Luke," in *The Queer Bible Commentary*, ed. Deryn Guest et al. (London: SCM Press, 2007), 529.

19. Maduro, "Once Again Liberating Theology?," 29.

to remain neutral: People were forced to respond to his call to join him in this new kingdom. Parables were Jesus's way of breaking into resistant minds with insights that stunned his hearers, not only with a surprise and twist, but also with shocking wisdom."[20] Thus, the most faithful reading of this text is the one that most startles us enough to engage anew with Jesus's intentions in telling the story. The point is that it is scandalous and therefore points us to God's dominion, to break into our "resistant minds" with the good news of mercy.

To be clear, the point of the stories is not to be shocking for their own sake. Rather, Jesus is challenging his hearers, and his modern readers, to point us more accurately at the nature of God's realm and the right actions we are to take. The shocking nature of the tale is meant to startle us into a greater awareness of what it means to live out the Greatest Commandments. As Carter Heyward points out in *Our Passion for Justice*,

> Jesus' life seems to have been steeped in his own strong sense that many human beings, in their common quest for God, had been searching in the wrong direction for the wrong kind of God, and hence had found neither God nor themselves.
>
> Seeking God, many had studied, memorized, and idolized scripture. Seeking God, many had immersed in religious traditions that they held precious. Seeking God, many had obeyed the ten commandments and other tenets of religious law. Seeking God, many had observed religious rituals on the sabbath. . . . Seeking God, many people in Jesus' time, much like many today, had looked to heaven rather than earth for something divine rather than human.
>
> And among them came Jesus, himself a good Jew, whose burning passion was to redirect the people's search for God, because Jesus seemed to know that God was to be found, known, and loved on earth, in whatever is fully human, rather than in the tomes of religious, sacred, or divine tradition.[21]

Jesus, in the parable of the Good Samaritan, is redirecting our spiritual search from the ways in which humans sought and seek for God through religious observances and sacred texts to the humanity that surrounds us. Thus, the place to seek for God is in the actions of others; when we look for the one who shows mercy, we find a person who is fulfilling Jesus's definition of what it means to be a neighbor and living out the Greatest Commandment. The parable of the Good Samaritan demonstrates that this is not to be found by following creeds, texts, or laws, but in human kindness and loving action where God is revealed.

Imagine a world in which, upon hearing that someone was Christian, people would assume that this person would stop and care deeply for a stranger, even when it was inconvenient and costly, because that is what Jesus taught us to do in seeking God. When religious groups and leaders exclude nonbinary and

---

20. Brian Stiller, *Preaching Parables to Postmoderns* (Minneapolis: Fortress Press, 2005), 15.
21. Carter Heyward, *Our Passion for Justice: Images of Power, Sexuality, and Liberation* (New York: Pilgrim Press, 1984), 94–95.

transgender people, they focus on a rigid cultural perspective on gender that runs counter to the biblical complexity on the topic and fails to follow the standard Jesus sets for neighborliness in this passage. The strictures of the culture wars do not allow us to embrace one another but instead posit rejection as faithfulness and paternalism as compassion.[22]

Jesus in this parable is calling us to understand that the Greatest Commandment—that which we need to know to thrive spiritually in consort with God's desire for us—is to love God and to love our neighbors as ourselves. It is in the mercy that we show to one another that we embody those commandments. Yet, as we pointed out earlier, the fact remains that transgender and nonbinary people are regularly rejected from communities of faith—or choose to leave these groups for fear of discrimination before they have to face that trauma and humiliation—at high rates. At public hearings, self-identified Christians are by far the most vocal opponents of bills to support trans rights (and often the only opponents) and the most vociferous proponents of bills to systematically strip public accommodation rights and medical support for young people.[23] This has the effect of both literally and figuratively removing trans people from community, so that we are not seen or acknowledged, much less treated as neighbor. As David Weekley writes,

> The lawyer in Jesus' parable wants to limit those who fall within the definition of neighbor. In response Jesus tells a story that removes all boundaries of the classification, offering an extreme example of inclusivity. Some people today, even those who follow Jesus, attempt to draw similar boundaries. There are those who attempt to place transgender and gender nonconforming people outside the circle of neighbor through legal actions, political activism, and religious dogmatism. Despite such endeavors the parable stands as a basic truth per Jesus: there is no one outside the definition of neighbor. Transgender and gender non-conforming persons are your neighbors.[24]

That is, despite the efforts to portray us as outside of society, and to enshrine this barrier into legislation, in God's view, we remain your neighbors.

In addition to using a highly marginalized figure as a main character to create a contrast between human society and the in-breaking dominion of God, Jesus lifts up the despised Other as Spiritual Exemplar. We are not just to be startled by the chasm of difference between God's realm and our human interactions

---

22. For example, the many references to "gender confusion" and an assumption that this "confusion" could be easily rectified with therapy or same-gender role models.

23. In my experience, this often takes the form of invoking the shibboleth that the passage of any legislation that upholds LGBTQ rights will result in the arrest of anti-gay and anti-trans pastors, dragged from their pulpits. This argues that any attempts to safeguard human and civil rights will, by extension, violate the right to free speech. One prime example, among many, is the testimony on the Matthew Shepherd and James Byrd Jr. Hate Crimes Prevention Act, S. 909, hearing before the Committee on the Judiciary, United States Senate, June 25, 2009, Serial No. J-111-33.

24. Weekley, *Retreating Forward: A Spiritual Practice with Transgender Persons* (Eugene, OR: Resource Publications, 2017), 10.

with one another; we are to emulate the Samaritan and "go and do likewise," to embody neighborliness. Jesus's story of these unexpected actions challenges and expands our categories of *who* might be our neighbor and offers concrete examples of how we should be a neighbor. What are the characteristics of the neighbor's response? The Samaritan truly saw the injured person lying beside the road; while others spotted a body and moved on, she stopped, engaged, and acted with care. She saw him as a human being in need rather than an inconvenience, potential ritual contaminant, or source of danger, as those who passed on by may have. She treated her neighbor as she herself undoubtedly would want to be treated if she were lying in pain beside the road, with deep care and hospitality. She provided material needs in an immediate and ongoing way until the person's health was restored and they were able to care for themselves. She offered safety and hospitality that allowed healing to take place. We are called to go and do likewise.

Other LGBTQ+ theologians have made the connection between queer hospitality and this passage. In his 1988 book, *Taking a Chance on God*, John McNeill writes,

> Hospitality is also a central theme of the New Testament. For example, Jesus tells his disciples: "And if anyone does not welcome you or listen to what you have to say, as you walk out of the house or town shake the dust from your feet. I tell you solemnly, on the day of Judgment it will not go as hard with the land of Sodom and Gomorrah as with that town" (Mt. 10:14–14). The text makes it clear that Jesus understood the crime of Sodom as inhospitality to strangers.
>
> Again, in chapter 10 of Luke, when someone asks Jesus, "Who is my neighbor?" he responds with the parable of the good Samaritan. Today, this parable might be paraphrased as follows: A man was mugged on 42nd Street and left in an alley close to death. A priest and a social worker passed by and saw him but did nothing because they were afraid. Then a transvestite saw him, went into the alley, picked him up, bound his wounds with her best scarf, called a taxi, and took him to the emergency room of a hospital. The parable would end in the very same way: with Jesus saying, "Go and do the same yourself."[25]

While McNeill's language reflects his time (we would say cross-dresser or drag queen, rather than transvestite), the meaning is certainly valuable. I wrote my trans versions of the Samaritan before I discovered McNeil's; I see in that a confluence of queer ideas, always committed to claiming our rightful place within the sacred stories and naming the centrality of the marginalized in God's vision of justice for our world. Many of us have been the outcast, the rejected, or the stranger and from those experiences, commit to ensuring that others are welcomed into community and cared for. Transgender people, especially transgender women of color, have done heroic work to share resources, offer housing

---

25. John McNeill, *Taking a Chance on God: Liberating Theology for Gays, Lesbians, and Their Lovers, Families, and Friends* (Boston: Beacon Press, 1988), 96.

and food, and meet the emergency needs of their sisters. They/we have created safe spaces where there were none and advocated fiercely for one another. Thus, it is easy to imagine our transgender Samaritan drawing upon these networks to offer hospitality and care.

Shore-Goss continues this theme and expands it in keeping with Jesus's radical vision of God's dominion. He writes,

> For McNeill queer hospitality is expressed in the parable of the Good Samaritan, where the Samaritan is a gay drag queen who picks up a man mugged on 42nd Street in New York City and who is passed by a Catholic priest and social worker (McNeill 1988: 96). But let's queer the text further than McNeill does. Imagine that the mugged man is the Catholic Cardinal or a televangelist such as Pat Robertson. The surprise comes in the love shown to someone who has actively persecuted the queer community and set up a climate of social violence. It communicates the intentional shock of the Samaritan parable and Jesus' injunction to love one's enemies. God's reign is radically inclusive, and Jesus tells his audience to imitate the compassionate Samaritan, a hated and despised outcast of his day. Queer hospitality, likewise, finds God present in the stranger, the enemy, or the homophobic religious leader.[26]

Can we imagine those we think of as transphobic or harmful to our community as possible Samaritans? For those of us for whom a transgender "Samaritan" is a welcome thought, we would do well to remember that we, too, are meant to be confounded. Whose helping presence on that road would shock us? What categories of people do we, as Maduro says, find "irrelevant, absurd or disturbing" or assume to be transphobic? If we believe, as I certainly do, that transgender and nonbinary people are truly heirs of our traditions, deserving the full value of our spiritual teachings, then we too can challenge ourselves to think of those whom we might stereotype and see in that person the Good Samaritan, a person who can embody Jesus's definition of the neighbor. Imagine if the story read like this:

After a long and troubling day, a trans woman decided to take a break on her way home and stopped at a park. She sat on a bench, listening to the birds and insects, and pondered life. Her mind elsewhere, she did not notice the group approaching her until it was too late to run. They descended on her, yelling hateful words, took her wallet and cell phone, beat her, and dumped her half-dead body in a ditch, leaving her there. She spent the night in agonizing pain, drifting in and out of consciousness. Early the next morning, two people passed on by, afraid of getting involved or wrapped in their own fears and anxieties.

Finally, the woman heard the roar of a pickup truck that pulled into a nearby parking space—it was big, painted red, white, and blue, with an eagle emblazoned on the side. From the bed of the truck, a Don't Tread on Me Flag fluttered in the wind. Out through the open windows, the truck's speakers were blaring talk radio with the latest conspiracy theories. Spotting the woman by

---

26. Goss, "Luke," 532.

the side of the road, the driver hopped out to investigate. Looking more closely, he saw the blood on her head and the tears in her clothes. He leaned down and gently shook the woman. She startled awake—pulling back in fear. The sight of that flag covered pickup truck was terrifying—she was sure that the violence was about to resume and thought she surely would not survive that. "It's okay now," he said, "shhhh." And she promptly passed out. As in our other stories, this Samaritan provided for her needs and ensured that she received care.

In Matt 5:38–44a (NRSVue), Jesus says,

> You have heard that it was said, "An eye for an eye and a tooth for a tooth." But I say to you: Do not resist an evildoer. But if anyone strikes you on the right cheek, turn the other also, and if anyone wants to sue you and take your shirt, give your coat as well, and if anyone forces you to go one mile, go also the second mile. . . . You have heard that it was said, "You shall love your neighbor and hate your enemy." But I say to you: Love your enemies and pray for those who persecute you.

Who are *our* enemies and how might they appear as a Samaritan on the road? For those of us who have been victims of prejudice and violence, this is truly challenging. But, as we have noted, perhaps that is what Jesus set out to do in this parable.

To conclude our trans envisioning of the characters in this story, let us turn to those who did not stop along the way. If we read these characters as nonbinary or trans, we might take into account their fears of being "read" or "clocked" as gender different and thus exposed to discrimination and hostility. We would think of how they might prudently weigh the risks about becoming the victim of violence themselves by getting involved in this situation. Or their lack of material resources because of the tremendously high levels of poverty in the community. You might notice that I offer a more sympathetic reading than many writers to the priest and the Levite who crossed to the other side of the road. It seems to me that Jesus would want us to see these characters in his story with deep compassion. After all, the point of the story is to illustrate what it means to treat others as we would want to be treated by them. If we—and surely we have—passed by someone in need, would we not want the circumstances that led to our aversion or avoidance to at least be considered? Might there not be legitimate reasons why we did not stop?

Martin Luther King Jr. preached on the parable of the Good Samaritan in sermons dating from 1954. He told a story about how he had been driving down a road in Georgia, one that bore a resemblance to the deserted Jericho Road in Jesus's telling. He saw a man in need and did not stop, because the risk felt too high, which he compared to those who passed on by the injured man. King went on to say,

> The first question that the Levite asked was, "If I stop to help this man, what will happen to me?" But the good Samaritan came by and he reversed

the question. Not "What will happen to me if I stop to help this man?" but "What will happen to this man if I do not stop to help him?" This was why that man was good and great. He was great because he was willing to take a risk for humanity; he was willing to ask, "What will happen to this man?" not "What will happen to me?"[27]

This putting the needs of others before our own, following the imperative to show mercy just as we would want to have mercy shown to us, is key to Jesus's teaching on and understanding of the Greatest Commandments. Again, we see this reversal as a central component of the parable. We are called to transition from fear to care, from self-interest to other-focus, to become the neighbor of those in need. I would argue, too, that there is peril to our spirits from failing to stop, just as there is risk to our bodies in stopping.

More than a decade later, speaking out against the Vietnam War in 1967 near the end of his life, King again spoke about the Good Samaritan. This time his message was more radical, as he urged his listeners to a revolution of values and orientation, to care more deeply for humanity than materialism and nationalism. In this speech, King raises the question not just of our responsibility to show mercy to those who have been injured but to ask why people are being beaten on the Jericho Road in the first place. He said,

> A true revolution of values will soon cause us to question the fairness and justice of many of our past and present policies. On the one hand we are called to play the Good Samaritan on life's roadside, but that will be only an initial act. One day we must come to see that the whole Jericho Road must be transformed so that men and women will not be constantly beaten and robbed as they make their journey on life's highway. True compassion is more than flinging a coin to a beggar. It comes to see that an edifice which produces beggars needs restructuring.
>
> A true revolution of values will soon look uneasily on the glaring contrast of poverty and wealth. With righteous indignation, it will look across the seas and see individual capitalists of the West investing huge sums of money in Asia, Africa, and South America, only to take the profits out with no concern for the social betterment of the countries, and say, "This is not just." It will look at our alliance with the landed gentry of South America and say, "This is not just." The Western arrogance of feeling that it has everything to teach others and nothing to learn from them is not just.[28]

Given the tremendous violence experienced by transgender people, we must ask ourselves not only what we can do to heal the damage done, but why it happens in the first place. This is urgent work. We must state, "This is not just." To care for the wounded is the initial step; to ask how the Jericho Road can be

27. Martin Luther King Jr. "The Three Dimensions of a Complete Life," Sermon Delivered at the Unitarian Church of Germantown, December 11, 1960, https://kinginstitute.stanford.edu/king-papers/documents/three-dimensions-complete-life-sermon-delivered-unitarian-church-germantown.

28. King, "Beyond Vietnam," New York, April 4, 1967.

transformed so that all can traverse it is the next. We begin that work by naming the injustice, violence, and the prejudice meted out against God's beloved nonbinary and transgender children. We continue it by recognizing that Jesus calls us to extend our compassion to restructuring society in ways that respect and value all of its members, including those at various points on the gender spectrum. When the Jericho Road is safe to travel for the most vulnerable members of society, it is available for all of us.

By seeing trans and nonbinary people as a significant part of this parable, we see new facets of a familiar story, both engaging our own sense of compassion and considering what actions embody mercy and neighborliness. A trans hermeneutic offers precious opportunities to (re)consider Jesus's methodology and pedagogy that turns the world upside down through this text. First, in the direct sense of showing that categories thought to be stable are not: enemies are to be loved, evildoers accommodated, persecutors to be prayed for, and Samaritans are spiritual exemplars. Nonbinary and transgender people are far more than the stereotypes that may evoke discomfort and hostility on both individual and societal levels. Jesus counts as neighbor and as exemplar the one who acts with mercy, rather than the exterior or demographic identity with which society labels them. For Jesus, the inner person, not the outer appearance, tells the truth. In the same way, transgender people assert that who we are, who we understand ourselves to be, and how God created us to be, is the truth. It is not the exterior but the interior in which personhood is revealed; the exterior can be made congruent with the interior, but not the other way around.

Trans people embody the fact that transition or migration between allegedly fixed categories of gender is entirely possible and, for those called to this path, a source of healing and a cause for celebration. Nonbinary people demonstrate that there are infinite paths between, among, and alongside the poles. Those who alter or circumvent allegedly fixed identities model for us Jesus's way of thinking: that the dominion of God is revealed by transforming our way of seeing the Other (and, in loving our neighbor as ourselves, our view of our own humanity as well). The first shall be last, the last shall be first. A trans hermeneutic is one that pushes us to think beyond the obvious to the subtle, just as Jesus points out that the key feature of neighborliness is not that this person is a Samaritan but that they show mercy.

This way of reading impacts our eight-year-old transgender girl by placing her firmly within the wider story of God's love, salvation, and grace. If she becomes hungry—and statistically as a transgender person, she is more likely to experience poverty and food insecurity—then if we offer her food, we offer Christ food. If she lacks clothing or water, and we give those to her, then we give them to Christ. If she falls prey to violence on the side of the road—and statistically as a transgender person, she is more likely to—then we are to bind up her wounds and care for her. In short, we are to treat her as we want to be treated ourselves. She is our neighbor. And we go on to ask, "what can we do to prevent this tragedy from ever happening again?"

Trans hermeneutics is, to me, to read the Bible for the explicit purpose of liberating humanity from the tyranny of oppressive gender norms, including those which devalue and debase transgender lives. Any theology we write or speak must be liberating to that eight-year-old girl whose grandfather is so worried about her, to a young transgender woman heading home from a long night of sex work, to the trans boy in the sixth grade who has a urinary tract infection because he cannot bear to use the girls' restroom, to the nonbinary teen who was thinking about suicide last night after being told that their way of being is not God's will. If we craft a theology powerful, compassionate, and truthful enough to save the lives of these children of God, we will be embodying the mercy that Jesus lifted up for us in the person of the Good Samaritan.

Chapter 6

Putting the "Trans" in Transfiguration in Mark 9:1–9

KATY E. VALENTINE

INTRODUCTION

It is high time to affirm the "trans" in the Transfiguration of Jesus. This is a cherished story for many Jesus followers, including trans Christians. Even so, several trans Christians surprised me when they brought up the Transfiguration as a significant story in their gender journey. Some felt that the corporeal changes that Jesus experiences in the Transfiguration could include gender transformation. They perceived their own bodily transformation of clothing, hairstyle, speech patterns, hormone therapy, or surgery as being similar to Jesus's transformation. Others for whom this passage was not initially significant felt resonance when presented with questions about it. This led to the primary question for this chapter: Is it possible to interpret Jesus's transfiguration in Mark 9:1–9 as a transgender experience? I theorize that the answer is "yes" when rooted in an analysis of metamorphosis stories in the ancient world.

In this chapter, I examine Mark 9:1–9 in several ways. To begin, I look at metamorphosis in the ancient world, led by a narrow focus on the word *metamorphoō* since it is the key word that describes Jesus's transformation in Mark 9:2. I then turn more broadly to examples of gender transformations of both gods and humans in the ancient world, followed by a trans interpretation of Mark 9:1–9. This Christian story can be seen within an ancient framework that makes gender transformation highly probable. Finally, I provide a theological reflection on the story in conversation with lived experiences of trans people today as well as scholarly voices.

METAMORPHOSIS IN ANTIQUITY

First, to set the scene: Mark 9:2 tells simply that Jesus *metemorphōthē* ("was metamorphized" or "was transfigured"). This powerful word evokes a sense of transformation, including bodily changes. Lexical definitions range from "transform" to "disguise" to "transfigured" of the mind or the body, but I narrow the focus here to corporeal transformations.[1] Within the New Testament, the word occurs only four times, two in the story of the Transfiguration in the Synoptic Gospels (Mark 9:2; Matt 17:2) with identical language: "He was metamorphized before them." The parallel story in Luke does not contain the language of *metamorphoō* but instead describes Jesus's face as becoming "other" in 9:29. In all three Synoptic versions, Jesus's clothes become white. Moses and Elijah join Jesus on the mountain, and the disciples are frightened; Matthew adds the detail that Jesus's face "shone like the sun."

The other two instances of *metamorphoō* in the New Testament are in the letters of Paul. The occurrence in Rom 12:2 is a brief encouragement to believers to be metamorphized in their minds but does not relate to corporeal transformations. Paul's use of *metamorphoō* in 2 Cor 3:18, however, does suggest a strong connection to the body. In this chapter, Paul contrasts the old and new covenants, appealing to the figure of Moses in an extended metaphor. Whereas Moses, representing the old covenant, had to cover his face with a veil when descending from the mountain in order to shield the Israelites from his glory (*doxa*), those in the new covenant can act boldly, presumably unveiled.[2] Paul concludes with the language of metamorphosis: "All of us, with unveiled faces, are being metamorphized (*metamorphoumetha*) into the same image from glory to glory" (3:18).[3]

Paul describes the ultimate metamorphosis of believers on the heels of a discussion about the body of Moses.[4] It would be easy to interpret Paul's use of *metamorphoō* as solely about the mind or spirit, but the close correlation to Moses and the descriptions of Moses's veil and shining face suggest otherwise. It is likely that Paul believed that the metamorphoses of Jesus's followers also

---

1. LSJ definitions include "transform" or "disguise," and even "to be transfigured" citing Matt 17:2.
2. Paul draws from LXX Exod 34:29 using the language of glory (*dedoxastai*).
3. Unless otherwise noted, all translations are my own.
4. Paul might refer to an oral version of the Transfiguration, but it is unlikely; Anthony C. Thiselton, *The First Epistle to the Corinthians: A Commentary on the Greek Text* (Grand Rapids: Eerdmans, 2000), 50.

included dramatic physical changes. Paul spends quite a bit of instructive time in 1 Corinthians focused on the bodies of believers: a man who lay with a prostitute (1 Cor 5:1–7), married believers who deny each other sex (1 Cor 7:2–5), circumcision (1 Cor 7:17–20), women's veils and men's heads (1 Cor 11:2–16).[5] Collectively, these strengthen the suggestion that the metamorphosis Paul envisioned included physical bodies.

The Hellenistic Jewish writer Philo also used the language of *metamorphoō* in a few instances. Philo describes Moses's protection of seven young maidens and their access to a watering place from a group of men (*Moses* 1.57). As Moses speaks, his appearance metamorphized (*metamorphoumenos*) to look like a prophet.[6] This language of metamorphosis is part of a wider understanding of Moses in Philo as a quasi-angelic being who descended to take the form of a human to teach the divine Law, and then reascends back to his angelic form.[7] Examples are numerous: Moses appears to remember lessons rather than learn them from his teachers;[8] he is "appointed" as a god with perfect control over his passions, and his own soul was in a perfect state before his death;[9] he also prophesies about what happens after death with special knowledge.[10] Moses as an angelic figure has particular resonance with Paul's description of him as one who surpassed an earthly existence and encountered God's glory emanating from his body.

The word *metamorphoō* appears a few times in later Hellenistic Jewish and Christian works. Ancient commentaries on the Transfiguration naturally use the word,[11] and in other instances the term is employed metaphorically or to emphasize a point about the transformation of the mind.[12] Regarding corporeal transformations, though, an interesting example comes up in the writings of the second century CE Christian writer Tatian. He quite clearly knows of the Greek metamorphosis stories, which he condemns to show the superiority of Christianity.[13] In his condemnation, Tatian confirms the corporeal understanding of metamorphosis. He describes Rhea who became a tree, Zeus who became a

---

5. I explore the corporeal complications of enslaved persons within the Corinthian community in Katy E. Valentine, *For You Were Bought with a Price: Sex, Slavery, and Self-Control in a Pauline Community* (Wilmore, KY: GlossaHouse, 2017).

6. Philo uses *metamorphoō* twice more: *Spec. Laws* 4.147 in a brief discussion on piety, right after the description of Moses's courage; piety is juxtaposed *to* Moses, but not *about* Moses. *Gaius* 95 describes the metamorphosis of Gaius (Caligula) into Apollo. Caligula dressed up like Apollo, which contrasts Philo's sincere depiction of Moses's transformation in *Moses* 1.57.

7. David Litwa orients Philo's transformation from human to angelic in the wider Greco-Roman conversation; M. David Litwa, *Posthuman Transformation in Ancient Mediterranean Thought: Becoming Angels and Demons* (Cambridge: Cambridge University Press, 2021), 74.

8. *Moses* 1.21.

9. *Sacrifices* 9–10.

10. *Moses* 2.291

11. Origen, *Cels.* 4.16; 6.76; *Comm. Matt.* 12.

12. Basil, *Ep.* 210.5, where he condemns hypostasis; Basil critiques Sabellius for believing that God was one substance who could "metamorphize" into the Father, the Son or the Spirit as needed; see Theophilus, *Autol.* 2.6 on the creation of the world.

13. Tatian, *Or. Graec.* 10.

dragon, sisters who are turned into trees, and Leto into a bird. He also references gods who become swans, or an eagle (Zeus) who kidnapped Ganymede, taking him to Olympus to become a cupbearer.

The Christian epistle to Diognetus (late second century CE) uses the word *metamorphoō* in a discussion about how raw materials such as silver and clay transform by way of iron and fire.[14] The letter attacks pagan idols, which the author asserts cannot *really* be gods because they are malleable and able to decay, using the language of transformation to dismiss their existence. A contemporary Christian writer, Clement (c. 150–c. 215 CE), describes the transformation of wild men (Gentiles and sinners) into believers through the song of heaven.[15] Several writings from the first to third centuries CE also continue along a similar trajectory. In the Testament of Solomon, *metamorphoō* describes the transformation of a demon into waves, but also intriguingly into a man (*anthrōpon*).[16] In the Testament of Abraham, Abraham angrily demands that Death teach him all of his metamorphoses (*metamorphosis*), including into a seven headed dragon.[17] Similarly, the composite Christian work *Ascension of Isaiah* also describes Jesus as being metamorphosized (*metamorphōthēnai*) into a human, presumably from spirit to flesh.[18] With the exception of the epistle to Diognetus, these instances of *metamorphoō* describes *bodies* that transform, and two of the examples specify a transformation into a human being, or *anthrōpon*.

More broadly in Hellenistic literature, several examples illuminate *metamorphoō* as corporeal transformation, often emphasizing bodily changes from human to animal. Diodorus Siculus 4.81 (first century BCE) relates the story of Acteon who is metamorphosized into a dog after angering Artemis. Plutarch (late first century CE) describes Smyrna's transformation into a myrrh tree by Aphrodite after she seduced her father unknowingly into her bed.[19] Pseudo-Apollodorus (first-to-second century CE) describes Zeus turning Io into a cow with the word *metamorphoō*[20] as well as Thetis' shape shifting into the forms of fire, water, and a beast.[21] Similar is the description of Nemesis, who was metamorphized into a fish to escape Zeus in *Deipnosophistae* (third century CE).[22]

These brief references show the widespread view of metamorphosis as physical, corporeal changes to and from elements, demons, humans, animals, and angels. None of the examples of *metamorphoō* included above give specific attention to gender with the possible exception of Jesus's incarnation as human in the later work *Ascension of Isaiah*, but the lateness of this work and the use of

14. *Diogn.* 2:3.
15. Clement, *Protr.* 1.
16. T.Sol. 16:2, 4.
17. T.Ab. 19:5.
18. *Mart. Ascen. Isa.* 3.13.
19. Plutarch, *Para.* 22; of interest is also Plutarch's discussion of Egyptian belief that souls are metamorphized into animals in *Mor.* 2.52B = *Isis/Osiris* 31B.
20. Apollodorus, *Hist.* 2.1.3; cf 2.4.1, 3.8.2.
21. Apollodorus, *Hist.* 3.13.3.
22. Athemaeus, *Deipn.* 8.334c=8.10.

anthrōpos rather than *anēr* weakens this argument. Additional stories, however, of humans and deities undergoing gender changes show how gender was understood to be at least partially mutable in the ancient world, to which I now turn.

THE WORLD OF GODS, HUMANS, AND GENDER TRANSFORMATIONS

The ancient world contains varied, almost dizzying, stories of gender transformation. These are embedded in the even wider array of metamorphosis stories, but here I narrow the focus to those that only include gender. Greek and Latin sources include myriad accounts exactly like those that Tatian would sarcastically critique: gods who transform into humans and occasionally humans who transform into gods; gods who turn human males into females or females into males, sometimes as punishment and other times in assistance; humans who become animals and vice versa. Gods and humans could shift across ages, genders, and species. Though the stories surveyed below do not use the word *metamorphoō*, they certainly *describe* metamorphosis. Such stories add to the scope of radical transformations in the ancient world, setting the scene for exploring the Transfiguration as a gendered experience.

Before diving into a selection of these stories, though, is a fair warning. Modern categories—gender transition, trans, cis, gender identity—do not map neatly onto the ancient world. At times, these terms even limit the way we think about gender today, as categories become less rigid and more fluid. Transfeminist scholar A. Finn Enke explores the limitations of words such as "cisgender" and "transgender," critiquing the way "cisgender" at times represents the stable norm of someone who really *is* the gender to which the trans person must strive. Some people who are defined, or may even self-define, as "cis" also do not feel that they fit into the box of normativity that cis sometimes implies. Enke critiques our current categories, suggesting that "the cis ally reduces 'trans' to the most oppressed and institutionally defined object fighting for recognition within a framework of identity politics and additive 'rights,'" making gender variance even more invisible.[23]

Enke's work strikes a chord, especially with me. I am not trans, but the cis label is not quite representative either, especially in conversation with ancient stories about what we see as transness. The invisible standards of "manhood" or "womanhood" affect everyone negatively. My own gender expression fits that of a cis woman, but even that category has wide expression and is always evolving. Yet, my own internal sense of gender is not limited to "woman" and is always changing, growing, and being shaped. As someone who looks to Jesus as an example, it is imperative that I am in a state of self-reflection, especially around

---

23. A. Finn Enke, "The Education of Little Cis: Cisgender and the Discipline of Opposing Bodies," in *The Transgender Studies Reader 2*, ed. Susan Stryker and Aren Z. Aizura (New York: Routledge, 2013), 243.

gender identity and perceived gender norms. Enke's caution that invisible standards of cis allies reduce trans to an objectified status remains true today, and this can only be broken by questioning the value of cis identity as an "arrival" point.

The obsession with neat categories of the body as fixed and stable—what many conservative religious traditions call "immutable"—color the analysis of ancient and modern transness. The fixation of men *changing* into women and women *transforming* into men reflects an obsession with genitalia as a gatekeeping tactic to analyze bodies that transform and determine who is a "real" man or a "real" woman.[24] Intense forms of gatekeeping today lead to transphobic laws, ostensibly about predatory men who might pose as women for sexual assault purposes of (white) women and girls. This covers up the actual existential anxiety about the violation of fixed binary categories, which has led to aggressive anti-trans legislation that attempts to moderate all nonbinary gender expression through the denial of gender confirmation services and support.

Enke's caution also holds true for the ancient Greek and Latin stories. Scholarship has unconsciously placed contemporary binary gender labels onto the ancient world. The ancient stories examined below contain a sense that the characters struggle to say something about their gender that the language or the framework of the writers could not quite capture. The limitations of languages, even those as precise as Greek and Latin and certainly one as imprecise as English, struggle to articulate gender satisfactorily. I, therefore, take the approach of appealing at times to contemporary categories such as gender identity, gender confirmation, trans man, trans woman, and transition. This is not to box in ancient characters or to point out their failure to live up to modern standards but rather to celebrate the gender variance that is often overlooked. I sometimes ignore Greek or Latin grammar to match the gender identity of the character as I perceive them. At the same time, some gender transformations are problematic, especially when the transformation is not tied to an identity. Are such gender transformations reflective of trans experiences, or do they belong to another category all together? For trans people today, gender transition or confirmation is generally thought of as a permanent change of the outward body to match the inward sense of gender. For gender fluid or nonbinary people, however, gender confirmation may be an ongoing journey where permanence of gender identity within a binary framework is not the key goal.[25] The stories examined below contain a multiplicity of ways to experience gender.

A striking story of gender transformation is visible as early as *The Odyssey* (c. 8th–6th century BCE). Athena becomes a young male to speak with Odysseus as

---

24. See my previous article, Valentine, "Examining Scripture in Light of Trans Women's Voices," in *The Oxford Handbook of Feminist Approaches to the Hebrew Bible*, ed. Susanne Scholz (Oxford: Oxford University Press, 2020), 511–12.

25. Some people may feel called to transition to one gender, and then back to another as described in Justin Sabia-Tanis, *Trans-Gender: Theology, Ministry, and Communities of Faith* (Eugene, OR: Wipf and Stock Publishers, 2018), 146–60.

she aids him on his journey back to Ithaca. Shortly thereafter, Athena changes back into a female goddess chiding Odysseus for not recognizing her.[26] Even while appearing as a human male, Athena's feet shine luminously,[27] and her godhead cannot help but shine through her bodily form. It is tempting to dismiss the story of Athena as a ruse, or a magical trick, but the word *demas* is used in both descriptions of Athena's gender shifts. This word describes physical bodies of humans and sometimes animals, both living and dead, not ethereal illusions. Athena's transformations are corporeal, though there is no indication of Athena's innate sense of gender as "male." Instead, the transformation is to benefit Odysseus.

Jumping forward in time and in language, there is the Latin author, Ovid (43 BCE–c. 18 CE). The monumental work *Metamorphoses* is a compendium of stories of people changing forms, two of which are relevant to this discussion. First is the story of Callisto, which describes a gender transformation of Jupiter, but for the purpose of rape, in sharp contrast to the helpfulness of Athena.[28] Callisto is a woman who does not enjoy typical feminine behavior, such as spinning or hair dressing. Instead, she is a huntress much like Diana. Jupiter transforms to appear as Diana to trick Callisto, which works in part because Callisto had an affinity towards the goddess. Callisto believes fully that Jupiter is Diana until he begins to kiss and embrace her. Though Callisto struggles against Jupiter, he rapes her, and she becomes pregnant with her son, Arcas. Later, she is rejected by Diana because of the pregnancy, and Callisto herself is turned into a bear by a jealous Juno.[29]

This story sounds alarms for contemporary readers familiar with arguments that fuel transphobic legislation in the modern "bathroom bills."[30] In the case of Callisto, Jupiter appears to fit this imagined role of a predatory man acting as a woman, though ancient audiences' sense of gender mutability or immutability was different than ours. It would be easy, but erroneous, to compare Jupiter to contemporary trans women or even gender fluid persons who have fluctuating gender expression. Intent, however, matters greatly. Jupiter is not motivated by assisting humans nor by an innate sense of gender, but by his own desire and control. In contemporary terms, he is a predatory god who abuses the gender transformation available to him in order to commit a heinous act.

The second story to explore from *Metamorphoses* is the more affirming one of Iphis.[31] Iphis, a gender-neutral name, is a female born to Telethusa and Ligdus.

---

26. He reasonably responds that she changes her appearance so often that it is difficult to know whether it's her or not (13.311–314). The Homeric Hymns also contain interesting metamorphoses; see Simon S. Lee, *Jesus' Transfiguration and the Believers' Transformation: A Study of the Transfiguration and Its Development in Early Christian Writings* (Tübingen: Mohr Siebeck, 2009), 24–30.

27. Homer, *Od.* 13.221–224.

28. Ovid, *Metam.* 2.405–531.

29. Ovid, *Metam.* 2.441–95.

30. K. C. Councilor, "The Specter of Trans Bodies: Public and Political Discourse about 'Bathroom Bills,'" in *The Routledge Handbook of Gender and Communication*, ed. Marnel Niles Goins, Joan Faber McAlister, and Bryant Keith Alexander (New York: Routledge, 2020), 274–88.

31. Ovid, *Metam.* 9.666–797.

Because her husband swore that he would kill a daughter, Telethusa hid Iphis' sex and raised her as a boy at the instruction of Isis. Iphis mourns his female sex and is troubled that he will not be able to marry his fiancée, Ianthe, wondering how he could be changed from a girl to a boy. Iphis's gender expression is that of a male though he has female genitalia. Iphis refers to himself as female, even though everyone else, including Ianthe, sees him and treats him as a man. Iphis's mother prays to Isis for a solution.

When Isis grants the request, Iphis's final physical transformation into a man begins. The temple shakes and moves with flashes of light and instruments making noise.[32] Iphis begins to walk with a different stride. His skin becomes darker, features more masculinized, hair shorter, and he has more vigor. The text reports "Iphis, who was a girl, is now a man!" and then simply "Iphis, a new man, gained his Ianthe."[33] Scholarship has interpreted this story as Ovid's condemnation of female-female sexual intercourse and celebration of conventional heterosexual marriage. However, Diane T. Pintabone points out that Ovid overturns expectations throughout this story. While Iphis seemingly adhered to ideal Roman values for women, such as sexual passivity, before the physical transformation, the very fact that no one questioned that Iphis was a man undercuts this stereotype.[34] Though Ovid essentializes some aspects of womanhood, he also shows Iphis as one who crosses the boundaries of gender, including the passion and sexual attraction he felt toward Ianthe in accord with traditional Roman expectations of men. The goddess Isis herself manifests Iphis's gender confirmation with a flourish of sounds, lights, and shakes.

Iphis may be based on the older Greek story of Leucippus, extant in Antoninus Liberalis's *Metamorphoses* (c. second century CE), a collection of stories with older source material.[35] In the story, Galatea is pregnant and is instructed by her husband to expose the child if it is a girl. Predictably, she gives birth to a female but decides to raise the child as a boy. She names the child Leucippus, who becomes beautiful and undeniably female in form; Galatea prays that the child be changed into a boy, granted by the Titan, Leto. Antoninus provides several tantalizing parallels, including the story of well-known Tiresias (discussed below) and the lesser known Caenis who became Caeneus by Poseidon, and Hypermestra, who sold her body as a woman and then became a man to bring food to her father.[36]

32. Ovid, *Metam.* 9.782–84.
33. Ovid, *Metam.* 9.790–91, 9.797.
34. Diane T. Pintabone, "Ovid's Iphis and Ianthe: When Girls Won't Be Girls," in *Among Women: From the Homosocial to the Homoerotic in the Ancient World*, ed. Nancy Sorkin Rabinowitz and Lisa Auanger (Austin: University of Texas Press, 2002), 275–76.
35. Antoninus Liberalis, *Metam.* 17. It is agreed that he uses older source material. For an English translation, see Francis Celoria, *The Metamorphoses of Antoninus Liberalis: A Translation with a Commentary* (London: Routledge, 1992). The story is also found in Nicander (second century BCE) but is no longer extant.
36. A poorly attested myth in *Hymn to Demeter* of Callimachus; see Celoria, *Metamorphoses*, 154, n. 203.

Stories of Tiresias are prevalent in antiquity. Famous as the blind seer, he was also known as a man who became a woman, albeit unintentionally. Gaius Julius Hyginus (first century CE) relates a short tale about a young Tiresias who was changed into a woman after he sees snakes copulating without mention of divine intervention,[37] a rare occurrence of a human male turning into a female.[38] Years later, Tiresias steps on the snakes in the same place upon oracular advice and is changed back into a man. Jupiter and Juno later have a dispute about whether men or women have more pleasure from human sexual relations. They ask Tiresias since he has experience as both, who answers that men have more pleasure. While embedded in a patriarchal framework, Tiresias' story hints that persons who have been both genders occupy a role as divine mediator, a role important to some transgender communities today.[39]

A few examples outside of mythological stories may reveal glimpses of everyday lives of gender variant people in antiquity. First is a Cyprian statue from Amanthus of a figure with breasts and a beard. This image is sometimes interpreted to be Aphrodite/Aphroditos[40] and other times as cultic personnel.[41] The Amanthus figure is the most well-known, though similar images sometimes with breasts and a phallus are found elsewhere in Cyprus, and one much later from seventh-century CE Corinth.[42] Limited literary evidence also describes a bearded statue with breasts, pointing to the worship of Aphrodite/Aphroditos on Cyprus.[43]

Such images have been named as androgynes, bisexual, dual-sexed, and hermaphrodites, an ancient term that describes a descendant of Hermes and Aphrodite who had both female and male genitalia and then applied more widely to similar individuals in the ancient world.[44] All of these terms betray a binary bias, particularly "hermaphrodite," which has been used as a derogatory term, both in antiquity and today. Now, the positive term "intersex" is preferred. Recent

---

37. The earlier Greek version may date back to Hesiod as reported by Phlegon of Tralles; see Luc Brisson, *Sexual Ambivalence: Androgyny and Hermaphroditism in Graeco-Roman Antiquity*, trans. Janet Lloyd (Berkeley: University of California Press, 2002), 116–17. Brisson's dated work uses old-fashioned terms, such as "sex-change," but remains useful for analysis.

38. Gaius Julius Hyginus, *Fabulae* 75.

39. Brisson comments that persons who are "dual-sexed" often perform the role of a mediator; see Brisson, *Sexual Ambivalence*, 115–17.

40. Aphrodite is suggested as a model for trans people today from a psychological perspective in Stella Fremi, "Aphrodite and Her Sisters," *Lancet Psychiatry* 3:2 (2016): 111–13.

41. Bettany Hughes, *Venus and Aphrodite: History of a Goddess* (London: Widenfeld & Nicolson, 2019), 75–77. Hughes sometimes uses "non-binary" or "double sexed" to describe the figures but stops short of a gender analysis.

42. See Bonnie MacLachlan, "The Ungendering of Aphrodite," in *Engendering Aphrodite: Women and Society in Ancient Cyprus*, ed. Diane Bolger and Nancy Serwint (Boston: The American Schools of Oriental Research, 2002), 365–66.

43. The late fourth-century CE writers Servius (*ad Aeneid* 2:632) and Macrobius (*Saturnalia* 3.8.1–3) both attest to Aphroditos with descriptions of a statue with breasts and a beard as an explanation for Vergil's reference to Aphrodite as a god (not goddess) in *Aen.* 2.632; see MacLachlan, "The Ungendering of Aphrodite."

44. See Anthony Spawforth, "Hermaphroditus," *OCD*; an origin story is related in Ovid, *Metam.* 4.285–395.

intersex advocacy pushes back against a gender binary that insists on either male or female. This same binary has clouded judgment and interpretation around evaluating the images of icons of Aphrodite/cultic personnel. Mary Weismantel critiques archaeology for imposing a binary gender model on artifacts, suggesting instead that a transgender archaeology needs to destroy "the layers of unsupported assumptions about sex and gender that encrust the archaeological record, and [free] the queerly formed bodies trapped underneath."[45] Weismantel advocates for scholars to "ungender" assumptions about ancient images and material evidence so that we do not project our modern entanglements around gender on the ancient world.

Certainly, the word "hermaphrodite" needs ungendering, as does similarly labeled material culture. A cultic official with a beard and breasts could certainly be intersex, or could also reflect an even broader gender variant range. It is certainly possible to imagine someone in the ancient world whose body did not match their gender identity commissioning a statue that resembled their ideal body. The images that have been interpreted as hermaphroditic could easily be more slippery, representing a deity who flowed between and among many gendered forms in antiquity.[46] Aphrodite/Aphroditos could take many transing forms, perhaps also bestowing the same ability on cultic leaders. While space precludes a full analysis of the deity here, I raise this as a suggestion that the iconography that has emerged suggests that actual people may have embraced and looked to Aphrodite/Aphroditos as a deity who understood and valued gender variance.

Greek medical literature also describes two fascinating cases in which a female body takes on characteristics of a male body. In the fourth century BCE, Hippocrates' *Epid.* 6.8.32 describes the case of the woman Phaethousa whose body became masculinized.[47] The case recounts that she bore a child prior to banishment by her husband. After missing her menses for a long time, her body took on characteristics associated with masculinity: hardened joints, hairiness, growth of a beard and a rough voice. Phaethousa died before the doctors could bring on her menses, which they most likely thought would be a cure for her condition. In the same text, another woman, Namusias, had the same symptoms and also died. Helen King points out that this case points to the question asked in the ancient world on "whether an individual could change sex spontaneously."[48] Limited attention to medical cases such as Phaethousa points to the ancient understanding of porousness between the male and female body in the ancient world, also

45. Mary Weismantel, "Towards a Transgender Archaeology: A Queer Rampage through Prehistory," in Stryker and Aizura, *The Transgender Studies Reader* 2, 320.

46. Fragments attributed to Aristophanes, 325a and b; briefly discussed in Hughes, *Venus and Aphrodite*, 75.

47. *Epid.* 6 is preserved in Galen plus Arabic sources; see Helen King, "Sex and Gender: The Hippocratic Case of Phaethousa and Her Beard," *EuGeSta: Gender Studies in Antiquity* 3 (2013): 124–42. See the translation in Hippocrates, *Epid.* 7 (Smith, LCL), 289–91. Cf. the case of Agnodice as told in Hyginus, *Fabulae*, 274.

48. King, "Sex and Gender," 126.

visible in the story of Tiresias, which signals the possibility of ancient gender changes, even involuntary ones.

The stories from ancient Greco-Roman literature provide a sampling of metamorphoses in which gender plays a crucial role, with numerous references to other lost stories. None of the above examples uses the language of *metamorphoō* specifically, but they do illustrate that gender transformations were part of the ancient imagination. Some examples are whimsical, such as Athena's transformation into a young male, in contrast to Jupiter's deceit. For Iphis, gender identity is important, and it is possible to speak of a gender transition that is confirmed with the assistance of Isis. Other short examples share in the complex world of gender transformations, showing bodies that are more mutable than a contemporary binary framework imposed on them often allows. The complex world of gender transformations in the ancient world was certainly not neat and tidy, any more than it is today. It is into this complexity that Jesus's journey on the mountain occurs.

THE TRANSFIGURATION

The Transfiguration in Mark 9:1–9 is situated firmly within the expansive framework of metamorphosis stories in the ancient world, including corporeal gender transformations. The story of Jesus's Transfiguration is beloved,[49] found in the Synoptic Gospels and hinted at elsewhere in the New Testament.[50] This chapter is by no means the first suggestion in scholarly and popular Christianity of Jesus as a trans figure,[51] and Cary Howie suggests that the Transfiguration may provide a template for trans people today, though without supporting exegesis.[52] My aim in this interpretation is to bring together strands of research around *metamorphoō* and the expansive stories of gender transformations in the ancient world, all while "ungendering" the Transfiguration.

While comparisons to other ancient metamorphoses have been an important part of research on the Transfiguration, attention to gender has been overlooked.[53] A few scholars have emphasized the critical importance of the body of

---

49. The Revised Common Lectionary reinforces this point with "Transfiguration Sunday" occurring on the final Sunday of Epiphany before Lent. The Transfiguration shifts the believer into a season of penitence and reflection, culminating in Holy Week and Easter. See a queer reading in Wendell Miller, Penny Nixon, and Randall Bailey, "Last Sunday after the Epiphany or Transfiguration Sunday, Year B," in *Out in Scripture: An Honest Encounter between LGBT Lives & the Bible: Epiphany, Year B* (HRC Foundation), 2023, https://hrc-prod-requests.s3-us-west-2.amazonaws.com/files/assets/resources/OutinScripture_Epiphany_YearB.pdf.

50. On possible allusions in John, see Dorothy A. Lee, *Transfiguration* (New York: Continuum, 2004), 100–111.

51. Especially in Virginia R. Mollenkott, *Omnigender: A Trans-Religious Approach* (Cleveland: Pilgrim Press, 2001). Also worth mentioning is a novel that envisions Jesus as a trans man but is also rife with supersessionism, Kristen Wolf, *The Way: A Girl Who Dared to Rise* (n.l.: Pixeltry, 2018).

52. Cary Howie, "On Transfiguration," *L'Esprit Créateur* 53:1 (2013): 158–66.

53. See especially Candida R. Moss, "The Transfiguration: An Exercise in Markan Accommodation," *BibInt* 12:1 (2004): 69–89. Moss also examines Persephone (Homer, *Od.* 13.312–314),

Jesus, such as Dorothy Lee: "it is precisely Jesus' transfigured body that discloses the face of God and the hope of God's future, addressing the concrete reality of a fearful, uncomprehending group of disciples and a tragic, unbelieving world."[54] The Western resistance to the body has stunted this direction of interpretation in favor of literary-theological interpretations with a focus on the ties of the Transfiguration to Jesus's baptism and resurrection.[55] Jesus's body, however, is crucial when interpreting the Transfiguration, especially in the Gospel of Mark where Jesus's body is crucified as a ransom (Mark 10:45). Jesus's body does not *point* to theological significance but rather *is* the significance of the story.

A gleaming starting place is the dazzling clothes of Jesus that signify a shift into godhead, explored expertly by Candida R. Moss.[56] Mark emphasizes Jesus's clothes with an unusual amount of detail. They are dazzlingly white so much that no one on earth could achieve this brilliance. These garments resemble Athena's transformation to herdsman, where her feet shine even as a human. Another relevant story that tells of a corporeal transformation is Demeter in her *Homeric Hymn* (seventh-to-sixth century BCE). Demeter becomes an old woman when she enters into house of Keleos, and then: "the goddess changed her stature and her looks, thrusting old age away from her . . . from the divine body of the goddess a light shone afar . . . so that the strong house was filled with brightness as with lightning."[57] The vocabulary is different from Mark, but the visual descriptions resonate. This is also true in Iphis's masculinization when lights flash and horns sound in Isis's temple. The pattern is clear; corporeal metamorphoses often include shining, flashing, brightness, and lights, *and* they sometimes include gender transformations. Jesus's clothes follow this pattern as they shine, gleam, and dazzle, firmly anchoring Jesus's divinity and signaling a potential gender transformation.

Another important element of the Transfiguration is the presence of ancestors, Moses and Elijah. The search for trans ancestors—or trancestors—is tried and true for gender variant people.[58] While perhaps a throwback to an earlier stage of trans awareness, trancestors still provide significant anchoring for trans communities today. An appeal to *ancient* sources, though, is relatively rare in the emerging trans canons; a cursory glance through the indices of both volumes of *The Transgender Studies Reader* yields very few entries for the ancient world or the Bible with Susan Stryker, Leslie Feinberg, and Mary Weismantel as exceptions. Weismantel also affirms how important it is to look for ancestors,

---

Demeter (*Homeric Hymn II* to Demeter 92–97, 101–102), and Aphrodite (*Homeric Hymn V to Aphrodite* 84–87). Also see the comprehensive appendix in Joel Marcus, *Mark 1–8* (New Haven, CT: Yale University Press, 2002), 1108–18.

54. Lee, *Transfiguration*, 2.

55. It is common to interpret the transfiguration with a literary-theological lens connected to Jesus's baptism and resurrection, or in a comparison to the kenotic hymn in Philippians. Succinctly stated: "Thus the transfiguration embraces both the opening of Jesus' ministry and its future cosmic culmination," in Mary Ann Tolbert, *Sowing the Gospel: Mark's World in Literary-Historical Perspective* (Minneapolis: Fortress Press, 1996), 204.

56. Moss, "Transfiguration."

57. *Homeric Hymn to Demeter*, 275–281 (trans. Evelyn-White, LCL).

58. See discussion in the introduction.

prompting the ungendering of modern gender assumptions when evaluating the ancient record so that those voices can emerge. As Weismantel declares, "the gender diversity of the past matters for transgender activism."[59] The gender binaries that we have placed *on* the ancient world have caused us to sometimes see a binary where fluidity may have existed.

Moses and Elijah are revealed to be just such trancestors in the Transfiguration. Moses has a strong connection with the word *metamorphoō* in both Paul and Philo, each time associated with physical change and transformation. Additionally, recent scholarship on Moses has suggested that he may be genderqueer, or gender ambiguous.[60] As recapitulated in 2 Cor 3, where Paul drives home the changes of Christian believers, Moses is a figure who dons a veil. Veils were women's wear for millennia in the ancient world, which Paul dispenses advice about in 1 Cor 11:5–7.[61] It is true that men sometimes wore face coverings such as masks or other ritual clothing, but the veil in Exodus serves as a garment of clothing usually associated with women. Through the veil, Moses becomes feminized, or queered. As Rhiannon Graybill observes, this shifts Moses into a particular state of intimacy with God "away from the category of normatively masculine. In covering his face, Moses further erases the specificity of his identity. He also makes his body into a concealed, private, interior space, thereby suggesting a move outside of ordinary masculine performer and self-presentation."[62]

More broadly than only the veil, Jennifer L. Koosed notes that Moses may be seen as a gender ambiguous character in other ways: "his gender shifts and changes—more 'masculine' as a leader of the people and husband to his human wife, more 'feminine' in his relationship to Yahweh—he is even cast as Yahweh's wife."[63] Roland Boer sees Moses and God in a homoerotic relationship, in which both Moses and God emerge with a gender identity of both masculine and feminine, perhaps even as nonbinary.[64] The gender and body of Moses is flexible and shifting in Exodus, and this is reflected in Paul, Philo, and Mark.

---

59. Weismantel, "Transgender Archaeology," 321.

60. Recent scholarship contains fascinating discussions around Moses's gender. Rhiannon Graybill explores the events in Moses's life in which his body is vulnerable, destabilizing hegemonic masculinity. She traces the fluidity of Moses's body, showing that the transformation in Exod 34 "distances him from the other Israelites, socially and physically, and makes him more like Yahweh" (see Rhiannon Graybill, "Masculinity, Materiality, and the Body of Moses," *BibInt* 23:4–5 (2015): 529–30). Koosed points out that Moses's relationship to YHWH may be seen in a wifely, or feminine, way; Jennifer L. Koosed, "Moses, Feminism, and The Male Subject," in *The Bible and Feminism: Remapping the Field*, ed. Yvonne Sherwood (London: Oxford University Press, 2017), 234. Also relevant are Howard Eilberg-Schwartz, *God's Phallus and Other Problems for Men and Monotheism* (Boston: Beacon Press, 1994); Brian Charles DiPalma, "De/Constructing Masculinity in Exodus 1–4," in *Men and Masculinity in the Hebrew Bible and Beyond*, ed. Ovidiu Creangă (Sheffield: Sheffield Phoenix Press, 2010), 36–53.

61. The verbal *katakalyptō* in 1 Cor 11:5–7, 13; the noun *kalymma* in 2 Cor 3:13–16.

62. Graybill, "Masculinity," 531. The Hebrew word that describes Moses's radiant face is the verbal *qāran*, similar to the cognate noun "horn," *qeren*, giving rise to interpretations of Moses with literal horns on his head. Graybill comments intertextually on this connection: "the light that streams forth is literally incorporated into Moses, becoming an extension of his body" (Graybill, "Masculinity" 530).

63. Koosed, "Moses," 234.

64. Roland Boer, "Yahweh as Top: A Lost Targum," in *Queer Commentary and the Hebrew Bible*, ed. Ken Stone (Cleveland: Pilgrim Press, 2001), 75–105. See also Koosed, "Moses," 234.

Similarly, Elijah undergoes a change from human to angelic in later Jewish and Islamic mystical traditions. The presupposition for this transformation is that Elijah does not die a physical death but instead is taken to heaven in a chariot of fire (2 Kgs 2:11), gradually becoming associated with the archangel Sandalphon.[65] While evidence for this post-dates the Gospel of Mark by several centuries, the later traditions of Elijah undergoing such a radical bodily transformation are more than suggestive.[66] It is uncertain if an earlier version of Elijah's transformation was available in the first century, but ancestral traditions build and take shape over time. Both Elijah and Moses appear in the role of ancestors with deep experiences of changing bodily forms.

Still more fascinating connections to the Transfiguration and bodily changes are found in stories in the early Christian apocrypha in which Jesus appears in multiple forms to followers. Often coined as "polymorphic" appearances,[67] such bodily changing theophanies occur in works such as the *Gospel of Peter*, *Gospel of Philip*, and *Acts of John*.[68] Paul Foster understands "polymorphism" as intimately related to singular instances of metamorphosis, usually in post-resurrection accounts.[69] It is the second century CE *Acts of Peter* that tells a charming story of Jesus's appearance directly connected to the Transfiguration. Peter recalls his own experience at the transfiguration, acknowledging that Jesus "was moved to show himself in another shape and to be seen in the form of a man."[70] After his retelling, a group of blind widows comes to Peter. He asks them to see Jesus with their inner eyes, then prays, after which the room brightens as if with lightning, and the people in the room were overwhelmed. The light enters the eyes of the widows and empowers them to see. The widows have visions of Christ in several different forms: as a young boy, as an old man and as an adolescent. While Jesus does not appear as trans in the early Christian apocrypha, it is apparent that early Christians were comfortable with Jesus in multiple bodily forms.

Mark is suggestive of Jesus's transness. Clothing, divinity, and trancestors offer a glimpse of potentiality for a trans identity. Other ancient stories are

---

65. A compilation in English is found in Howard Schwartz, *Tree of Souls: The Mythology of Judaism*, annotated edition (Oxford: Oxford University Press, 2007), 197–98. The Jewish sources are b. ʻErub 45a; b. Moʼed Qaṭ. 26a; Seder Olam 2, 17; Zohar 2:197a; Genesis Rabbah 21:5; Pesiq. Rab Kah. 9:76a.

66. A wide view of Jewish and early Christian literature shows corporeal transformations. Humans turn into angels, such as Enoch from Gen 4–5 becoming the angel Metatron in Pseudepigraphal and Rabbinical materials. Similar angelic transformations happen to Adam, Seth, Enoch, Noah, Melchizedek, Jacob, Moses, and David. Such a transformation does not include gender, but it points to the tradition of bodily transformation in association with religious contexts in early Christianity and Judaism. See chapter 3 in Kevin P. Sullivan, *Wrestling with Angels: A Study of the Relationship between Angels and Humans in Ancient Jewish Literature and the New Testament* (Leiden: Brill, 2004).

67. Lee defines polymorphy as the ability of gods to appear in multiple forms, sometimes simultaneously, through the process of metamorphosis in Lee, *Jesus' Transfiguration*, 176.

68. Paul Foster, "Polymorphic Christology: Its Origins and Development in Early Christianity," *JTS* 58:1 (2007): 66–99.

69. Foster briefly explores the Transfiguration in Matthew; Foster, "Polymorphic Christology," 67.

70. *Acts of Peter* 20 in Wilhelm Schneemelcher, ed., *New Testament Apocrypha, Vol. 2: Writings Relating to the Apostles Apocalypses and Related Subjects*, trans. R. Mcl Wilson, rev. ed. (Louisville, KY: Westminster John Knox Press, 1992), 303.

forthright about gender transformations of both gods and humans, and interestingly, the stories explored above do not comment on the rarity of such an event or on any fixed category of gender that is being violated. If, however, a gender transition is visible in the Transfiguration, why would Mark simply not say so? A few reasons might exist. Mark is naturally terse with the famous emphasis on secrecy. The Gospel alludes and foreshadows rather than drawing outright conclusions; Mark is an instructive Gospel precisely *because* it shows rather than tells. Whether the Transfiguration originates as a pre-Markan tradition or is an original composition, it is multifaceted, with Jewish and Greek motifs that draw the reader in to the *experience* of the event. Ancient listeners would have been clued in automatically about the multiple layers of metamorphoses from Hellenistic Jewish and Greco-Roman stories. The contemporary trans Christians who initially alerted me to the possibility of a trans Jesus in the Transfiguration likewise sensed the possibility. All listeners to the Gospel can understand the body of Jesus in the Transfiguration without having to be told directly *what* the body of Jesus is.

Yet the most obvious clue that a gender transformation occurs is the very body of Jesus. To reiterate, the combination of the word *metamorphoō*, the inclusion of body-changing Moses and Elijah, plus the divine theophany packs a punch that points to the very body of Jesus. Something happens to Jesus's body that leaves the disciples terrified.[71] The combination of the powerful vocabulary and the setting of a divine revelation might suggest to ancient readers that Jesus's body undergoes a radical change, similar to Athena, Tiresias, Moses, Elijah, or Iphis. The bright lights, the uncontained godhead of Jesus, and the presence of other body-changing ancestors leads to an unspoken suggestion that Jesus is a deity who is transgender, and more than this, multi-gendered. Not only this, Jesus is also a deity who affirms all listeners past and present of the Gospel. Jesus becomes "she" and "they."

The time-honored connection of the Transfiguration to the baptism and resurrection strengthen this connection. The transness of the story brings together the past, present, and future, securing Jesus as trans woman. The link to the past begins with the arrival of the trancestors and in the echo of Jesus's baptism with the divine pronouncement in 9:7: "This is my Son, the Beloved." This raises a sticky point. If Jesus is, as I propose, experiencing a gender transition, why would God still call Jesus "Son"? I see several possibilities within a trans framework to understand this pronouncement. First, the refusal of a parent to identify a child by their proper pronouns and name after transition is depressingly common. Many trans people experience dead naming, where friends and family refuse to use their chosen name and pronouns. Perhaps God here is an example of an obtuse parent, or a deliberately stubborn one, who doesn't recognize the gender identity of the child. A second possibility is a softer suggestion; God

---

71. A helpful analysis is George Aichele and Richard Walsh, "Metamorphosis, Transfiguration, and the Body," *BibInt* 19 (2011): 263.

is *unaware* of Jesus's gender expression or confirmation. A cloud overshadows Jesus, the ancestors, and the disciples in 9:7, and it is possible that God does not see Jesus's femme, or multi-gendered, form through the thickness of the cloud; in this case, Moses and Elijah serve to protect Jesus from a potentially disapproving parent. A third possibility illuminates the gender complexity of Jesus's transfiguration, namely that Jesus has expressed themselves as *all* genders in the resurrected form, including a male form, a female form, a nonbinary form, an intersex form, and more. In this case, calling Jesus "Son" is incomplete but certainly not inappropriate.

The Transfiguration also points forward to the resurrection, and it is commonly understood that the disciples witness a resurrected Jesus. Some scholars postulate that what terrifies the disciples is a vision of the resurrected body of Jesus.[72] While this is possible, it is a weak argument; why should a resurrected body produce terror unless they are also seeing a crucified body? As Moss points out, the reactions of humans in the presence of a divine body changing event often produces fear,[73] and, indeed, a rapidly changing body would naturally be unsettling.

Yet, this is not all. The connection of the Transfiguration to the baptism and resurrection of Jesus also exists apart from normal linear time. The past, present, and future distill into a particular moment outside of time defying a linear and binary understanding of either the body or gender. This is a queer time, a trans time, in which the past and future reveal the many gender identities that Jesus can inhabit.[74] Such a revelation is possible in this protective, trans space in which trancestors support Jesus and the resurrected body of Jesus is visible. With linear time set aside, Jesus can experience a resurrected trans body, plus more, experiencing the full range of human possibility. Jesus, indeed, becomes ungendered. The return to normal time is indicated in 9:8 when the disciples suddenly no longer see the trancestors, but only Jesus. While the disciples do not comprehend, the readers *are* able to understand what the text does not say explicitly: Jesus is trans, and she is glorious.

WHAT DIFFERENCE DOES IT MAKE?

What difference does it make if "trans" is revealed in the Transfiguration? Above I cultivate an analysis to suggest that the ancient context supports a reading of Jesus as trans in Mark 9:1–9. Some dimensions of the interpretation, though, live in the realm of theological imagination. These are in conversation with the

---

72. For instance, "we have to see the Transfiguration as being in some sense connected with the Resurrection of Jesus. . . I am of the opinion that in the Transfiguration the disciples receive a vision of how Jesus will be after his resurrection" (Chris Knights, "Metamorphosis and Obedience: An Interpretation of Mark's Account of the Transfiguration of Jesus," *ExpTim* 121:5 [2010]: 220).

73. Moss, "Transfiguration."

74. See the delightful exploration of time in Jaeda Calaway's chapter in this collection.

historical and theoretical analysis above, but not limited to it. Historical analyses may reveal the transness of the story, but trans experiences also illuminate the story in new ways. The potentiality of a trans experience at the Transfiguration casts a wide net for trans visibility among believers who value this story.

The connection of the Transfiguration with the resurrection brings up significant points that are relevant to trans Christians. Again, Mark's Gospel is a classic example of showing rather than telling. As explored above, clothing (*ta imatia*) in 9:3 indicates Jesus's godhead and transformation. The term is a plural and can mean either an outer garment, such as a cloak, or simply stand as a gender-neutral word for generic clothing. The same word is used at the crucifixion to refer to the garments that are divided by casting lots (15:24). Clothing is again important in the sparse resurrection story in Mark with the appearance of the young man in a white (*leukos*) robe, echoing the divinity of Jesus's clothes in the Transfiguration. This thread of clothing occurs in stories where Jesus undergoes radical transformation: Transfiguration, death, and resurrection. Clothing as a sign of resurrection has theological significance, especially for trans people for whom new wardrobes often mark significant points of transition.

The trancestors also provide important support for Jesus as she transitions. Moses and Elijah both experience bodily transformations from human to angel, and Moses is a genderqueer, veil-wearing prophet/prophetess. The desire of many trans people for trancestors to support their gender confirmation has been noted, particularly by Weismantel and others, and Jesus is no exception. Both Moses and Elijah could provide guidance for Jesus in the startling transformation from human to divine and male to female. Moses, in particular, could provide support for Jesus as she reckons with her body in various stages of transition. In an imaginative rendering of the scene, Moses might have assisted Jesus in adjusting her veil, or given her advice on what clothing to wear for the circumstances.[75]

Clothing and trancestor support are present for Jesus's gender confirmation. For many trans people, gender confirmation *is* a resurrection that is not metaphorical but concretely tangible. Countless trans individuals have told me that transition saved their lives from suicide or social death. Trans bodies often metamorphize and change, gloriously, not in one divine moment but over weeks, months, or years to have the exterior body match an inward identity. The suggestion of Jesus's changing body, inclusive of a femme, intersex, or a nonbinary body, is an affirmation but not a prescription for trans bodies today. Jesus's own dazzling, queer, trans body in the Transfiguration connects the past, present, and future, showcasing the body in its many forms and stages of transition. Trans Christians indeed *are* like Jesus when they transition their clothing, hair, styles, and bodies. The resurrection that the Transfiguration points to occurs in the individual lives of trans believers in the process of resurrection through transition, gender confirmation, and living authentically.

75. A common motif in stories of gender confirmation today is advice from elders about what to wear, and the light-hearted often humorous stories of dressing with the care of one who has navigated this road before.

Another element that bears further reflection in lived experience is that of the strict instruction to the disciples to keep the Transfiguration secret in 9:9. While certainly adhering to the Markan theme of secrecy, this also has another layer. Some trans readers may experience this instruction as one to stay hidden and closeted. Others, though, may see it as confirmation of their own privacy, an invitation to be selective about revealing their own transformations. This is a crucial means of safety for many trans people who face risks due to gender expression. The order to the disciples to keep quiet serves as a safety mechanism for Jesus and to empower trans Christians to be selective with whom they trust their trans stories until the day arrives when all see the beauty of the trans body of Jesus.

Circling back to the original question: Is it possible to interpret the Transfiguration as a transgender experience? Undoubtedly, yes. The ancient sources point to the dazzling array of gender transitions and transformations in the ancient world, and seeing Jesus as another figure who appears as both god and trans is supported in the milieu of ancient evidence. For those invested in the incarnation of Jesus, this is good news. The weight of evidence shows a gender transformation in the timeless space of the Transfiguration, but undoubtedly this space is not *limited* to Jesus as trans. Gender analysis should always be intersectional, and the future contributions of the Transfiguration in terms of race, dis/ability, and class analyses are doors that will open even wider as ancient characters continue to be ungendered. It is my hope that reading the Transfiguration as a trans experience is empowering for readers of all gender identities.

Chapter 7

Grace, Truth, and Danger
Toward an Africana Queer Trans-Figuration of John 1:14

MINENHLE NOMALUNGELO KHUMALO

AND ERIC A. THOMAS

IN THE BEGINNING WAS THE TRANS*[1]

In this essay, we read the Gospel of John in solidarity with Black and brown nonbinary, gender nonconforming, and trans* persons whose lived experiences have been underrepresented in biblical studies.[2] We are Black queer scholars whose research, pedagogy, and embodiments prioritize activist interventions for the freedom, flourishing, and futures of queer people of color, in and across African diasporas. In our praxis of Africana queer futurity, the liberation of the community, and striving toward multiple versions of life more abundant in our everyday living, as in Jesus's proclamation in John 10:10, we are incomplete without our trans* siblings. In consideration of the Johannine prologue, we

---

1. Throughout this essay we use *trans** as a descriptive term to signify a multiplicity of subject positions within the spectrum of transgender lived experiences. Following Tompkins, "Trans* is thus meant to include not only identities such as transgender, transsexual, trans man, and trans woman that are prefixed by trans- but also identities such as genderqueer, neutrios, intersex, agender, two-spirit, cross-dresser, and genderfluid." Avery Tompkins, "Asterisk," *TSQ* 1:1–2 (2014): 26–27.

2. This essay is revised from a paper presented at the Society for Biblical Literature Annual Meeting in San Diego, 2019.

acknowledge biblical scholarship that reads Jesus as Wisdom/Sophia,[3] as a crossdressing drag king,[4] and as Jesus's "coming out as the Word of God."[5] This essay contributes to these discourses from the intersection of Africana queer biblical interpretation and transgender studies as "an attempt to think more precisely about the connections within blackness and transness in the midst of ongoing black and trans death and against the backdrop of the rapid institutionalization of trans studies."[6]

From the beginning, we declare that Black Trans Lives Matter, and so does radical allyship in care. Our intervention bears witness to the grace, truth, and danger inherent in Black trans* lives through the transitivity[7] of the Johannine Jesus. We offer our allyship in care through the spirit of IsiZulu *ukuhlanganisa* that we define as the practice of bringing together and bringing connection between, with the strength of the struggle, for the purpose of our well-being. Africana queer well-being is linked with communal care webs that are embodied through intra-dependent physical and spiritual wholeness, as defiant and resilient practices of joy.[8] Our allyship as biblical scholars with the trans* community is a joy that we take with us, even as we name and disrupt the dangers that biblical (mis)readings have produced for queer and trans* experiences. This is a joy that we understand to be inextricably linked to *just* (as in justice) being and livable lives. Our allyship with trans* communities acknowledges that queer, trans, disabled, and indigenous people of color "stand at crossroads, between both the gifts and the unexpected, inevitable collapses of work, and we have the opportunity to dream and keep dreaming ways to build emergent, resilient care

---

3. See, for example, Raymond E. Brown, *The Gospel according to John I–XII* (Garden City, NY: Doubleday, 1966); Adela Yarbro Collins, "New Testament Perspectives: The Gospel of John" *JSOT* 22 (1982): 47–53; Martin Scott, *Sophia and the Johannine Jesus* (Sheffield: Sheffield Academic Press, 1992); Sharon Ringe, *Wisdom's Friends: Community and Christology in the Fourth Gospel* (Louisville, KY: Westminster John Knox Press, 1999); Colleen M. Conway, "Gender Matters in John," in *A Feminist Companion to John*, vol. 2, ed. Amy-Jill Levine with Marianne Blickenstaff (Cleveland: Pilgrim Press, 2003), 79–103; Shelley Matthews, Cynthia Briggs Kittredge, and Melanie Johnson-DeBaufre, eds. *Walk in the Ways of Wisdom: Essays in Honor of Elisabeth Schüssler Fiorenza* (Harrisburg, PA: Trinity Press International, 2003); and Johnson-DeBaufre, *Jesus among Her Children: Q, Eschatology, and the Construction of Christian Origins* (Cambridge, MA: Harvard University Press, 2005).

4. Tat-siong Benny Liew, "Queering Closets and Perverting Desires: Cross-Examining John's Engendering and Transgendering Word across Different Worlds," in *They Were All Together in One Place?: Toward Minority Biblical Criticism*, ed. Randall C. Bailey, Tat-siong Benny Liew, and Fernando F. Segovia (Atlanta: SBL, 2009), 251–88.

5. Robert E. Goss, "John," in *The Queer Bible Commentary*, ed. Deryn Guest, et al. (London: SCM Press, 2006), 550.

6. C. Riley Snorton, *Black on Both Sides: A Racial History of Trans Identity* (Minneapolis: University of Minnesota Press, 2017), 7.

7. Following Snorton, "transitive [should be defined] not only as a term that articulates the quality of 'passing into another condition, changeable, changeful; passing away, transient, transitory,' but also in terms of the mechanics of grammar, in which the transitive refers to the expression of an action that requires a direct object to complete its sense of meaning." Snorton, *Black on Both Sides*, 5. We read the Johannine Jesus's scriptural trans-formations as both indicting and exceeding concrete notions of gender, capitalistic productivity, and imperial Christian heteronormative teleology.

8. See Leah Lakshmi Piepzna-Samarasinha, *Care Work: Dreaming Disability Justice* (Vancouver: Arsenal Pulp Press, 2018).

webs."[9] Following Lindsey Stewart, the insistence of joy is also a Black queer refusal of "the impulses (or, more strongly, mandates) to emphasize sorrow and mute joy, to dial down our pleasure and turn up our pain, in pursuit of white, northern liberal allies."[10] In this essay, then, we take up the allied practice of sharing joy as a practice that "forms a bridge between the sharers which can be the basis for understanding much of what is not shared between them, and lessens the threat of their difference."[11]

Furthermore, we recognize that this essay is more than an interpretive study in contextual biblical hermeneutics; it understands that life and death decisions are made according to how marginalized communities reclaim and redeploy scriptures for generative theological use. In this ethos, we are inspired by Justin Sabia-Tanis who writes:

> I have heard a number of trans folks state that, for them, transition was primarily a spiritual process. This assessment is not true for all trans-gendered people, of course. For some of us, however, transitioning is a time of deepening spirituality and a journey to come home to ourselves in body, mind, and spirit. This time can include a sense of learning more about the divine as we learn more about ourselves, and may mean finally coming to terms with the idea of being a child of God, put on this earth for a purpose, or simply arriving at self-acceptance. While some people may view religious faith as contrary to the development of a transgendered identity, for many of us faith is a critical component of our transitions and the strength that we draw upon to live in this world as gender-variant people.[12]

Following Sabia-Tanis above, we contend that the process of transitioning can be understood as a time filled with divine grace, as we seek to live into our truth (cf. John 1:14), cognizant of the dangers of being misread or misunderstood. Africana queer time is unapologetically out of synch with straight time.[13] Rather, it is almost always communal potential time. In solidarity with our trans* siblings, we appreciate that all of us are at various points of being and becoming, regardless of gender identity or expression. This epistemological and spiritual counter-knowledge disrupts cis-gendered notions that one goes from

---

9. Piepzna-Samarasinha, *Care Work*, 35.

10. Lindsey Stewart, *The Politics of Black Joy: Zora Neale Hurston and Neo-Abolitionism* (Evanston, IL: Northwestern University Press, 2021), 8.

11. Audre Lorde, "Uses of the Erotic: The Erotic as Power," in *Sister Outsider: Essays and Speeches* (Trumansburg, NY: Crossing Press, 1984), 56. See Eric A. Thomas, "The Futures Outside: Apocalyptic Epilogue Unveiled as Africana Queer Prologue" in *Sexual Disorientations: Queer Temporalities, Affects, Theologies*, ed. Kent L. Brintnall, Joseph A. Marchal, and Stephen D. Moore (New York: Fordham University Press, 2018), 90–112.

12. Justin Sabia-Tanis, *Trans-Gender: Theology, Ministry, and Communities of Faith* (Eugene, OR: Wipf and Stock Publishers, 2018), 130.

13. "Queerness's time is a stepping out of the linearity of straight time. Straight time is a self-naturalizing temporality. Straight time's 'presentness' needs to be phenomenologically questioned, and this is the fundamental value of a queer utopian hermeneutics. Queerness's ecstatic and horizontal temporality is a path and a movement to a greater openness to the world" (José Esteban Muñoz, *Cruising Utopia: The Then and There of Queer Futurity* [New York: New York University Press, 2009], 25).

point A to point B and arrives (e.g., female to male, novice to scholar, secular to sacred). Race, class, gender, language, geography, citizenship, and access to resources (monetary, medical, spiritual, communal) are among the factors that complexify the time of becoming. On the risks of being innocently or intentionally misunderstood, we learn from Audre Lorde who writes, "I have come to believe over and over again that what is most important to me must be spoken, made verbal and shared, even at the risk of having it bruised or misunderstood. That the speaking profits me, beyond any other effect."[14] We speak with respectful care in this essay in solidarity with those who are yet to come into their own voices at the intersection of biblical studies and transgender studies.

Yet, in our time, there is a sense of urgency to attend to Black trans* life, not in the policing of becoming but in the protection of (current and prospective) being. Anti-transness and Anti-Blackness in global public policies inject a lethal linearity and rigidity in the interpretations of being that moves passages of time against the beauty of becoming. In the spirit of *ukuhlanganisa*, following Amaryah Shaye's thinking, we take on a refusal to reconcile with straight time and its demands. Instead, we seek collective mobilizations (physically, socially, epistemologically, politically, linguistically, etc.) of life more abundant that is not about "being made a something" but finding joy in the vast possibilities of *just* being and becoming.[15]

In our interpretation, the Johannine Jesus is a transitive figure who by divine necessity inhabits multiple iterations of differing becoming. He is *ho logos* (the Word; John 1:1) that becomes *sarx* (flesh; 1:14) and is theologically deadnamed and outed first by John the Baptist, then by John's disciples, as the lamb of God who takes away the sins of the world—*ho amnos tou Theou ho airōn tēn hamartian tou kosmou* (1:29; 1:36). Deadnaming is the act of stubbornly or maliciously referring to a person, especially of trans* experience, by a name they no longer use for themselves, as in the name assigned to them at their birth. It is a violent act of trans-antagonism that rejects a trans* person's "I AM-ness." Examples of deadnaming include family members of origin that do not accept the names trans* folks choose for themselves, media reports of trans* murders that misgender and refer to the victims by their deadnames, and in legal circumstances, including the academy, places of employment, and identification materials (i.e., drivers licenses, passports).[16] In our essay, deadnaming is also understood as an expropriation of trans* being and becoming that violently reimposes stagnant heteronormative temporal linearity in and through misnaming/misgendering. It is a practice that (rein)forces hetero-chrononormative interpretations of bodies at the expense of trans* life, a forced reconciliation of difference that refuses

14. Lorde, "The Transformation of Silence into Language and Action," in *Sister Outsider*, 40.
15. See Amaryah Shaye, "Refusing to Reconcile, Part 2," https://womenintheology.org/2014/02/16/refusing-to-reconcile-part-2/.
16. Austen Hartke offers, "A note for trans allies: . . . It's never polite or appropriate to ask a trans person what their birth name was. If they feel comfortable enough with you to volunteer that information, they'll do it in their own time and in their own way." *Transforming: The Bible and the Lives of Transgender Christians* (Louisville, KY: Westminster John Knox Press, 2018), 75.

to connect to other(ed) being and becoming. In resistance to this, we use the isiZulu notion *ukuhlanganisa* (that is the practice of bringing together people, resources, and strategies into communal care webs for the sake of liberation) to name nonreconciliatory connections to difference and multiplicity, similar to Roberto Che Espinoza's perception of diffraction, which they deploy as a methodology for "combining disparate strands of thinking and being (and becoming) and finding a particular style of relationality in the in/betweenness of difference."[17] In Bantu theology, the naming of *umuntu* (human/person) is an extension of the naming of *ubuntu* (humanity/personhood) and understood to function as a copula to being.[18] That is, naming words do not mark an essentialized ontological existence, but denote (personal) referential formulations that perform *ukuhlanganisa*, bringing connections between human beings and the wider motions of being to and from humanizing life forces. Thus, deadnaming/misnaming/misgendering, within a Bantu ontological perspective, is a repudiation of the connections to life force and humanity that are constructed by different naming/gendering.

The theological deadnaming of Jesus in the Fourth Gospel attempts to interpolate Jesus's identity as the Passover lamb that was slain for the atonement of the world's sins. This idea of Jesus is necessary for those who believe in a sacrificial formation of salvation, that Jesus as the lamb of God who is born to die, helps construct a certain Christian identity that requires his shed blood on behalf of *their* salvation. We note that a similar investment in trans* death helps to reify heteronormative, hypermasculine, hyperfeminine, and internalized homophobic notions of "straight life," especially in the intersection of race, sexuality, class, gender, and religion. For some people, initiating trans* death is salvific, in order to know themselves as hegemonically masculine and feminine. This is a melancholic construction of identity where, according to Judith Butler, cis-gendered "masculinity and femininity within the heterosexual matrix are

---

17. Roberto Che Espinoza, "Difference, Becoming, and Interrelatedness: A Material Resistance Becoming," *CrossCurrents* 66:2 (2016): 282–83.

18. Valentin-Yves Mudimbe, *The Invention of Africa: Gnosis, Philosophy, and the Order of Knowledge* (Bloomington: Indiana University Press, 1988), 160. In the English language, copulae connect subjects to subject complements. For example, when one says, "I am trans*" and "I am Black," the copula "am" does not function as an expression of an essentialized state in the subject or the complement, but marks connections that can be made across subjective being. Hence, "am" can fully connect the subject, "I," to "trans*" and "Black" (and any other relevant subject complement) without contradiction. In isiZulu, the copula verb "to be" is not used in the present indicative form "am," instead isiZulu (and other Bantu languages) form copulative nouns using copulative particles, compounded with noun prefixes. For example, if one where to say "I am human" in isiZulu, they would use the copulative noun "ngingumuntu"—ngi (noun prefix, "I") + ngu (copulative particle, "am") + muntu (singular noun, "human"). Thus, the conception of ubuntu as copula does not name an essentialized state of human being, but is used as a term that indicates the historically present possibilities of human connection within the wider networks of being. So, when the concept of *ubuntu* is translated into English as "I am because we are," the phrase is translating a copulative noun that is not just naming subject relations but demonstrating that subjective identity is always a copulative formation of persons in communal modes of personhood.

strengthened through the repudiations that they perform."[19] Jesus never names himself the lamb of God in any of his "I AM" statements in the Gospel of John. From the moment of his outing and deadnaming in John 1:29, 36 and forward, Jesus is in mortal danger from attacks by the *religious leaders* on the one hand (5:16–18; 7:30, 32, 45–49; 8:59; 10:31, 39; 11:45–57; 18:1–5; 19:7, 12, 15–16), and state-sanctioned murder on a Roman cross on the other hand (19:1–5, 17–37). In the process of his transition, Jesus becomes a resourceful intermediary for his community as the bread of life (6:35); the light of the world (8:12); the door (10:9); the good shepherd (10:11); the resurrection and the life (11:25); the way, the truth, and the life (14:6); and the vine (15:5), much in the ways that the Street Transvestite Action Revolutionaries (in the 1970s), the Sylvia Rivera Law Project, the Trans Youth Equality Foundation, the Emergency Release Fund, and the Movement for Black Lives, among many others, are resourceful intermediaries for the trans* community.[20] In this regard, we interpret the precarious lived experiences of Black and brown trans* folk, illuminated by the Johannine Jesus, as a figural representation of trans* experience that likewise expresses grace (*charis*), truth (*alētheia*), and danger. In our Africana queer interpretation, Jesus's "I AM" statements are more than metaphors. They speak directly to and respond with resources for the needs of his community. These acts of radical care are not confined by straight time, neither are they defined by the deadnaming. Jesus, here, is practicing *ubuntu*, by claiming and practicing an identity that humanizes and empowers life-agency.[21] It reconnects dehumanized people to sacred being and becoming. Therefore, "I AM because we are" to the extent that Jesus's human incarnation cannot be fully understood or appreciated without the human communities he enters into. Jesus, in transitions from the Son of Humanity (*ho huios tou anthrōpou*; 1:51; 3:13–14; 5:27; 6:27, 53, 62; 8:28; 9:35; 12:23, 34; 13:31), to crucified Christ (19:1–5, 17–37), to resurrected Savior (20:1–31), indicates both the dangers of the material recognition of a trans* figured body and the insistence that death does not have the final word. We conclude that a politics of resilience and practice of allyship with radical care is crucial in order to stand with our trans* siblings. In other words, Black Trans Lives Matter!

BLACK TRANS LIVES MATTER

When the original version of this essay was presented at the Gender, Sexuality, and the Bible section of the Society for Biblical Literature's national meeting,

---

19. Judith Butler, "Melancholy Gender-Refused Identification," *Psychoanalytical Dialogue* 5 (1995): 170.

20. For more information, see The Sylvia Rivera Law Project, https://srlp.org/; The Trans Youth Equality Foundation, http://www.transyouthequality.org/; The Emergency Release Fund, https://www.emergencyrelease.org/; Movement for Black Lives, https://m4bl.org, especially https://m4bl.org/policy-platforms/end-the-war-trans/.

21. See n. 18.

the Human Rights Campaign (HRC) reported that at least twenty-seven trans* people had been murdered in 2019.[22] Most of them were Black transgender women younger than thirty years old. We speak some of their names: Dana Martin, Ellie Marie Washtock, Jazzaline Ware, Ashanti Carmon, Claire Legato, Muhlaysia Booker, Michelle "Tamika" Washington, Paris Cameron, Titi Gulley, Chynal Lindsey, Chanel Scurlock, Zoe Spears, Brooklyn Lindsey, Denali Berries Stuckey, Tracy Single, Bubba Walker, Kiki Fantroy, Jordan Cofer, Pebbles LaDime Doe, Jamagio Jamar Berryman, Itali Marlowe, Brianna "BB" Hill, Nikki Kuhnhausen, Yahira Nesby, Tracy Single, Bailey Reeves, Layleen Polanco, and Bee Love Slater. It is important to note that these are victims whose deaths have been reported; far more go unreported or misreported.

On Friday, September 6, 2019, transgender and nonbinary activist, actress, and model Indya Moore, one of the stars of the FX television show *Pose,* commemorated their deaths by wearing a pair of elaborate earrings that included a photo of each victim. She wore them because she was a guest of honor at the Daily Front Row Fashion Media Awards. The occasion, which was sponsored by fashion house Louis Vuitton, celebrated *Elle* magazine's cover of the year on which Moore appeared in the June 2019 issue. The event is significant because Moore is the first transgender person to appear on the cover of American *Elle* magazine. Moore began their remarks as follows, "All of our lives are so expensive, including mine and people like me. . . As you all know—or not—I am Black and I am trans. Some of you may be uncomfortable with the politics of my speech, and I won't apologize for that, because my life is politics."[23] Indeed, for most people of trans experience the personal is not only political, but often *necro*-political. Banners that demand "Stop Killing Trans People" are deployed on social media platforms, at marches and rallies, and even on T-shirts. Even though popular television shows and streaming series like "*Pose,*" "Orange Is the New Black," and "RuPaul's Drag Race" have introduced specially curated versions of trans, gender nonconforming, and drag experiences to wide audiences, the everyday flesh and blood experiences of the unfamous (or infamous) are much more precarious. As CeCe McDonald notes:

> I feel like trans women are being acknowledged and are in the spotlight in ways that are not just about depicting trans women as stereotypes. We're human beings. But this trans visibility also puts trans women in unsafe positions. With the height of trans visibility has also come the height of trans violence and murder. And so it's very important for people to acknowledge that yes, it is important to see these figures in the spotlight,

22. Human Rights Campaign, "Violence against the Transgender Community in 2019," https://www.hrc.org/resources/violence-against-the-transgender-community-in-2019 (accessed September 28, 2019).
23. Sabienna Bowman, "'Pose' Star Indya Moore's Earrings Paid Tribute to Black Transgender Women who Were Murdered in 2019," September 7, 2019, https://www.bustle.com/p/pose-star-indya-moores-earrings-paid-tribute-to-black-transgender-women-who-were-murdered-in-2019-photos-18734027.

but it is also necessary to recognize that this "trans tipping point" is bringing an unsettling rate of violence toward trans women.[24]

Correspondingly, the HRC reports that most victims of fatal violence "were killed by acquaintances, partners and strangers, some of whom have been arrested and charged, while others have yet to be identified. Some of these cases involve clear anti-transgender bias. In others, the victim's transgender status may have put them at risk in other ways, such as forcing them into unemployment, poverty, homelessness and/or survival sex work."[25] The ubiquitous dangers faced by trans* people relate to their personal everyday contexts, to the extent that trans* lives, with gendered presentations that follow different trajectories of becoming, have come to embody violent, all-too-frequently fatal, marginalization. In truth, for trans* people, the personal is often indeed necropolitical.

Jin Haritaworn, Adi Kuntsman, and Silvia Posocco in the collected volume *Queer Necropolitics* define the term (necropolitics) as "a concept-metaphor that illuminates and connects a range of spectacular and mundane forms of killing and of 'letting die' while simultaneously radically reimagining the meanings, purchase, and stakes inherent in 'queerness' as a category of analysis and critique."[26] Jasbir Puar, in her readings of Michel Foucault, Judith Butler, and Achille Mbembe, centers race and sexuality simultaneously for the reproduction of relations of living and dying to "keep taut the tension between biopolitics and necropolitics."[27] Puar defines biopolitics as relating to "the management of life—the distribution of risk, possibility, mortality, life chances, health, environment, quality of living—the differential investment of and in the imperative to live."[28] Conversely, necropolitics can be understood to concern questions of "death decoupled from the project of living—a direct relation to killing that renders impossible any subterfuge in a hallucinating disavowal of death in modernity."[29] In other words, in cisheteronormative culture, lives worth caring for and protecting are filtered through the sieves of race, gender, sexuality, nationalism, and U.S. sexual exceptionalism. These same sieves dictate the distributions of death and dying. Because of this, we are attentive to the conditions of living and dying that Black trans* people experience in the United States. These existential factors form the basis of queer color critique that is elaborated in transgender studies.

We assert that Black trans* persons are killed and let die for several reasons including (but not limited to): 1. Trans antagonist and queer-phobic rejection from their communities of origin; 2. Marginalization, erasure, and racial discrimination within the hierarchy of LGBTQIA+ politics and organizing; 3.

---

24. Miss Major Griffin-Gracy and CeCe MacDonald in Conversation with Toshio Meronek, "Cautious Living: Black Trans Women and the Politics of Documentation," in *Trap Door: Trans Cultural Production and the Politics of Visibility*, ed. Tourmaline, Eric A. Stanley, and Johanna Burton (Cambridge, MA: MIT Press, 2017), 26.
25. HRC, "Violence against the Transgender Community in 2019."
26. Jin Haritaworn, Adi Kuntsman, and Sylvia Posocco, "Introduction," in *Queer Necropolitics* (New York: Routledge, 2014), 4.
27. Jasbir Puar, *Terrorist Assemblages: Homonationalism in Queer Times* (Durham, NC: Duke University Press, 2007), 35.
28. Puar, *Terrorist Assemblages*, 32.
29. Puar, 33.

Systematic vulnerability to obtain legal employment, health care, state-issued identification, and basic advocacy. As Dean Spade writes, "the most marginalized trans populations have the least protection from violence, experience more beatings and rapes, are imprisoned at extremely high rates, and are more likely to be disappeared and killed."[30] It is with this existential reality that we redact the Johannine prologue. The transing of Word to flesh, *logos* to *sarx*, crucified Christ to resurrected Savior, is a becoming of grace, truth, and danger for lives marked for death. Recognizing the divinity of a becoming that conquers the world for the cultivation of intra-dependent communities of care approaches Marquis Bey's theorization of *traniflesh*. According to Bey:

> Traniflesh emerges as an impossibly possible space where we know not what will arise because it does not rely on normative framework. As an emergent force and "capacitating structure for alternative modes of being," traniflesh offers different formations and matterings, different and differing subjectivities, of material and symbolic life. Traniflesh is an otherwise way of being that exceeds the categorizing logics of race and gender, that exceeds "identities" and (dis)organizes around subversive world-building.[31]

Reading Jesus as a transitive figure (the transfiguration) in the Gospel of John allows us to imagine an impossibly possible space in which trans* siblings and allies find freedom, flourishing, and futures informed by life and life more abundantly.

SOME TRANS* THEOLOGICAL IMPLICATIONS OF JOHN 1:14 IN GRACE/TRUTH/DANGER

And the Word became flesh and dwelled among us, and we have seen his glory, the glory as of a father's only son, full of grace and truth.[32]

Our assertion of the Johannine Jesus's transfiguration as divine motion through grace, truth, and danger for the purposes of life and life more abundantly invites liberative theological reflection. In what follows, we bring together (*hlanganisa*) thoughts on the implications of the incarnation for communities who have been variously afflicted by hegemonic and erotophobic Christologies that are invested in the abjection of flesh, especially trans*, queer, Black, and brown flesh. Womanist theologian JoAnne Marie Terrill describes the incarnation of Jesus—the event of divine Word becoming flesh—as "God's *with-us-ness* (that is, God's

---

30. Dean Spade, *Normal Life: Administrative Violence, Critical Trans Politics, and the Limits of Law* (Durham, NC: Duke University Press, 2015), xiv.
31. Marquis Bey, "Black Fugitivity Un/Gendered," *The Black Scholar: Journal of Black Studies and Research* 49:1 (2019): 57.
32. Unless otherwise noted, all translations are our own.

decision to be *at-one* with us)."[33] Allen Dwight Callahan furthers this point by stating, "the incarnation has happened in history and in community; the incarnation has happened '*in us.*'"[34] In summary of these points, Eboni Marshall Turman writes, "acknowledging that 'Christ dwells in' humanity allows for an understanding of how grace can be given to humankind."[35] Furthermore, M. Shawn Copeland writes, "Jesus mediated God's presence among us through a body marked by race, gender, sex, sexuality, culture, and religion."[36] Within African (Bantu) Christologies, Jesus's incarnation in the flesh and "in us"—especially as a figure that mediates divine presence—also allows him to become our ancestor.[37] Although these African Christologies are still very attached to melancholic constructions of identity that characterize Jesus as "the perfect victim,"[38] a queer affirming vision of Bantu theology sees Jesus's ancestral character as one that inspires re/connective mediations of being. Our gestures to a queer affirming Bantu theology acknowledge the relative silence around transgender experience in African religious discourse. By presenting approaches to Bantu ontology and African Christologies, in the context of our allyship with Black trans* folk, we point to the urgent need for the transing of African theologies in light of African queer-phobia that perpetuates the violence of "corrective rape,"[39] constructs antihomosexuality legal and public policy,[40] and generally forwards a language that claims "gays are worse than terrorists."[41] As we understand trans* experience in these contexts, including in Sabia-Tanis above, we see the divine spark that sets one on the journey to harmonize their physical embodiment and gendered performance as an authentic presentation of self, is the process of Word becoming or transitioning into flesh. The process of coming home to ourselves is the becoming of Word enfleshed in a community of care, and thus, a practice of re/connecting to divine enfleshment guided by a memory of Jesus as *trancestor*.[42]

33. JoAnne Marie Terrell, *Power in the Blood? The Cross in the African American Experience* (Maryknoll, NY: Orbis Books, 1998), 125.
34. Allen Dwight Callahan, "The Gospel of John," in *True to Our Native Land: An African American New Testament Commentary*, ed. Brian Blount, Cain Hope Felder, Clarice J. Martin, and Emerson B. Powery (Minneapolis: Fortress Press, 2007), 187.
35. Eboni Marshall Turman, *Toward a Womanist Ethic of Incarnation: Black Bodies, the Black Church, and the Council of Chalcedon* (New York, NY: Palgrave Macmillan, 2013), 47.
36. M. Shawn Copeland, *Enfleshing Freedom: Body, Race, and Being* (Minneapolis: Fortress Press, 2010), 83; Sabia-Tanis, *Trans-Gender*, 130.
37. See Timothy Palmer, "Jesus Christ: Our Ancestor?" *African Journal of Evangelical Theology* 27 (2008): 65–75.
38. Kwesi Dickson, *Theology in Africa* (Maryknoll, NY: Orbis, 1984), 197.
39. Harvard Political Review, "South Africa's 'Corrective Rape' Problem," https://harvardpolitics.com/south-africas-corrective-rape-problem/.
40. Kapya Koama, "Beyond Adam and Eve: Jesus, Sexual Minorities and Sexual Politics in the Church in Africa," *JTSA* 153 (2015): 7–12.
41. Pambazuka, "Kenya: Bishop Says Gays Are Worse than Terrorists," https://www.pambazuka.org/gender-minorities/kenya-bishop-says-gays-are-worse-terrorists.
42. Lewis Reay defines the term *transcestor* as "an elision of trans and ancestor to signify those transgender characters and people who provide a history and prove that we have always been here" (in Reay, "Towards a Transgender Theology: Que(e)rying the Eunuchs," in *Trans/formations: Controversies in Contextual Theology*, ed. Marcella Althaus-Reid and Lisa Isherwood [London: SCM Press, 2009], 149 n. 1).

I'M (BE)COMING OUT! I WANT THE WORLD TO KNOW[43]

In the queer joy of biblical pleasures with language, we were wondering if there is something to be said about the translation of the verb *egeneto*[44] in John 1:14 and the presence of *erchomai* in John 1:27, 29?[45] To be clear, the question arises from Minenhle's rusty recognition of the Greek verb, an unwillingness to let a pun pass us by, and a consequent confusion about the relation between "became" and "came to pass." In the joyful queer art of failure to perform biblical philology, we consider these questions as a way of transing linguistic norms within biblical studies. As the question of *egeneto*'s translation in this context developed, we landed with a need to emphasize that it is important that Jesus as a trans* figure, is one who became and is becoming, rather than one who *came to pass*.[46] Yet it is also true that Jesus, the one through whom all things came into being (*panta di' autou egeneto*—1:3), filled with gracious transtemporal timing, is both coming after (*ho opisō mou erchomenos*—1:27) and toward ([*ton Iēsoun*] *erchomenon pros auton*—1:29) John the Baptist, when he is "clocked"[47] by the necropolitical logic of deadnaming Jesus the lamb of God (1:29, 36). Divine timing is circumscribed by a straight time that demands his death, disallowing the opportunity of simply becoming the Word made flesh. He cannot come to pass, and his passing continuously initiates the danger he will ultimately encounter upon crucifixion. As Kenyan novelist Ngũgĩ wa Thiong'o has noted, colonial impositions of European languages have forced colonized people to borrow constructions of meaning from the affective contexts of colonizers, thereby prioritizing the bodily capacity for meaning making of colonizers over that of indigenous peoples. For Ngũgĩ, and indeed for this essay, too, colonial significations are "branded" onto colonized people and are still repeated and preserved in the languages that we use (i.e. Lamb of God).[48] Different becoming and passing have entangled material forms for trans* people, recognizing, as Roberto Che Espinoza has, that "Language has by far been used to colonize bodies. In fact, the coloniality of language is one such strategy in controlling bodies."[49] Similarly, John the Baptist's annunciation brands Jesus with a (mis)recognition of his identity that is repeated and preserved in the language of biblical interpretation

---

43. This is a play on Diana Ross's legendary song, "I'm Coming Out," written by Nile Rogers, that has become an iconic queer anthem.

44. *Egeneto*, third-person singular aorist middle of *ginomai*, often translated as "to come into existence; to be created, exist by creation" as in, "the Word *became* flesh." Wesley J. Perschbacher, ed. *The New Analytical Greek Lexicon* (Peabody, MA: Hendrickson Publishers, 1990), 80.

45. *Erchomai*: first-person singular middle/deponent meaning to come, to go, to pass.

46. *Egeneto* is often translated as "was" or "came" or "happened"; for example, John 1:14.

47. "Clocked" in Black/brown transgender slang means that one is recognized as trans. If one is "unclockable," it means they can pass in public without their trans status being known or revealed. Dawn Ennis in *The Advocate* (February 4, 2016) writes, "for those of us in the trans world, the term 'clocked' is used to reflect that someone transgender has been recognized as trans, usually when that person is trying to blend in with cisgender people, and not intending to be seen as anything other than the gender they present." See "'Clocking' as Realizing or Understanding," https://www.merriam-webster.com/words-at-play/clock-new-senses-verb-usage.

48. Ngũgĩ wa Thiong'o, *Something Torn and New: An African Renaissance* (New York: Basic Civitas Books, 2009), 14.

49. Espinoza, "Difference, Becoming, and Interrelatedness," 281.

and liturgical practice. Thus, it would be significant that the *logos* transitions to *sarx* with a "coming to pass" that is entangled, at least for us, with language that triggers an awareness of questions of conformity with punitive, and even carceral notions of trans*ness and the necropolitics of passing. This necropolitics of passing literally means the difference between life or death, freedom or incarceration, for our trans* siblings. When Word becomes flesh through terminology that has linguistic relation to temporal spectrums of becoming, and marks a *logos* that has indeed become *sarx*, that is a Jesus whose time has not come. This necropolitics of passing is given (trans*) figuration in the Gospel of John. This strikes us as a question that may have consequences for thinking about the quasi-eschatological nature of queerness, to the extent that queerness is already but not yet. That is, we can make general associations of what transness and queerness are across space and time, but the specificities of queerness in space and time do not always move or synch with hegemonic chrononormativity. The Johannine Jesus's coming and becoming are in service to life and life more abundantly (10:10).[50]

Traniflesh Dwelling among Us

Marcella Althaus-Reid's *Indecent Christology* imagines a people's identity outside of heterosexualism and a Christ outside of binary categorical limitations. She writes, "In a Christology of a Bi/Christ we are considering two things. First, the reality of people's identity outside heterosexualism, and second, a pattern of thought for a larger Christ outside binary boundaries... In Christ there is a conjunction of divinity and humanity, and there is not just *The Christ* but a diverse Ultra-Christ, incarnated [located] in our specific time and communities."[51] The koine Greek verb *skēnoō* which is often translated as "dwelled" also means "tabernacle," or "spreads a tent." Althaus-Reid notes, "tents can change shape in strong winds, and their adaptability rather than their stubbornness is one of their greatest assets. The beauty of this God/tent symbolic is that it can help us to discover Christ in our processes of growth, the eventual transformations through unstable categories to be, more than anything else, a Christ of surprises."[52] The dangerous truth of this tent imagery for trans* folks is that "home" is not always a place where there is safety. Trans* people in their resilient adaptability reimagine home in various ways that are not necessarily homes of origin (as in he came to his own—John 1:11), rather home is where the trans* person is received (as in "I no longer call you slaves/servants.... Instead, I call you friends"—John 15:15). Horace L. Griffin, Episcopal minister and professor of pastoral care took up this scripture as the starting point for his monograph *Their Own Receive Them Not: African American Lesbians and Gays in Black Churches*.[53] John 1:11

---

50. John 10:10: "The thief comes only to steal and kill and destroy. I came that they may have life, and have it abundantly."
51. Marcella Althaus-Reid, *Indecent Theology: Theological Perversions in Sex, Gender, and Politics* (London: Routledge Press, 2000), 117.
52. Althaus-Reid, *Indecent Theology*, 120.
53. Horace L. Griffin, *Their Own Receive Them Not: African American Lesbians and Gays in Black Churches* (Cleveland: Pilgrim Press, 2006).

foreshadows chapter 15 where Jesus tells the disciples, "If the world hates you, remember that it hated me first . . . they will do these things to you on account of my name because they do not know him who sent me" (John 15:21). Multiple forms of violence have been done to trans* and queer people substantiated by hegemonic Christianity in the name of "a" Jesus whose *lambnesia* causes him to forget the plights of sexual and gender outlaws to heteronormativity.[54]

Jesus does not conform to singular being in the Gospel of John, and in fact John's Jesus does not conform to any of the other Jesuses in the New Testament. His speech is entirely different from the Synoptic Jesuses, and John's Jesus disrupts the canonical ordering of Jesus's being. This nonconformity means that John's Jesus becomes a different Jesus, who becomes different things at different times, even though his time, most of the time, has not come. Those differences unfold in context, an imperial context, to be exact, and they breed specific dangers. Even as the Gospel offers the high Christology of a preexisting incarnating logos, John's Jesus is seen as an important intervention in the tendency to ontologize Jesus into fixity. The Christology of the Gospel of John relocates processes of inclusion and exclusion in the navigation of Jesus's identity and community from formations of the flesh to ethical-spiritual formation while always attending to the material conditions of such formation.

Drawing on Althaus-Reid, this leads us to question whether the different nonconforming, arguably disorderly, becoming of the Johannine Jesus makes him an indecent Jesus, or does it make the Gospel of John an indecent Gospel, to the extent that the different nonconforming becoming of the Johannine Gospel exposes and is simultaneously fraught with grace, truth, and danger. We are also considering that it is worth noting that the figure of Jesus in the structural form of the narrative is often indistinguishable from the narrator. Not because we want to emphasize anything related to the question of the historicity of John's Jesus, but to note that the figure of Jesus in the Johannine Gospel is distinct but entangled. His identity is known, expressed, and actualized—in all its glory—through the context of the Johannine community, yet also, at risk of being consumed by and sacrificed for the community (as in the Gospel context and later church practices of Holy Communion). The Gospel of John, despite the interests and investment in Jesus, the preoccupation with witnessing his divinity, leaves the figure of Jesus vulnerable to a uniquely thorough exploitative and violent consumption of the perceived specialty of his divinity. These investments function to serve the community of Jesus's allies in his present and future con/textual temporal locations at the expense of his life both in word (text) and flesh (historical context). In other words, Jesus's identity is at risk of exploitation in both the context of the gospel story as well as in communities through history who have interpreted and made use of him. This issue indicates the need for us, as allies to trans* folks in our own contexts, then, to configure the lines of our own becomings along with the practices and narratives thereof

---

54. See Thomas, "The Futures Outside."

in relation to trans* figures in such a way that we are not consumptive voyeurs of trans* figured glory at the expense of trans* life, especially in a contemporary context where trans* folk are both more visible/famous than ever and also are in more danger than ever.

TRANIFESTING GRACE AND TRUTHS

We want to emphasize that fulfilling grace and truth means taking on a politics of resilience and practice of allyship with radical care. This involves the recognition of the complexity of time, the complexity of language, and the complexity of being and becoming that acknowledge trans* truths. Jesus in the Johannine resurrection narrative (20:1–18) models this care for Mary Magdalene. After Peter and the Beloved Disciple realize that the tomb is empty, they go home, but Mary remains behind and so does Jesus. Similarly, in the process of writing this essay Eric has waited for me (Minenhle) as I attend to the work of living, writing a dissertation, as well as caring for a child and self under the impoverishments of capitalist heteronormativity. I interrupt the rhetorical flow of our joint thinking in this essay to honor and rejoice in a queer academic consideration of care that Eric has embodied for and with me time and time again. This a practice of Africana queer futurity that holds space for each other in recognition of the different pacing of becoming. The crucified Christ trans*figures into the resurrected Savior not through divine transmutation, but through attentive care to Mary's trauma. As trancestor, Jesus connects us to radical practices of healing and provides resources and support for new visions of life, particularly where there has been harm. *Ukuhlanganisa*, that is, bringing this together in modes of solidarity with trans* studies and everyday experiences, we, too, can build activist networks of communal freedom, flourishing, and futures. Intra-dependent coalitions of care can be imagined and embodied when we recognize each others' grace and truths. In this regard, allyship for us means that we must be willing to transform those parts of ourselves, our practices, and our language that negate life and bring violence to processes of becoming. The importance of this mutual responsibility of working toward transformed and transformative arrangements of care is highlighted by Leah Lakshmi Piepzna-Samarasinha when they say:

> But as I hear my friends talking about how they're sure they'll die young, I wonder if changing the narratives around care might change their expectations of dying young. I think about what it would take to continue to build communities of care, where caring for each other is something we actually practice and build the structures to hold. I think of Loree Erickson's mutual aid care collective and how it is both a model of being cared for when the state fails and a place so many people in Toronto get brought into disabled community that is deeply joyful, sexy, and fun in a way that many people don't think of when they think of care. When I try to explain the care collective to folks outside Toronto, there's a silence—it's because

they can't quite imagine someone asking for and receiving help, including help that sees you naked and helps you with intimate acts, without shame and with joy. And I wonder—how would our belief that we could live rich, long disabled lives worth living change if we created more mutual aid collectives?[55]

As the Movement for Black Lives states, "Black life and dignity require Black political will and power. Despite constant exploitation and perpetual oppression, Black people have bravely and brilliantly been a driving force pushing toward collective liberation."[56] Black lives will not matter until Black trans* lives matter. Indeed, the mattering of all life is incomplete until Black trans* lives matter. This connects with Bey, who writes:

> Black and trans reference *movement* and cultivate space to live, to become-as-being, in this movement. They reference the process by which gender is unmoored and unmade as an otherwise way to become a subject in excess of gender. As we become, both in unanticipated ways and in ways imposed upon us, in addition to ways we self-determine, there is a displaced and ethereal movement within us that yearns to breach the bounds of this body that has been made without our consent.[57]

Ukuhlanganisa means to simultaneously name and speak to African contexts as we attend to the realities of queer folk in the African diaspora. Queer and trans* antagonisms across Africa and African diasporas are substantiated by hegemonic religious imaginations that deny grace and truth. These globalized movements of trans*phobia and erotophobia must be interrupted, disrupted, unsettled, and reimagined. As Sarojini Nadar and Adriaan van Klinken observe, "Religion is widely considered as one of the major forces fueling negative perceptions about and attitudes toward LGBT people, and particularly in Africa, religious moral claims against sexual diversity are combined with claims that such sexual diversity is 'un-African' and a Western import."[58] As biblical scholars of African descent, caring for ourselves and our communities of accountability, in and out of the continent, means taking on the commiment to interpret our texts in the name of life more abundantly for our people. This includes constructing counter narratives to cis-gendered heteronormative hegemony.

Thus, all the above points to the fact that realizing and enfleshing the vision of futures filled with abundance, nurtured by justice, and characterized by freedom necessitates collective mobilization that is open to being trans*ed. We insist that the repudiation of transness is not only dangerous to trans* lives, but it also stands in direct contradiction to common goodness and the movement

---

55. Piepzna-Samarasinha, *Care Work*, 131–32.
56. Movement for Black Lives, "End the War on Black People," https://m4bl.org/end-the-war-on-black-people/.
57. Bey, "Black Fugitivity Un/Gendered," 55.
58. Sarojini Nadar and Adriaan van Klinken, "'Queering the Curriculum': Pedagogical Explorations of Gender and Sexuality in Religion and Theological Studies," *JFSR* 34:1 (2018): 102.

of humanizing life forces for all human beings (*ubuntu*). Without a transing of our social, political, economic, and academic arrangements we, knowingly or unknowingly, bind ourselves to necropolitics and further systemic death-dealing. Academic guilds of biblical studies—as predominantly white cis-het institutions—have a duty of reparation for the harms biblical interpretation has caused. Above all else, the academic study of the bible must attend to the histories of violence we have inherited through our participation in the reading of a book that has been the basis of incalculable iterations of fatal discrimination, dehumanization, oppression, and negation. To be clear, as Michael Joseph Brown states, "I could have asserted that African American biblical hermeneutics needed to include the distinctive social location of black gays and lesbians, transvestites, and the transgendered, into their interpretive program, and many would have nodded in assent. If, however, the possibility of such a hermeneutical perspective rests entirely on the presence of these individuals in the guild, then their voices may never be heard."[59] That is, the work of subverting the narrative of white, cis-gendered, heteronormative hegemony cannot be left to Africana queer folk to do alone. Heteronormative cis-gendered whiteness must also be willing to transform itself for the sake of allyship. The duty to transform biblical narratives and biblical attitudes is, as it has always been, a matter of life and death. Our Africana queer hermeneutic responds to this duty with a defiant insistence on futures filled with joy and life more abundant for all of us, that cannot be realized without our trans* siblings!

---

59. Michael Joseph Brown, *Blackening of the Bible: The Aims of African American Biblical Scholarship* (Harrisburg, PA: Trinity Press International, 2004), 178.

Chapter 8

Trans Historiography and the Problem of Anachronism
Eunuchs and Other Non-men in Matthew 19:1–15 and 1 Corinthians 6–7

REBECCA WIEGEL

This chapter articulates a method of reading that can recover a history for trans people beyond the bounds of the modern, Western invention of that term. It will do this in several steps. First, it will articulate in brief the major problem with such efforts. Second, it will critically summarize and decenter modern, Western trans narratives to make room for a more abstract category. Third, it will assert a definition for an abstract, analytic category of "trans" suitable for use across cultures and in premodern settings. Fourth, it will turn to Matt 19:1–15 and then 1 Cor 6:9–7:40 (Christ's provocative praise of eunuchs for the kingdom of heaven and Paul's valorization of sexual renunciation) as helpful test cases for this analytic category—test cases that will both show this method at work in close readings and, at the same time, show how close readings in this vein can productively interpret biblical passages for feminist, queer, and trans readers of the text while remaining attentive to the text's literary and historical context.

In terms of the problem of anachronism, Elizabeth Reis, in her article on teaching transgender history, rightly comments that "Historians typically criticize those who use the past selectively to support political agendas."[1] Indeed,

---

1. Elizabeth Reis, "Teaching Transgender History, Identity, and Politics," *Radical History Review* 88 (2004): 166–77.

most of the earliest examples of trans historiography amount to identity politics.[2] Given that, like women's history and LGB history, trans people's stories were largely ignored or erased in twentieth-century historiography in the interest of modern cisheteronormative and androcentric politics, this search for the usable past is entirely understandable and deeply sympathetic. That does not, however, make it good history.[3] The social historian rightly wants to respect the identity categories of historical figures themselves—to take into account the purposes of the writers of a given time period and the huge range of means by which cultures construct and enforce sexual difference. There is due caution to avoid "colonizing" the past by the imposition of our categories, which contain our cultural narratives and assumptions, all of which threaten to distort the past in the interest of the present. This becomes more directly colonial when it is performed upon the pasts of non-Western societies.[4]

Recognizing this basic problem and the real danger of anachronism, Reis does propose a way to reframe the project; she states:

> While mindful of the perils of viewing history merely as a usable past, we must remain open to the beneficial influences of a "usable present." Present concerns enhance historical study, enabling us to see the past in a different

---

2. This can be seen in a diverse range of writings, starting with Richard Green, "Mythological, Historical, and Cross-Cultural Aspects of Transsexualism," in Harry Benjamin's seminal 1966 work *The Transsexual Phenomenon*, now reprinted in *Current Concepts in Transgender Identity*, ed. Dallas Denny (New York: Garland Publishing, 1998), 3–14. Green's work treats all past historical phenomena of gender crossing as being, in essence, transsexualism. In contrast, Leslie Feinberg, *Transgender Warriors: Making History from Joan of Arc to Dennis Rodman* (Boston: Beacon Press, 1996), interweaves significant personal narrative with a sweeping survey of transgender history—this identifies all surveyed trans people not as transsexuals, but as resistors against problematic hierarchies like monotheism, imperial politics, capitalism, and gender normativity. More recently, see G. G. Bolich, *Transgender History and Geography* (Raleigh, NC: Psyche's Press, 2007); and *Transgender and Religion* (Raleigh, NC: Psyche's Press, 2009), which operate on a straightforward (if problematic) equivalence between transgender phenomena and historical examples of cross-dressing.

3. Those who do theorize transgender historiography recognize this problem. See Genny Beemyn, "A Presence in the Past: A Transgender Historiography," *Journal of Women's History* 25 (2013): 113–21; and also her chapter "Transgender History," in *Trans Bodies, Trans Selves*, ed. Laura Erickson-Schroth (Oxford: Oxford University Press, 2014), 501–36, though her focus in both cases is on American history.

4. Thankfully, there is an abundance of truly superb scholarship dealing with trans phenomena outside of Western contexts that is deeply conscious of its post-colonial position, often criticizing Western scholarship on precisely this point. See Afsaneh Najmabadi, *Professing Selves: Transsexuality and Same-Sex Desire in Contemporary Iran* (Durham, NC: Duke University Press, 2014). *The Transgender Studies Quarterly* has also published several thematic issues that cope with issues of post-colonialism (Volume 1.3 in 2014), translation (Volume 3.3–4 in 2016), and non-Western contexts (like Volume 5.3 "Trans-in-Asia, Asia-in-Trans" in 2018). See also Howard Chiang, ed. *Transgender China* (New York: Palgrave MacMillan, 2012); in particular Chiang's introductory theoretical work, "Imagining Transgender China," on pages 3–19. See also Evan B. Towle and Lynn M. Morgan, "Romancing the Transgender Native: Rethinking the Use of the 'Third Gender' Concept," in *The Transgender Studies Reader*, ed. Susan Stryker and Stephen Whittle (New York: Routledge, 2006), 666–84. Finally, see Finn Enke, "Transgender History (And Otherwise Approaches to Queer Embodiment)," in *The Routledge History of Queer America*, ed. Don Romesburg (New York: Routledge, 2018), 224–36, especially 229–30, for brief comments on this feature of trans historiographic writing.

light, to imagine and reconstruct it in new ways, and to search our sources for the answers to different questions.⁵

The search for a "usable present" rightly leads us to trans narratives as presenting a distinctive, underutilized modern and postmodern heuristic for exploring the past. Reis certainly views it so, arguing that "Transgender history . . . is the history of sexuality. It is the history of gender. Women and men cannot enter the space between gender boundaries or cross them—behaving, appearing, or passing as the other sex—unless those borders have first been demarcated."⁶ A history of gender non-conformers can help cisgender people identify the past boundaries of their own history. Queer theorist historians have also long found utility in the figure of the trans person for disrupting the notion of an immutable gender binary, enabling the queering of the past.⁷

This utilization of the figure of the modern trans person in the service of cis or queer projects, however, almost always values trans people precisely for their unintelligibility and marginality. Trans narratives, it would seem, ought also to function as a usable present for trans people themselves (binary or nonbinary) in a way that illuminates the past. Finn Enke, in his chapter on transgender historiography in the *Routledge History of Queer America*, comments that in order for modern trans narratives to function in this way "it has also been necessary to establish that transgender *is* a culturally specific social category; that is, there is a *history* of transgender as a twentieth-century US phenomenon and its roots in a

---

5. Reis, "Teaching Transgender History," 169.
6. Reis, 168.
7. There is no room to survey all the relevant literature here, but for a survey of queer theory's use of the figure of the trans person up through the mid-1990's, see Jay Prosser, *Second Skins: The Body Narratives of Transsexuality* (New York: Columbia University Press, 1998), 21–60. Prosser surveys Eve Sedgwick, Kobena Mercer, Cherrie Moraga, Gloria Anzaldúa, Teresa de Lauretis, Sue-Ellen Case, Jonathan Dollimore, Marjorie Garber, and especially Judith Butler. See further Patricia Elliot, *Debates in Transgender, Queer, and Feminist Theory: Contested Sites* (Farnham: Ashgate Publishing, 2010), 33–59, who brings this survey up to 2009, in particular analyzing how one strand of trans theorizing (which Elliot labels "transgender" as opposed to "transsexual") internalizes this queer usage of the figure of the trans person. Several scholars of early Christian studies make productive use of this "queering" potential of trans phenomena. For example, see Stephen J. Davis, "Crossed Texts, Crossed Sex: Intertextuality and Gender in Early Christian Legends of Holy Women Disguised as Men," *JECS* 10 (2002): 1–36; Kristi Upson-Saia, *Early Christian Dress: Gender, Virtue, and Authority* (London: Routledge, 2011), in particular 85–89; Virginia Burrus, *The Sex Lives of Saints: An Erotics of Ancient Hagiography* (Philadelphia: University of Pennsylvania. Press, 2004), 145; on cross-dressing saints and Burrus, *Begotten, Not Made: Conceiving Manhood in Late Antiquity* (Stanford: Stanford University Press, 2000), 80–133, for her queering / trans-ing presentation of Gregory of Nyssa. See also Mathew Kuefler, *The Manly Eunuch: Masculinity, Gender Ambiguity, and Christian Ideology in Late Antiquity* (Chicago: University of Chicago Press, 2001) in its entirety, but especially the final two chapters on pp. 206–82. See also Bernadette Brooten, *Love Between Women: Early Christian Responses to Female Homoeroticism* (Chicago: University of Chicago Press, 1996), 1–72. This is not to critique the quality of these works, which have all been deeply influential in my own scholarly formation, but to say that in their attentiveness to questions of attire, sexual object choice, and gender they tend to use past examples of gender transgressive behavior as a means of queering or destabilizing our present gender binary and that this focus, while admirable, leaves room for additional analysis of these trans people / trans phenomena in their own right.

particular cultural (not universal) epistemology."[8] In other words, to establish an analytical category of "trans" that can work across time and culture, the current predominant, Western narratives must be decentered. In order for this present essay to do this work of decentering, it makes sense to start with the two major trans narratives of the twentieth and twenty-first century in the Western world: those surrounding the concept of the "transsexual," and those surrounding the concept of the "transgender person."[9]

DECENTERING WESTERN TRANS NARRATIVES: THE TRANSSEXUAL AND TRANSGENDER DIVIDE

As Joanne Meyerowitz persuasively argues in her 2002 book *How Sex Changed*, the notion of a transsexual emerged in the mid-twentieth century as a product of a complicated interplay between popular media, trans people themselves, and medical-psychological professionals. Each had to negotiate its interests and positions around the others. The doctors' research and credibility impacted public discourse, but the researchers themselves were also products of that public culture and brought its assumptions to their work. Doctors did not, indeed could not, merely fiat the truth of their categories; instead, they drew their narratives from the letters and first-hand reports of trans people themselves. Trans people, in turn, were motivated to give the professionals what they were looking for because those professionals functioned as gatekeepers in the trans person's pursuit of hormones and surgery. Likewise, the press sought out stories about trans people (giving them a degree of influence in their self-presentation), but the press sought them out in order to sell newspapers and books—this deeply informed what sorts of stories they featured. Similarly, trans people took pains to communicate themselves in terms that the mainstream culture would find intelligible—they wanted respectability, employment, and physical security.[10]

8. Enke, "Transgender History," 228.

9. Elliot, *Debates in Transgender, Queer, and Feminist Theory*, 33–59, uses this same schema for classifying trans theorists of the 1990s and 2000s. This is certainly an oversimplification of terms and categories that shift and overlap; see Mary Alice Adams, "Traversing the Transcape: A Brief Historical Etymology of Trans* Terminology," in *Transgender Communications Studies: Histories, Trends, and Trajectories*, ed. Leland G. Spencer and Jamie C. Capuzza (New York: Lexington Books, 2015), 173–86. For my own purposes of broadly describing the self-interpretive stories used by twentieth century trans people, the TS / TG divide is likewise neither exhaustive nor nuanced enough. For clear evidence of this, see especially David Valentine, *Imagining Transgender: An Ethnography of a Category* (Durham, NC: Duke University Press, 2007). The *insufficiency* of these categories, however, only further serves my point here that these various schemas and narratives employed by trans people to render their embodiment intelligible are culturally specific. There is not one that is ontologically "true" and the others that are varying degrees of "false," but rather *even the modern conceptualization of trans people* already demonstrates the contingency of specific trans narratives.

10. Joanne Meyerowitz, *How Sex Changed: A History of Transsexuality in the United States* (Cambridge, MA: Harvard University Press, 2002). Meyerowitz shows the interweaving of these distinct influences throughout the text, but see especially chapter four, "A 'Fierce and Demanding' Drive," 130–67, for its discussion of trans people's self-reporting through letter writing and their strategic navigation of both medicine and the media. Najmabadi notes a similar dialectical process at

Thus, in the case of mid-twentieth century trans people, the prevailing norms of a strict sex binary, heteronormativity, bio-centric understandings of sexual difference, psychoanalytic understandings of the interior life, and post-war enthusiasm for American individualism produced "the transsexual narrative" by the end of the 1960s. In this narrative, the transsexual knows of their cross-gendered identity from their earliest memories, wants nothing to do with the genitals they were born with (avoiding all sexual contact prior to surgery), wants to be strictly heterosexual after transitioning, fervently pursues *full* medical transition (hormones and surgeries), and performs their new white middle-class heteronormative gender role flawlessly (to the point that no one knows their past as a trans person).[11]

Postmodernity's challenge to the structures of cis-hetero-normativity and bio-essentialist notions of sexual difference likewise unsettled the stability of trans peoples' attempts to render themselves intelligible within said structures. Because transsexuals needed, in the 1950s and '60s, to make their stories intelligible to conservatives who rejected them, it became possible to see trans people as re-inscribing precisely those conservative categories. Their (perceived) conformity to normative gender roles, their (perceived) complicit participation in the exploitative sexual objectification of women, their (perceived) rejection of homosexual identities in favor of heteronormative privilege—all of this became justification for a feminist and queer rejection of transsexuals.[12] If gender were merely performative, and sex was gender all along, then how could one "be" one gender to such a degree that it mandated transitioning to the *full* citation (social and medical) of the gender of one's identity? Wouldn't that reinscribe the harmful illusion of gender-as-ontological?[13] Cressida J. Heyes' monograph *Self-Transformations* responds to these critiques in her chapter "Feminist Solidarity after Queer Theory:

---

work in Iran surrounding trans people: "The filtering process [distinguishing authentic transsexuals from illicit homosexuals] has become possible through the condensed workings of legal, Islamic jurisprudential (*fiqhi*), and biomedical / psycho-sexological discourses and through the work of various structures... which we often call 'the state.' This complex authorizing nexus has made the category of transsexual intelligible and acceptable; at the same time, the process of distinguishing between 'trans-' and 'homo-' in part depends on trans persons' own actions and narratives, and thus on their self-definitions and self-productions" (*Professing Selves*, 15–16).

11. See Meyerowitz's chapter 6, "The Liberal Moment," (*How Sex Changed*, 208–54) for a detailed articulation of the fragile triumph of this narrative in the late 1960s and early 1970s, especially centered around the formation of clinics at several major universities with diagnostic criteria. Meyerowitz comments, "The criteria demonstrated professional standards to those critics who cast the doctors as charlatans. They helped the doctors select patients carefully and thus avoid potential lawsuits from those who might regret the surgery. They also allowed doctors to figure out how to choose a handful of patients from the hundreds who asked for surgery" (*How Sex Changed*, 224).

12. Several writers summarize how elements of radical feminism and gay liberation turned against trans people (trans women in particular). For basic overviews, see Meyerowitz *How Sex Changed*, 255–68; and Susan Stryker, *Transgender History* (Berkeley, CA: Seal Press, 2008), 91–120.

13. Here I jump ahead of the second wave critiques of trans people, which often depended on some version of biological essentialism, and instead supply a more current line of critique based out of queer theory based on a questionable reading of Butler. Elliot summarizes these most recent critiques as well as how they (problematically) build on the older second wave criticisms (in *Debates in Transgender, Queer, and Feminist Theory*, 1–32).

The Case of Transgender."[14] Against trans-exclusionary writers, she argues that they "draw on the classification of transsexuality as a mental 'disorder' to make their case. . . . They construct trans people as lacking both agency and critical perspective."[15] This allows the "reductive characterization of the transsexual as the dupe of gender," as reinforcing gendered stereotypes, leading to the "conclusion that transgender politics writ large has no feminist potential."[16] This, Heyes argues, is guilty of "persistently foreclosing all possibilities for political resistance to a disease model."[17]

This notion of "resistance" did indeed form one way that trans people sought to render themselves intelligible within this new framework of post-structuralist gender criticism. They sought to bring transgender, as a term, into close alignment with queer, with narratives of disruption (as opposed to conformity);[18] this alignment fit well with how queer theory used trans narratives already.[19] By deploying the term "transgender" in a new way as an umbrella term that could incorporate, but deemphasize the older transsexual narrative,[20] trans people argued that they were *not* "reinscribing" harmful gender norms or "invading" gender specific-spaces. Rather, they were queering or disrupting cis-heteronormativity and doing, thereby, much needed heavy lifting in the work of gender liberation. This "transgender" narrative of queering, disruption, and liberation appears abundantly in the literature of the last two and a half decades,[21] with a few notable objections.[22]

These two narratives (in short, the "transsexual narrative" and the "transgender narrative") have created a bifurcation within the trans community itself, though, since the transgender narrative struggles at some level to account for

14. Cressida J. Heyes, *Self-Transformations: Foucault, Ethics, and Normalized Bodies* (Oxford: Oxford University Press, 2007), 38–62.
15. Heyes, *Self-Transformations*, 39.
16. Heyes, 40.
17. Heyes, 39.
18. See especially Sandy Stone, "The *Empire* Strikes Back: A Posttranssexual Manifesto," in *Body Guards: The Cultural Politics of Gender Ambiguity*, ed. Julia Epstein and Kristina Straub (New York: Routledge, 1991), 280–304. Stone's manifesto, often seen as a founding document of transgender studies in the current academy, argues for precisely this positioning of trans people as a means of answering the feminist anti-trans polemicists of the preceding decades.
19. See n. 7 above.
20. Stryker, *Transgender History*, 36–40 discusses how this term originally denoted a category distinct from transsexuals (rather than an umbrella category inclusive of transsexuals among other nonconformers). See also Adams, "Traversing the Transcape"; and Stryker "Transgender History, Homonormativity, and Disciplinarity," *Radical History Review* 100 (2008): 145–57, in particular 146.
21. Elliot concisely summarizes many of these thinkers and their works (in *Debates in Transgender, Queer, and Feminist Theory*, 1–59).
22. These include figures that Elliot terms transsexual theorists (as opposed to transgender theorists), including Prosser, *Second Skins*, and Viviane Namaste, *Invisible Lives: The Erasure of Transsexual and Transgendered People* (Chicago: University of Chicago Press, 2000). There is also still a vibrant discourse on caring for trans people in medical and psychological literature that, in many ways, operates outside the more radical paradigms of queer studies. See, for example, Randi Ettner, Stan Monstrey, and Eli Coleman, eds. *Principles of Transgender Medicine and Surgery*, 2nd ed. (New York: Haworth Press, 2016), as well as the website and literature of the *World Professional Association for Transgender Health* (WPATH).

trans people who focus on the *body*, who seek medical transition under a disease paradigm. It has difficulty situating those who *do* seek a place within the gender binary, since this new narrative implicitly accepts the presuppositions of the anti-trans feminists (implying that surgeries physically literalize gender norms) while simply arguing that trans people stand outside the scope of that critique. Many trans people, quite emphatically, continue to identify with the narrative of medical-social transition along the axis of a gender binary—even if many now avoid the term "transsexual." At this point, there exist two contradictory narratives side by side. In one sense, people within mainstream culture still understand trans people as *being* one sex trapped in or erroneously assigned to the opposite sex; at the *same time*, in another sense, people in mainstream society routinely see trans people as exemplars of the breakdown of sex-binary essentialism. These two notions at minimum exist in tension, if they are not outright contradictions of one another.

In seeking to secure a liveable existence, trans people do make strategic use of both of these narratives, but it would be a mistake *either* to see them as being "dupes" of either system *or* as purely cynical strategists. Again, I turn to Heyes for a useful summary statement. She argues that: "It may well be the case that a larger institutional history creates those subjects, but that does not make their experience any less real or deeply felt on an individual level."[23] People, as subjects, *internalize* and genuinely *identify* with their cultural narratives (just as we internalize our native language). Heyes continues that this:

> suggests a complex intermediate space, where individuals are thrown into particular subject-positions that are the contingent product of larger historical dynamics, within which they work to resist or exceed norms that are simultaneously the conditions of their own possibility.[24]

By this statement, Heyes rightly places trans people's agential choices within the same context as everyone else's. All people exist in this intermediate state as subjects who make choices based on the cultural horizons available to them. The intelligible norms serve both as limiting conditions and the basis for resistance. As Susan Stryker and Aren Aizura describe in the introduction to the *Transgender Studies Reader 2*, "'gender identity' is understood as the psychical internalization and somaticization of historically contingent modes of embodied personhood."[25]

This fundamentally destabilizes any claim to one or another narrative as being an ontological reality—we can see "transsexual" and "transgender" as two

---

23. Heyes, *Self-Transformations*, 57.
24. Heyes, 57.
25. Stryker and Aren Z. Aizura, "Introduction: Transgender Studies 2.0," in *The Transgender Studies Reader 2*, ed. Stryker and Aizura (New York: Routledge, 2013), 8. Thus, they continue: "*transgender* is intimately bound with questions of nation, territory, and citizenship, with categories of belonging and exclusion, of excess and incorporation, and with all the processes through which individual corporealities become aggregated as bodies politic."

examples of the same phenomenon. Like all people, trans people make strategic choices as embodied subjects in order to secure intelligibility within their historical context. Their choices take place in an ever-looping dialectic between the limitations and possibilities presented by their embodiment and their cultural horizons. Much in the way that human neurobiology creates the potential for language acquisition, but language itself remains entirely a social construct variable across time and space, so also does gender identity both *depend on* and *dialogue with* the enculturated body. Only embodied people make and experience culture, and all people live within culture; the enculturated body stands as an irreducible complexity. Cultural categories like sexual difference stand as limited, imperfect attempts to render embodied experiences intelligible within the social sphere. They are socially constructed, but not made up in a purely imaginative vacuum. They have to make sense to the embodiment of those who make use of those social categories; they have to fit the natural limiting condition of the body itself. Put more simply, human bodies present a finite number of features upon which cultures can construct meaning, even as the combination of these differentiating features leads to a near infinite variety of possible social constructions. Transsexual narratives and transgendered narratives are *two* attempts to communicate the *same embodiment* in, by analogy, two different cultural languages.

Therefore, when I say that this perspective destabilizes seeing the transsexual or transgender narrative as ontologically valid, this perspective *also invalidates any attempt to use that destabilization as a means of discrediting trans people* since their agential choices proceed in precisely the same conditions and limits as cis people. As a useable present, the fact that trans narratives shift with the cultural structures of sexual difference empowers us to find trans people in history prior to the invention of the term itself. Meyerowitz implicitly understands this as possible; her history of transsexuality begins in the pre-war period decades before that term was coined and shows a direct growth from that pre-transsexual conceptual space to one where such an identity could be explicitly claimed. Meyerowitz does not hesitate to call these pre-WWII people part of the "history of transsexuality" or "transgendered subjects." Clearly, though, many of these people could never have identified with those terms. What is it, then, that makes this claim legitimate if not the common pattern they share with later self-identified trans people of attempting to render intelligible the lived reality of their enculturated body, with all its complex cross-gendered movement?[26]

26. Emily Skidmore recognizes that her work makes a similar maneuver, in *The Lives of Trans Men at the Turn of the Twentieth Century* (New York: NYU Press, 2017), 10–11. Enke likewise recognizes that this categorical ambivalence could extend to figures often viewed as predecessors to modern LGB people who, in this light, may also count as trans as well as LGB—he specifically references the presence of gender non-conforming people in George Chauncey's seminal *Gay New York: Gender, Urban Culture, and the Making of the Gay Male World, 1890–1940* (New York: Basic Books, 1994); and in Elizabeth Lapovsky Kennedy and Madeline D. Davis' equally influential *Boots of Leather, Slippers of Gold: The History of a Lesbian Community* (New York: Routledge, 1993) (in "Transgender History," 224–27).

DEFINING TRANS AS AN ANALYTIC CATEGORY

The impact of the above decentering of current mainstream Western narratives is significant. Whether one imagines gender as a social construct or biological essence, whether one sees human sexual difference as an immutable binary, a mutable binary, a spectrum, or any other structure, whether one locates someone's "true" sex (or gender) in chromosomes, genitals, hormones, neuroanatomy, reproductive capacity, sexual capacity, sexual orientation, social assignment, internal sense of identity, or in any other possible feature, trans people will still exist and will make use of these available differentiating structures to make sense of their bodies—just like cis-gendered people must do. It is not adherence to one or another narrative, one or another structuring of sexual difference, that makes someone trans; this means it is *not* an internal sense of gender identity that makes someone trans since that notion belongs to modernity and postmodernity, with their notion of the gap between depth and surface, and their emphasis on absolute individualism, the agential subject, or personal existentialism.[27]

What makes a trans person identifiably trans for the historian is the *act of transition* or the *desire for that act*—however expressed. Following Judith Butler's notion of intelligibility, I agree that societies seek ways to make sense of bodies—given that we as a species reproduce via sexual reproduction, behaviors *around* sex provide a ripe opportunity for articulating or organizing these structures. Given how it demonstrates the situatedness of all claims to knowledge, and the ties of those claims to assertions of power, post-structuralism shows how fraught, contradictory, and socially immanent these apparently essential categories actually are; but that does not inhibit my project here. Rather, it empowers it. Precisely *because* the categories of intelligibility shift from era to era, culture to culture, and place to place, we must anticipate that those who *transition between or away from* those categories will likewise look different in each era, each culture, each place. Indeed, given how inconsistent or problematic the categories themselves are, we may expect trans people to look different or construe themselves differently even within the same socio-historical-cultural location.

It is necessary to be quite clear about this chapter's intentions here. The definition of "trans" proposed here must be held purely as a scholarly construct. It is a scholarly category useful for historical analysis but must not be imagined as a transplantation of modern trans narratives into the lives of past people who could not possibly identify with that narrative. In one sense, this is the same maneuver proposed by Joan W. Scott in her work on situating "gender" as a useful category for historical analysis,[28] though I thoroughly agree with J. Boydston's caution that we ought first consider gender as a question to be posed

---

27. Najmabadi asks: "What does saying 'I am trans / gay / lesbian' mean when the question of 'what am I' does not dominantly reference an I narrativized around a psychic interiorized self, but rather an I-in-presentation at a particular nexus of time and place?" (*Professing Selves*, 9).

28. Joan W. Scott, "Gender: Still a Useful Category of Analysis," *Diogenes* 225 (2010): 7–14.

rather than as a categorical given.[29] With that said, on the basis of the useable present summarized and analyzed above, historians can call someone in the historical record "trans" in this limited sense if that historical person, having been assigned to one position of sexed or gendered intelligibility, seeks to transition to another position of sexed or gendered intelligibility *or*, finding their cultural categories insufficient, seeks out a quasi or unintelligible space. That is it—that is the single criterion; specific enough to refer exclusively to transgender people, flexible and abstract enough to be appropriately contextualized to the specific social reality under inquiry. It is necessary in that someone who does not transition or desire to transition would not fit the "trans" prefix; it is sufficient in that anyone clearly engaging in or desiring to transition would qualify as trans in a rather unproblematic fashion.

APPLYING THE CATEGORY: EUNUCHS FOR THE KINGDOM OF HEAVEN AND OTHER NON-MEN

Can this definition make useful analytical distinctions in premodern texts, though? Given that this volume deals with trans hermeneutics in biblical studies, it seems appropriate at this point to turn to two particularly provocative biblical examples: the eunuchs for the kingdom of heaven in Matt 19:12 and then Paul's valorization of sexual renunciation in 1 Cor 6–7.

Unique to the Gospel of Matthew, Matt 19:12's discussion of three types of eunuchs has, until recently, generally been assumed to be a metaphorical reference to renunciation in general[30] or to the embracing of celibacy along with a renunciation of marriage.[31] A significant stream of recent scholarship has

---

29. Jeanne Boydston, "Gender as a Question of Historical Analysis," *Gender and History* 20 (2008): 558–83.

30. A. E. Harvey, "Eunuchs for the Sake of the Kingdom," *HeyJ* 48 (2007): 1–17, see pp. 12–15. See also John Nolland, *The Gospel of Matthew: A Commentary on the Greek Text* (Grand Rapids: Eerdmans, 2005), 781, who leans, but does not commit, to Matt 19:12 implying celibacy and renunciation of marriage, preferring instead to see this as a complex metaphor with several interpretive applications.

31. J. D. Hester, "Eunuchs and the Postgender Jesus: Matthew 19.12 and Transgressive Sexualities," *JSNT* 28 (2005): 13–40, see p. 17 nn. 4–6 for an excellent survey of this common interpretation. David Turner argues, with respect to Matt 19:12, that "celibacy is only for divinely gifted people" (See Turner, *Matthew* [Grand Rapids: Baker Academic, 2008], 463.) Turner also shows a desire (possibly motivated by Protestant theological concerns) to avoid forbidding marriage in general or ascribing any moral superiority to celibacy, and likewise wanting to avoid any association of Matt 19:12 with "asceticism" (*Matthew*, 464). See also: David E. Garland, *Reading Matthew: A Literary and Theological Commentary on the First Gospel* (New York: Crossroad, 1993), 201; R. T. France, *The Gospel of Matthew* (Grand Rapids: Eerdmans, 2007), 711–25; Craig Evans, *Matthew* (New York: Cambridge University Press, 2012), 342; Anna Case-Winters, *Matthew* (Louisville, KY: Westminster John Knox Press, 2015), 240; Larissa Tracy, "Introduction: A History of Calamities: The Culture of Castration," in *Castration and Culture in the Middle Ages*, ed. Tracy (Cambridge: D. S. Brewer, 2013): 1–28, see p. 9; Jack Collins, "Appropriation and Development of Castration as a Symbol and Practice in Early Christianity" in Tracy, *Castration and Culture in the Middle Ages*, 73–86, see p. 73.

challenged that long-standing view by pointing out both that early reception of this saying by Christians included literal self-castration,[32] and that the general view of eunuchs in classical antiquity saw them not as celibate but as provocatively sexual.[33] We do not, however, need to make Matt 19:12 about *either* renunciation *or* a transgressing of gender boundaries. Instead, the renunciations argued for in Matt 19:1–15 as a whole can be read as transgressing gender boundaries.

In medical literature from the Hippocratic corpus (fifth–fourth century BCE) onward, children were presexual and, therefore, somewhat analogous to eunuchs by virtue of having less obviously sexed bodies (both developmentally and in terms of reproductive potential). Similarly, we see a set of three reflections on human sexual difference within Matt 19:1–15—marriage/divorce, then eunuchs, then children. The message seems to be that *if* one engages in marriage, that it is acceptable and God-given, but that it is better (if one is so called) to be like eunuchs or like children. Thus, though Jesus cites Gen 1:27 here, the binary is not strictly between male and female, but between man and not-man (a category to which a woman, eunuch, or child belonged). The marriage/divorce discussion of Matt 19:1–9 carries these gendered overtones because the power to divorce was not gender neutral; it belonged to the man by right.[34] Jesus, in Matt 19:1–9, takes away the scriptural-theological support for that male prerogative, then compares this to infertility and literal, physical emasculation in 19:12. Finally, he positively cites children—at best *potential* men. Women's power within marriage is unchanged by Matt 19:1–9, and women could not be emasculated surgically (their gendered status could not be lowered in analogous fashion). The shift in power, the movement across the barrier created by social institutions predicated on sexual difference, is entirely in the direction of a male giving up his male power in favor of a less powerful position as an androgynous figure. The man is to join categorically with the not-man.[35]

---

32. Tracy, *Castration and Culture in the Middle Ages*, 10; and Collins, "Appropriation and Development of Castration," 80–85 provide basic argument to this effect. The best survey, though, comes from Daniel Caner, "The Practice and Prohibition of Self-Castration in Early Christianity," *VC* 51 (1997): 396–415, see pp. 396–407, citing a series of ancient witnesses: Justin Martyr's *Apology* 29.1–2; Basil of Ancyra's *On Virginity* 61–62; the canons of Nicaea I (325); the Apostolic Constitutions; Athenagoras' *Leg. pro Christ* 33.2–4; Eusebius' dubious account of Origen's castration (*Hist. eccl.* 6); the *Acts of John* 53–54; Origen's *Comm.Matt.* 15.3 (in turn citing the *Maxims* of Sextus); Tertullian's rejection of self-made eunuchs as having a dualistically negative attitude toward material creation; Epiphanius' *De Fide* 13.5; and John Chrysostom's *Comm.Chap 5 Ep. to Gal.* 3.717.

33. Rick Talbott, "Imagining the Matthean Eunuch Community: Kyriarchy on the Chopping Block," *JFSR* 22 (2006): 21–43, see p. 41. See also Hester, "Eunuchs and the Postgender Jesus," 24. Cp. Caner, "The Practice and Prohibition of Self-Castration," 396 (citing Basil of Ancyra's *On Virginity* 61). See especially the overview of the sexuality of eunuchs provided by Kuefler, *The Manly Eunuch*, 96–102.

34. Deut 24:1–6 assumes it is only a male initiating or issuing a certificate of divorce, so regardless of actual practice in first century Judean Palestine under Roman Law, this is the assumed context of discussion because it centers around Torah—Deut 24:1–6 versus Gen 1:27.

35. This is both a positive and a negative point. Negatively, one may rightly lament that this makes the passage silent on the concerns and needs of those already *in* the not-men category; they remain respectively powerless and are serving here merely as points of comparison for the powerful men whom the passage addresses. However, more positively, one may see here a delightful reversal

Thus, to paraphrase it briefly, the conversation of Matt 19:1–15 seems to proceed as follows: the Pharisees ask Jesus to weigh in on the question of a man's power to initiate divorce; Jesus presents an opinion that strips the man of virtually all authority with respect to that question; the apostles (perhaps wryly) offer that perhaps one should simply give up marriage all together then; Jesus counters that on this logic they should just give up on manhood all together, becoming like eunuchs or children. Matt 19:12 is not *either* about renunciation of marriage *or* about renunciation of sexual difference; both the traditional reading of renunciation and the interpretation of Matt 19:12 attuned to ancient gender categories exist because both are legitimate concerns present in the text. The shift here is not to eliminate one set of concerns or the other, but to see how they are one and the same within the logic of Matt 19:1–15 as a whole.

This is to say that while those who are born eunuchs or made eunuchs by the hands of men do not qualify as "trans" under the proposed definition of this essay, those who become eunuchs for the sake of the kingdom of heaven absolutely do count as trans whether one understands this as a literal or metaphorical emasculation. The point is precisely the movement from one intelligible category (patriarchal, androcentric manhood) to another (that of the non-men). Provocatively, then, even movements which do not seem to our eye to be phenomenologically analogous to transgender narratives—a movement from marriage to virginity, in this case, or in 1 Cor 6–7—may provide legitimate material for the history of trans people.

This reading of Matt 19 (and then also 1 Cor 6–7) makes an argumentative reply to a question posed by Ambrose of Milan: "Be it allowed however that they [i.e. women] should imitate the nature of the more worthy sex [i.e. men]; but why should men choose to assume the appearance of the inferior?"[36] This rhetorical question points to the prevailing androcentrism that universally characterized early Christianity. If any transition were tolerated, it was to be that of women becoming like men, never the reverse. The simple fact is that all our examples of early saints crossing gender boundaries or transitioning gender roles were assigned female at birth and, through transition, emulated masculine virtue. In contrast, accusations of effeminacy were used to shame political and religious competitors (as in Elagabalus or the *galli*).

Teresa Shaw summarizes this attitude within early Christian asceticism by stating that "Even within the lofty visions of genderless and bodiless unity, femaleness defines and constricts the goals of ascetic piety. Femaleness is that which must be overcome to achieve male rank, it provides the symbolic language

---

of the early Christian trope of the "manly woman"; whereas for that trope femininity itself is problematic (since masculinity is a literal synonym of virtue in Latin and Greek), here it is *actually* male power itself that receives attention for its problematic divisiveness. The passage may not do much work for those engaged in theological advocacy for trans and intersex people, but it does legitimately serve as a resource for those engaged in deconstructing institutionalized male privilege since it is precisely that privilege which this passage, in this reading of it, seeks to confront.

36. Ambrose *Letter 69* (Letter 15 in the Corpus Scriptorum Ecclesiasticorum Latinorum 82 1:112).

for the fall and the power of death as well as for the ascetic's subordinate relationship to Christ."[37] Benjamin Dunning, similarly, bases his reception history of Pauline sexual anthropology on the correct notion that, for early Christianity, "the sexual binary is one that puts woman at a decided disadvantage to man, placing her a further step removed from the image of God and the realm of reason, virtue, and incorruptibility."[38] This hierarchy creates a problematic feminine "excess" when, in Paul's anthropology, the two main figures are the fallen Adam and the risen Christ. In Dunning's reading, early Christian responses to this problem of how to figure women in that male symbolic frame fell into roughly two camps: those that sought to absorb the female into the male (to "make Mary male"), and those that sought to provide a parallel, valorized, but inferior place for the female within the scheme.

I seek here to point to a third option, related to both of those outlined by Dunning and prefiguring Shaw's observation that early Christian asceticism used femaleness not only as something to overcome but also as the symbolic framework for articulating the submission of all ascetics (including male ones) to Christ. Dunning's framework misses one possible direction of transition: that of the male vacating his male prerogative and social status in order to become un-male on some level, as explored in this chapter. Without challenging the scholarship that correctly observes early Christianity's androcentric framework, this third interpretive option opens up a possible valorization of the female and feminine as something worth transitioning *into* and not merely *away from*. It answers St Ambrose's rhetorical question; rather than accepting his presupposition that there is no valid reason for a man to emulate women, this chapter argues that early Christianity in fact presented a powerful framework for just such a gendered transition. I argue for this alternative interpretive option in both Matt 19 and 1 Cor 6–7.

In 1 Cor 6:9–7:40, Paul provides a lengthy discussion of sexual ethics that seeks to valorize sexual renunciation while still defending marriage as acceptably Christian. In 1 Cor 6:13, he says that the body is "for the Lord." In 6:19–20, he tells his audience, "You are not your own; you were bought with a price."[39] He repeats this again in 7:23: "You were bought with a price; do not become the slaves of humans." Paul lays out his approach to Christian sexual ethics in these two chapters by relying on a metaphorical comparison between slavery and the Christian life, a comparison that was relevant in the first century because an enslaved person's sexual desire could distract them from their jobs, vexing owners.

Columella, Paul's contemporary, twice discusses the sex life of the foreman, himself enslaved (the *vilicus*), in his agricultural manual *De re rustica* (*Rust.*).

---

37. Teresa M. Shaw, *The Burden of the Flesh: Fasting and Sexuality in Early Christianity* (Minneapolis: Fortress, 1998), 252–53.
38. Benjamin Dunning, *Christ without Adam: Subjectivity and Sexual Difference in the Philosophers' Paul* (New York: Columbia University Press, 2014), 21.
39. Unless otherwise noted, all translations are my own.

He tells owners to give the *vilicus* a woman, a *contubernalis mulier* to "keep him within bounds" (*contineat eum, Rust.* 1.8.5). Much later (*Rust.* 11.1.14) he warns owners against letting a *vilicus* engage in sexual indulgence (*venereis amoribus*), since it undermines their focus and reduces the master's ability to control the *vilicus*. In contrast, when Columella (in Book 12) justifies the marital sex of free people, the focus is on procreation; this is unsurprising since procreative, faithful marriage was politically significant in the early Roman Empire.[40] The sexuality of enslaved people, though, was categorically different—it was a tool to be used or discarded for the benefit of the master.

In 1 Cor 6:9–7:40, Paul appears much closer to Columella's discussion of the sexuality of the enslaved than he does to other ancient Jewish and Greco-Roman views of the marital sex of free people. Nowhere in these verses does Paul attempt to justify marriage through an appeal to procreation, the goodness of sexual desire itself, or the unitive companionship it can provide. Instead, "Because of cases of sexual immorality [*dia tas porneias*], each man should have his own wife and each woman her own husband" (1 Cor 7:2, NRSVue). In 1 Cor 7:7 Paul states, "I wish that all were as I myself am," namely, unmarried—but 1 Cor 7:9 concludes that if two people "are not exercising self-control, they should marry. For it is better to marry than to burn." Paul knows that marriage divides one's loyalties (7:32–35), but that is preferable to the risk that *porneia* might remove one from the household of Christ entirely (6:9–16). One cannot be a "slave" in the house of God if one is not in the household at all (7:22, NRSVue). Like Columella, Paul's concern is "to promote good order [*euschēmon*] and unhindered devotion [*euparedron*] to the master" (7:35). The function of monogamy in 1 Cor 6:9–7:40 is to keep people *in Christ's house* so that they can serve God and be saved.[41]

Paul's justification of both marriage and sexual renunciation, though, works by flattening the power gap, in this specific instance, between men and women. Paul asks his audience, even if they are free-born, to think of themselves in terms of slavery—this is in particular a significant loss of power for free, adult men who might otherwise expect to have rightful ownership of their bodies as well as the bodies of those living in their household.[42] There is, then, a movement

---

40. Paul Zanker, *The Power of Images in the Age of Augustus*, trans. by Alan Shapiro (Ann Arbor: University of Michigan Press, 1988), 156–62. See also Beth Severy, *Augustus and the Family at the Birth of the Roman Empire* (New York: Routledge, 2003) in its entirety, but especially 50–56.

41. Figured in terms of the general resurrection in 6:14.

42. Thus, my focus on the Corinthian men's gendered transition here holds less in common with previous readings of this letter that have juxtaposed the Corinthian women with present-day trans people and practices (including Joseph A. Marchal, "The Corinthian Women Prophets and Trans Activism: Rethinking Canonical Gender Claims," in *Bible Trouble: Queer Reading at the Boundaries of Biblical Scholarship*, ed. Ken Stone and Teresa J. Hornsby [Atlanta: SBL, 2011], 223–46; "Female Masculinity in Corinth?: Bodily Citations and the Drag of History," *Neot* 48:1 (Fall 2014): 93–113; or *Appalling Bodies: Queer Figures Before and After Paul's Letters* (New York: Oxford University Press, 2020), 30–67, but resonates somewhat with queer readings of these men found in: Gillian Townsley, *The Straight Mind in Corinth: Queer Readings across 1 Corinthians 11:2–16* (Atlanta: SBL Press, 2017).

or transition along a gendered power axis lurking behind Paul's argument here, the same transitional movement that appears in the discussion of early Christian marital ethics in Matt 19:1–15, again from man to not-man.

Matt 19, though, like 1 Cor 6–7, is not *strident* in demanding this renunciation—it is for those who are called to it, a sort of supererogative Christian ascesis worthy of emulation but necessarily mitigated for pastoral reasons for those unable to live up to those demands. Matthew's Jesus also makes pastoral allowance with respect to divorce, saying that a man may still divorce his wife in cases of *porneia*—though the question of how to interpret *porneia* remains an open one—and that becoming a eunuch for the kingdom is for those who are able to accept it.

Returning to my general point, in both of these cases a renunciation is made that could be described as a movement from one kind of gendered category (patriarchal, androcentric manhood) to another gendered category (one of the non-men). Paul's justification of sexual renunciation in 1 Corinthians 6–7 appears to flatten the power gap between gendered categories. Likewise, while those who are born eunuchs or made eunuchs by the hands of men in Matt 19 do not seem to transition on any level, those who become eunuchs for the sake of the kingdom of heaven absolutely do *transition* from the male position to the not-male position—whether one understands this as a literal or metaphorical emasculation. The point is precisely the movement from one intelligible category (patriarchal, androcentric manhood) to another (that of the non-men). In terms of social-justice advocacy today, this interpretive insight carries both positive and negative potential meanings. Negatively, one may rightly lament that this makes both passages silent on the concerns and needs of those already *in* the not-men category; they remain respectively powerless and are serving here merely as points of comparison for the powerful men whom the passage addresses.

However, more positively, one could cite these passages as part of an answer to Ambrose's rhetorical question: "why should men choose to assume the appearance of the inferior?" The eunuch passage in Matt 19 in particular provides a delightful reversal of the early Christian trope of the "manly woman"; whereas for that trope femininity itself is problematic (as indicated by both Dunning and Shaw), here it is *actually* male power itself that receives attention for its problematic divisiveness. The passage may legitimately serve as a resource for those engaged in deconstructing institutionalized male privilege. In this reading of it, Matt 19 seeks to confront precisely that privilege. Provocatively, then, even movements which may not seem to be phenomenologically analogous to transgender narratives—a movement from marriage to virginity, in these cases—may be productively analyzed with the historically flexible and contextual category of "transition." We must attend to the specific ways that cultures construct their intelligible categories and the specific ways that people may act upon or articulate their embodiment and desire in dialogue with those categories.

Contrary to the presumption implied within Ambrose's rhetorical question, both of these texts valorize on some level the act of transition along a gendered axis from male to female or, at minimum, to non-male. This is parallel to, though not identical with, early Christianity's elevation of the feminine into the masculine—one of the interpretive maneuvers pointed to by Dunning. Though predating the Christian ascetics studied by Shaw by several centuries, we are closer in these texts to what she identifies as the use of "femaleness" to articulate "the ascetic's subordinate relationship to Christ." First Cor 6–7 certainly fulfills this function by positing all Christians as enslaved people in God's household—all occupy this subordinate, therefore inherently female, position before God. Matt 19:12, though, in defending sexual renunciation through the figure of the eunuch-for-the-kingdom, already begins to position that gendered transition as an act not only of submission but of *imitation* since, in Matthew's Gospel (as in most others), Jesus is unmarried.

We must attend to the specific ways that cultures construct their intelligible categories and the specific ways that people may act upon or articulate their embodiment and desire in dialogue with those categories, including those who act in transition (or desire to act), in movement from one intelligible category (patriarchal, androcentric manhood) to another (that of the non-men). Once one begins looking for people who act or aim to move in this way, one might be surprised by just how many people in religious texts fit this single, specific criterion necessary to my suggested definition of trans as a category of literary analysis in historical texts. Thus, the experiences of trans people in our own culture may provide a useable present for a successful reinterrogation of the past—a reinterrogation made particularly necessary because of the ways that other constructions of the past, especially the Judeo-Christian scriptures, are employed against trans people and other sexual minorities in our own time period.

Chapter 9

This Is My Glorified Body
Pauline Transitions

JAEDA C. CALAWAY

In this essay, I develop a hermeneutic of transgender resonance and dissonance between Paul's evocation of a glorified resurrection body in 1 Cor 15 and modern trans embodiments. Paul's transformative imagery and *morphosis* terminology that refer to the social and embodied transformations of dying and rising with Christ resonate with how modern trans people undergo social and embodied transitions as we die daily to our old selves, bend binaries, and rise into our glittery glorified trans bodies. In the process, these transitions reveal how trans temporalities' curves and hairy entanglements bend, double, reverse, dilate, and contract time in nonlinear ways. Yet Paul's androcentrism and delay of the embodied transformation into the future strike a dissonant note for trans embodiments. Instead, I find greater resonance with the partial reconstructions of the Corinthian women prophets in our embodiments that are simultaneously always already resurrected and in a state of perpetual becoming.

"Resolve to know that in you is the capacity to be transformed."[1]

---

1. Origen, *Dialogue with Heraclides* 13.19–20; trans. M. David Litwa (*Posthuman Transformation in Ancient Mediterranean Thought: Becoming Angels and Demons* [Cambridge: Cambridge University Press, 2020], 94). This essay originated as a talk at the Annual SBL Meeting in Denver on

Let me tell you a mystery. In the Spring of 2002, I sat in my Sexuality and Christianity class as an undergraduate at Illinois Wesleyan University, in which my professor, April DeConick, explained that when Jesus said in the resurrection we will be equal to the angels (Matt 22:30; Luke 20:27–28), that meant we would all be "male."[2] Though "assigned male at birth," I've had a persistent sense of being somehow female since I was around five. I would pray every night for God to turn me into a girl by the next morning since I was ten. The constant whisper in the back of my mind telling me I was a woman never went away. As a teenager, I decided to suppress this impulse; I was going to hide who I was and hoped I could muffle this voice forever. Nonetheless, I had hoped that I would get to be a woman in the afterlife. Sitting in a classroom in Shaw Hall at the age of twenty-one as I listened to DeConick explain that in ancient Jewish and Christian literature, angels were always figured masculine, and, therefore, Jesus's saying implied a masculine afterlife for everyone, my heart sank. More than anything, I wanted to be a woman, even if deferred until the resurrection; at that moment, I thought I never would be.[3] So I sublimated my impulse to become a woman into the study of ancient texts of transformation, and April DeConick and Alan Segal unwittingly became my guides.

Here I offer a transgender touch across time to Paul's rich evocation of resurrection in 1 Corinthians 15 as I undergo a social and embodied gender metamorphosis.[4] As of this writing, I have been publicly transitioning for a little over

---

November 20, 2022, the Transgender Day of Remembrance / Resilience, and my birthday. I want to thank Jay Twomey for asking thoughtful questions and offering me encouragement that day. Since then, Caryn Tamber-Rosenau and Joseph Marchal have encouraged me to develop my ideas on transgender time, and Skyler McGee has expanded my thinking on a hermeneutics of resonance and dissonance.

2. See, e.g., Jub 5:1–7, where the higher orders of angels are circumcised and angels that have sex with human women (cf. Gen 6:1–4) assumes angelic maleness; Kevin Sullivan, "Sexuality and Gender of Angels," in *Paradise Now: Essays on Early Jewish and Christian Mysticism*, ed. April D. DeConick (Atlanta: SBL Press, 2006), 214–18. Turid Karlsen Seim and Jorunn Økland note that "not all believers in the resurrection believed in the resurrection of women. Some believed that women would be resurrected as men or as 'genderless' beings still defined in masculine terms" (Turid Karlsen Seim and Jorunn Økland, "Introduction," in *Metamorphoses: Resurrection, Body, and Transformative Practices in Early Christianity*, ed. Seim and Økland [Berlin: De Gruyter, 2009], 6).

3. I had not yet read John Milton: "For spirits when they please / Can either sex assume, or both; so soft . . . And works of love or enmity fulfil (*Paradise Lost*, I.423–431).

4. "Touch across time" is from Carolyn Dinshaw, *Getting Medieval: Sexualities and Communities, Pre- and Postmodern* (Durham, NC: Duke University Press, 1999), 47. Discussing Margery Kempe's queerness, her own queerness, and the relationship between past and present queerness, Dinshaw writes, "What is left out, that residue, is the leavings of categories, the queer; and queerness is just that relation of unfittingness, disjunctiveness—that uncategorizability, that being left out. Queerness denotes a relation that can be specified in a given time and place . . . and can be traced across time" (*Getting Medieval*, 158). Cf. DeVun's "deep history": "Placing the premodern and modern in conversation allows us to recognize a pattern in thinking about human bodily diversity that continues, and perhaps recurs, in science and medicine across a long chronological framework. . . . Parallels between past and present, while not absolute, speak to an expanded timeline of efforts to manipulate bodies to fit the binary sexual and social categories of male and female. A deep history helps us to shine a light on harmful and even violent practices in the past, as well as to make further challenges to ones that exist even today" (Leah DeVun, *The Shape of Sex: Nonbinary Gender from Genesis to the Renaissance* [New York: Columbia University Press, 2021], 203–4).

two years. I am liminality embodied, partially transitioned, a gooey chrysalis. Transition reflects my desire, this impulse I have had my entire life, to *become*—to rearrange my own flesh into something greater.

In reading Paul's account of resurrection from a trans perspective, I do not speak for all trans people, whether binary or nonbinary. I do not speak for all trans women or trans fems. I speak for what resonates with me on a deep, visceral level. As Leah DeVun writes concerning past and present nonbinary bodies, "we should allow the past and present to resonate productively. In that resonance we might find that our contemporary debates about the body are less new and exceptional than they first appear. Such resonances may help us pose more critical questions about our own world."[5] Even with my own resonance with these themes, I hope that others, trans or cis, will also find much that resonates with their own selves. The themes I unfold jump out to me because I am trans, but they are not exclusively trans.

Why Paul? I never liked him much. I even started my career studying Hebrews partly to avoid Paul.[6] But in my emerging embodiment, Paul's letters queerly resonate with my transgender experience. As I rise into my glorified body, Paul's letters provide a reservoir of language and imagery for my transformation.

Yet might this be too obvious a place for a transgender reading? Wouldn't it be more interesting to take a passage that has no clear transgender resonances and read it with a transgender "lens," "gaze," or—my preferred term—"touch" to reconsider it without cis-normative assumptions like Deryn Guest has done with 2 Kings 9–10?[7] Or use the analytic category "gendered category transgressors" as Jane Nichols and Rachel Stuart do in their analysis of Jacob's crossing of gendered categories.[8] But I'm not going to recover gender variant people in biblical literature as other scholars have already adroitly done when examining figures like Jacob, Yael, Tamar, Jezebel, Jesus, or the Ethiopian eunuch.[9]

---

5. DeVun, *Shape of Sex*, 162.

6. Jaeda C. Calaway, *The Sabbath and the Sanctuary: Access to God in the Letter to the Hebrews and Its Priestly Contexts* (Tübingen: Mohr Siebeck, 2013).

7. Deryn Guest, "Modeling the Transgender Gaze: Performances of Masculinities in 2 Kings 9–10," in Teresa J. Hornsby and Guest, *Transgender, Intersex, and Biblical Interpretation* (Atlanta: SBL Press, 2016), 45–80.

8. Jane Nichols and Rachel Stuart, "Transgender: A Useful Category of Biblical Analysis?" *JIBS* 1:2 (Spring 2020): 1–24. Yet "transgender" can operate as an analytical category rather than as a descriptive self-identification to refer to anyone who moves away from their assigned gender; see Susan Stryker, *Transgender History: The Roots of Today's Revolution*, rev. ed. (Seal Press, 2017), 1; cf. Susan Stryker and Aren Z. Aizura, "Introduction: Transgender Studies 2.0," in *The Transgender Studies Reader 2*, ed. Stryker and Aizura (New York: Routledge, 2013), 11; DeVun, *Shape of Sex*, 159–60. DeVun (*Shape of Sex*, 1–15) uses "nonbinary sex" as an analytic term for all gender variances throughout history that cross, blur, and disrupt how the gender binary is constructed at that time.

9. Nichols and Stuart, "Transgender," 1–24; Samuel Ross, "A Transgender Gaze at Genesis 38," *JIBS* 1:2 (Spring 2020): 25–39; Rebekah Dyer, "Envisioning Fire Theophanies as Gender-Neutral Expressions of Selfhood," *JIBS* 1:2 (Spring 2020): 40–60; Aysha W. Musa, "Jael Is Non-Binary; Jael Is Not a Woman," *JIBS* 1:2 (Spring 2020): 97–120; Melissa Harl Sellew, "Reading the *Gospel of Thomas* from Here: A Trans-Centred Hermeneutic," *JIBS* 1:2 (Spring 2020): 61–96.

Instead, I look around me. My heart breaks daily as I breathe in an ever-present atmosphere of transphobic violence, murder, microaggressions, and legislation. In this context, I reach out to hope. While any relation to hope can become cruel,[10] this hope is positional and strategic, as, to paraphrase Italo Calvino, I find the things in the inferno that are not inferno and give them space.[11] In that way, it is like Sara Ahmed says of her own willful optimism, that it is "a way of holding on, of not giving up."[12] As José Esteban Muñoz argues, the "idea of hope . . . is both a critical affect and a methodology."[13] Queer people are supposed to be melancholic, and trans people are supposed to feel the psychological pain called dysphoria. In this context trans hope, joy, and euphoria are resistance; they are revolutionary.[14] So let me be obvious, because I need a moment to revel in the fact that I was sown a boy, but I am rising a woman; I was assigned male but am claiming my femaleness. It is the same flesh and blood, soul and spirit, but in a more pleasing arrangement.

SOCIAL TRANSITIONS

I am going to do something Alan Segal could have never imagined when he took me on as his graduate student: I am going to trans his reading of Paul.[15] While others have offered queer readings of Paul,[16] Segal's body of work has some-

---

10. Lauren Berlant, *Cruel Optimism* (Durham, NC: Duke University Press, 2011), 1–3; cf. Sara Ahmed, *Willful Subjects* (Durham, NC: Duke University Press, 2014), 173–74. *Pistis* can become a cruel relation, as Jimmy Hoke (*Feminism, Queerness, Affect, and Romans: Under God?* [Atlanta: SBL Press, 2021], 187–200) demonstrates.

11. Italo Calvino, *Invisible Cities*, trans. William Weaver (San Diego: Harcourt, 1974), 165: "The inferno of the living is not something that will be; if there is one, it is what is already here, the inferno where we live every day, that we form by being together. There are two ways to escape suffering it. The first is easy for many: accept the inferno and become such a part of it that you can no longer see it. The second is risky and demands constant vigilance and apprehension: seek and learn to recognize who and what, in the midst of the inferno, are not inferno, then make them endure, give them space."

12. Ahmed, *Willful Subjects*, 174.

13. José Esteban Muñoz, *Cruising Utopia: The Then and There of Queer Futurity*, 10th Anniversary Edition (New York: New York University Press, 2019), 4.

14. As Lopez says, "Being and acting queer necessitates . . . a shift in focus from how to deal with what is to how to imagine what is possible" (Davina C. Lopez, *Apostle to the Conquered: Reimagining Paul's Mission* [Minneapolis: Fortress Press, 2008], 14); or as Crawley has evoked the "otherwise possible" in Black queer joy; Ashon T. Crawley, *Blackpentecostal Breath: The Aesthetics of Possibility* (New York: Fordham University Press, 2017), 3; *The Lonely Letters* (Durham, NC: Duke University Press, 2020), 88, 145–49, 202.

15. On "transing" see Max K. Strassfeld, *Trans Talmud: Androgynes and Eunuchs in Rabbinic Literature* (Oakland: University of California Press, 2022), 14–15; "Transing Religious Studies," *JFSR* 34:1 (2018): 37–53. The term derives from Susan Stryker, Paisley Currah, and Lisa Jean Moore, "Introduction," *Women's Studies Quarterly* 36:3–4 (Fall/Winter 2008): 13.

16. E.g., Lopez, *Apostle to the Conquered*, 11–16; Joseph A. Marchal, *The Politics of Heaven: Women, Gender, and Empire in the Study of Paul* (Minneapolis: Fortress Press, 2009); *Appalling Bodies: Queer Figures Before and After Paul's Letters* (New York: Oxford University Press, 2020); Gillian Townsley, *The Straight Mind in Corinth: Queer Readings across 1 Corinthians 11:2–16* (Atlanta: SBL Press, 2017); Hoke, *Feminism, Queerness, Affect, and Romans*.

thing unintentionally queer about it as it questions and crosses boundaries.[17] His crossings were conversion, ascent, and death. Among the transformations he charts, let's add gender as well.

In what follows, I will cling to, lean against, and push and pull like taffy Segal's thesis that Paul's conversion was both a social and spiritual transformation.[18] As I transition, I am undergoing two overlapping transformations: a bodily metamorphosis and a social reorientation. Paul's letters likewise enjoin a resocialization as one joins the nascent Jesus-following community and envision a bodily transformation of resurrection.

I will, however, leave behind the language of "conversion" central to Segal's thought. Whatever Paula Frederiksen has to say about terms we should abandon,[19] "conversion" is a triggering word for many queer and trans people, myself included, due to "conversion" therapy, a form of psychological torture used against LGBTIQ people. So, let's jettison "conversion."

There is Stendahl's preferred alternative: a call.[20] Acts frames Paul's about-face vis-a-vis early Jesus followers as a prophetic call.[21] Paul refers to himself as called (1 Cor 1:1–10).[22] Justin Sabia-Tanis, similarly, has spoken of gender as a call.[23] Joy Ladin compares her transition to a prophetic call; in her case, Jonah.[24] Yet it is not *only* a call; it is a radical social reorientation.[25] Segal concedes partly to Stendahl: "Paul was both converted and called."[26]

Since I've answered my own calling to transition, I have been disoriented and reoriented. Sara Ahmed writes, "In order to become oriented, you might suppose that we must first experience disorientation."[27] The moment I said "I'm really a woman," and someone else was in the room with me—in this case, my partner—I felt the earth move under my feet. As Ahmed continues, "disorientation happens when the ground no longer supports an action. We lose ground, we lose our sense of how to stand; we might even lose our standing. It is not only that queer surfaces support action, but also that the action they support involves

---

17. Kimberly B. Stratton and Andrea Lieber, eds., *Crossing Boundaries in Early Judaism and Christianity: Ambiguities, Complexities, and Half-Forgotten Adversaries: Essays in Honor of Alan F. Segal* (Leiden: Brill, 2016).

18. On resocialization, see Alan F. Segal, *Paul the Convert: The Apostolate and Apostasy of Saul the Pharisee* (New Haven, CT: Yale University Press, 1990), 74–79; 72–114 more generally.

19. Paula Fredriksen, "Mandatory Retirement: Ideas in the Study of Christian Origins Whose Time Has Come to Go," *SR* 35 (2006): 231–46.

20. Krister Stendahl, *Paul among Jews and Gentiles and Other Essays* (Minneapolis: Fortress Press, 1976), esp. 7–23; cf. Segal, *Paul the Convert*, 5–6.

21. Acts 9:15–17; 22:14–16; 26:16–17; resembling Jer 1:5–11; Isa 6:1–9; and parts of Ezek 1.

22. Dale B. Martin, *The Corinthian Body* (New Haven, CT: Yale University Press, 1995) 56–58.

23. Justin Sabia-Tanis, *Trans-Gendered: Theology, Ministry, and Communities of Faith* (Cleveland: Pilgrim Press, 2003), 4, 146–60.

24. Joy Ladin, *The Soul of the Stranger: Reading God and Torah from a Transgender Perspective* (Waltham, MA: Brandeis University Press, 2018); "In the Image of God, God Created Them: Toward a Trans Theology," *JFSR* 34:1 (2018): 53.

25. On (auto)biographical reconstruction of a "convert," see Segal, *Paul the Convert*, 12, 28–29.

26. Segal, *Paul the Convert*, 6, 285–300; cf. Lopez, *Apostle to the Conquered*, 119–37.

27. Sara Ahmed, *Queer Phenomenology: Orientations, Objects, Others* (Durham, NC: Duke University Press, 2006), 5.

shifting grounds, or even clearing new ground, which allow us to tread a different path."[28] I lost and gained direction at the same time. I have also lost social status in some ways while gaining it in others. As I answer that call to transition, I see and walk through the world differently.

My interactions with most people have changed. Some stare as they see a mixture of masculine and feminine elements in my clothing, demeanor, body shape, facial features, and my voice. This might be something akin to "genderfuck."[29] Others read me as wearing drag and call me, "sir." Most people read me as a woman and call me "ma'am." As I continue to transition, the misgendering has decreased and the correct gendering has increased, especially from those who did not know me prior to my transition.

My relationships with many—not all—cishet men have become awkward. Male colleagues who used to be friendly with me no longer look me in the eye. Some pretend I am not there. Others glare at me. Others are curious. My interactions with most—not all—other women, queer, and trans people have strengthened, as if an invisible barrier has melted away. Trans students ask my advice on how to navigate transitioning at college. I receive advice from them as well. Others come up to me in public—having "clocked" me—and ask my pronouns. I have welcomed this newly embodied way of moving through spaces and interacting with others and their varied embodiments. As I come out, I change, but the world around me changes too, acquiring a new shape.[30]

So what happens when we think beyond "conversion" and even "calling"? What happens if we think of Paul's resocialization in terms of social transition? He discusses such a social transition using the physical terminology of *morphosis*.[31]

> Rom 12:2: "Do not be conformed to this age, but be transformed [*metamorphousthe*] by the renewal of your mind, so that you may examine what is the will of God, the good and the preferred and the perfect."[32]

> Gal 4:19: "my little children, with whom again I am in labor pains until Christ be formed [*morphōthē*] in you!"

> Phil 3:10–11: "To know him and the power of his resurrection and the sharing of his sufferings, co(n)forming [*symmorphizomenos*] in his death."

In Romans 12, Paul speaks out against conformity to this world or age (*aion*). It is odd in context, since this statement appears in a passage otherwise pregnant

28. Ahmed, *Queer Phenomenology*, 170.
29. Erin Runions, *How Hysterical: Identification and Resistance in the Bible and Film* (London: Palgrave Macmillan, 2003), 93–114.
30. This resonates with Sara Ahmed's "lesbian landscape": "The lesbian body does not extend the shape of the world, as a world organized around the form of the heterosexual couple. Inhabiting a body that is not extended by the skin of the social means the world acquires a new shape and makes new impressions" (*Queer Phenomenology*, 20).
31. Segal, *Paul the Convert*, 22–23.
32. Unless otherwise noted, all translations are my own.

with Paul urging his audience to conform to Romanness (e.g., Rom 13:1–7).[33] Yet Paul likely sees acquiescence as temporary as this age recedes and a new age takes its place. One ought to be "out of place" or rather "out of time" in this age. One's actions—here "holy"—mark one as different, as nonconforming, as queer. By not conforming, one enables the small opening of a potential for change, transformation. In Galatians 4, Paul transes himself to become a laboring mother to the Galatians. The father seems to be Christ, who will—according to ancient embryology—provide the form or the mold into which the Galatians will be re-formed. Finally, Philippians 3 blurs the processes of social and physical transition, since participation in Jesus's death and resurrection enables both; this process is *symmorphosis*, which I have rendered as "co(n)forming." One could render it merely as "conforming." But it is different from "being conformed" (*syschematizesthe*) in Rom 12:2. Instead of conformity to this age, it is conforming to Christ in Christ's death in order to realize the power of resurrection. This last example, however, is not merely social but also indicates a bodily co-emerging, which leads to a potential translation of a sociobiological co-forming rather than only a social conforming. To be "in Christ" includes both a social and bodily transition. By using the term *transition* for both social and embodied processes, I find a resonance, a partial touch across time. In addition, Paul plants a seed of hope for a bodily transformation.

BODILY TRANSITIONS

Dying Daily

In 1 Cor 15:35–57, Paul encases his discussion of attaining a glorified body in death. For resurrection, death is a prerequisite. Just before talking about the transformative quality of resurrection, he switches between literal and figurative death: "Daily I die" (15:31).[34] Paul elsewhere blurs the differences between literal and figurative death through baptism, participating in Christ's death so that one can likewise experience Christ's conquest of death in his resurrection (Gal 2:19–21; Rom 6:1–10).[35]

Literal and figurative death is a daily part of the trans experience. November 20 is the Transgender Day of Remembrance / Resilience, when we reflect upon victims of transphobic violence. The week before I came out of the closet in the fall of 2021, I sat at the reference desk in the library reading the obituaries of

---

33. Hoke (*Feminism, Queerness, Affect and Romans*, 11–77) discusses Paul's "Romanormativity." Later they write, "Paul's theology is *Roman without Rome*" (186).

34. Marchal calls this a "perpetually necropolitical status" (Marchal, "How Soon is (This Apocalypse) Now? Queer Velocities after a Corinthian Already and a Pauline Not Yet," in *Sexual Disorientations: Queer Temporalities, Affects, Theologies*, ed. Kent L. Brintnall, Marchal, and Stephen D. Moore, [New York: Fordham University Press, 2017], 50).

35. Segal, *Paul the Convert*, 133–38.

trans folks who had been murdered in 2021.³⁶ I held back tears as I was surrounded by colleagues and students who knew nothing of my internal turmoil. I came back to my work area and noticed that my colleague Elora Agsten was staying later than usual, because she was going to a party. I plopped down in the seat next to her, pulled out my phone with a picture of me *en femme*, and told her if I went to the party, I would go like this.

The act of coming out is an apocalypse, an "unhiding." It leads to a reorientation of social relationships and modes of embodiment. At that moment, to my colleague I was no longer a man; I became a woman in her eyes. I died to my male persona. I came out fully at work the next week, and I have lived my life as a woman ever since. The next thing I knew, I was called into the Dean of Faculty's office. She had come up with a list of things to make my institutional transition smoother. I died to my old self even more. I came out to my parents in late January 2022. Shaking like a leaf in the wind, I read a letter I had written to them. Within three days, my dad was calling me Jaeda. I told my sister, brother-in-law, and nieces in late February 2022. At that point, the last remaining social thread holding me back was cut. I finally legally changed my name to Jaeda on November 3, 2022. Many trans people often even refer to their pretransition name as their "deadname," though I call it my "birth name." Jaeda rises as I slough off the persona I had cultivated for decades, and I am renewed.³⁷

> Death has been swallowed in victory.
> Where, O death, is your victory?
> Where, O death, is your sting?
> (15:54–55)

Yet in the midst of my life-saving, soul-saving series of symbolic deaths, literal deaths still surround us as much as they did when I first came out. My heart breaks daily as transphobic violence increases in the form of physical violence, anti-trans legislation, and harassment. Unfortunately, death still has its sting for us. Nonetheless, as I die daily to my previous male persona and am transformed, becoming who I always was to begin with, Jaeda, who had been hidden, is now revealed in a new gender apocalypse.

CURVY TIME: TRANS TEMPORALITIES IN PAUL

My *embodied* gender revelation resonates with Paul's transformative terminology and imagery. In addition to the passages mentioned, Paul says in Phil 3:21, that Christ "will transform [*metaschēmatisei*] the body [*sōma*] of our humiliation

---

36. C. Riley Snorton (*Black on Both Sides: A Racial History of Trans Identity* [Minneapolis: University of Minnesota Press, 2017], vii–xiv), discusses the recounting of the deaths of trans people, especially trans women of color, and its racial genealogies.

37. Sabia-Tanis (*Trans-Gendered*, 142) speaks of the ways in which Christian trans people relate their transition to dying and rising with Christ.

so that it may be co(n)formed [*symmorphon*] to the body of his glory [*tō sōmati tēs doxēs autou*]."³⁸ *Morphosis* is emphatically embodied. While Paul uses *morphosis* vocabulary elsewhere, he strangely omits it in 1 Corinthians 15. He resorts to transformative *imagery*. Through these images, one is "sown" and "raised" and "becomes"; one even shall be "changed" (*allagesometha*).

This terminology of "changed" emerges at the end of the passage, where Paul returns to another major theme: flesh. He had started with the flesh—there are different kinds of flesh (1 Cor 15:39)—but reached a conclusion that flesh and blood cannot inherit the kingdom (1 Cor 15:50). Flesh and blood are perishable, but the kingdom is for those who rise imperishable. Then Paul writes:

> Look, I will tell you a mystery!
> All of us will not sleep,
>   but all of us will be changed (*allagesometha*)
>   in an atom (*en atomoi*)
>   in the twinkling of an eye
>   at the last trumpet
>   For the trumpet will blast
> and the dead will be raised imperishable
> and we will be changed (*allagesometha*).
>   (1 Cor 15:51–52)

This passage shows a dissonance between the language of instantaneous transformation and the imagery of transformation as a process of sowing and raising. Which is it?

Since my dissertation, I have enjoyed toying with time; I like its curves, dilations, contractions, and bending.³⁹ Though not explicit in my previous works, I have engaged queer temporalities.⁴⁰ Queer temporalities have multiple trajectories and overlaps; they can be disorienting touches across time; they can also recognize and resist "chrononormativity." Along with my earlier readings of physical curvatures, performative temporalities, and narrative chronotopes with a dose of my own life, they inspire my transgender temporalities.⁴¹ Because I am a trans woman, I prefer to call trans time "curvy time," but it can also be quite "hairy." Curvy time highlights the ways in which temporalities are not

---

38. Segal, *Paul the Convert*, 63; Elizabeth A. Castelli, *Imitating Paul: A Discourse of Power* (Louisville, KY: Westminster John Knox Press, 1991), 106. Paul also uses *metaschematizein* in 1 Cor 4:6; cf. *sysmatizesthe* in Rom 12:2, translated as "conformed."

39. Calaway, *Sabbath and the Sanctuary*, 18–20 nn. 63–67.

40. Dinshaw, *Getting Medieval*; Dinshaw, *How Soon Is Now? Medieval Texts, Amateur Readers, and the Queerness of Time* (Durham, NC: Duke University Press, 2012); see Marchal, "How Soon is (This Apocalypse) Now?" 45–58; Hoke, "Unbinding Imperial Time: Chrononormativity and Paul's Letter to the Romans," in Brintnall, Marchal, and Moore, *Sexual Disorientations*, 68–83. In addition, see Marchal, "'Making History' Queerly: Touches across Time through a Biblical Behind," *BibInt* 19 (2011): 373–95; and, "Female Masculinity in Corinth? Bodily Citations and the Drag of History," *Neot* 48:1 (2014): 93–113.

41. Note a "touch across time" as a kind of resurrection (Dinshaw, *Getting Medieval*, 47); see further Calaway, *Sabbath and the Sanctuary*, 18–20 nn. 63–67. Strassfeld, *Trans Talmud*, 151–81, develops "eunuch temporality."

straight: their overlaps, their doubling, their switchbacks, their entanglements, their *curves*.[42]

How might a trans person experience time's curvatures and hairy entanglements? Elizabeth Freeman introduces the concept of "chrononormativity." In chrononormativity "time binds" various forms of embodiment to social (re)production: the "straight time" of marriage, reproduction, and childrearing operates within a capitalist system of production that impacts daily, weekly, and yearly rhythms as well as generational time and inheritances. Queer temporalities find alternative rhythms at work.[43]

My own life experience partly participates in what Jack Halberstam similarly calls "repro-time" ("reproductive time") and yet exceeds it. I am married, have kids, and am trying to raise them as best I can (repro-time), but I am a trans woman who is attracted to other women (both trans and cis) and nonbinary people. Halberstam notes that many cishet people are in "queer time,"[44] and many LGBTIQ people are in repro-time.[45] But just as chrononormativity or repro-time arranges embodiment through temporal regulations, my embodiment is both shaped by and pushes back against these socio-temporal regulations. I am too Bakhtinian, however, to see queer temporalities as solely in opposition to chrononormativities or repro-time;[46] they are dialogical with one another. Trans embodied experience is fluid; it flows, can become congealed, and flow again; it swirls within and through multiple simultaneous temporalities, both normative and disruptive, ultimately unsettling both.[47]

Individual trans lives bend time differently; there are variances and patterns among trans folks, depending upon when, if, and how they transition. There is the apparent linearity of pre-transition, transition, and post-transition, which trans people use as a short-hand. Yet with a closer examination of any trans person's life one finds sets of overlapping transitions: social, legal, medical, and surgical. Not all of these transitions line up, nor are they in the same sequence for everyone. I started my social transition before hormones, whereas others

---

42. Roberto Che Espinoza writes, "My body is a borderland, a paradox of being and becoming" (*Body Becoming: A Path to Our Liberation* [Minneapolis: Broadleaf, 2022], 18).

43. Elizabeth Freeman defines "chrononormativity": "By 'binds,' I mean to invoke the way that human energy is collated so that it can sustain itself. By 'time binds' . . . I mean that naked flesh is bound into socially meaningful embodiment through temporal regulation: binding is what turns mere existence into a form of mastery in a process I'll refer to as *chrononormativity*, or the use of time to organize individual human bodies toward maximum productivity" (*Time Binds: Queer Temporalities, Queer Histories* [Durham, NC: Duke University Press, 2010], 3; emphasis original).

44. Jack Halberstam, *In a Queer Time and Place: Transgender Bodies, Subcultural Lives* (New York: New York University Press, 2005), 5, 152–54.

45. Freeman, *Time Binds*, xv.

46. As in Halberstam, *In a Queer Time and Place*, 1. Halberstam gets closer to this when discussing how rural or small town "alternative sexual communities" operate in proximity to rather than distinction from [cis]-heterosexualities (39).

47. Compare Judith Butler, *Undoing Gender* (New York: Routledge, 2004), 217: "As a consequence of being in the mode of becoming, and in always living with the constitutive possibility of becoming otherwise, the body is that which can occupy the norm in myriad ways, exceed the norm, rework the norm, and expose the realities to which we thought we were confined as open to transformation."

start hormones without telling anyone that they are even transitioning. Not every trans person undergoes every kind of transition. Not all trans people will get surgery; some do not want it while others may desire it but it remains out of reach for health, monetary, or legislative reasons. Instead of being linear, we see a bunch of wibbly wobbly, intersecting lines that curve back on themselves.[48]

While intense in the first couple years, I will always be transitioning in some way. I am always "coming out" to someone. Socially, some people refuse to believe that I am a trans woman until they see me in my flesh. Bodily, my hormone treatments will continue to alter my body in increasingly subtle ways; I am in a state of perpetual becoming, as we all are. My becoming, however, is marked in our society.[49]

Trans time, moreover, doubles as past and present collide.[50] While Halberstam carves out queer time as extended adolescence,[51] those who transition after natal puberty experience a second puberty: I am becoming both a pubescent girl and a middle-aged woman at the same time, which can be quite disorienting.

Trans time also can fast forward or reverse. Closeted trans people age quickly—the stress of the closet is intense; moreover, many closeted trans people self-medicate through drugs and alcohol in order to numb themselves. Throughout my life, people have noted how I seemed much older than I was or how serious my demeanor was. Yet a lot of transitioning people appear to age backwards. My former supervisor asked me: "how do you keep looking younger?" The release of the pressure of the closet and the boost in hormones, if one transitions in that manner, give us a more youthful appearance. Moreover, people note I am much happier now. I smile more, and not because men tell me to do so; a former colleague once noted that she didn't know that I could smile until I began my transition.

My timeline is no longer a line; it is all mixed up, doubled, reversed, with overlapping, intersecting, and looping threads. As Eliza Steinbock has written, "The embodiment of trans time might be fractured, discontinuous, and layered: At any rate, it goes against the presumption of a linear, enduring sense of self-sameness associated with cis identity."[52] DeVun speaks of nonbinary bodies as in "tension," defining "tension" as "where bodies and genders meet." DeVun's

---

48. Because of this, S. J. Crasnow ("'Becoming' Bodies: Affect Theory, Transgender Jews, and the Rejection of the Coherent Subject," *Crosscurrents* 71:1 [March 2021]: 57) refers to trans temporalities as nonlinear and rhizomatic. As Moore, Brintnall, and Marchal write: "Past, present, and future are the interflowing, ever-shifting sites where happiness, joy, shame, loss, mourning, disgust, despair, hope, pride, and victory are experienced and processed" (Moore, Brintnall, and Marchal, "Introducing Queer Disorientations: Four Turns and a Twist," in Brintnall, Marchal, and Moore, *Sexual Disorientations*, 4).

49. Crasnow, "'Becoming' Bodies," 49–62. Butler states, "Life histories are histories of becoming, and categories can sometimes act to freeze that process of becoming" (*Undoing Gender*, 80); on perpetually coming out, see Eve Kosofsky Sedgwick, *Epistemology of the Closet*, Updated with a New Preface (Berkeley: University of California Press, 2008), 68.

50. Cf. Dinshaw, *How Soon is Now?*, 64.

51. Halberstam, *In a Queer Time and Place*, 152–54, 174–76.

52. Elizabeth Steinbock, "Embodiment," in *The Sage Encyclopedia of Trans Studies*, volume 1, ed. Abbie E. Goldberg and Genny Beemyn (Los Angeles: Sage Reference, 2021), 230.

nonbinary "tension" suspends, compresses, and ruptures time, makes time double over, returning to origins, but looks forward to renewal.[53] Halberstam expresses the paradox of trans-ness by noting that while *queer* time is compressed with a diminished future, the plasticity of *transgender* embodiment becomes futurity itself.[54]

How do time's curves and hairy entanglements relate to how I read Paul? Change is instantaneous, but it isn't at the same time. He says it is in an instant, moment, or literally "atom." It is in the twinkling of an eye. Yet his imagery indicates a process. The disjunction between terminology and imagery creates a ripple in Paul's text. The word translated as "moment" is *atomos*. It means "uncuttable." This word intensifies time's immediacy, irreducibility, and infinite smallness.[55] Time cannot get any smaller, faster, or briefer. To update Paul's scientific terminology, it is a quantum event.

By contrast, his agricultural imagery of resurrection dilates time. It slows things down to a seasonal level through sowing, watering, growing, and harvesting (15:35–38, 42–49). Paul portrays such a processual transformation elsewhere. In Philippians 3, the term *symmorphosis* indicates a continual process.[56] Second Cor 3:12–4:5 likewise lays out a gradual transformation. In 2 Cor 3:18, Paul writes:

> And all of us, with unveiled faces, mirroring the glory of the Lord, are being transformed into the same image from glory to glory [*tēn autēn eikona metamorphoumetha apo doxēs eis doxan*].

A gradual transformation reverberates throughout Paul's letters to the Philippians and the Corinthians. Returning to 1 Corinthians 15, this physical transformation contracts and expands time—an eternity in a moment. Similarly, Halberstam writes that queer time "expands the potential of the moment."[57] Why from one perspective could it be an instant and from another a slow process through the quanta of trans temporalities?

Firstly, the difference is determined by death; to the living, it appears instantaneous. "We" are changed; but the dead are raised imperishable (cf. 1 Thess 5:2–4). While cis people likely are drawn into Paul's first-person plural "we" of the living, trans people are marked by death, having socially died to their pre-transition self, while finally arising at last to life. There is, therefore, a transgender resistance to Paul at this point, because it is awkward to identify with Paul's "we." While he suggests "we" includes "all of us," just as there are those of us now who resist his "we," there were surely those then who did not want to be co-opted into his "we."

53. DeVun, *Shape of Sex*, 206–7.
54. Halberstam, *In a Queer Time and Place*, 2, 18; Halberstam attributes this position to others.
55. Liddell and Scott, s.v., "ἄτομος."
56. Segal, *Paul the Convert*, 141–42.
57. Halberstam, *In a Queer Time and Place*, 2.

At the same time, Paul's "we" was driven by an apocalyptic present. For trans people, there is a queer urgency,[58] but the reason is a bit different: it is because our resurrection is *always already happening*. Again, unlike in 1 Corinthians 15, our resurrection is not deferred until the ever-receding tomorrow; our resurrection is now and is an ongoing emergence. In this way, trans people may find a fleeting resonance in Antoinette Clark Wire's reconstruction of the Corinthian women prophets' views of the transformation of resurrection as either something that has already occurred or is currently unfolding rather than a future event. They have already reclaimed God's image and likeness, and obtained their glorified spiritual body in Christ through baptism. Paul's deferral of the resurrection status until the future in 1 Corinthians 15 does not even accord with his other writings which also show a current unfolding (e.g., 2 Cor 3:18).[59] In this current and ongoing transformation, the future of repro-time recedes and chrononormativity's intergenerational binding loosens, as our embodied transformation becomes futurity itself.[60]

Secondly, the paradox may be resolved with the process of transformation beginning with joining the community and making Christ your Lord, but the "instant" being the final step of the transformation.[61] Segal writes, "Dying and being resurrected along with Christ in baptism is the beginning of the process by which the believer gains the same image of God, his *eikon*."[62] I would rephrase Segal; instead, one's social transition catalyzes one's embodied transition into the image of God.

Or it could be the opposite: a moment of change at baptism leads to a processual transformation into God's image. Segal writes: "Paul uses the term *morphosis* to express the true Christian life. . . . This suggests that the formation of the likeness of Christ is both a punctal event, which is marked by baptism, and a durative process, which will culminate in the second coming, the parousia."[63] It's possible all of these solutions are true according to varying angles. The slippage of metaphorical death (baptism) and literal death with resurrection complicate how one resolves the paradox of the momentary yet processual transformation. It mirrors a trans person's transition that alternates between punctal events (initial coming out or surgery) and ongoing transformations (ongoing coming out

---

58. Halberstam, *In a Queer Time and Place*, 2.
59. Antoinette Clark Wire, *The Corinthian Women Prophets: A Reconstruction through Paul's Rhetoric* (Minneapolis: Fortress Press, 1990), 123, 131, 161, 163–76, 184–85. She cites Gal 3:27–28 as well as the dying and rising with Christ that Paul develops throughout his correspondences but distinctly not in 1 Corinthians (Gal 2:19–20; 2 Cor 4:7–14; 5:14–15; Rom 5:3–11; 7:6; 8:10–11; Phil 3:10–11). See the present state of resurrection in Col 2:12–15.
60. Halberstam, *In a Queer Time and Place*, 18.
61. Engberg-Pedersen's analysis of Paul's transformation language is representative of this two-stage view, though he views it as a cognitive change (partial transformation) that leads to the resurrected bodily change (full transformation); Troels Engberg-Pedersen, "Complete and Incomplete Transformation in Paul: A Philosophical Reading of Paul on Body and Spirit," in Seim and Øklund, *Metamorphoses*, 123–46.
62. Segal, *Paul the Convert*, 64; cf. 151–58.
63. Segal, 151.

or HRT—hormone replacement therapy). Paul's simultaneous instantaneous-and-ongoing *morphosis* resonates with how I, a trans woman, *transition*: both *morphosis* and *transition* entwine social and embodied transformation that simultaneously compresses and dilates time in curvy and hairy ways.

BENDING THE BINARY

In 1 Cor 15:42–49, Paul develops his transformation imagery with a series of binaries between what is sown (*speretai*) and what is raised (*egeiretai*). We are sown perishable, in dishonor, weak, physical, a soulish body, earthly, and dusty, but will be raised imperishable, glorious, powerful, a spiritual body, and heavenly; that is, sparkly.[64] There is a discontinuity between the fleshly and glorified bodies. What is raised is not the same as what was sown, though it derives from it. It disrupts any sense of a continuous self.

Binary thinking was deeply rooted in Paul's own time and remains so in ours.[65] Cavan Concannon notes: "Paul's repeated binary constructions . . . serve to other his opponents, perceived or real, and these binaries, in turn, are deployed by modern scholars when they interpret Paul's letters."[66] These binaries are always asymmetrical, with one side valued and the other devalued. While balanced in phrasing, they are unbalanced in weight, but, thereby, they unravel when examined closely.

In the center of the series is the regularly mistranslated pairing of the "soulish body" (*soma psuchikon*) and the "spiritual body" (*soma pneumatikon*). While earlier in 1 Corinthians, Paul presents this as a simple binary of "soulish" versus "spiritual" (1 Cor 2:6–3:5; esp. 2:14),[67] here Paul presents it as two compound concepts (soulish body and spiritual body) with three terms: body, soul, and spirit. Both soul and spirit are embodied (cf. Rom 8:18–25), and spiritual things have a subtle materiality. So one has embodied spiritual materiality.[68]

What is assumed is flesh. Paul mentions flesh before and after this passage. Before, he looked at different kinds of bodies, flesh, and glories. Again, three terms—not two. Here we have body, soul, and spirit: three elements and not two. So, we are juggling five terms: body, flesh, glory, soul, and spirit. But this becomes simplified since flesh and blood will be discarded (cf. Rom 13:14). While there is a fragmentation and disruption of self indicated by the transformation Paul describes, embodiment—rather than psyche or spirit—provides

---

64. Other Pauline binaries include body/spirit, law/grace, law/spirit, death/life, sin/love, loss/gain; Castelli, *Imitating Paul*, 103–4; and Martin, *Corinthian Body*, 127.

65. Segal, *Paul the Convert*, 66, 126–27.

66. Cavan Concannon, "Reading Paul Obliquely: Reading against the Grain in a Latourian Pluriverse," in *After the Corinthian Women Prophets: Reimagining Rhetoric and Power*, ed. Joseph A. Marchal (Atlanta: SBL Press, 2021), 101.

67. Martin, *Corinthian Body*, 63.

68. Martin, 21–25, 106–7, 120, 122, 126–27; Wire (*Corinthian Women Prophets*, 170) notes the soul being on the side of decay.

continuity, even if the kind of embodiment changes.[69] As terms come in and out of the equation, embodiment, whether fleshly or glorious, ensouled or spirited, weaves throughout the passage, providing a baseline into which all beings return and find renewed expression.

BECOMING SHINY: GLORY AND IMAGE

The ultimate expression of transformation is a shiny body. After I came out of the closet on campus, Jenny Barker-Devine, the chair of my old department, gave me a gift. It was a pink, sparkly scarf. She said she got it because it is sparkly, just as I am now. My Dean of Faculty told me that while Jared's eyes always looked absent, Jaeda's eyes radiate. This observation is common among trans people. If a trans person is willing to show a pre-transition photo alongside a current photo, other trans people look mainly at the eyes, their deadness in pre-transition photos and their fire and life in the current photos.

Between the frame of death and the center of transformation, Paul places "glory" (*doxa*). Although Paul uses a series of images based upon the sowing and reaping metaphor, in the resurrection one does not reap what one sows, but something much greater: "you do not sow the body that is to be... but God gives it a body as he has chosen" (15:37–38). Shifting from bodies, Paul speaks of different kinds of flesh. Then the language switches from flesh to glory, though still maintaining an embodied connection. Glory gathers many connotations throughout 1 Corinthians. Earlier in the letter, it resembles "honor."[70] Here, however, with the astral imagery, "glory" reflects "brightness." It's sparkly and shiny!

Firstly, Paul uses the word "glory" in terms of heavenly bodies but then shifts to characterize the resurrection body. A sparkly body draws upon the *kavod* traditions—the bright appearance of the likeness of the glory of the Lord in Ezekiel 1. But the point for one in transition is not merely that one sees the *kavod*, but that we *become* the *kavod*. This builds upon Dan 12:3, which states that the wise will shine like the brightness in the sky; it is the reward of the righteous whose lives had been cut short (cf. 2 Bar 51:10).

Secondly, for Paul, the "martyr" who has achieved this is Christ, attracting the language of "glory" and "image" in Philippians and 1 and 2 Corinthians.[71] In Phil 3:21, Paul speaks of Jesus's "body of Glory," to which his followers are

---

69. cf. Jorunn Øklund, "Genealogies of the Self: Materiality, Personal Identity, and the Body in Paul's Letters to the Corinthians," in Seim and Øklund, *Metamorphoses*, 91–94, 105–6; Vigdis Songe-Møller, "'With What Kind of Body Will They Come': Metamorphosis and the Concept of Change: From Platonic Thinking to Paul's Notion of the Resurrection of the Dead," in Seim and Øklund *Metamorphoses*, 118–19; Engberg-Pedersen, "Complete and Incomplete Transformation in Paul," 128–29.

70. Wire, *Corinthian Women Prophets*, 120; Øklund suggests a translation here of "aura" ("Genealogies of Self," 91).

71. Segal, *Paul the Convert*, 59–61, 151–58.

assimilated. Christ is the "Lord of Glory" (1 Cor 2:8), and Paul speaks of the glory of Christ, the likeness of God (2 Cor 4:3, 6, 17). He is the image of the Lord (2 Cor 4:4; Col 1:15) and the form (*morphe*) of God (Phil 2:6; cf. 2 Cor 3:18).

Thirdly, by participating in Christ's death and resurrection, one also becomes shiny. This happens by transformation into Christ's image, embodying Christ's glittery glory. Paul speaks of being transformed into the image of Christ and into the image of God (Rom 8:29; 1 Cor 3:18; 15:49; Col 3:9). In 1 Cor 15:49, this happens for those who are "in Christ."[72]

With these three steps, Paul argues that we will arise as the image of the shiny heavenly human. We become the *kavod*.

TRANS/FORM

When I told my parents that I always wanted to be their daughter, they asked me how this impacts how I read the Bible—as one does. I said the Bible resonates a lot more with me now. Resonance is not about faith or fidelity, though it can include those things. It is not even about the hope that I seek. It is about attraction. Reading certain texts strikes a chord, and that chord causes something to vibrate within me due to my accumulated embodied experiences, which include my transgender embodiment. It does not strike all my chords nor do all biblical passages have equal resonance. Other passages make me deeply uncomfortable, and I should explore the dissonance that erupts. Most passages create varying combinations of resonance and dissonance, simultaneously attracting and repelling.

There is an undercurrent of trans-ness to Paul, though a problematic one. As I read Paul as a trans woman, his androcentrism elicits dissonance. Paul could never imagine a transition from male to female as a movement into glory as 1 Cor 11:7 makes clear; but that is what it is for me. Perhaps it is more akin to the Corinthian women prophets and their rise into their present glory.[73] As Shelly Matthews argues for the Corinthian women prophets, "Shifting from an emphasis on crucifixion to resurrection, their elevation is articulated as the experience of Christ's rising in them."[74] As Wire notes, they put on Christ, God's image,

---

72. Jesus is never called "the Glory of God," but one does see "glory" or "the glory" in letters speaking of Christ or the Son (Jas 2:1; Phil 3:21; 4:19; 1 Cor 2:8; Rom 6:4; 9:23; Eph 1:17–18; Col 1:27; 2 Cor 4:4; 1 Tim 1:11; Heb 1:3; Segal, *Paul the Convert*, 10). Paul speaks of only men being in the image of God in 1 Cor 11:7, ignoring that both male and female are made in the image of God (Gen 1:27). Wire (*Corinthian Women Prophets*, 29–30, 116–34, 137–38) has noted this elision is due to the Corinthian women's own citation of this same tradition; see Marchal, "How Soon," 52–53; Marchal, "Female Masculinity" 108.

73. Marchal, "How Soon," 56; for "taking on the female/feminine" to transcend, see Townsley, *Straight Mind in Corinth*, 112–14. Wire (*Corinthian Women Prophets* 29–30, 116–34) notes that the Corinthian women prophets likely spoke about God's image and glory in a different manner than Paul, which is why Paul cites the tradition.

74. Shelly Matthews, "Hearing Wo/men Prophets: Intersections, Silences, Publics," in Marchal, *After the Corinthian Women Prophets*, 51.

which inaugurated "a new reality lacking the privilege of male over female."[75] *As* (trans) women, we also push back against these androcentric assumptions and rise into our gynomorphic glory.[76] There is, therefore, a partial touch across time, a resonance, between the social and physical transitions that emerges from Paul's interactions with different people in the Corinthian community and that I am living.

1 Corinthians 15 is a ripple in the spacetime fabric, much like the "open heaven,"[77] queerly dilating our otherwise regular temporalities and opening up possibilities of transformation. It is a revelation that allows me to unfold myself to myself and to others in a new apocalyptic moment. My transition is not *en atomoi* for me. It is a fight; it is multiple sowings and raisings. I don't just die daily; I choose new life daily. I have been sown. I am stretching out to rise. I am "in the moment" rather than momentary. I can return to my twenty-one-year-old self sitting in my Sexuality & Christianity class at Illinois Wesleyan and say, "don't worry; you're going to make it; you don't have to wait for the resurrection; you will become the woman you always knew you were. You have been sown male at birth but will rise a woman. And you will shine!"

---

75. Wire, *Corinthian Women Prophets*, 126.

76. As Matthews writes, "Recognizing gender identity along a continuum rather than according to a simple binary, and recognizing gender as performative rather than a biological given, has enabled scholars to complicate reconstructions of the wo/men among Paul's interlocutors, including reconstructions of how they might have resisted his prescriptions concerning gender conformity" ("Hearing Wo/men Prophets," 63).

77. Ezek 1:1; Isa 64:1; Matt 3:16; Mark 1:10; Luke 3:21; Rev 4:1.

Chapter 10

Captive Genders, Fugitive Flesh, and Biblical Epistles
Trans Approaches to Ancient Apostles and Assemblies in the Afterlives of Enslavement and Imprisonment

JOSEPH A. MARCHAL

For many interpreters, readers, and receivers of biblical texts and traditions, Paul's letters look like an ideal space to encounter, even celebrate forms of gender variability, transitivity, or minoritization. After all, the oft-celebrated apostle to the gentiles (or nations), ostensibly transgressing ethnoracial divisions between Jews and gentiles (in Christ), also projects certain forms of gender transitivity, particularly when he depicts himself as laboring, birthing, and nursing the letter recipients (Gal 4:19; 1 Thess 2:7; 1 Cor 3:1–2).[1] Indeed, this might resonate with what some might depict as a present-day "tipping point" of representation and inclusion for trans people. In that context one can understand the excitement in discovering a potentially gender variant apostle presented with newfound visibility. Yet, while the previous decade or so has been characterized as a period of arrival or inclusion, it has also been a period of persistent, even resurgent violence against trans and, or, gender-nonconforming people.

1. See the stirring work in Beverly Roberts Gaventa, *Our Mother Saint Paul* (Louisville, KY: Westminster John Knox, 2007); Davina C. Lopez, *Apostle to the Conquered: Reimagining Paul's Mission* (Minneapolis: Fortress, 2008); and Brigitte Kahl, "Gender Trouble in Galatia?: Paul and the Rethinking of Difference," in *Is There A Future for Feminist Theology?*, ed. Deborah F. Sawyer and Diane M. Collier (Sheffield: Sheffield Academic, 1999), 57–73; and Kahl, "No Longer Male: Masculinity Struggles Behind Galatians 3.28?" *JSNT* 79 (2000): 37–49; inter alia.

A range of trans activist and academic groups has highlighted this coincidence, of violence *with* visibility (for further context, see also the Introduction). The occasional mass media attention paid to a few celebrated public figures does little to improve or mitigate the precarious living conditions for the vast majority of trans people. Engaging and transforming those conditions, then, requires a shift in focus toward broader, collective, and participatory efforts. In the present context trans activists aim to address the root causes of higher rates of unemployment and homelessness, harassment and assault, criminalization and incarceration, often by contextualizing them within longer histories of imprisonment and enslavement. This, in turn, can redirect our focus when we turn back to Paul's letters, noting the violence and the visibility and shifting attention from the celebrated few to the conditions of larger collectives. In developing an approach from the intersections of critical race, trans, and abolitionist practices, this essay is informed by the experience and expertise of (formerly) incarcerated trans women and their networks of support and solidarity, critique and transformation, to resituate captive genders and fugitive flesh negotiating greater precarity and proximity to death. This approach requires reassessing Paul's letters, tracking how the letters reflect practices of communication and coordination of other apostles and wider networks of assemblies among those impacted by imprisonment and enslavement, the people beside Paul, both named and unnamed in these epistles and their interpretations.

MOVING VISIBILITY AND VIOLENCE TOWARD TRANSITIVITY AND FUGITIVITY

Taking my cues in part from recent reflections on trans cultural production and representation, I open here in much the same way Tourmaline, Eric A. Stanley, and Johanna Burton cautioned in launching their influential *Trap Door* collection: highlighting the recurrent pairing of apparent visibility with institutional and interpersonal violence.[2] The current "doors" of visibility, always on the terms of racial and economic respectability, also coincide with "traps" of violence, especially for trans women of color. In short, reflexive projects aiming toward trans liberation must also engage the overlapping force multipliers of racism and incarceration, their brunt unevenly borne by trans people. What might appear as an incongruity or paradox, then, looks and feels more like a persistent proximity to precarity, a proximity that is symptomatic of larger dynamics and longer patterns. This is likely why much trans writing, theorizing, and organizing[3] builds upon Ruth Wilson Gilmore's definition of racism

---

2. Tourmaline, Eric A. Stanley, and Johanna Burton, "Known Unknowns: An Introduction to *Trap Door*," in *Trap Door: Trans Cultural Production and the Politics of Visibility*, ed. Tourmaline, Stanley, and Burton (Cambridge, MA: MIT Press, 2017), xv–xxvi.

3. As reflected in Dean Spade, *Normal Life: Administrative Violence, Critical Trans Politics, and the Limits of Law* (Durham, NC: Duke University Press, 2015); Eric A. Stanley and Nat Smith, eds., *Captive Genders: Trans Embodiment and the Prison Industrial Complex* (exp. 2nd ed.; Chico,

as "the state-sanctioned or extralegal production and exploitation of group-differentiated vulnerability to premature death."[4] Dean Spade describes the ways trans resistance and transformation can elaborate on this vulnerability in attending to the distribution of life chances, or "who lives, for how long, and under what conditions."[5] If an analysis attends to those most (frequently) harmed by forces that are imposed on all of us, one can see that disparities in life chances have not improved, and in many instances have only increased, even in recent periods of ostensible progress, recognition, or inclusion. Countering the disparities growing out of this group-differentiated vulnerability to premature death, then, requires altering their overlapping root causes, including poverty, homelessness, police violence, and imprisonment.[6]

This is why abolition has been proposed as one of the main necessary nodes in trans and, or, as queer struggles,[7] given its potential to make a greater impact for more trans and, or, as queer folks than other recent goals, like legalizing same-sex marriage. Grappling with the wide-ranging and long-lasting effects of carcerality emphatically addresses the everyday violence that recurs alongside the cycles of (limited) visibility. Recent, higher-profile efforts, like the international campaign to free and support CeCe McDonald,[8] have certainly bolstered the overlaps and connections between collectives working toward trans liberation and prison abolition.[9] Yet, these struggles have an extended lineage within trans and queer histories, as reflected in the life and work of Miss Major Griffin-Gracy (among others). Miss Major not only participated in the Stonewall rebellion (of 1969) but was further politicized in the wake of the Attica prison rebellion when she was imprisoned in the 1970s, and continued working at those intersections, directing organizations like the Transgender, Gender Variant, and Intersex Justice Project, TGIJP.[10] Of course, Stonewall itself, and the forms of resistance before it, including the uprising at Compton's Cafeteria (in 1966),[11] were responses to harassment and intimidation, criminalization and incarceration.

CA: AK Press, 2015); and C. Riley Snorton, *Black on Both Sides: A Racial History of Trans Identity* (Minneapolis: University of Minnesota Press, 2017), inter alia.

4. Ruth Wilson Gilmore, *Golden Gulag: Prisons, Surplus, Crisis, and Opposition in Globalizing California* (Berkeley: University of California Press, 2007), 28.

5. Spade, *Normal Life*, 7.

6. Morgan Bassichis, Alexander Lee, and Dean Spade, "Building an Abolitionist Trans & Queer Movement with Everything We've Got," in Stanley and Smith, *Captive Genders*, 23. See also Spade, *Normal Life*, 32.

7. See, for example, Stanley, "Fugitive Flesh: Gender Self-Determination, Queer Abolition, and Trans Resistance," in Stanley and Smith, *Captive Genders*, 9.

8. See, for instance, CeCe McDonald, "'Go beyond Our Natural Selves': The Prison Letters of CeCe McDonald," ed. Omise'eke Natasha Tinsley, *TSQ* 4:2 (2017): 243–65.

9. Miss Major Griffin-Gracy, CeCe McDonald, and Toshio Meronek, "Cautious Living: Black Trans Women and the Politics of Documentation," in Tourmaline, Stanley, and Burton, *Trap Door*, 23.

10. See Jayden Donahue and Miss Major Griffin-Gracy, "Making It Happen, Mama: A Conversation with Miss Major," in Stanley and Smith, *Captive Genders*, 301–13; and Toshio Meronek and Miss Major Griffin-Gracy, *Miss Major Speaks: Conversations with a Black Trans Revolutionary* (London: Verso, 2023).

11. See Susan Stryker, *Transgender History* (Berkeley, CA: Seal Press, 2008), 63–78.

Two of the better-known leaders at Stonewall, Sylvia Rivera and Marsha P. Johnson, subsequently founded Street Transvestite Action Revolutionaries (STAR) to house, clothe, and feed homeless trans young people (see also the Introduction). STAR's organizing was frequently coalitional and multipronged yet remained persistently and often urgently focused on the criminalization and incarceration of trans and queer people, particularly Black and Latinx trans women.[12] One of Rivera's most famous speeches, the "Y'all Better Quiet Down" speech at New York's Christopher Street Liberation Day in 1973, called out an increasingly "mainstreaming" or respectable focus for mostly white gay and lesbian rights by specifically stressing incarceration:

> I've been trying to get up here all day, for your gay brothers and your gay sisters in jail! They're writing me every motherfuckin' week and ask for your help, and you all don't do a god damn thing for them. Have you ever been beaten up and raped in jail? . . . . I will no longer put up with this shit. I have been beaten. I have had my nose broken. I have been thrown in jail. I have lost my job. I have lost my apartment for gay liberation, and you all treat me this way?[13]

Rivera's relatively short intervention was frequently punctuated by the phase "in jail" (seven times) in order to emphasize the status of their gay, lesbian, and trans brothers and sisters who were (re)currently incarcerated. The ethos and actions of STAR, and groups like them, underscore the longer and intertwined histories of antiracist, abolitionist, trans, and queer struggles, while undermining any narratives about sequential progress (including proclamations that trans rights are now "what's next" in civil rights).

The extended, interrelated lineages of these struggles then trouble straightforward narratives about visibility or arrival.[14] Indeed, claims about the historic representation or visibility of trans people have the potential to pass over not only violence, but also the past! Morgan M. Page, for example, stresses how: "The media that make us visible simultaneously obscure our presence in history by continually framing trans people as new, as a modern, medicalized phenomenon only now coming to light in the topsy-turvy post-gay marriage world."[15] Trans approaches to history and time then might be shaped more by loops of

12. See especially Roderick A. Ferguson, *One-Dimensional Queer* (Cambridge: Polity Press, 2019), 18–45.

13. Sylvia Rivera, "'Y'all Better Quiet Down': Sylvia Rivera's Speech at the 1973 Liberation Day Rally," in *Street Transvestite Action Revolutionaries: Survival, Revolt, and Queer Antagonist Struggle* (Untorelli Press, 2013), 30. https://theanarchistlibrary.org/library/ehn-nothing-untorelli-press-street-transvestite-action-revolutionaries. For an important critique, however, of this compilation, and the politics of preservation and citation, see Tourmaline, "On Untorelli's 'new' book," March 13, 2013, https://thespiritwas.tumblr.com/post/45275076521/on-untorellis-new-book. Unfortunately, this Rivera speech is not featured on Tourmaline's indispensable blog thespiritwas.tumblr.com.

14. See also Abram J. Lewis, "Trans History in a Moment of Danger: Organizing within and beyond 'Visibility' in the 1970s," in Tourmaline, Stanley, and Burton, *Trap Door*, 57–89.

15. Morgan M. Page, "One from the Vaults: Gossip, Access, and Trans History-Telling," in Tourmaline, Stanley, and Burton, *Trap Door*, 135.

mediated consumption, less sequential or progressive than cyclical. Jacob Lau, for instance, highlights how trans representations have been shaped by the time of the commodity, particularly in the deployment of celebrity culture. From Christine Jorgensen, through Thomas Beatie, Chaz Bono, to Caitlyn Jenner, "trans* histories and cultural production tend to go through cyclical patterns of 'rediscovery' and commodification every couple of years in American media."[16] The history of trans is marked by a perpetual return of the past in the form of presents that erase these repetitions.

Abolitionists adopt the term "abolition" now, in part, to call up one element of these loops or cycles or, rather, one set of repetitions that are a perpetuation of racism: the longer histories of captivity and exploitation that link imprisonment to enslavement. C. Riley Snorton's field-shifting historical work, *Black on Both Sides*, resituates both of these institutional sites of violence and offers a broader and more disparate genealogy for both transness and Blackness, and their transitive interrelations (see also the Introduction). Their transitivity indicates certain directional qualities, pointing in two ways. The first might be the more obvious, as the word transitive connotes passing, changing, and transience. The second meaning of transitive makes Snorton's approach more distinctive since it draws "in terms of the mechanics of grammar, in which the transitive refers to the expression of an action that requires a direct object to complete its sense of meaning."[17] Transitivity points toward, is even directed against, objects, and thus is historically related to the commodification, the quantification, the thingification of Black people.

Enslaved people in particular have been passed, transferred, and transmitted; these were an inseparable part of the transatlantic imperial, colonial, and gendered past time (and this transitivity persists in a series of ways). Snorton traces how "the fungibility of captive flesh produced a critical context for understanding sex and gender as mutable and subject to rearrangement."[18] Enslavers used the flesh of enslaved people as objects of experimentation, in order to reorient their anatomical sense of sex and gender. Yet, enslaved people (and those living in their not-yet-past) cannot be reduced to how they are acted upon as objects or things. Indeed, Snorton shows how frequently "cross-dressing" and other forms of cross-gender comportment are featured in accounts of flight from slavery. Flesh is not only the clinical object, as Snorton reflects: "I pursue flesh as a capacitating structure for alternative modes of being by tracing the various ways black figures made use of fungibility for fugitive movement, such that flesh became their instrument to engender interstitial spaces of reprieve, as in what Harriet Jacobs called her 'loophole of retreat.'"[19] Enslaved people could use their

16. Jacob Lau in M. W. Bychowski, et al., "Trans*historicities": A Roundtable Discussion with M. W. Bychowski, Howard Chiang, Jack Halberstam, Jacob Lau, Kathleen P. Long, Marcia Ochoa, and C. Riley Snorton. Curated by Leah DeVun and Zeb Tortorici." *TSQ* 5:4 (2018): 658–85, 665. Page also highlights this cyclical pattern within trans history ("*One from the Vaults*," 143).
17. Snorton, *Black on Both Sides*, 6.
18. Snorton, 12.
19. Snorton, 53.

object status for flight. In those times, then, enslaved people passed, so as to transmit themselves, used their fungibility to (begin to) transfer their status—to move from captivity to (something akin to) freedom.[20]

These loopholes in the (always already, but often unacknowledged) racialized history of transitivity signify otherwise upon the cyclical, or looped quality of trans histories and temporalities. Racist structures and practices haunt some normalizing claims about progress for and inclusion of trans (and queer) folks now. Among other factors racialization accounts for the coincidence of visibility and violence, some of those doors that are traps, as violence is especially, spectacularly-yet-ever-so-frequently visited upon trans women of color. This ongoing vulnerability to premature death reflects the lingering ghosts of racism and enslavement and manifests in the "death-in-waiting" of incarceration. Snorton, though, traces how various (formerly) enslaved and imprisoned people negotiated their transitivity as also fugitivity from both enslavement and its carceral afterlives.

CAPTIVE, FUGITIVE FLESH OF HAGAR, ONESIMUS, AND EPAPHRODITUS

If we remain haunted by such ghosts in our own approaches to materials like Paul's letters,[21] what can, or even should we do with times like these (then and now) within these loops and coincidences, the proximities of visibility and violence, traps and doors, of transitivity and fugitivity? On the one hand, I can understand the potential appeal of a gender transitive apostle, as in Paul's letter to the Galatians, when he casts himself as a "mother" to the recipients, laboring to deliver them (4:19).[22] Here, Paul might be an ancient prefiguration of Thomas Beatie, a trans man whose experience birthing three children was splashed across tabloid and mainstream publications in the first decade of this century.[23] Previously, I have wondered if this moment in Galatians rhetorically figures Paul as a drag and/or transgender mother, in the house of Paul,[24] which would certainly

---

20. See Harriet Jacobs, *Incidents in the Life of a Slave Girl*, ed. L. Maria Child (Boston: Published for the Author, 1861), 84-85.

21. On haunting in biblical interpretation, see especially Denise Kimber Buell, "God's Own People: Specters of Race, Ethnicity, and Gender in Early Christian Studies," in *Prejudice and Christian Beginnings: Investigating Race, Gender, and Ethnicity in Early Christian Studies*, ed. Elisabeth Schüssler Fiorenza and Laura Nasrallah (Minneapolis: Fortress, 2009), 159–90; and Buell, "Hauntology meets Post-Humanism: Some Payoffs for Biblical Studies," in *The Bible and Posthumanism*, ed. Jennifer L. Koosed (Atlanta: SBL, 2014), 29–56. For some initial reflections on haunting in relation to trans temporalities in biblical interpretation, see Joseph A. Marchal, "Melancholic Hopes, Trans Temporalities, and Haunted Biblical Receptions: A Response," *BibInt* 28:4 (2020): 495–515.

22. Unless otherwise noted, all translations are my own.

23. See Mel Y. Chen, "Everywhere Archives: Transgendering, Trans Asians, and the Internet," in Tourmaline, Stanley, and Burton, *Trap Door*, 147–49.

24. See, for example, Marchal, "Queer Approaches: Improper Relations with Pauline Letters," in *Studying Paul's Letters: Contemporary Perspectives and Methods*, ed. Marchal (Minneapolis: Fortress,

give a whole new resonance to *Pose*'s lead character, Blanca Rodriguez, and her House of Evangelista. The representation of an ancient transgender evangelizer could offer a strategic doorway to inclusion. Yet, a range of trans activists and scholars encourage us to interrogate on what terms and into what corridors we will be directed at yet another, breathless rediscovery, now of a celebrity apostle and saint.[25]

These moments are only fleeting in the epistles, since in terms of kinship Paul tends to cast himself in a recurrently paternal mode. So, on the other hand, we should proceed with caution, as the letters persistently call up and cast aspersions on a series of other gender troubled figures—gender variant females, castrated and enslaved bodies, barbaric foreigners—echoing the ambient ethnoracial stereotyping of the Roman imperial context.[26] These figures also show up in Galatians, particularly the castrated and enslaved bodies. Just a breath after Paul briefly toils as a mother, he develops a longer and more significant argument on the basis of two other mother figures, Hagar and Sarah (4:22–5:1). Their bodies become vessels of his extended allegory, as he winnows down aspects of the Genesis traditions around these women. He recapitulates some of the exploitation and violation of those materials, even as he further reduces both female figures to receptacles, of Abraham's seed and Paul's unnerving apocalypse, as opposed symbols of flesh and freedom, enslavement and kyriarchal inheritance. Both of these women have been thingified, but most especially the enslaved woman Hagar, as he capitalizes upon the bodies, both hers and her child's, and demands a renewed repetition of Hagar's enforced flight (4:30). In a disturbing loop, he calls up these two figures, making them briefly visible again, but does so to recast them as symbols of something else, and only to cast them out again.[27]

As with Paul's thoughtless punning and negotiation over the enslaved Onesimus in the letter to Philemon,[28] these letters reflect and reduplicate the perspective of enslavers who used the flesh of enslaved people as objects of experimentation. Onesimus is most certainly become transitive, an object to

---

2012), 220–21; Marchal, *Appalling Bodies: Queer Figures before and after Paul's Letters* (New York: Oxford University Press 2020), 76–78; building upon Lopez, *Apostle to the Conquered*, 142–46.

25. For trans readings that are more enthusiastic about Paul's arguments in Galatians, see especially Virginia R. Mollenkott, *Omnigender: A Trans-religious Approach* (Cleveland: Pilgrim, 2001), xii–ix, 85, 113–14, 192; Justin Tanis, *Trans-Gendered: Theology, Ministry, and Communities of Faith* (Cleveland: Pilgrim, 2003), 80–83; and Austen Hartke, *The Bible and the Lives of Transgender Christians* (Louisville, KY: Westminster John Knox, 2018), 156–65. For a less celebratory approach to this letter by and for trans and queer folks, see Melissa Harl Sellew and Joshua Reno, "Galatians," in *The Queer Bible Commentary*, Second Edition, ed. Mona West and Robert Shore-Goss (London: SCM, 2022), 644–62.

26. See Marchal, *Appalling Bodies*.

27. For an important meditation on the operation of Hagar as an enslaved person treated as a fungible object in Galatians, see Amaryah Armstrong, "Of Flesh and Spirit: Race, Reproduction, and Sexual Difference in the Turn to Paul," *Journal for Cultural and Religious Theory* 16:2 (2017): 126–41. For an engaging reassessment of the operation of Hagar in Galatians, as opposed to the Septuagint, as one route for reassessing ideas about human precarity, see Jennifer A. Glancy, "Hagar as/against Bare Life," *JFSR* 37:1 (2021): 103–21.

28. See Marchal, "The Usefulness of an Onesimus: The Sexual Use of Slaves and Paul's Letter to Philemon," *JBL* 130:4 (2011): 749–70.

be exchanged, sent, and negotiated between various owning figures, fungible particularly with regard to the benefits he provides Paul (vv. 11, 13, 20), a human object, owned, but incurring owing (vv. 13, 18, 19), and thus requiring an accounting (vv. 18–20). A similar dynamic is at work in the letter to the Philippians, in which Paul writes rather instrumentally about Epaphroditus the (likely) enslaved apostle of the Philippian assembly.[29] Both Onesimus and Epaphroditus are apparently already in transit: dispatched by Paul with the letter back to their respective assembly communities (Phlm 12, 14, 17; and Phil 2:25, 28–29), but emphatically for Paul's own purposes. The circumstances of Epaphroditus' life were precarious, even dire; in traveling to Paul, he became so ill that he was "near death"—his proximity to death is stressed twice in the span of just four verses (2:27, 30). Yet, even Epaphroditus's near-death experience is about (this) God's mercy to Paul (2:27), allaying Paul's anxieties (2:28), and fulfilling the Philippians' obligation to Paul (2:30). Paul stresses *their* lack (*hysterēma*, 2:30), even as both of these letters reflect Paul's concerted efforts to accept support from these communities without being vulnerably indebted to either of them.[30] In the epistles these other, enslaved figures—Hagar and Onesimus and Epaphroditus—are objects (re)circulated and exchanged, mostly reduced to rhetorical occasions for Paul working out ideas and practices of embodiment and authority, debt and patronage.

Paul's brief gender transitivity becomes visible in a new way given the more persistent violence of his arguments, where enslaved, mutilated, and castrated people are but object lessons of those who would (in his mind at least) oppose him (see also Gal 5:12; Phil 3:2). Their minoritized figurations coincide rather than conflict with proximate, even embedded Pauline claims about "birthing" at least some of the Galatians (Gal 4:19) and "begetting" the enslaved Onesimus (Phlm 10), another chilling reminder of the other way to make more enslaved people outside of conquest. These claims are buffeted by surrounding anxieties about flesh, especially in Galatians (4:13–14, 23, 29; 5:16–25), but also in Philippians (1:22–24; 3:3–4) and briefly in Philemon (v. 16). Flesh helps Paul summon the specter of violent containment, expulsion, and even extermination. He repeatedly dissociates himself from flesh (Gal 1:16; Phil 3:2–4) and seeks to eliminate its influence in the assembly communities that receive these letters. Linked not only with weakness and those Paul opposes (Phil 3:2–4), but also with enslaved bodies (Gal 4:23, 29), improper desires (Gal 5:16–17, 24), and the vices that exclude one from inheriting the kingdom (Gal 5:19–21), flesh is tainted by its association with desire, weakness, enslavement, inferiority, or,

---

29. On these roles, see Katherine A. Shaner, *Enslaved Leadership in Early Christianity* (New York: Oxford University Press, 2018).

30. On the economic dynamics routed through Epaphroditus in this exchange, see Jennifer A. Quigley, *Divine Accounting: Theo-Economics in Early Christianity* (New Haven, CT: Yale University Press, 2021), 51–64. For other queer reflections on this feminized lack and other aspects of the exchange surrounding Philippians, see Marchal, *Philippians: Historical Problems, Hierarchical Visions, Hysterical Anxieties* (Sheffield: Sheffield Phoenix, 2014).

in short, ancient claims about "the feminine."[31] This cluster of associations for flesh recalls the feminized "lack" (*hysterēsis*) Paul tries to avoid sticking to himself (in Phil 4:11–12) by placing it back on the Philippians instead (2:30). In a related fashion, Paul claims to prefer leaving this life in the flesh (1:22–24), but remains, and later insists that he has no confidence in the flesh, even as he has many reasons, even more than others (3:3–4). The irony of such rhetorics is that Paul wrote that letter (and the one to Philemon) while imprisoned (Phil 1:7, 13–17; Phlm 1, 9–10, 13, 23), as captive flesh—though affectively, one could hardly tell!

A receptivity to what still haunts these texts and traditions requires responding to and rejecting the gendered, sexualized, racialized, and colonized terms of visibility they offer, their doors of entry that exceptionalize a select few and estrange those from the rest who are debased and degraded, often to be expelled or eliminated. If one is looking for ways to negotiate trans proximity to precarity, to address and prevent the forms of harm that accompany some groups' greater vulnerability to premature death, then Paul's letters are treacherous sites, symptomatic of the coincidence of violence with (limited) visibility. Their arguments about flesh, and particularly the captive flesh of Hagar and Onesimus (and possibly Epaphroditus), are not adequate for the task of addressing the violence that so shapes trans lives, the structural and quotidian problem that various critical, coalitional, and even abolitionist trans political projects aim to address by focusing on diminished life chances.

CAPACITIES OF CAPTIVE FLESH TOWARD FREEDOM

Against Paul's prevailing tendency, then, we should reconsider the capacitating potential of flesh, both fungible and fugitive, alongside Snorton. I would like to momentarily return to Paul's experiments with flesh and at times a metaphorical sort of enslavement and freedom in this vein. In particular, I remain curious about those places where he insists on warning others away from the capacities of flesh, asserting that his version of "us" are "not having confidence in the flesh" (Phil 3:3), or "For you yourselves were called to freedom, brothers, only do not use your freedom as a starting point (or occasion) for the flesh" (Gal 5:13). Enslavers might experiment with flesh, but scholars like Snorton show how we can reverse the flow of these experiments—flesh can become an occasion for certain efforts toward freedom.

Enslaved people lived in and through transitivity in all kinds of ways. Paul's letters to Philemon and to the Philippians claim to transmit Onesimus and

---

31. For related suspicions and critiques about Paul's arguments in this letter from womanist perspectives, see Angela N. Parker, "One Womanist's View of Racial Reconciliation in Galatians," *JFSR* 34:2 (2018): 23–40; and Jennifer T. Kaalund, "'You Can't See What I See': Black Bodies in Galatians," in *Stony the Road We Trod: African American Biblical Interpretation*, Thirtieth Anniversary Expanded Edition, ed. Cain Hope Felder (Minneapolis: Fortress, 2021), 324–38.

Epaphroditus, respectively, with the letters themselves. The shorter of these letters is harder to understand but seems to promise to transfer Onesimus back to another owning figure (perhaps even asking for Onesimus to be returned to Paul), possibly after Onesimus already took fugitive action, at least according to one common, if still fraught, historical contextualization.[32] Another possibility, however, is that Onesimus was, like Epaphroditus, sent to Paul. This possibility is increased when one recognizes what else the letters have in common beyond their instrumentalized approach to these (formerly) enslaved people: they are both written from prison. This coincidence of enslaving and incarcerating dynamics not only ties these ancient letters to those trans people whose diminished life chances are impacted by more recent versions of enslavement and imprisonment (and their interrelations). The presence of these violent institutions in these ancient networks also points to alternative practices of solidarity for addressing these disparities, including the ever-present, if still variable, resistant potentials of fugitive action. Scholars typically speculate as to whether Onesimus was a fugitive before reaching Paul in prison, but so far as I know, few (if any) have considered how enslaved people carried these letters, in and out of prisons, and further still, how an enslaved person, treated as an object, could have taken a range of fugitive actions with an object that is a letter.[33] Given their diminished life chances, and their dwelling within a zone between consent and coercion, what other deliberate calculations could Onesimus and Epaphroditus have made with and to these letters—taking flight, refusing delivery, excising or emphasizing elements, inscribing additions, choosing one or another mode of resistance, improvisation, or redirecting support toward others trying to negotiate diminished life chances?

Trapdoors remind us that there are paths besides entrance and exits. These letters as objects can be taken elsewhere, including by people who have been thingified, to places not known to the author later acclaimed as apostle. Paul himself already transposed one fungible person into another place in a most obvious fashion: through his allegorical redeployment of the captive flesh of Hagar. His rhetorical aims do not foreclose the possibilities for how other people with captive flesh would have heard and received and used the objects that were and are "his" letters. Indeed, Paul's letters have already been transposed and reconfigured in the intersections between trans and, or, as prison abolitionist movements, particularly within their prison letter-writing programs!

32. See John Byron, *Recent Research on Paul and Slavery* (Sheffield: Sheffield Phoenix, 2008), 117–30.

33. Recent studies have stressed the indispensable role of enslaved people's labor and skill in the production and transmission of these texts, including Emerson Powery, "Reading with the Enslaved: Placing Human Bondage at the Center of the Early Christian Story," in *Bitter the Chastening Rod: Africana Biblical Interpretation After Stony the Road We Trod in the Age of BLM, SayHerName, and MeToo*, ed. Mitzi J. Smith, Angela N. Parker, and Ericka S. Dunbar Hill (Lanham, MD: Lexington/Fortress Academic, 2022), 71–90; and Candida Moss, *God's Ghostwriters: Enslaved Christians and the Making of the Bible* (New York: Hachette, 2024).

TRANS PRISON LETTER PROJECTS

Once organizing is refocused to address the disparities in life chances for trans people, the higher rates of imprisonment and (or as) violence faced by trans people, in and out of carceral institutions, come to the fore. Finding ways of directly supporting imprisoned trans people requires communicating and coordinating with them. As a result, a range of political, nonprofit, and student-run groups have created pen pal programs to link and build relationships between people in and out of prison.[34] These efforts are but one way to resist what trans and abolitionist advocates (biblically) describe as the "exile" logic of incarceration,[35] how the prison-industrial complex removes people from society and, in turn, directs our attention away from the conditions these people face in prisons. Letter writing is an especially important strategy for resisting and mitigating the effects of this logic, as it counters the already common isolation of imprisoned people, an isolation that is often exacerbated for trans people due to factors at work outside and inside of prisons. Trans people in prison often have limited support from family or friends, due to estrangement or their own precarious health, employment, transportation, or economic situation. Trans and, or, as gender nonconforming people are also more frequently subject to isolation in a SHU (a secured housing unit), a form of predominantly solitary confinement, where people the system deems either too vulnerable or too violent for the larger prison population are segregated from them with next to no human contact.[36] SHU remains one of the main ways to handle trans and, or, as gender nonconforming people, particularly when trans women are imprisoned predominantly among men. The letters sent to and from trans people in SHU can be the main or even the only form of social contact they have.[37]

Having and building relationships, then, is essential for trans people surviving life during and after imprisonment. The relationships forged and fostered by this correspondence raise the odds that they can access necessary resources within prison (particularly when they are subject to violence or deprived of healthcare or even adequate food) and in preparation for life after they have served their sentence. The provision of this access is not solely due to the efforts of heroic individuals, as these programs are extensions of collective struggles that aim to (further) connect often overlapping oppressed communities.[38] Groups like Prison Activist Resource Center (PARC), for example, connect people in prison and their families and friends with resource packets and directories

---

34. See some of the discussion in Spade, *Normal Life*, 135–38.
35. See Spade, *Normal Life*, 116, 135, and 137.
36. For one helpful description of practices around SHUs, specifically in relation to Ashley Diamond's incarceration and organizing, see Stanley, *Atmospheres of Violence: Structuring Antagonism and the Trans/Queer Ungovernable* (Durham, NC: Duke University Press, 2021): 104–8.
37. See Grace Dunham, "Out of Obscurity: Trans Resistance, 1969–2016," in Tourmaline, Stanley, and Burton, *Trap Door*, 112.
38. On countering the "hero mindset," see Bassichis, Lee, and Spade, "Building an Abolitionist Trans & Queer Movement," 32–34.

through both mail and online formats.³⁹ Such efforts extend their impact in multiple directions, as the replies from people in prison often indicate that they share these resources with many others imprisoned alongside them, while the stories from their letters increase comprehension of their conditions to those outside of prison. Connecting people not only counters exile and isolation, then; it can also expose the violent conditions of imprisonment to those outside.⁴⁰ Letter-writing practices create opportunities for mutual education and leadership development for all those involved. As Miss Major stressed about TGIJP, they extended their pen pal programming to additional materials sent to people in prisons with the aim of aiding reentry and fostering networks for mentorship and leadership.⁴¹ Letter-writing projects are a common practice and strategic priority for a range of trans, queer, and abolitionist groups, including Hearts on a Wire (in Pennsylvania), the Bent Bars Project (in Britain), the Prisoner Correspondence Project (in Canada), the Write to Win Collective (in Illinois), the Freedom to Live (F2L) network (in New York), and Black and Pink (more than a dozen regional chapters).

These projects are hardly limited to letter writing, linking these practices to circulating newsletters and reading materials, skill-share projects, relief funds (for food and clothing), sharing resources, and housing after incarceration. The replies from people in prison also reach beyond the epistolary format. As reflected in the artwork archived by Black and Pink, their correspondents in prison often improvise with the letters and envelopes as their expressive media.⁴² Ashley Diamond even created and smuggled out a series of digital videos to document the violence she faced in her Georgia prison cell.⁴³ As with PARC's (and many other groups') resource sharing, Diamond's own efforts connected her with other people in prison, as she found a way to build an intra-prison network to pass her twenty-five second segments between other people in prison and ultimately posted them online as *Memoirs of a Chain Gang Sissy*.⁴⁴ Thus, the groups within these interrelated movements build networks of support and demonstrate the capabilities of people in prison. Other circulating materials like newsletters reflect their interests and investments, including specialized sections or separate zines focused on topics like sexuality or religion, further connecting people within and outside of prisons.

Still other organizations that focus on trans-led solidarity and abolition in their practices, like the Sylvia Rivera Law Project (SRLP), also reflect the longer histories of these efforts. Even Rivera's famous "Y'all Better Quiet Down" speech (part of which I quoted above) stressed the initiative taken by gay and especially trans people in jail. Nearly from the start, Rivera notes:

39. See https://www.prisonactivist.org/
40. Spade, *Normal Life*, 135–6; and Stanley and Smith, *Captive Genders*.
41. See Donahue and Griffin-Gracy, "Making It Happen," 306–8, and http://www.tgijp.org/.
42. See some samples in Dunham, "Out of Obscurity," 111–13.
43. See Stanley, *Atmospheres of Violence*, 101–8.
44. Posted to YouTube in parts. See Part 1 here: https://www.youtube.com/watch?v=YwuhEF7_-yI.

> They're writing me every motherfuckin' week and ask for your help, and you all don't do a god damn thing for them... And they write STAR, not the women's group. They do not write women. They do not write men. They write STAR, because we're trying to do something for them.[45]

Rivera hardly gives up on reaching her audience that day, reminding them that they can still join STAR to help the people who were in jail, recalling some of them by name: "do not forget Bambi l'Amour, Andorra Marks, Kenny Messner, and the other gay people that are in jail."[46]

The number of groups focused on these collaborative and collective projects over the years indicates the range and extent of imprisonment and (or as) violence faced by trans and gender nonconforming people. In more recent years the ongoing work of Miss Major and CeCe McDonald stress how extraordinary and yet still so common these conditions are, particularly for trans women of color. Now we are fortunate to have a selection of McDonald's prison letters published by an academic journal. Her letters are compelling for several reasons, including their insights into carceral isolation, coalitional activism, and theological reflection, which I can only treat briefly. Indeed, McDonald's letters reference Paul's letters, even as they reveal the specific masculinity of Pauline appeals and the fraught pursuit of interpersonal support.[47] Her letters reflect the creation of an alternative kinship as well as the violence she first suffered at the hands of family.[48] Yet, both Miss Major and McDonald refuse to individualize their experience or allegorize women to pit them against each other or pose them in different directions; they both stress the ubiquitous violence that links trans women to all other women.[49] In reflecting on a growing adaptability, McDonald's prison letters also reframe and exceed the too brief Pauline references to gender variation and adaptability, while her reference to missing the anniversary of the march led by Dr. Martin Luther King, Jr. subtly links her letters to previous cycles of signifying upon biblical letters, as King consciously modeled his own letters from prison on Paul's prison letters.[50] Thus, these letters reflect not only a set of biblical resonances, but the transformative potential of solidarity, as McDonald was connected to networks of support through these letters, and they provided her and others opportunities to connect her trial and treatment to ongoing dynamics of violence and injustice. Where she could have been trapped in the cycles of violence that still constrain trans lives and too many others', these practices began to create trapdoors, clever modes of resisting and eventually (partially) escaping debilitating and death-dealing conditions.

45. Rivera, "'Y'all Better Quiet Down'," 30.
46. Rivera, 30.
47. McDonald, "'Go beyond Our Natural Selves,'" 247, 251, and 252.
48. McDonald, 248, and 263–64.
49. Griffin-Gracy, McDonald, and Meronek, "Cautious Living," 32; and McDonald, "'Go beyond Our Natural Selves,'" 258.
50. McDonald, 259, and 264.

TRANSMISSIONS BETWEEN EPISTLES AND APOSTLES

To be sure, the contents of these letters are invaluable for their insights into a range of interrelated issues and potential strategies for facing them. Yet, the creation and circulation of the letters themselves are also clear reminders of how McDonald, like other trans people in prison, survive and participate in larger networks and ongoing practices of support and solidarity. As a result, the resonances among prison letters across the centuries can move in multiple directions. McDonald's letters not only recall and occasionally cite the Pauline letters canonized in various collections of Christian scriptures, but they can also help us to see (again) how those ancient prison letters also reflected broader networks and their embodied practices in precarious conditions. Such an approach resonates not only with decades of feminist and womanist approaches to these letters,[51] but my own adaptation of this approach here explicitly builds upon the insightful connections made by Arminta Fox, whose important study places Paul as one captive apostle alongside other people in prison and constructs a more complicated picture of the assembly communities.[52] From this vantage point, then, the letters themselves are small, if still significant signs that the assembly communities that sent their own apostles and epistles practiced this support for people in prison, many of whom would be vulnerable to potentially premature death. Being incarcerated in that time and place certainly translated to diminished life chances for most. Dying in prison was relatively common in the ancient Roman imperial world, and people in prison were dependent upon outside support for their food and other necessities.[53]

---

51. For a few feminist and womanist examples focused on the many other women (and unmen) in these assembled networks, see: Antoinette Clark Wire, *The Corinthian Women Prophets: A Reconstruction through Paul's Rhetoric* (Minneapolis: Fortress, 1990); Elisabeth Schüssler Fiorenza, "Paul and the Politics of Interpretation," in *Paul and Politics: Ekklesia, Israel, Imperium, Interpretation: Essays in Honor of Krister Stendahl*, ed. Richard A. Horsley (Harrisburg, PA: Trinity, 2000), 40–57; Cynthia Briggs Kittredge, "Rethinking Authorship in the Letters of Paul: Elisabeth Schüssler Fiorenza's Model of Pauline Theology," in *Walk in the Ways of Wisdom: Essays in Honor of Elisabeth Schüssler Fiorenza*, ed. Shelly Matthews, Kittredge, and Melanie Johnson-DeBaufre (Harrisburg, PA: Trinity, 2003), 318–33; Arminta M. Fox, *Paul Decentered: Reading 2 Corinthians with the Corinthian Women* (Minneapolis: Lexington/Fortress Academic, 2019); Parker, "Feminized-Minoritized Paul? A Womanist Reading of Paul's Body in the Corinthian Context," in *Minoritized Women Reading Race and Ethnicity: Intersectional Approaches to Constructed Identity and Early Christian Texts*, ed. Mitzi J. Smith and Jin Young Choi (Lanham, MD: Lexington, 2020), 71–87; Marchal "Slaves as Wo/men and Unmen: Reflecting upon Euodia, Syntyche, and Epaphroditus in Philippi," in *The People Beside Paul: The Philippian Assembly and History from Below*, ed. Marchal (Atlanta: SBL Press, 2015), 141–76; and Marchal, *Appalling Bodies*.

52. Fox, "Decentering Paul, Contextualizing Crimes: Reading in Light of the Imprisoned," *JFSR* 33:2 (2017): 37–54. Though the approach taken by Schellenberg commendably aims to deemphasize the apologist theological approaches to the depiction of Paul's imprisonment in Acts (and how scholars trust this depiction as a source for letters like Philippians), it almost entirely avoids or brackets these feminist approaches to this letter and, as a result, does not pursue any of the other people (aside from the occasional nod to networks, yet always as about their support of Paul). See Ryan S. Schellenberg, *Abject Joy: Paul, Prison, and the Art of Making Do* (New York: Oxford University Press: 2021).

53. See Craig S. Wansink, *Chained in Christ: The Experience and Rhetoric of Paul's Imprisonment* (Sheffield: Sheffield Academic, 1996), 33, 43–46, 78–84. For some historical connections about

Thus, the letters and the people sent into prison accompanied material support for people in prison. In many ways, the enslaved people sent were themselves a form of ongoing support to allow for imprisoned people's survival. People like Epaphroditus and Onesimus and other unnamed enslaved apostles bore those risks with and in their own bodies. They put their own flesh on the line to facilitate potential forms of freedom, or at least stave off despair and death, for others. Their embodied actions can demonstrate, to some (quite possibly to us?), that they were much more than how the letters and the ambient kyriarchal context portrayed enslaved people from conquered and colonized groups. According to the common ethnoracial stereotyping of the ancient Roman imperial context, Onesimus and Epaphroditus would have been characterized by their enslaved, ethnoracial, embodied, and thus specifically gendered vulnerability; they would have been considered "unmen."[54] This vulnerable status of many enslaved people was physically marked on parts of their bodies, cast as cut off (Gal 5:12) or as mutilated (Phil 3:2). Paul's rhetorics tend to repeat and reinscribe these practices, degrading and dividing people from each other and their own flesh. It is unsurprising, then, that Paul more frequently denies or downplays his own vulnerable situation, and specifically his own imprisonment. Yet, one can read against the grain and, if one proceeds carefully, transitively, even fugitively, one can notice the places where the letters cannot help but index their movement within larger networks, how assembled collectives collaborated toward other ends.

Certainly, Paul makes some manifest efforts to dissociate from (what he calls) the flesh (Phil 3:3; and Gal 5:13). Intriguingly, Galatians specifically associates flesh with enslavement and fugitivity, if negatively, treating Hagar as a debased point of contrast (4:22–30). But there are at least two other ways to proceed from this rhetorical combination, building upon Snorton's focus on the fungibility of captive flesh. Thus, along one path, Hagar's fungibility is crucial context for the letter's neighboring, if brief, characterization of the gender variant "mothering" apostle Paul (4:19); Hagar's fungibility could be what allows this only-temporary mutability. Along another, critical path, though, we can return to this same nexus for fugitive flesh and resist the flow of its following rhetorics to see how the actions of enslaved people like Hagar have been and can be the occasion and means toward freedom struggles for more than one apostle (contrary to assertions like Gal 5:13 and Phil 3:3). At the very least, we can, with Miss Major and CeCe McDonald, resist the impulse to individualize or allegorize, pitting women against each other, and instead note some of the common forms of violence that link trans women to all other women. This capacity questions and counters the persistent patriarchal strategy of juxtaposing two "types"

---

incarceration as punishment, see Matthew D. C. Larsen and Mark Letteny, *Ancient Mediterranean Incarceration* (Berkeley: University of California Press, 2025).

54. For further connections between ethnoracial rhetorics and the criminalization of conquered and minoritized people in the Roman colonial contexts for biblical materials, see Jeremy L. Williams, "'I am a Human': Racializing Assemblages and Criminalized Egyptianness in Acts 21:31–39," in Smith, Parker, and Dunbar Hill, *Bitter the Chastening Rod*, 91–107. For one, initial treatment of Epaphroditus as an "unman," see Marchal, "Slaves as Wo/men and Unmen."

of women against each other, as evident in the allegory of Hagar and Sarah in Galatians 4 as it is currently among far too many loud transphobic voices from both the right and the left. Instead, an experience of violence can direct one's attention, not toward a celebrated if limited mode of visibility for a select few, but a visibility that recognizes, connects, and thus acts toward countering others' related, if varying, vulnerability to violence.

For a critical, coalitional, or abolitionist trans political project, Paul's letters remain vexing sites, given the ways they briefly note yet diminish the significance of Paul's imprisonment. Particularly in the case of Philippians, Paul insists on his ability to transcend this precarious situation (1:12, 18; 4:11–13). However, when one reads such incarcerating dynamics more transitively and fugitively, the letters clearly indicate how dependent the imprisoned Paul was, given how much he tries to avoid that association and obligation, while insisting that other people actually owe him (Phil 1:24–25; 4:17–19; Phlm 19–21). In contrast to this rhetorical and organizing habit, a range of trans activists and alliances have drawn attention to the multiple impacts of carceral institutions and ideologies on trans, queer, and, or, as gender nonconforming folks for decades. Like other formerly incarcerated Black or Latinx trans women, Sylvia Rivera, Miss Major, and CeCe McDonald agitated beyond their own individualized gendered freedoms, recurrently recognizing and then reinforcing collective sources of support and solidarity. At minimum, this involves resisting "the hero mindset" and not forgetting those still captive in carceral institutions. This is one reason I have attempted to craft a counter-memory of Epaphroditus and Onesimus and Hagar, just a few of the people beside Paul, named and unnamed, who struggled from, within, and around imprisonment and enslavement.

Indeed, once more the letters themselves contain intriguing traces—of people moving from, among, within, and between assembly communities at multiple sites, including in and out of prisons. Paul names fewer people around the edges of Philippians than he does elsewhere, likely because this is the more extended instance of how he negotiates the support he receives even as he aims to evade his own obligation in return.[55] The closing greetings subtly delineate three different, if potentially overlapping, sets of people: "all the brothers who are with me" (4:21), "all of the holy ones" (4:22), and "especially those from Caesar's household" (4:22). Scholars have speculated as to how the last of these groups could help to specify the site of Paul's imprisonment, but it is also possible that the first set, the siblings with Paul, are meant to differentiate the other people in prison alongside Paul from a larger set of assembly members. The closing of the letter to Philemon is more explicit in naming Epaphras as Paul's "fellow prisoner" (v. 23), as well as four other coworkers, Mark, Aristarchus, Demas, and Luke

---

55. On the affects of interest and indebtedness among more recently incarcerated and racially criminalized populations, particularly within "faith based" prison programming (and/as the afterlives of slavery in the Americas), see Erin Runions, "Immobile Theologies, Carceral Affects: Interest and Debt in Faith-Based Prison Programs," in *Religion, Emotion, Sensation: Affect Theories and Theologies*, ed. Karen Bray and Stephen D. Moore (New York: Fordham University Press, 2020), 55–84.

(v. 24). While we might presume that the latter were not also imprisoned, they were likely among those, with Onesimus, in a network of people providing support to keep these imprisoned assembly members alive.

Though Philemon and Philippians are the two traditionally labeled "prison letters of Paul," still other letters reflect the vulnerability to this kind of violence within the networks of these assemblies, as Arminta Fox highlights in her arguments connecting Epaphroditus to several other named figures in the greetings within the letter to the Romans.[56] These extended greetings close that letter by highlighting Andronicus and Junia not only as "fellow prisoners," but also "outstanding among the apostles" before Paul was "in Christ" (16:7). Prisca and Aquila also "risked their necks for my life" (16:4), a likely colloquialism for risking execution. Moving both of these references alongside those toward the end of Philemon and Philippians demonstrates the broader vulnerability to violence and limited life chances, repeatedly associated with imprisonment, for a wider set of people beyond Paul. Further, the frequency of these references to people in, alongside, and occasionally out of prison indicates coordinated efforts to connect with those inside and support their survival. These assembled negotiations of imprisonment could have been another node, beside the more frequently treated collection for Jerusalem, that linked various assembly communities in multiple cities dwelling within the broader Roman imperial atmospheres of violence.[57] The aim here, then, is not to laud new heroic exceptions, either among the many different prisoner correspondence projects in the present or the networks that created and circulated support with and through ancient apostles and epistles. Rather, these people and practices reflect how common imprisonment and other modes of imperial violence were (and are, if in altered forms). Their quotidian regularity, like the violence and vulnerability overwhelmingly faced by many trans people now, should not lessen one's anger, horror, or determination to counter these forces. Indeed, the history of imprisonment and enslavement includes various fugitive efforts to resist these institutionalized forms of violence.

Any potential, ancient versions of such fugitive efforts toward survival, resistance, or freedom could be indexed by the movement of enslaved apostles like Epaphroditus and Onesimus. In the epistles we now call "Paul's," these other enslaved figures are depicted as thingified entities, themselves recirculated and exchanged, and thus mostly rhetorically reduced as elements for one apostle to assert his relative indifference and invulnerability, his occasional adaptability to reinforce his authority. Yet, we can resituate how people like Epaphroditus are moved into the arc of arguments like those that stressed how very close he came to death (Phil 2:27, 30). This precarious risk, his diminished life chances and proximity to death, link him with many others beside Paul, like Prisca and Aquila, or Andronicus and Junia. This association pulls our picture of these

---

56. See especially Fox, "Decentering Paul," 48–51.
57. On one helpful, and thus potentially analogous treatment of that collection as a counterimperial effort, see Sze-kar Wan, "Collection for the Saints As Anticolonial Act: Implications of Paul's Ethnic Reconstruction," in Horsley, *Paul and Politics*, 191–215.

people out of a strictly "Pauline" orbit into broader, if at times tentative and temporary, assembled yet improvised networks. Epaphroditus can be compared and connected with them not only because he was more like these other outstanding apostles mentioned in Romans, but also because the picture we are assembling in connecting their efforts traces the wider networks of support and solidarity in which they acted. This support and solidarity would have been enabled and embodied by the fugitive transitivity of so many of these named and unnamed people, like and unlike Onesimus and Hagar and Epaphroditus, their attempts to act even when constrained within carceral systems that (tried to) hold them captive. Their fugitive efforts did not deny the risks involved in negotiating coercive conditions, even when and if those who benefitted from, even survived by, such support still emphasized their attempt as a form of feminized lack (*hysterēma*)—as Paul did in constructing a reply about the Philippians' apostle Epaphroditus.

The enslaved apostolic vulnerability involved with moving into prisons and drawing dangerously close to death is also then a form of gender variability, transitivity, or minoritization. For Paul this feminized lack typifies Epaphroditus as a representative of a broader group, the Philippian assembly members, even as such arguments also unwittingly demonstrate how apostles are inextricably linked to and interdependent with collectives. In trying to connect people and (other) resources to engender the survival and support of people in, out, and around prisons, the assemblies and the apostles (like these) would not be evading or downplaying a gendered lack or embodied vulnerability. They would be recognizing these and organizing around addressing greater and interrelated degrees of precarity and proximity to death faced by some. Rather than seeking identity and identification with a transgender Paul, we can see a kind of transmission between incarcerated trans people and other, ancient captive flesh like Epaphroditus and Onesimus and Hagar, and the wider networks that assemble around them. Broader trans modes of support and solidarity help us to track the ways these epistles and apostles were parts of ongoing practices of communication and coordination among the many impacted by imprisonment and enslavement. We might do well, then, to not forget these fugitive forms of gendering and those who demonstrate the embodied capacities of such joint efforts, keeping them in transit so that we might challenge and change the conditions for those who still unevenly face the interrelated impacts of transphobia and its force multipliers of racism and incarceration. Instead of downplaying these impacts, or dividing and degrading those who grapple with them, these various letter-writing people and practices show us neglected signs of transmission and necessary strategies, beyond recognition, for the transformation of trans people's life chances, if we but give it a chance.

Chapter 11

Considering the Body with the Gospel of Thomas

MELISSA HARL SELLEW

The Gospel of Thomas has been a site of interest for those considering the place of the body in early Christian discourse since its discovery and first publication two generations ago. Questions of gender and gender variance have come to play a significant role in interpreting this ancient text, including recent readings from a transgender perspective.[1] As we shall see, there is ample evidence that Thomas has a severely negative view of the physical body—part of its general disdain for material existence in this world—and a correspondingly positive view of the soul or spirit. Nonetheless, it may well be that such a starkly binary understanding of the Gospel's anthropology is incomplete.

I notice a broad range of feelings and attitudes these days regarding the value of our bodies and physical existence, especially amongst transgender and otherwise gender variant people such as myself. Encounters with variant bodies and genders in literature and other art forms can activate strong emotions for those of us who fear we fit poorly within mainstream notions of bodily shapes and

---

1. A significant early intervention was that of Richard Valantasis, *The Gospel of Thomas* (New York: Routledge, 1997); on trans-related issues see particularly Melissa Harl Sellew, "Reading the *Gospel of Thomas* from Here: A Trans-centred Hermeneutic," *JIBS* 1:2 (2020): 61–96, with further literature discussed there.

sizes. In my own case, the strong emphasis that I have put on Thomas's rejection of materiality in close readings over many years[2] can lead to a dismissal of the worth of our bodily existence. I now suspect that such an approach cedes too little space to the text's stirring call for transformation of the human being. It seems time to offer a reading that seeks to provide a bit more nuance and balance to this topic. To what extent can or should the Gospel of Thomas be read as a text of hope for any of us, whatever our bodily expressions?

From the point of view of the lived experience of many trans, gender-variant, racialized, disabled, and other too-often marginalized people, Thomas's call for renewal of one's essence, through the metaphor of constructing a new, ungendered body, might best be heard as a call for spiritual liberation, whatever the visible state of our embodiment. Perhaps some could find a place of stability, equilibrium, peace, even joy while inhabiting their body, whatever its externals and internals might be, rather than accede to an utter dismissal of our material existence. Despite all the challenges that people with gender nonconforming bodies may encounter most every day—contingent tolerance, strained interactions, or outright threats to our survival—we still need to move about in public bravely and hope to thrive despite our difference(s) from the norm.

In this essay I explore how it might be possible both to acknowledge the Gospel's demurral of the ultimate worth of our physical, material bodies and yet perhaps still find elements of hope and renewal for an attentive and sympathetic gender-variant reader of the text. After all, however strained or even perilous the relationship with our embodied selves might be, we rely on those very bodies to carry us through the world day by day. In the words of the poet, the spirit is an "Airy and shapeless thing, / it needs / the metaphor of the body."[3]

In a recent article, I pressed the point that from my own perspective as a white woman of transgender experience, Thomas's emphasis on the authentic self being located in our soul or spirit (terms used as close synonyms there) could be felt as potentially liberatory.[4] Coupled with its relentless devaluation or even rejection of our fleshly bodies as temporary entrapment in materiality, Thomas might sketch out a more hopeful picture for those of us who have long felt just that sort of dissonance between our inner understandings and how our external, bodily selves might be thought—mostly by others, and too often through scrutiny of our genitals—to determine who we truly are. "Salvation" from the

---

2. Melissa [née Philip] Harl Sellew, "Death, the Body, and the World in the Coptic Gospel of Thomas," *StPatr* 31 (1997): 530–34; "Jesus and the Voice from Beyond the Grave: *Gos. Thom.* 42 in the Context of Funerary Epigraphy," in *Thomasine Traditions in Antiquity: The Social and Cultural World of the Gospel of Thomas*, ed. Jon Ma. Asgeirsson, April D. DeConick, and Risto Uro (Leiden: Brill, 2006), 327–56; "Reading Jesus in the Desert: The *Gospel of Thomas* Meets the *Apophthegmata Patrum*," in *The Nag Hammadi Codices and Late Antique Egypt*, ed. Hugo Lundhaug and Lance Jennot (Tübingen: Mohr Siebeck, 2018), 81–106; and "The Gospel of Thomas and the Synoptics," in *The Oxford Handbook of the Synoptic Gospels*, ed. Stephen Ahearne-Kroll (Oxford: Oxford University Press, 2023), 223–42.

3. Mary Oliver, "Poem," first published in her collection *Dream Work* (New York: Grove Atlantic, 1986).

4. Sellew, "Reading *Thomas* from Here."

constraints and pain of our materiality, including the sorts of disquiet or self-loathing so many of us feel and have felt with regard to our bodies, would then not require complete disengagement or denial of our true selves, to the point of self-harm or suicidal thoughts in far too many cases.[5]

Liberation might instead (or also) involve recognition and celebration of something valuable in our inner, less visible selves. As Laurel C. Schneider writes, "The liberation of queer sexualities" (to which I would add queer/ed gender identities) "from temporal narratives of both heteronormatively framed reproductivity *and* maturity is dependent on the death of dominant expectations for both."[6] This "death" would require our defiant refusal of the regnant cis-heteronormative world's judgment of our supposed "confusion" or "self-deception" or "self-directed preoccupations" as we struggle to overcome the culture's oppressive values that center normative body types and their correlations with presumed gender identity.

In this Gospel's mythopoetic imaginary, its singular offer of "salvation" would mean transcending our bodily specificities, working to attain a return to a non-material, spiritual plane, at home with divine presence. This version of heaven is pictured by Thomas as a locus of Light and Life beyond this created order, where one regains a form of preexistence involving simplicity and unity of being (Gos. Thom. 3; 11; 18; 49; 50; 61b; 77; 85; 106; 111).[7] As a "single one," the Thomasine Christian should thus hope to assimilate to the status of "Living Spirit" beyond or outside of gender, inspired by the example of Jesus (Gos. Thom. 114), and thus be recognized alongside "him"[8] on "entry into the kingdom" as another "child of the Living Father" (Gos. Thom. 3). One point of great interest to a trans reading is how this Gospel portrays such "offspring"—beginning with Jesus—as no longer embodied, and thus as no longer projecting gender, indeed no longer fitting within any gender.[9] Where we find our end, our spiritual home, is where we began, before our fatal fall into captivity in fleshly bodies (Gos. Thom. 18). Spirit is not material for Thomas and thus has no gender.

The introspective process of "salvation" in this Gospel's economy begins a long, arduous, and potentially quite lonely process of seeking and (perhaps)

---

5. Other trans folk hold more nuanced or positive views of embodiment. See e.g., Austen Hartke, *Transforming: The Bible and the Lives of Transgender Christians*, 2nd ed. (Louisville, KY: Westminster John Knox, 2023); or some of the informants discussed by Katy E. Valentine, "Examining Scripture in Light of Trans Women's Voices," in *The Oxford Handbook of Feminist Approaches to the Hebrew Bible*, ed. Susanne Scholz (Oxford: Oxford University Press, 2020), 508–23.

6. Laura C. Schneider, "More Than a Feeling: A Queer Notion of Survivance," in *Sexual Disorientations: Queer Temporalities, Affects, Theologies*, ed. Kent L. Brintnall, Joseph A. Marchal, and Stephen D. Moore (New York: Fordham University Press, 2018), 267, emphasis original.

7. For the texts see Bentley Layton and Harold W. Attridge in *Nag Hammadi Codex II, 2–7*, vol. 1 (Leiden: Brill, 1989). Translations from the Greek and Coptic of Thomas and the New Testament are my own, avoiding gender exclusive language as possible.

8. I mark my use of the pronoun "he, him, his" for the Jesus of Thomas with "scare quotes," since Jesus's gender is unclear in the text apart from the specific and distinct grammatical limits of the Greek, Coptic, and English languages.

9. Discussed more thoroughly in Sellew, "Reading *Thomas* from Here," esp. 87–90, and "Thomas and the Synoptics," 235–36.

finding one's own true self. "Let the one who seeks keep seeking until they find," through a journey featuring trouble, wonder, and ultimately (one hopes) self-fulfillment (Gos. Thom. 2). There are strong resonances here with many trans people's experiences, in particular our own complex, sometimes treacherous, often confusing, and too frequently isolated attempts at self-understanding, self-acceptance, and, for many of us, public assertion of our true gendered selves. For Thomas, the goal is to free oneself from the limits of the physical body and (re-)unite with the source of divine Life and Light outside this material realm. One will accomplish this by digging deep down within to find, recognize, and free one's true self.

There is no specific ritual act in view that would bring one into an elect community, be that baptism or a sacred meal. There are no theological claims that must be assented to, or declarations of belief that need be made, such as the Pauline "Jesus is Lord, and God raised him from the dead" (Rom 10:9) or the Johannine assertion that authentic existence (frequently pictured as "eternal life") requires belief that Jesus is the Christ and Son of God (20:31). Instead, we find in Thomas a tight focus on the individual and one's need to engage in exploration of the self to discover their heavenly origin.

The Gospel repeatedly devalues the material order, including human bodies, in favor of extolling our true, spiritual selves, currently exiled from the realm of divine Light while entombed in mortal flesh. Jesus declares, "Whoever understands the world has found a corpse, and whoever has found a corpse is superior to the world" (Gos. Thom. 56; cf. 80). Jesus states further, "If the flesh came into being because of spirit, that would be a marvel. But if spirit came into being because of the body, that would be a marvel of marvels! Indeed, I am amazed at how this great wealth [the spirit] has come to dwell in this poverty [the flesh]" (Gos. Thom. 29; cf. 87). Sexual reproduction, childbearing, and conventional family life are repeatedly disparaged (Gos. Thom. 16; 49; 55; 79; 99; 101).

Thus the case for Thomasine disdain for our fleshly existence is quite strong. Indeed, the world we inhabit, far from being a place of sun-filled life and divine favor, as is claimed by the opening page of the book of Genesis, and most of its interpreters, instead is viewed as something dead and dark.[10] The first enfleshed human being, formed from the dust or muck (Gen 2:7), was not worthy of the gift of immortality, or so this Gospel has Jesus judge: "Adam came into being from a great power and a great wealth, but he was not worthy of you. For had he been worthy, he would not have tasted death" (Gos. Thom. 85). When humanity took on the fleshly materiality of our world, and with that began to express sex and gender in our bodies, this transition triggered our true and tragic fall from heavenly existence, a descent entailing alienation from divine

10. This negative view of our created cosmos is not sufficient to designate Thomas as "gnostic," as is still sometimes suggested. *Thomas* lacks the mythopoetic fantasies that typify many gnostic texts. See e.g., Antti Marjanen, "Is Thomas a Gnostic Gospel?" in *Thomas at the Crossroads: Essays on the Gospel of Thomas*, ed. Risto Uro (Edinburgh: T&T Clark), 107–39; further Sellew, "Death, the Body, and the World" and "Jesus and the Voice from Beyond the Grave."

Spirit—a nonmaterial force pictured here and elsewhere in Thomas as "power" and "wealth."

And so it seems likely that the well-known parable of fashioning a new human being via replacement of body parts in Gos. Thom. 22 speaks not of actual, physical hands, feet, genitals, or eyes. Rather, the process of "making the two one, the inside like the outside, and the outside like the inside . . . and the male and the female one and the same" evokes a metaphorical transformation of ourselves into a spiritual, nonmaterial, ungendered unity or singularity. As Thomas has Jesus go on to say, "Blessed are the solitary and elect, for you will find the kingdom. For you are from there, and to it you will return" (Gos. Thom. 49).

Jesus challenges "his" audience, both those mentioned within the text as well as those of us standing outside it, to recognize themselves as not defined by (or limited to) mortal bodies, but instead as "offspring of the living Father" (Gos. Thom. 3), as remarkable spirits imbued with divine Light, "one out of a thousand, two out of ten thousand" (Gos. Thom. 23). Then Jesus explains, "There is light within a person of Light, and it gives light to the whole world. If it does not give light, that person (that world) is darkness" (Gos. Thom. 24b). Later "he" advises, "If they ask you, 'Where have you come from?' say to them, 'We have come from the Light, where the Light came into being of its own accord and stood and appeared in their images.' If they say to you, 'Is that you?' say, 'We are its offspring and we are the chosen of the Living Father'" (Gos. Thom. 50). Return to the Light will entail transformation of one's material existence into a spiritual being beyond or without gender (Gos. Thom. 22; 114). This is the Thomasine analogue to other Christian and Christian-adjacent images of rebirth, renewal, or resurrection.

Evaluation of the anthropology and antimaterialist ideology of Thomas can be skewed by debates over the proper theological, literary, and historical contexts in which we should place and interpret the text.[11] We have three partial fragments of the Greek original, all dating from the early to mid-third century, whereas a Coptic translation inscribed in a late fourth-century manuscript provides the only full witness to the Gospel.[12] Quite unlike the narrative structures of the New Testament Gospels, Thomas simply presents a series of more than one hundred statements attributed to Jesus, offered with little or no context or explanation. Its literary format as a collection of proverbs, parables, and obscure remarks likely found its greatest appeal and use as a spark for interrogation of the self and the world. Whether its readers were solitary ascetics or members of some sort of ancient Christian study group, we can say that "Thomas's manner

---

11. Recent, reliable, and balanced treatments of the central questions include Stephen J. Patterson, *The Gospel of Thomas and Christian Origins: Essays on the Fifth Gospel* (Leiden: Brill, 2013); Simon Gathercole, *The Composition of the Gospel of Thomas: Original Language and Influences* (Cambridge: Cambridge University Press, 2012); Gathercole, *The Gospel of Thomas: Introduction and Commentary* (Leiden: Brill, 2014); Ivan Miroshnikov, *The Gospel of Thomas and Plato: A Study of the Impact of Platonism on the "Fifth Gospel"* (Leiden: Brill, 2018), 25–37.

12. Manuscript details in Layton and Attridge, *Nag Hammadi Codex II, 2–7*, vol. 1, 2–5, 96–99.

of presentation lends itself well to the inquiring minds of readers who seek inspiration of a more probing sort.... The Gospel of Thomas could be characterized as a spiritual guide that activates a 'hermeneutical soteriology.'"[13] The opening claims of the text demand close attention to the words of Jesus so as "not to taste death" (Gos. Thom. 1).

The only surviving complete version of Thomas was found in Egypt, bound up in Nag Hammadi Codex II with other Christian-adjacent noncanonical literature, part of a cache with a dozen other books, whose varied content produces an atmosphere of esoteric wisdom that scholars frequently label as "gnostic" or "heretical." This physical proximity of Coptic Thomas in a context dominated by noncanonical scripture and mystical and speculative treatises still suggests to many readers that its proper conversation partners (so to speak) would be authors of Valentinian, Hermetic, Manichaean, or other persuasions that are considered out of the mainstream (and thus uninteresting) by much of the scholarship on Christian origins. Such an approach loses sight of the Gospel's thematic connections with central New Testament authors in matters both somatic and spiritual. To be sure, Thomas has its own specific take on the role and meaning of Jesus and differs from the broader scriptural tradition in questioning the "goodness" of the material creation; but as it relates to the ultimate value of the immortal spirit versus the perishable flesh, Thomas is far from idiosyncratic compared to most early Christian viewpoints, let alone "heretical." As the Apostle Paul puts it, "Flesh and blood cannot inherit the kingdom of God, nor does the perishable inherit imperishability" (1 Cor 15:50).

This sort of attitude is in fact shared broadly by Thomas with Paul and his contemporary Christian and Jewish texts. This widespread perspective imputes the highest value to our spiritual components while relativizing or diminishing the worth of our bodily selves. It is a sensibility that finds its starting point in the generally dualistic tendency prevalent in much philosophical and religious literature of the late Hellenistic and early Roman periods, including protocanonical texts.[14] Despite their differences, we can find significant similarities in this respect between Thomas and such writings as the Pauline epistles, the Gospel of John, or the treatises of the Jewish interpreter Philo of Alexandria, as will be explored below. There is of course considerable diversity in how one author or another will express the generally Platonizing contrast between things that are eternal, noetic, spiritual, invisible, and/or intangible, as contrasted with other things that are temporary, mortal, accessible to the physical senses, and

---

13. Sellew, "Thomas and the Synoptics," 228, with further literature cited there.

14. For a range of ancient Greek and Roman (including Jewish) positions on this theme contemporary with Thomas, see David T. Runia, *Philo of Alexandria and the "Timaeus" of Plato* (Leiden: Brill, 1986); John Whittaker, "Platonic Philosophy in the Early Centuries of the Empire," *ANRW* 2:36.1 (1987), 81–123; John Dillon, *The Middle Platonists, 80 B.C. to A.D. 220* (Ithaca, NY: Cornell University Press, 1996); Troels Engberg-Pedersen, ed., *From Stoicism to Platonism: The Development of Philosophy, 100 BCE–100 CE* (Cambridge: Cambridge University Press, 2017). On Thomas more specifically, see especially Jon Ma. Asgeirsson, "Conflicting Epic Worlds," in Asgeirsson, DeConick, and Uro, *Thomasine Traditions in Antiquity*, 155–74; Patterson, *Thomas and Christian Origins*, 32–91; and Miroshnikov, *Thomas and Plato*.

bound by the limitations of earthly existence and our daily bodily needs for shelter, sustenance, and a supportive community. And yet we will also see that a total, all-encompassing negativity with regard to our embodied materiality can be its own trap.

As mentioned, Thomas lacks reference to the saving need for communal rituals or adherence to credal proclamations that we see in many New Testament authors. Despite this contrast, the Gospel's viewpoint on the spirit vis-à-vis the flesh appears less alien when set alongside close parallels to be found in some more familiar, canonical writings. Paul, for instance, apparently drawing in part on popular philosophy,[15] will at places differentiate aspects of human understanding or wisdom and of existence, using a ranking of human capabilities in terms of *spirit, mind, soul,* and *flesh,* as he does most famously early on in 1 Corinthians. Both the soul and the flesh seem to be of material substance in Paul's understanding, whereas for Thomas the soul and the spirit both seem to be nonmaterial entities.

> We have not received the *spirit* of the world, but rather the *spirit* that comes from God. . . . Indeed, what we speak is not through words taught by human wisdom but through teachings of the *spirit*, explaining *spiritual* matters to *spiritual* people [*pneumatikoi*]. A *soul*-person [*psychikos*] does not receive what comes from God's *spirit*—for there is foolishness in such people, and such things are discerned *spiritually*. . . . I could not speak to you as though to *spiritual* people, but as to *fleshly* ones [*sarkinoi*]. . . and you are still *fleshly*. (1 Cor 2:12–14, 3:1–3)

In Romans 7, Paul portrays a human struggle between the "sinful flesh" and the interior forces of spirit and mind (which as in Stoic thought have material aspects). He regrets human tendencies to sin in and with "this body of death," under the power of "the flesh" while holding out hope that through incorporation into the (immaterial) body of Christ one might live the life of the spirit (7:4–6): "For we know that the law is spiritual; but I am of the flesh, sold under sin. . . . I know that nothing good dwells in me, that is, in my flesh. . . . For I joyfully concur with the law of God *in the inner person*, but I see a different law *in the members of my body*" (7:14, 18, 22–23).

As is well known, Paul constructs a complex metaphorical process of death, re-creation, and rebirth to picture "salvation," with a special focus on the believer

---

15. From among a vast literature relevant to Paul and this topic, see e.g., Abraham J. Malherbe, *Paul and the Popular Philosophers* (Minneapolis: Fortress Press, 1989); Stanley K. Stowers, *A Rereading of Romans: Justice, Jews, and Gentiles* (New Haven, CT: Yale University Press, 1994); Engberg-Pedersen, ed., *Paul in His Hellenistic Context* (Minneapolis: Fortress Press, 1995); Walter Burkert, "Towards Plato and Paul: The 'Inner' Human Being," in *Ancient and Modern Perspectives on the Bible and Culture: Essays in Honor of Hans Dieter Betz*, ed. Adela Yarbro Collins (Atlanta: Scholars Press, 1998), 59–82; Engberg-Pedersen, *Paul and the Stoics* (Louisville, KY: Westminster John Knox Press, 2000); Emma Wasserman, *The Death of the Soul in Romans 7: Sin, Death, and the Law in Light of Hellenistic Moral Psychology* (Tübingen: Mohr Siebeck, 2008); Engberg-Petersen, *Cosmology and the Self in the Apostle Paul: The Material Spirit* (Oxford: Oxford University Press, 2010); Stowers, "The Dilemma of Paul's Physics: Features Stoic-Platonist or Platonist-Stoic?" in Engberg-Pedersen, *From Stoicism to Platonism*, 231–53.

somehow or other sharing in the death and resurrection of Christ: "For through the law I died to the law, that I might live to God. I have been crucified with Christ; and it is no longer I who live, but Christ lives in me" (Gal 2:19–20a). It is significant in this regard that experience in the body has critical meaning for Paul, whether ethically or spiritually. The formal ritual of baptism both analogizes and effects transformation: "Don't you know that all of us who have been baptized into Christ Jesus have been baptized into his death? Therefore, we've been buried with him through baptism into death, in order that as Christ was raised from the dead through the glory of the Father, so we too might walk in newness of life. For as we have been united with him in the likeness of his death, certainly we shall be also in the likeness of his resurrection" (Rom 6:3–5; cf. the "baptismal formula" of Gal 3:28).

This Pauline focus on the salvific power of Christ's death—actualized in the rituals of baptism and the Eucharist—is quite foreign to the thought world of Thomas, which gives no space to the role of bodily suffering, even that of Jesus, or of sacred actions that are felt to activate its holy power. "Only by foreknowledge of the New Testament Gospels . . . would a reader of Thomas realize that Jesus was to meet a gruesome death at the hands of the Romans, framed as a divinely required sacrifice to redeem the world of sin, and yet was somehow able to transcend death through resurrection. In other words, the 'Jesus Christ crucified, and him alone' preached by Paul (1 Cor 2:2) is not the subject of the Gospel of Thomas."[16]

On the other hand, Paul shares much else with Thomas, as when the self-proclaimed Apostle to the Gentiles develops his contrast between the fleshly body as a site of death and the spiritual body—inhabited by the divine Spirit—as full of life in Romans 8. One's *mind* is seen as the instrument by which one can direct either fatal or life-giving values and choices: "Those who exist according to the *flesh* set their *minds* on the things of the *flesh*, but those who exist according to the *spirit* set their *minds* on the things of the *spirit*. For the *mind* set on the *flesh* is death, but the *mind* set on the *spirit* is life and peace. . . . However, you are not *in the flesh* but *in the spirit*, if indeed the Spirit of God dwells in you. . . . And if Christ is in you, though *the body is dead* because of sin, yet *the spirit is alive* because of righteousness" (Rom 8:5–6, 9–10).

Paul also shares with Thomas a rejection of hierarchical family life, including marriage, sexual reproduction, and the raising of children, a system highly valued in their ancient Mediterranean culture (and ours). This lack of positive interest in "flesh" and its workings may offer space for queer and trans-sensitive readings. For example, as Joseph A. Marchal comments in connection with 1 Corinthians, "Significant aspects of Paul's argumentation seem oddly compatible with some of the more recent queer critiques of reproductive futurity. Paul imagines a constantly diminishing future, one in which he proves quite disinterested in a life organized around the predominant Roman imperial expectations for family, inheritance, and child rearing."[17]

---

16. Sellew, "Thomas and the Synoptics," 226.
17. Joseph A. Marchal, "How Soon Is (This Apocalypse) Now? Queer Velocities after a Corinthian Already and a Pauline Not Yet," in Brintnall, Marchal, and Moore, *Sexual Disorientations*, 50.

For example, famously, Paul shows no interest in childbearing and rearing as a main purpose or rationale for marriage, a view he makes patent in 1 Corinthians 7—a rather shocking omission in his context once we recognize it. His acceptance of marriage comes merely as an ethical safe haven for cross-sex couples besotted with erotic desire (1 Cor 7:1–9). His radical disinterest in raising children is explained in part by Paul's urgent expectation of an apocalyptic break into history, what he terms "the impending crisis" of a "world passing away" (1 Cor 7:26–31). As the nearness of the End faded away more and more into the distance in subsequent decades and generations, however, some of Paul's followers and imitators made corrections on this point, and a more traditional view of family was ultimately given scriptural authority. This tendency is visible in such texts as Ephesians or the Pastoral Epistles (e.g., Eph 5:25–6:9; 1 Timothy 2–3), including an insistence on a father's mastery of his wife, his children, and enslaved household members. Competing ascetical tendencies of other authors inspired by Paul were ultimately tamed or restricted to a spiritual elite, as we see play out in the development from a strict demand for celibacy for all Christians in the second-century *Acts of Paul and Thecla* toward a more culturally normative view in the fifth-century *Life and Miracles of St. Thecla*.[18]

The ultimate transformation from the material to the spiritual in Paul's own imaginary will of course come at the resurrection he looks for at the end of time, when believers will see themselves, more specifically their essences, transformed from "earthly" to "heavenly" bodies. His attempt to persuade the assembly in Corinth that some sort of resurrection of the body will truly occur may offer Paul's closest parallel to the sort of spiritual transformation that Thomas has Jesus talk about. In the apostle's framework, this event is tied to the apocalyptic eschatology that so imbues his thought (and will be redirected internally and individually by Thomas—as well as in the Gospel of John).

At the "last trumpet" believers will be awakened and/or lifted up, and one's earthy, perishable, dishonorable, weak body of flesh and soul will be replaced with heavenly, imperishable bodies of spirit, according to Paul's Adam / Christ pattern:

> There are indeed heavenly bodies and earthly bodies, but the glory of the heavenly is one, and the glory of the earthly is another. . . So indeed it is written, "The first human, Adam, became a living *soul*," the last Adam a life-giving *spirit*. However, the *spiritual* is not first, but the *soul*-like,[19] then the *spiritual*. The first human is from the earth, *earthy*; the second human is from heaven. . . . And just as we have borne the image of the earthy, we shall also bear the image of the *heavenly*. . . . This *perishable* must put on the *imperishable*, and this *mortal* must put on *immortality*. . . . (1 Cor 15:40–52; cf. Gos. Thom. 85 on the inferiority of the enfleshed [earthy] human being Adam)

---

18. See Scott F. Johnson, *The Life and Miracles of Thecla: A Literary Study* (Cambridge, MA: Harvard University Press, 2006); Andrew S. Jacobs, *The Life of Thecla: Apocryphal Expansion in Late Antiquity* (Eugene, OR: Cascade Books, 2024).

19. Paul here uses the term *soul*-like (*psychikon*), which is typically translated in this context as "physical" or "material."

For Thomas, Jesus is also "from heaven" and "spiritual" in nature; but, as mentioned, in this Gospel there is no hint of a baptismal or eucharistic reenactment of "his" death and resurrection.

The death of Jesus figures not at all in Thomas; indeed, messiahship of any sort goes unmentioned. Any weak remnants of the apocalyptic eschatological discourse found in Paul and the Synoptic Gospels are directed in Thomas toward the inner person and away from the drama of Judean life. Thomas shows no interest in the fate of historical Israel or Jerusalem or even its Temple,[20] let alone the reported resurrection of a vindicated Christ.[21] What we find instead of those prominent Pauline and Synoptic themes is how the reader or audience is called to follow the example of a Jesus with a vanishing connection to Judaism, working beyond or outside the specificities of a particular cultural ethnicity to attain self-recognition of one's spiritual, heavenly origins and essence, and thereby effect and enact return to the heavenly realm.

Whether this spiritual ascent is imagined by Thomas to be possible within this earthly life or only at death is unclear. In any case, the Gospel has Jesus disparage anxiety over temporal or historical eschatology. When the disciples ask "him," "How will our end come to be," Jesus retorts, "Have you discovered the beginning that you look for the end? For where the beginning is, that's where the end will be. Blessed is the person who takes their stand at the beginning—that person will know the end and will not taste death" (Gos. Thom. 18). Instead of an imminent apocalyptic event, renewal is already possible in the present: "The disciples said to 'him', 'When will the repose of the dead come about, and when will the new world come?' 'He' said to them, 'What you look forward to has already come, but you do not recognize it'" (Gos. Thom. 51; cf. 113). Thus, one's true existence (what John pictures as "eternal life" in John 3:16; 4:14; cf. 20:31) need not wait for some sort of deferred afterlife.

In fact, the Gospel of John[22] provides another set of fascinating theological parallels, as when it has Jesus spell out the stark contrast between flesh and

---

20. On this interesting Thomasine disinterest and lacuna, see most recently Sellew, "Thomas and the Synoptics," esp. 232–38.

21. Cf. Maia Kotrosits's evocative comment in connection with the (Paulinist) Gospel of Mark: "Christian theology has so often historicized its triumphalism in the Jesus who is vindicated on the cross through the earliest gospel, the anxious and uncertain subtext of the empty tomb exchanged for a lightness unbearable in its own way. . . . Having to go on is a privilege, and often a terrible one" (Kotrosits, "Queer Persistence: On Death, History, and Longing for Endings," in Brintnall, Marchal, and Moore, *Sexual Disorientations*, 140).

22. On John's resonances with Platonism and Stoic thought, seemingly mediated by Philo or a similar source, see Thomas H. Tobin, "The Prologue of John and Hellenistic Jewish Speculation," *CBQ* 52 (1990): 252–69; George van Kooten, "The 'True Light which Enlightens Everyone' (John 1:9): John, Genesis, the Platonic Notion of the 'True, Noetic Light' and the Allegory of the Cave in Plato's *Republic*," in *The Creation of Heaven and Earth: Reinterpretations of Genesis 1*, ed. van Kooten (Leiden: Brill, 2005), 149–94; Gregory E. Sterling, "'Day One': Platonizing Exegetical Traditions of Genesis 1:1–5 in John and Jewish Authors," *SPhilo* 17 (2005): 18–40; John Ashton, *Understanding the Fourth Gospel*, 2nd ed. (Oxford: Oxford University Press, 2007); Gitte Buch-Hansen, "*It Is the Spirit that Gives Life*": *A Stoic Understanding of Pneuma in John's Gospel* (Berlin: De Gruyter, 2010); Engberg-Petersen, *John and Philosophy: A New Reading of the Fourth Gospel* (Oxford: Oxford University Press, 2017); Miroshnikov, *Thomas and Plato*, 16–25. Douglas Estes cautions against

spirit in terms reminiscent of those expressed by both Paul and Thomas: "It is the *Spirit* that gives life; the *flesh* profits nothing" (John 6:63). John's Jesus also speaks dismissively of physical, sexual reproduction: "Unless one is born of water and spirit, a person cannot enter the kingdom of God. That which is born of flesh is *flesh*; that which is born of Spirit is *spirit*" (3:5–6). In light of these claims, it is intriguing that the divine Word, which is said to be generative and luminescent (1:1–5), is described both in Thomas and in John's opening lines as taking its place in our material world in the form of enfleshed humanity "that came to dwell among us" (John 1:14; cf. Gos. Thom. 24; 28; 77). As C. Riley Snorton notes in the context of reading theorist Judith Butler alongside the Prologue to John, "Matters of flesh and word—of signification and ontology—are tied in scripture and theory through a complex temporality that presents origin by way of existence."[23] Furthermore, when Jesus as Spirit and Light becomes enfleshed in this material place in John's thought world, this contingent embodiment as human will necessarily evoke a sense of gender, along with other characteristics thought to be visible in that flesh.

At the same time, John's Jesus, who is pictured as "the Light that shines in the darkness" (1:5), judges in his nighttime conversation with Nicodemus that "the Light has come into the world, and people loved the darkness rather than the light; for their deeds were evil. For everyone who does evil hates the light. . . . But the one who practices the truth comes to the Light" (3:19–21). John's Jesus (addressed explicitly as male and Judean by the Samaritan woman, as in 4:9, 11, 15) repeatedly yearns to leave this earthly, material realm for return to the spiritual, heavenly plane that he inhabited before "the Word became flesh and dwelt among us" (1:14). This Jesus declares plainly "I have come down from heaven," sent here by God (6:38). "For a little while longer I am with you, then I go to the one who sent me" (John 7:33; 14:28; 16:5, 16). Jesus, in sum, embodies the divine Light that shines in the cosmic darkness: "While I am in the world, I am the Light of the world" (9:5); "For a little while longer, the Light is among you. Walk while you have the light, that darkness may not overtake you" (12:35). In Thomas, similarly, Jesus declares "I am the Light which is above all things" (Gos. Thom. 77), explaining how "he" "exists from the [divine] undivided" (Gos. Thom. 61), and "took my place in the midst of the world and appeared to them in the flesh" (Gos. Thom. 28). As in John, here too in Thomas Jesus is in essence a spiritual being who speaks of "his" expectation and desire to return to "his" divine home—along with his followers (Gos. Thom. 38; 49; 50).

Hellenistic Jewish writers like the first-century philosopher Philo of Alexandria also provide rich material with which to compare and explain these views of spirit and flesh in John and Thomas. Philo interpreted the opening pages of Genesis as having provided a Mosaic template for Plato's theories of a transcendent

---

overplaying the dualistic thought world of John's Gospel in view of the text's ironic-laden rhetoric: "Dualism or Paradox? A New 'Light' on the Gospel of John," *NTS* 71 (2020): 90–118.

23. C. Riley Snornton, *Black on Both Sides: A Racial History of Trans Identity* (Minneapolis: University of Minnesota Press, 2017), 52, citing Butler's *Gender Trouble* alongside John 1.

spiritual-noetic realm as contrasted with our material-tangible existence; scholars debate how directly or indirectly the Thomas Gospel draws from Philonic-style biblical scholarship.[24] Philo read Genesis 1 as reflecting an initially created world (*kosmos*) existing only on the noetic, immaterial plane, indeed in the "mind of God," while Genesis 2 narrates the subsequent enfleshment and embodiment of humanity in our earthly, material, and mortal realm; this view has interesting analogues with how Thomas views the stark division between heaven and earth. But the adherence of authors like Paul, John, and Philo to a Scriptural model of divine creation, alongside the influence of Platonist thought,[25] entails a godly, benign origin for material existence. This means that all these aspects, spirit, mind, soul, and flesh, though of different value, can each be viewed in a partly positive way. All, including the flesh, are central to the makeup and essence of the human being.

Is this also a possible reading of Thomas? The answer is not obviously *yes*. Instead, as we have seen, in a partial analogue to Paul's notion of a new existence "in Christ," or the Johannine Gospel's metaphor of "rebirth from above" (3:3), Thomas imagines a re-formation of the human that involves moving on from one's somatic existence toward a newly immaterial spiritual essence. Therefore, while our bodily experience is quite central to both Paul's and John's notions about human identity and the processes of salvation, including a sharp focus on the physical sufferings of Jesus, this is clearly not the case for Thomas, which makes no reference to Christ's Passion or Resurrection. There is thus no reason to model one's own bodily woes on those of Jesus, as Paul suggests he does in several places, including Galatians (6:17); 2 Corinthians (4:7–12); and Philippians (3:7–11). Instead, Thomas invites us to follow Jesus on a journey of interior scrutiny and self-reflection in hopes of achieving divine self-recognition. This perspective leaves materiality beside one and behind one, and thus entails a diminishment of the value of one's bodily existence. Thomas promotes a view that calls into question the worth of anyone's expression of identity in the body, whether they be gender-variant or not.

Right from the start of the text, Jesus puts forth this challenge in Thomas: "The one who seeks should not stop seeking until they find. And if and when

---

24. *De opificio mundi*. For background on this question see esp. Runia, *Philo of Alexandria: On the Creation of the Cosmos according to Moses* (Leiden: Brill, 2001), along with Richard A. Baer, *Philo's Use of the Categories Male and Female* (Leiden: Brill, 1970); Runia, *Philo and the "Timaeus"*; Sterling, "Platonizing Moses: Philo and Middle Platonism," *The Studia Philonica Annual* 5 (1993): 96–111; on Philo and Thomas: Patterson, "Jesus Meets Plato: The Theology of the *Gospel of Thomas* and Middle Platonism," in *Das Thomasevangelium: Entstehung—Rezeption—Theologie*, ed. Jörg Frey, Enno Edzard Popkes, and Jens Schröter (Berlin: De Gruyter, 2008), 81–205; Miroshnikov, *Thomas and Plato*; Ian Phillip Brown, "Where Indeed Was the Gospel of Thomas Written? Thomas in Alexandria," *JBL* 138 (2019): 451–72.

25. Well discussed by Stevan L. Davies, "The Christology and Protology of the Gospel of Thomas," *JBL* 111 (1992): 663–82; April D. DeConick, *Seek to See Him: Ascent and Vision Mysticism in the Gospel of Thomas* (Leiden: Brill, 1996), 21–24; Elaine Pagels, "Exegesis of Genesis 1 in the Gospels of Thomas and John," *JBL* 118 (1999): 477–96; cf. Ismo Dunderberg, *The Beloved Disciple in Conflict? Revisiting the Gospels of John and Thomas* (Oxford: Oxford University Press, 2006).

they find, they will be disturbed. And if and when they are disturbed, they will marvel, and will reign over all."[26] The contingency of this process is too little recognized by commentators: the grammar of the promise is introduced by a syntactic form that in both Greek and Coptic communicates uncertain, even anxious conditionality, which is why I offer the admittedly awkward English version "when (if)" or "if and when."[27] There is no assurance offered that one will actually be able to seek and then to find, as though this were a mechanical or so-called magical ritual process.

The difficult, uncertain journey of self-scrutiny and discovery that Jesus describes in Thomas has striking analogies with the experiences of many trans and gender-variant people. We seek to gain self-understanding in the face of painful dissonance between the identities others try to assign us, and that our reception in the world further amplifies, in contrast with our strongly felt inner gender truths. The road to self-acceptance is all too often blocked by denial, doubt, embarrassment, and disturbance. But if it can be achieved, self-recognition can bring a person out of the darkness of despair into the lightness of being that is suggested by Thomas's opening lines: seeking can lead to disturbance, yes, but ultimately also to wonder, and repose. As we read, "If and when you come to know yourselves, then you will become known" (Gos. Thom. 3). That is, God will know and recognize you; God and you will recognize each other.

Some might suggest that internal, preferably silent and private self-recognition of one's true gender could—perhaps indeed should—be sufficient, that measures taken to alter how others perceive our exterior selves are unnecessary and even self-indulgent. (I myself have heard some tentative and more blatant expressions of this attitude directed at my own moves to live publicly in accordance with my gender.) Isn't it enough, some people might say, to "know oneself" internally, and perhaps spiritually, without insisting on troubling, confusing, and frightening others with our problems? And this is where the dismissal of the importance of physical, bodily identity that I see in Thomas could likely collide with the lived experience of other trans and gender-variant people. Our experience of the world must shape our valuation of the text. Shouldn't trans people take deep pride in our identities, including our own physicality? Cannot trans people express our truths in visible, bodily ways, and do so gladly and safely? True to the bodies we inhabit as well as to our self-understanding? While Thomas offers avenues to spur self-knowledge that can bolster narratives of trans and nonbinary self-discovery, the Gospel may fall short for many in the way it elides the bodily expression of this interior knowledge and the public assertion of one's gender as truly felt.

---

26. Gos. Thom. 2 in its Coptic version. A Greek version survives in Papyrus Oxyrhynchus 654, lines 17–19, concluding with the achievement of repose.

27. The Coptic of Gos. Thom. 2 employs the indefinite temporal marker with the conditional: *auo hotan efshankhine*. The underlying Greek from P. Oxy. 654 conveys the identical contingency (at least as restored by Attridge in Layton, *Nag Hammadi Codex II*, vol. 1, 113). The same significant uncertainty is conveyed in the key logion Gos. Thom. 22, to which I return below.

Certain realms of bodily experience in modern American culture (at least) that I have not addressed directly in my previous work on Thomas, beyond brief gestures, include the often-dire intersections of race, ethnicity, age, class, and (dis)ability. The dangers faced daily by Black trans women, in particular, who share in frighteningly elevated ways in the pervasive potential vulnerability of any female-identified person, whether in public or domestic spheres, complicate the picture of self-discovery created in Thomas. How does any gender-variant individual balance their right to express their femininity (as one example) in public with confidence and pride, while also feeling at least some level of personal safety? Access to medical care, including body-altering hormones or surgery, is contingent at best, dependent as it so often is on one's financial, employment, and familial statuses. Trans people's journey into publicly accessible and publicly acceptable presentations of our true identities can face severe obstacles based on age (too young? too old?), insecurity in food, employment, or housing, and/or lack of support from family or one's broader community, including faith communities. These difficulties are reduced or multiplied based on numerous factors well beyond most individuals' control.

It is therefore a sign of considerable privilege for a white, middle-class trans woman, such as myself, to want to imagine a more meaningful form of existence focused on my inner self in the Thomasine manner, since my exterior self, in most regards, carries with it deeply rooted aspects of privilege and diminished vulnerability in so many spheres of daily life "in the flesh."[28] I realize and acknowledge that the daily bodily experience of multiply vulnerable trans or otherwise gender-variant people could well evoke different and quite possibly more entangled responses to Thomas's disparagement of fleshly existence and promotion of interior selfhood than feels true for me. Though our contemporary concept of racialized identity does not fit the thought world and system of values prevalent in the Mediterranean context of Thomas's world, the lives and worldviews of those resident in contemporary America, at a minimum, are affected deeply and, for too many of us, oppressed tragically, by the forces of racialized and ableist notions of human worth. From a social justice perspective, in the incisive words of Audra Lorde, "There is no such thing as a single-issue struggle because we do not live single-issue lives."[29]

In this light, the response of many trans people to how the Gospel of Thomas directs us away from our material to another, (merely?) spiritual identity could likely be quite different from my own. One of the most significant advances of collective work toward equality and liberation, at least in the North American context, has been how powerfully, indeed joyfully, folks assert the beauty and

---

28. In my own case, as an older white woman with a supportive employer and family, with access to the best medical care, the challenges have been much less daunting than for many others. See further Sellew, "Traversing the Society of Biblical Literature While Trans," in *Women and the Society of Biblical Literature*, ed. Nicole L. Tilford (Atlanta: SBL Press, 2019), 231–38; "Reading *Thomas* from Here," 62–63.

29. Audre Lorde, *Sister Outsider: Essays and Speeches* (Trumansburg, NY: Crossing Press, 1984), 138.

strength of existence in bodies outside the norms of the regnant Eurocentric, straight, normatively abled, cis-male-oriented value system. Assertions of self-worth in the face of dislike, disapproval, and oppression can express both a yearning and an achievement. Self-respect and self-acceptance may often give rise to a potent rebuke of attempted dismissal or rejection, powered by an eloquent assertion of one's place in the world. Should not this move toward self-love and self-assertion also be made manifest in the lives and bodies of trans and other gender nonconforming people? From this standpoint, the value or relevance of Thomas's severely antimaterialist ideology is potentially open to question for many trans or gender-variant readers.

Here is where Jesus's challenge set out in the list of transformations in Gos. Thom. 22 holds promise—for those who wish it: that a trans person might reconfigure one's physical self into a new body, possibly one that better conforms with one's true gender, or possibly one that leaves gender difference and specificity behind ("no longer male and female"). Though here and elsewhere I personally have read the imagery of that parable as symbolic or metaphorical, that the language points to spiritual transformation instead of material alteration, some would find the notion of a physical replacement of body parts to be affirming of their choices: "If and when you make the male and the female one and the same, so that the male not be male nor the female, female . . . then you will enter the kingdom."[30] Some interpret this pronouncement as potentially validating the sorts of medical interventions, whether through hormonal therapy, surgical reconstruction, or other means, that many trans people look toward to refashion our bodies to escape the shape and anatomical elements of the bodies we "were born with." We might seek to enter our own versions of the Kingdom of Heaven in our own true gender(s), expressed by many of us, in part, through our trans male or female or agender bodies.

And yet it is indeed erasure of gender, beginning with female gender, that the text seems to expect. At the very close of the Gospel, Jesus replies to Simon Peter's demand that "he" "make Mary leave us, for women are not deserving of life," by insisting that human bodies that read as female must somehow "become Living Spirits resembling *you* males" (Gos. Thom. 114). Even male bodies will seemingly not, in and of themselves, have achieved that higher spiritual level, since Jesus distinguishes "his" own person and gender both from that of women (for whom Mary stands in at this point in the text)[31] and of men (whom Peter represents). In the viewpoint of the Gospel of Thomas, or so Richard Valantasis has argued,[32] Jesus pioneers some sort of third gender that combines elements of the female and the male, and so the Thomasine Christian must do so as well, if they hope to "enter the kingdom." A more compelling reading, in my view, is

---

30. See for example the trans folks found in the works cited in footnote 5 above.
31. Mary's role in this passage is as a "placeholder" for any woman, as is argued persuasively by Anna Cwikla: "Placeholders, Lessons, and Emasculators: The Literary Function of Women in Early Christian Texts" (PhD dissertation, University of Toronto, 2024), 58–66.
32. Valantasis, *The Gospel of Thomas*, 10–11.

that Thomas sees Jesus not as third-gendered but instead as beyond or outside of human gender categories altogether, along the lines of Philo's reading of the immaterial "image of God" of Genesis 1, even as the temporary "embodiment" of divine Spirit and Light.[33]

The path to salvation, then, in the Thomasine theology, allows for and perhaps demands attention to the physical body, while looking ultimately to transformation of the human person from an enfleshed, gender-specific, mortal, material form into an imperishable, spiritual, asomatic and thus ungendered essence. And, importantly, for Thomas, there is no need for deferral of the attainment of acknowledgment of one's authentic identity until some distant or even imminent eschatological event. The salvific journey can and must happen in the here and now. For some of us, even if not for all, this means the bodies that carry our hidden spirits can be celebrated.

For a trans individual living contingently in their physical embodiment, it seems that the Jesus of Thomas recognizes that humans of any, all, or no gender/s could be on a path toward enlightenment, self-understanding, and, if so desired, escape from the limitations of material existence. While alive in this created, mortal plane, so Thomas would suggest, any and all human bodies struggle with their physicality—female bodies more than male, to be sure, and disabled and/or differently gendered folks even more—but all may and likely do struggle, none the less. And so, in light of Thomas's rendering of inevitable bodily struggle in the human quest to ascertain our spiritual essence, the non-normative, unusual, possibly monstrous-seeming bodies that convey trans and gender-variant folks about in this material world may ultimately not appear to be quite so alien.[34] None of us lives a single-issue life. Perhaps, through our shared versions of embodiment, we, the gender diverse, as with the variously (dis)abled, may offer ourselves to be simply seen, and, one hopes, to be viewed positively. We would thus embody some of the more accessible and self-aware exemplars of living in and through the challenges, confusions, and joys that must be faced and experienced for anyone striving to be authentically human, body and soul.

---

33. See further Sellew, "Reading *Thomas* from Here," esp. 75–80.

34. Alluding to the work of Valérie Nicolet, when she writes, "The presence of monsters at the outskirts of biblical texts highlights the need for a critique of the Bible's participation in the creation of a patriarchal society and culture" ("Monstrous Bodies in Paul's Letter to the Galatians," in *Bodies on the Verge: Queering Pauline Epistles* ed. Joseph A. Marchal [Atlanta: SBL Press, 2019], 135).

Chapter 12

Achilles Breaks Gender

Tertullian's Trans Monster Making in De Pallio

KY MERKLEY

Growing up in a devoutly Christian home as a transgender youth, I was often directed to Deuteronomy as a corrective for my desire to wear feminine clothing. Deut 22:5, after all, was clear in its injunction that "The woman shall not wear that which pertaineth unto a man, neither shall a man put on a woman's garment: for all that do so are abomination unto the LORD thy God" (KJV). As a child, this verse seemed clear. I had no idea how many different ways this verse had been understood throughout the long history of Christianity.[1] Within Christian thought, the relationship between gender, identity, and clothing has never had a single, simple answer. As I've argued elsewhere, gender is a hyperobject—a concept so massive that we cannot easily comprehend more than a small part of it.[2] When dealing with gender as a hyperobject, the temptation is

---

1. For example, Thomas Aquinas in *Summa Theologiae II* provides a list of excuses that would permit crossdressing (*Secunda Secundæ Partis*, 169), multiple Byzantine Saints were women who lived as male monks—for this see in particular Roland Betancourt, *Byzantine Intersectionality: Sexuality, Gender, and Race in the Middle Ages* (Princeton, NJ: Princeton University Press, 2021), and Martin Le Franc wrote in the *Champion des dames* an entire section defending Joan of Arc's change of clothing. More examples will follow in this chapter.
2. See Ky Merkley, "Writing Trans History with an Ethics of Care, While Reading Gender in Imperial Roman Literature," *Gender and History* 36:1 (2024): 5–6.

to take what we know today and assume that gender has always been that way. For this reason, modern conceptions of gender have found points of comparison with Tertullian, the first Latin Church Father (late second/early third century CE). Tertullian believed in rigid gender boundaries, and his conception of gender has been highly influential in the Latin west. Such rigidity has made it easy to map modern conceptions of gender onto Tertullian. By analyzing a single one of Tertullian's works, *De pallio*, this chapter aims to demonstrate why this is a mistake, as Tertullian's ideas on gender are a direct response to Roman ideas of masculinity. At the same time, the kind of gendered polemic that Tertullian constructs in *De pallio* made gender nonconforming people monsters in a similar way to how trans women are rendered monstrous today. Through a close reading of *De pallio*, we can view in the past similar means of policing gender and gender performance, even if the reasons for policing gender are different from today.

Clothing and morality were closely tied together by many early Christian authors. As Kristi Upson-Saia notes in *Early Christian Dress: Gender, Virtue, and Authority*, "At times, dress was assumed to be an extension of the wearer's soul, whether one's clothing exhibited his inherent self-mastery or self-indulgence."[3] Yet, an important distinction concerning clothing, gender, and identity emerges between Clement of Alexandria writing in the Greek east and Tertullian writing in the Latin west. Clement imagined a world in which gendered clothing could be unnecessary, a world in which women would become strong enough to wear manly clothes ("For as it is common to both [male and female] to require things to cover them, so also their coverings ought to be similar" *Paedagogus* 2.9).[4] Tertullian, on the other hand, believed wearing the clothing of the other sex was a lie, a deception against Nature and God.[5] As we will see, *De pallio* is entirely dedicated to examining the relationship between morality, clothing, nature, and God. Tertullian concluded that to change one's clothing is to change one's very nature and is, therefore, against God's will. Tertullian's conclusion was adopted by other Latin Church Fathers: Cyprian, Ambrose, and Jerome all continue to perpetuate the idea that wearing the clothing of the other sex is a lie—an idea central to many modern readings of Deut 22:5.[6] The fact remains, however, that when Tertullian delivered *De pallio*, he was speaking in a specific cultural context, to a specific audience of Roman citizens (who were ethnically Punic and Berber) in the North African city of Carthage, and refuting specific practices—Roman masculinity and its tendency to gender flexibility.

3. Kristi Upson-Saia, *Early Christian Dress: Gender, Virtue, and Authority* (New York: Routledge, 2011), 5.
4. Translation here by Philip Schaff, *ANF*, vol. 2.
5. As one good example see Tertullian, *De spectaculis*, 23.
6. For a rapid general overview see G.G. Bolich, *Transgender and Religion* (Raleigh, NC: Psyche's Press, 2009), 71–77.

INTRODUCING *DE PALLIO*

In Roman imperial culture, the clothing an individual wore carried tremendous meaning. Clothing mattered: it signaled gender, social class, political or juridical importance, and citizenship—it created a clear sense of exclusion or inclusion in the Roman social world.[7] To wear the wrong clothing in the wrong setting was a serious social *faux pas* that betrayed a rustic breeding and lack of *Romanitas* (those ideals and cultural practices that defined what it meant to be Roman). The appropriate Roman attire for public addresses was the toga; yet, in the text of *De pallio*, which is presented as a speech that was delivered in the forum of Carthage, Tertullian says that he is wearing not a toga but a *pallium*—a cloak of Greek and North African style associated with Greek intellectualism, philosophy, and Carthaginian history. Tertullian's first rhetorical move in *De pallio* is purposefully dressing in the wrong clothing. This choice shattered expected social norms, and Tertullian knew that his choice would require an explanation—setting up the excuse to deliver an entire speech condemning the toga and Roman conceptions of masculinity.

De pallio centers around this critique of the toga, an object that embodied Roman cultural identity, moral values, and masculinity. By attacking the toga as a cultural object, Tertullian lays siege to the very notion of *Romanitas*. Indeed, *Romanitas* and the toga are difficult to separate: Virgil's *Aeneid* goes so far as to define the Roman people as "the togaed people" (*Aen.* 1.296, *gentemque togatam*). Because the toga was such an important symbol, the right to wear the toga was heavily regulated and policed.[8] Once permitted, the toga allowed its wearer entrance into the Roman world. This strict regulation and enforcement rendered the toga a clear, visible marker of hierarchy.[9]

On the other hand, wearing the wrong clothing carried serious social consequences. Cassius Dio reports that Fronto, on suddenly finding out that one of his court cases had already begun, rushed to court and arrived still wearing his dining robes—perhaps the modern equivalent of having your attorney show up to court wearing a velvet smoking jacket. The presiding judge ironically greeted the mis-dressed Fronto with *vale* (the evening greeting) instead of *salve* (the official greeting)—a biting enough rejoinder that the story deserved to be recorded.[10] Additionally, Septimius Severus is said to have committed the error of going to an imperial banquet in a *pallium* and was only saved from

---

7. See Jonathan Edmondson, "Public Dress and Social Control in Late Republican and Early Imperial Rome," in *Roman Dress and the Fabrics of Roman Culture*, ed. Jonathan Edmondson and Alison Keith (Toronto: University of Toronto Press, 2008), 22.
8. See Edmondson, "Public Dress," 21–28, for a rich discussion on the place of the toga in Roman society.
9. For example, Ap., *Flor.* 8.2. For further discussion see T. Corey Brennan, "Tertullian's *De Pallio* and Roman Dress in North Africa," in Edmondson and Keith, *Roman Dress and the Fabrics of Roman Culture*, 261.
10. See *Cassius Dio* 69.18.3.

social embarrassment by the loan of one of the emperor's own togas.[11] So, when Tertullian, as a well-educated public speaker, arose to deliver a public address from the *rostrum* dressed in the wrong clothing, he was making an obvious and dramatic statement.

WHY IS CLOTHING SO IMPORTANT TO TRANSGENDER STUDIES?

Initially, Tertullian's change of clothing may not seem intimately connected with transgender identities; but of course, personal identity, social identity, and clothing are all intimately connected—tied up in what we today call "gender." When clothing matches an expected social identity, normative bodies are granted normative genders.[12] In fact, the phrase "granting someone a gender" betrays an important truth: gender is given to us by others. Hil Malantino in *Trans Care* declares gender an act of supplication, something we plead for, something that needs to be returned and granted in order to become truly real.[13] This means that gender is never *achieved*; instead, gender is a process—an ongoing actualization of identity through the outward expression of gendered (i.e., normatively expected) actions with the hope that the gendered act will be recognized and accepted. Nonetheless, "normatively expected" actions differ greatly depending on race, ethnicity, class-status, and citizenship along with a host of other categories. As much as we might try to split gender into a clear binary (or even spectrum) built around anatomy, countless additional factors and coinciding identities, each with their own societal pressures and expectations (stereotypes), modify and change our conceptions. While it might be easy to assume that such a nuanced approach to gender is a modern phenomenon, Tertullian's *De pallio* takes this same approach by proposing new norms that unite Christianity with Punic conceptions and practices of gender.

De pallio weaponizes normative ideals to create new rules around how social and cultural categories are defined and bounded. This reveals an important truth: to study gender is to study categorization. Indeed, what is Gender Studies but a study of the history of categorization, its arbitrary and capricious functions, and its—unjust and often horrifying—consequences? The word "gender" itself reveals in its origins the truth that to study gender is to study categorization: the English word "gender" developed as early as the fifteenth century to mean "the male-or-female sex."[14] Before that, gender simply meant "kind" or "sort," a class of things that share certain traits, retaining its meaning from the Old French *gendre* and the Latin *genus*. In fact, "gender" and "kin" share the same

11. SHA *Hadr.* 22.4, for a discussion on the passage see Edmondson, "Public Dress," 24.
12. C. Riley Snorton, *Black on Both Sides: A Racial History of Trans Identity* (Minneapolis: University of Minnesota Press, 2017).
13. Hil Malatino, *Trans Care* (Minneapolis: University of Minnesota Press, 2020), 36–37.
14. See "gender, n." *Oxford English Dictionary Online*, June 2022, Oxford University Press.

Proto-Indo European root, *-gene*. Gender, in its most fundamental sense, is a way of distinguishing those who are like us—our kin. Too often, to achieve or to recognize gender means that first we must identify and define those who are not like us—the Other.

Some of the best work of the last several years in transgender studies has been dedicated to searching for ways in which the Other has been used to define gender.[15] Following Claire Colebrook's call to define trans not as a category but a *lack* of category (which creates the potential to create new categories), I often use trans potentiality as a tool for deconstructing and analyzing the process of categorization.[16] For understanding Tertullian, this tool has been particularly fruitful. In the world of the Roman Empire, clothing and internal identity were closely linked, though the specific relationship between clothing and internal identity was heavily contested.[17] In *De pallio*, Tertullian linked his attack on the toga and *Romanitas* to a failed Roman masculinity. After demonstrating the ways in which normative Roman conceptions of masculinity have morally failed, Tertullian attempted to shift ideas surrounding identity, clothing, and masculinity away from distinctly Roman norms and instead worked to establish a Christian concept of gendered identity that is still recognizable and influential today.

CLOSE READING OF *DE PALLIO*

Due in part to the ambiguous societal place and position of the *pallium* in Roman Carthage, *De pallio* has elicited significant academic consideration—as well as occasional consternation. Vincent Hunink even went so far as to proclaim that "the *De pallio* is one of the strangest texts ever written in Latin" in his 2005 commentary.[18] Should this article of clothing be read as a social marker of class and education? A sign of philosophy? A boundary marker of ethnic identity?[19] Understanding the cultural place of the *pallium* seems essential for any reading of this text. Rather than attempt to define precisely what semiotic place the *pallium* occupies, however, I will focus on what it is *not*—for despite any answers to the questions above, the *pallium* is not the *toga*.

Starting with the assumption that *De pallio* serves as a rhetorically brilliant proselytizing effort "to win over the Carthaginian audience to Christianity,"[20] I

---

15. Besides Snorton's *Black on Both Sides*, Leah DeVun's *The Shape of Sex: Nonbinary Gender from Genesis to the Renaissance* (New York: Columbia University Press, 2021); and Betancourt's *Byzantine Intersectionality* provide excellent examples of how fruitful this approach can be.

16. Claire Colebrook, "What Is It Like to Be Human," *TSQ* 2:2 (2015): 228.

17. For one excellent example, see Chris Mowat, "Don't Be a Drag, Just Be a Priest: The Clothing and Identity of the Galli of Cybele in the Roman Republic and Empire," *Gender and History* 33:2 (2021): 296–98.

18. See Vincent Hunink, *Tertullian De Pallio: A Commentary* (Netherlands: Brill, 2005), 9.

19. David E. Wilhite, *Tertullian the African: An Anthropological Reading of Tertullian's Context and Identities* (Berlin: De Gruyter, 2007), 140. For the broader discussion see 139–45.

20. See Brennan, "Tertullian's *De Pallio*," 267.

see in *De pallio* a clear rejection of *Romanitas*.[21] In his broader works, Tertullian saw the conciliation of Christian faith and social life in Carthage (i.e., *Romanitas*) as a problem that necessitated prevention: Tertullian feared that a multiplicity of social identities would erase the important distinctions of "being Christian."[22] The purposeful creation of marked cultural differences between the hegemonic practices of *Romanitas* and a proper Christian life is a natural extension of this thesis. By choosing not to wear the toga and then defending that choice, Tertullian is rejecting not only Roman identity, but also Roman modes of *being* masculine.

In order to present this thesis, Tertullian has a lot of ground to cover: proving that clothing can and should change; spelling out when a change of clothing is immoral; establishing the *toga* as a failed symbol of morality; presenting the *pallium* as a better symbol of morality; and then finally tying the *pallium* to Christianity. The following outline lays out the argument of the text providing a macro view of how Tertullian structured his argument in *De pallio*:

1. Tertullian questions why he has received condemnation for wearing the *pallium*. The Carthaginians used to wear the *pallium* and, in the right circumstances, they still do. By adopting the *toga*, they've bowed to the Roman yoke.
2. Rather than condemn the Carthaginian change of clothing from *pallium* to *toga*, Tertullian argues that change is natural and, in truth, essential to the world: even Nature changes its appearances. He asks the Carthaginians why they are condemning change in a man while accepting change in nature.
3. Further examples of change: Humanity was created naked and then later clothed itself. Clothing exists in many different forms and the *pallium* is worn almost everywhere—even sometimes by Romans.
4. The rules for when changing clothing is wrong are presented with negative examples. These include Achilles, Hercules, Cleomachus the boxer, as well as kings and Caesars. When clothing is no longer policed or proper, disaster follows.
5. The *pallium* is superior to the *toga*, easier and more comfortable to wear; it represents a better life, a philosophical life disengaged from public life and Rome. This makes the *pallium* the proper dress with which to condemn Roman excesses.
6. Clothing is a powerful moral symbol. The *pallium* represents learning, philosophy, and morality. This might not convey the glory of the *toga*, but the *toga* also may adorn gladiators and sex-workers; therefore, the *pallium* is superior. And it has become even greater now since it adorns the Christians.

As we can see, the first three sections of the speech focused on the fact that clothing does change, that the Carthaginians themselves have changed theirs, and that there is nothing dishonorable in their (or Tertullian's) change of dress. Once this precept—that clothing can and should change—has been set down, Tertullian established the rules for when it should not be changed.

21. This argument follows Keith Bradley's chapter "Romanitas and the Roman Family: The Evidence of Apuleius' Apology," in *Apuleius and Antonine Rome* (Toronto: University of Toronto Press, 2012), 41.
22. Eric Rebillard, *Christians and Their Many Identities in Late Antiquity: North Africa 200–450 CE* (Ithaca, NY: Cornell University Press, 2012), 9.

ACHILLES IN *DE PALLIO*

Tertullian's negative examples—establishing when a change of clothes is immoral or wrong—were drawn from stories fundamental to Roman masculinity and heroism. In the process, Tertullian created a comparative critique of Roman masculinity versus Punic (and, as will later be established, Christian) norms. Tertullian's first example is the tale of Achilles on the island of Scyros, in which Achilles famously dressed and lived as a maiden. This act is encouraged by his mother, who was trying to protect him from dying in the Trojan War. For his account of the story, Tertullian relied heavily on the version told in Statius's *Achilleid*.[23] Tertullian, however, transforms Statius' complicated and fluid conception of Achilles' gender into a cautionary tale where a change of clothing represents the immoral, monstrous, or wrong:

> Thus, the Larissan hero broke nature by turning into a maiden. . . . You, permitting it, might endure the solicitude of a mother, if he was still a child; but certainly, at this time he was already hirsute, certainly at that time he had privately proved himself a man [a euphemism], yet he endured wearing the stola, arranging his hair, putting on makeup, consulting the mirror, softening his neck, and even effeminizing his ears by piercing them, which his bust at Sigeum preserves. (4.2)[24]

Tertullian's critique doesn't hold back at all: Achilles broke nature, an assault against God himself—a point emphasized immediately before this passage: "Custom should give faithfulness to the times, Nature should give faithfulness to God" (*Det consuetudo fidem tempori, natura deo*, 4.2). When Tertullian has Achilles *break* nature, he uses the verb *concutio*, which has a range of semantic meanings: to shake violently, to shake to its foundations, to shatter, etc. Tertullian often used *concutio* in his works forcefully, as a literal or metaphorical earthquake that causes radical upheaval.[25] By using the word in this passage, Tertullian drives home the serious nature of Achilles' actions.

Tertullian then reduces hundreds of lines of Statius's *Achilleid* down to just a couple lines of plot synopsis. This summary artfully emphasizes that Achilles has no excuse for his actions—namely, his becoming a maiden. Comparing translations of this synopsis helps to elucidate the effect that Tertullian's abridgement creates. Peter Heslin's translation of *De pallio* emphasizes how Tertullian's account is a synopsis of the *Achilleid*:

> You would be able to stand it if it was while he was still a boy, putting up with his mother's fussing; but he kept it up, even after he had sprouted some stubble and had performed the job of a man for someone in secret.[26]

---

23. Following P. J. Heslin, *The Transvestite Achilles* (Cambridge: Cambridge University Press, 2005), 270–72.
24. Unless otherwise noted, all translations are my own.
25. *Concutio* has very strong connotations within Tertullian. See Tertullian, *Apol.* 21.20, 25.7, 31.2 for literal earthquakes, *Apol.* 50.14 for another metaphorical example.
26. Trans. by Heslin, *The Transvestite Achilles*, 277.

Achilles is first allowed to dress as a *virgo* when he is a boy, because of his mother's concern, and only comes under attack when he persists in this action after achieving puberty and having sex with Deidamia. Yet, Heslin's translation doesn't necessarily account for the rapid temporality created by *iam . . . iam . . . adhuc*. This repeated use of *iam* (meaning "now/at this moment") flattens this narrative into what can seem to be a single temporal moment, an effect which Vincent Hunink's translation emphasizes:

> One may willingly tolerate, in the case of a little boy, a mother's concern. But no doubt he was already covered with hair, no doubt he had already secretly proved himself a man to somebody, when he still put up with a woman's flowing robe.[27]

Hunink's translation strips any excuse for Achilles to dress as a woman from the very beginning: "One may . . . but no doubt." While Heslin's translation emphasizes Tertullian's use of Statius' narrative, Hunink's choice highlights how Achilles' potential excuses for being a woman have been stripped from him. My translation of the text attempts to balance the two approaches, capturing the narrative created by Heslin's translation while also retaining the singular temporal moment, which Hunink emphasizes. I find the rhetorical effect created by the rapid pace of *iam, iam, adhuc* essential to translate since this strips away the potential excuses that Statius provides for his Achilles to dress as a maiden in the *Achilleid*.

Statius's *Achilleid* clearly establishes Achilles as a boy (*puer*).[28] Tertullian reduces hundreds of lines to a single sentence, temporally flattening the narrative and thereby refuting the excuse of youth. While a reader might tolerate (*feras*) that a boy would listen to his mother, we have no reason to tolerate it anymore: he has gone through puberty and had sex within a single moment. This leaves Achilles no excuse. He has become a woman. Tertullian's language is explicit: Achilles *concussit naturam mutando in virginem*. Achilles shook the very foundations of nature itself by changing into a maiden.

ACHILLES IN THE ACHILLEID

This condensed, instantaneous change stands in stark contrast to how the *Achilleid* frames Achilles' feminine embodiment. In the *Achilleid*, Achilles' mother Thetis hides Achilles in the court of Lycomedes (on the island of Scyros) by having Achilles live as a maiden. Before Achilles goes to Scyros, Statius repeatedly emphasizes that Achilles is a boy (*puer*) who explicitly occupies a liminal place between masculinity and femininity. As a result, multiple characters express hopes or fears regarding the outcome of this embodiment, framing the *Achilleid* around if and how Achilles has changed as a result of his feminine embodiment.

27. Trans. Hunink, Tertullian, *De pallio*.
28. *Achill.* 605; see also *Achill.* 229, 302.

Three options are presented: (1) Achilles has changed into a woman and this is a moral wrong; (2) Achilles has changed into a woman and this is the desired outcome; or (3) Achilles has not changed at all. Calchas, seeing Achilles' feminine garb in a dream, fears the change will permanently affect Achilles' inner nature and declares, "Oh no! He's gone . . . snatched away. Who is this shameful maiden here now?" (534–35). On the other hand, Thetis, his mother, wants Achilles' externally adopted dress to change his internal identity. She explicitly bids Lycomedes, the king of Scyros, to "Break her by ruling her and hold the difficult-to-teach maiden to her sex" (355–56). On leaving Scyros, Thetis concludes with a prayer that Achilles *might be* a maiden of pious Lycomedes.[29] Finally, Achilles always sees himself as male. As a boy, he is only driven to don women's garb as a way to get close to Deidamia, struck by desire for the first time.[30] Later, feeling that his manliness is being wasted, he exhorts himself to be a man and rapes Deidamia. He justifies this act by telling her that his shameful clothes and feminine behavior were a stratagem for her sake, and that he will lay waste to the whole city if her father is not pleased with this arrangement.[31]

Statius's *Achilleid* engages in a dialectic between two seemingly opposed positions. Achilles doesn't believe his feminine dress affects his manliness or identity, while Calchas and Thetis view Achilles *as* a maiden and wonder whether this change will be permanent. These opposed positions on identity, embodiment, and clothing permeate Roman society. Contemporary philosophical arguments between the Stoics and Platonists questioned if changing clothing could change one's very identity.[32] The Platonic position on embodiment was that a change in embodiment changed the self. Stoic conceptions of selfhood, on the other hand, represent self-identity as persisting even if a material body is changed. In the *Achilleid*, Achilles is striving to prove the Stoic position correct. Yet, Achilles is not all unique in his desire to prove that he can remain *a man* while dressing otherwise. The Latin elegiac lover attempts to embrace femininity in order to arise more masculine after being victorious in love, and Roman depictions of Hercules see in his adoption of woman's clothing the potential for him to become even more manly or for his masculinity to be damaged.[33] Achilles' internal position in Statius' *Achilleid* follows these same rules. He has donned women's garb in order to keep him safe, entered femininity and learned its rules; but so long as he can continue to assert masculine power, his identity as a man is ultimately protected. If Achilles had failed to reassert his identity, perhaps Calchas's fears that maybe Achilles was never really a man at all would have been proven true.

The competing opinions around clothing and identity create a complicated interplay essential to traditional Roman conceptions of masculinity: clothing *might* change the self entirely; it *might* dangerously alter external perceptions of

---

29. *Achill.* 396
30. *Achill.* 301–304.
31. See *Achill.* 638–639 and 657–660.
32. Christopher Gill lays out these positions excellently in *The Structured Self in Hellenistic and Roman Thought* (Oxford: Oxford University Press, 2006), 67 by using a philosophical problem found in Philo (LS 28P).
33. DeVun, *The Shape of Sex*, see in particular ch. 1.

self with severe consequences; or it *might* lead to no change at all.[34] All of these conceptions are delightfully encapsulated in the double meaning of the Latin word *habitus*: clothing *and* inner nature. The doubled nature of *habitus* is a crucial element for understanding Roman masculine norms, one in which I see a potential tool that invites—even demands—to be played with.

Roman masculinity has a central definition, a set of norms that define it, yet *real Roman men* ought to be able to transgress those norms; *real men*, you see, define what "man" means in the first place. For Roman men, straying from a masculine *habitus* becomes a somewhat risky "game," which can be used to prove one's own masculinity if played correctly—a useful tool in a world where unquestionably *being* a *vir* (a word I would translate as a *real man*) was of central importance. In poetry, the elegiac lover subordinates and effeminates himself to his love interest yet exerts masculine violence to return to masculinity if things ever go too far.[35] Similarly, Corey Brennan sees the "heterosexual *effeminatus*" as a purposeful adoption, "a deliberate social stance in which the principal aim was conspicuously to display one's heightened *urbanitas*."[36] Statius's text is another example of this "game"—clothing could, and can, affect one's identity, but a real man will still remain a man and can be interpellated and called forth by other men—as happens with Achilles.

TERTULLIAN REJECTS THE GAME

Tertullian is not interested in this complicated interplay. In *De pallio*, Achilles's change is so complete that an entire life living as a woman seems a possibility, arguing in 4.2 that "if after such a jolt she had still continued being a maiden, she could have married." Achilles had changed her *habitus*. Once the change was made, Tertullian implies, this *habitus* should not have been changed again:

> The monstrosity is doubled, from a man, he was a woman, and soon after from a woman she was a man. The truth should not have been negated, nor the conceit confessed. Either change of *habitus* was bad. One was against nature, the other against safety. (4.2)

---

34. This creates a fluid and complex conception of masculinity in the Roman imaginary. For those interested in better understanding Roman conceptions of gender (and its fluid and sometimes ambiguous identity) Brooke Holmes' *Gender: Antiquity and Its Legacy* (Oxford: Oxford University Press, 2012) provides a good overview of gender in Roman thought. For explicitly trans readings, Domitilla Campanile, Filippo Carlà-Uhink, and Margherita Facella, eds. *TransAntiquity: Cross-Dressing and Transgender Dynamics in the Ancient World* (London: Routledge, 2017); and Allison Surtees and Jennifer Dyer, eds., *Exploring Gender Diversity in the Ancient World* (Edinburgh: Edinburgh University Press, 2020) provide a solid introduction to transgender studies in classics.

35. Other examples of this abound. Anthony Corbeill, *Nature Embodied: Gesture in Ancient Rome* (Princeton, NJ: Princeton University Press, 2004), 114–16 shows how masculine *habitus* and *actio* in oratory can reflect purposeful genderbending as male orators would purposefully use feminine *actio* and then return to the masculine; or Monica Silveira Cyrino, "Heroes in D(u)ress: Transvestism and Power in the Myths of Herakles and Achilles," *Helios* 31:2 (1998): 207–41, which lays out the conception of paradigmatic heroic crossdressing (conveniently for us based on Hercules and Achilles).

36. Brennan, "Tertullian's *De Pallio*," 265.

In fact, *natura* provides Tertullian his central definition of when a change of clothing is wrong or not. Immediately before the Achilles episode, he defines when a change of clothing is wrong:

> To change one's *habitus* only approaches fault if one's nature is changed rather than custom. There is a significant difference between the honor due to time and religion. Custom should give faithfulness to the times, Nature to God. (4.2)

This plea to *natura* creates a clear dichotomy between changes that are proper and moral, and a change that is not.

In addition to the summary of Achilles's genderbending, *De pallio* provides two other explicit examples for changes of dress that are *against* nature and thus are inappropriate: the hero Hercules crossdressing at the command of Omphale, the queen of Lydia, and the boxer Cleomachus. Tertullian declares Hercules' adoption of femininity to be even more shameful than Achilles's: "It is more shameful yet that lust transformed the dress of a man" (4.3).

While *habitus*, with its clear connection between clothing and nature, has been the central focus of Tertullian's argument, at this point Tertullian switches to a discussion of *cultus*. This is a fascinating decision, particularly since, as noted above, Achilles' change is tied to *habitus*—a word which extends far beyond a mere external change to inner identity. Hercules's change, however, is of *cultus*—a word tied to culture, ornament, and clothing rather than internal nature. The use of the word *cultus* rather than *habitus* marks Achilles's and Hercules's changes as different: Achilles "passed" and lived as a woman, while Hercules momentarily donned Omphale's clothing. Hercules's choice is more shameful because he has no excuse, other than his "lust." While Hercules is rendered less manly because of his clothing, Omphale does not become more masculine by donning male clothes. Rather, Tertullian emphasizes that Hercules's clothing needed to be modified in order to be worn by a woman. An entire passage is dedicated to how the skin of the Nemean Lion must be perfumed and washed so that it is soft enough, and feminine enough to be worn by Omphale. Hercules intentionally chose, with no excuse, to enter femininity and deserves condemnation for the morally wrong choice rather than the adoration that the Carthaginians heap upon him.[37]

In the Cleomachus example, morality and proper dress are linked even more explicitly. Cleomachus's departure from masculine dress and comportment, according to Tertullian, is occasioned by his submission to anal sex: "with an incredible change he flowed from the masculine, having submitted himself to anal sex and more"[38] (4.4). Cleomachus's submission to being penetrated leads

---

37. See *Pall.* 4.3
38. J. N. Adams specifically cites this example in his discussions of both *caedo* and *intercus* as a clear example of sexual metaphor in the *Latin Sexual Vocabulary* (Baltimore: John Hopkins University Press, 1990), 145–48.

him away from the masculine entirely, a *vir* is by his very nature impenetrable; Tertullian implies that his adoption of a feminine *habitus* is a natural consequence. If the adoption of feminine dress is the natural consequence of unmanly action, as Tertullian suggests, then clothing and moral uprightness are directly linked. Just as Achilles' adoption of feminine clothing and mannerisms almost led to marriage as a woman, Cleomachus's unmasculine submission literally led him away from masculinity and to the complete adoption of femininity.

The examples of Hercules and Cleomachus effeminizing themselves "for lust" serve as the bridge for Tertullian to talk about effeminacy and immorality. Tertullian covers a lot of ground as he continues his list of moral failings that lead to effeminacy. In addition to lust, greed, vanity, and pride are all listed as reasons for effeminacy—with many of these vices tied directly to the wealth and excess of Rome.[39] Tertullian creates a clear argument that masculinity, masculine norms and dress, and morality are all inextricably entwined and that Roman masculinity lacks moral uprightness.

By doing this, Tertullian is not attacking typical Roman norms (for it was generally agreed even in Rome that dress and morality were linked) as much as elite Roman male practices, even literary or imagined ones.[40] Tertullian subtly decenters Rome as the defining agent for masculinity and instead centers Christian conceptions of morality against Roman excess. This excess, then, is centered around the symbol of the toga.

Tertullian's attack on the toga was well placed. Even well-known social critics such as Martial and Juvenal complained that wearing the toga was an onerous social duty.[41] Martial goes so far as to declare the "work of the toga without end" (3.46.1). The "work of the toga" encompassed a great number of formal aspects of Roman life; for example, clients had to wear the toga to the daily salutation of their patrons as well as to banquets and other events. To wear the toga was to inject oneself into Roman life and place oneself into a clear class hierarchy.[42] And wearing the toga was an exhausting affair even for the elite: Pliny, whose elite upbringing brought him into proximity of the emperor Trajan, discussed how freeing it was to go to the countryside and escape constantly wearing the toga.[43]

It's impossible to separate the discourse of the toga, with its unspoken rules and complicated sets of expectations, from Roman conceptions of masculinity. At the same time, the symbol of the toga could be sullied and needed to be protected, since in the wrong circumstances wearing the toga marks immorality:

39. See 4.6 with its direct attack on the caesars, 5.5 with its mention of M. Tullius's excessive spending on furniture, Drusillanus and excessive spending on food, 5.6 and an attack on Hortensius for eating peacock, 5.7 "I speak not at all of Neros, Apiciuses, and Rufuses." Examples abound.

40. See, for example, Seneca, *Contr.* pr. 8–9.

41. Also, the "futile weariness of the toga" (*vanae taedia . . . togae*, Martial 3.4.6). For a good discussion of this, see Michelle George, "The Dark Side of the Toga," in Edmondons and Keith, *Roman Dress and the Fabrics of Roman Culture*, 102. Both Martial and Juvenal compare the togaed clients to enslaved people (see Fanny Dolansky, "*Togam virile sumere*: Coming of Age in the Roman World," in Edmondson and Keith, ed. *Roman Dress and the Fabrics of Roman Culture*, 104).

42. See Dolansky, "*Togam virile sumere*," 96.

43. See Pliny, *Ep.* 5.6; Jonathan Edmondson, "Public Dress," 23, has a brief discussion of this passage.

prostitutes wear the toga, and Cicero attacks Marc Antony for taking up the toga and rendering it womanly (see Cicero *Phil.* 2.44). The status of the toga can be usurped and social rank broken by wearing the wrong clothing.[44] This complicated interplay between unspoken social rules and the policing of the toga makes the entire system susceptible to misinterpretation and critique by outsiders, a circumstance that Tertullian takes full advantage of in *De pallio*.[45]

By wearing a *pallium*, Tertullian breaks free of this discourse and reminds his audience of the "special regard" that old Carthage had for the pallium.[46] At the same time, Tertullian's evisceration of Roman masculinity and immorality demands a new source for social mores. By changing his own *habitus*, Tertullian presents himself as an example of a new moral order. As Brennan notes, "Tertullian's central concern, I would argue, is that his audience ought to change their *habitus* in the sense of chang[ing] their 'attitude of mind.'"[47]

In the final section of *De pallio*, Tertullian prepares his audience for his proselytizing message. If Roman dress is a yoke and Roman masculinity and morality are shams, a better way needs to be offered. Tertullian's answer is, of course, Christianity. While Roman conceptions of elite masculinity relied on norm-breaking and fluidity, Christian masculinity comes to desire complete male adherence to norms. Gender might still be tenuous and malleable (not fixed), but maleness comes to represent spiritual advancement.[48] This sentiment reaches a crescendo in the Gospel of Thomas's declaration that women must become men to enter the kingdom of heaven:

> Look, I will guide her to make her male, so that she too may become a living spirit resembling you males. For every female who makes herself male will enter the kingdom of Heaven. (Gos. Thom. 114)

In *De pallio*, Tertullian strengthens these conceptions by linking masculinity, morality, and spiritual progression to the concept of *natura*. All things that act according to nature must also be following the will of God. The opposite, then, must also be true. In, *De corona militis* (1.5), Tertullian declares:

> All which is against Nature deserves to be branded as monstrous among men, but among us it is to be condemned also as sacrilege against God, the Lord and creator of Nature.[49]

---

44. See Brennan, "Tertullian's *De Pallio*," 261–62.
45. See Andrew Gallia, "The Vestal Habit," *CP* 109:3 (2014): 222 for a discussion of the unspoken rules surrounding the wearing of the toga.
46. Brennan, "Tertullian's *De Pallio*," 263.
47. Brennan, "Tertullian's *De Pallio*," 263.
48. Elizabeth A. Castelli, "'I Will Make Mary Male': Pieties of the Body and Gender Transformation of Christian Women in Late Antiquity," in *Body Guards: The Cultural Politics of Gender Ambiguity*, ed. Julia Epstein and Kristina Straub (London: Routledge, 1991), 32–34. See also Kathryn Leigh Phillips, "'You Are Correctly Called a Man, Because You Act Manfully': A Transgender Studies Approach to Gender-Crossing Saints in Late Antiquity" (PhD dissertation, University of California Riverside, 2020), 15.
49. Trans. Philip Schaff, *ANF* 3.96.

By appealing to *natura*, Tertullian invokes Stoicism's central tenet to live in accordance with nature. Seneca and Epictetus both provide clear examples of this sentiment. Seneca declares that "The one goal of all good people is to live in consistency with nature" (*consentire naturae, Ep.* 66.41) and Epictetus that "Nothing bad by nature happens in the world" (*Enchiridion* 27). *Natura*—and the importance of order in the world—serves as a readily accessible bridge between Christian thought and the Roman world. But Stoicism does not align well with Tertullian's own beliefs regarding clothing and identity. In order to draw on Stoic conceptions of *natura*, Tertullian must realign *natura* to adhere to Christian thought more closely.

REDEFINING NATURA AND GENDER

To recap, Tertullian uses *De pallio* to present a complete argument that norms surrounding clothing and dress should be a part of "the natural order" (*natura*). First, he establishes that Nature itself has the "solemn duty" to change *habitus* (2.1) and therefore change (including changing clothing) is a natural part of the world. While change might be natural, Tertullian emphasizes that *natura* should be, and is, the guiding element for how the world works.[50] Then unexpectedly the story jumps to Achilles. In order to introduce Achilles' story, Tertullian establishes that:

> Therefore, to alter one's *habitus* approaches criminal negligence [*culpa*], if Nature itself should [attempt to] be changed [*mutetur*], rather than custom. (4.1)

The present tense subjunctive verb *mutetur* highlights the sheer impossibility—hence my addition of "attempt to" in my translation—of changing Nature, while *culpa* with its strong legal connotations (determining when negligence is criminal or not) grounds the sentence in the legal reality of the here and now.[51] This language, therefore, puts Achilles on trial for his change of clothing: Achilles, by changing his dress against nature (*adversus naturam*), broke nature (*concussit naturam*) and a crime committed against nature is one also committed against God. Tertullian's final use of *natura* in *De pallio* stresses that it is a human duty to police and control what can be expressed in society: "such clothing, which departs from Nature and modesty, deserves to be sharply looked at, pointed out, and exposed to ridicule" (4.8). *Natura*, and its strict normativity, is now established as the guiding force for what clothing is appropriate to wear or not—a radically different idea of *natura* from the Stoic belief that clothing did not affect one's nature.

50. He uses the word *natura* to establish the importance of the natural order (wool being colored naturally [3.6]; nature suited the Carthaginians for agriculture [4.1]).
51. See Richard Gamauf, "Culpa", in: *Brill's New Pauly: The Classical Tradition*, ed. Manfred Landfester, English edition by Francis G. Gentry (Leiden: Brill, 2006).

The groundwork for this redefinition of *natura* had long since been laid for Tertullian by other Christian writers. The Pauline injunction in Rom 1:26 not to go against nature (*para phusin* in Greek, *contra naturam* in the Latin Vulgate) and Deut 22:5's command against wearing the clothing of the other sex both provided a clear set of rules that could make masculine dress an appropriate part of nature and masculinity itself.

That said, other Christian writers did not necessarily go that far. In fact, Clement of Alexandria provides the argument that gendered clothing should not even exist (*Paedagogus* 2.9):

> I say, then, that man requires clothes for nothing else than the covering of the body.... For as it is common to both to require things to cover them, so also their coverings ought to be similar... if the female sex, on account of their weakness, desire more, we ought to blame the habit of that evil training, by which often men reared up in bad habits become more effeminate than women. But this must not be yielded to. And if some accommodation is to be made, they may be permitted to use softer clothes... these superfluous and diaphanous materials are the proof of a weak mind, covering as they do the shame of the body with a slender veil. For luxurious clothing, which cannot conceal the shape of the body, is no more a covering. For such clothing, falling close to the body, takes its form more easily, and adhering as it were to the flesh, receives its shape, and marks out the woman's figure, so that the whole make of the body is visible to spectators, though not seeing the body itself.[52]

Clement sees clothing itself as merely a covering and protection, though he does allow women some concessions in their clothing since they *are weaker than men*. Clement sees, in an ideal world, no difference between the clothing of the sexes. His interpretation of Deut 22:5 found in *Stromata* 2.18 continues this same line of reasoning—masculinity represents a higher morality, but clothing is not itself moral or immoral. Being effeminate, however, is:

> What reason is there in the law's prohibiting a man from wearing woman's clothing? Is it not that it would have us to be manly, and not to be effeminate, neither in person and actions, nor in thought and word? For it would have the man, that devotes himself to the truth, to be masculine both in acts of endurance and patience, in life, conduct, word, and discipline.[53]

Tertullian draws a much firmer line. Clothing and its inherent gendered distinctions are a part of Nature itself and must be followed, a train of thought that Tertullian continues in his comment on Deut 22:5 (*De spectaculis* 23):

> The Author of Truth hates all that is false; he regards as adultery all that is unreal.... Then, too, as in his law it is declared that the man is cursed

52. Trans. Philip Schaff, *ANF* 2.264–265.
53. Trans. Philip Schaff, *ANF* 2.365–366.

who attires himself in female garments, what must be his judgement of the pantomime, who is even brought up to play the woman![54]

Manliness is once again pitched as that which is moral, but now the act of changing clothing is presented as a lie—and therefore against both God and Nature. In *De pallio*, Tertullian uses Achilles's change of *habitus*—and its corresponding movement away from maleness—to create an abomination that deserves condemnation.

CONCLUSION: TRANSGENDER ACHILLES

Where the traditional Roman perception of inappropriate clothing treated it as a potential marker of effeminacy, immorality, and a failure to truly be a *man*, Tertullian takes these views one step further. Where there was once fluidity and flexibility available to masculinity, now any movement away from normativity is a crime against nature itself. *De pallio*'s argumentation has reached its natural conclusion. If wearing clothing that goes against nature (and therefore God) is a moral wrong, not only does normativity in dress need to be encouraged but its violation policed:

> A *habitus* that goes against nature and modesty, merits a fixed gaze, pointing fingers, and disapproving nods. . . . But with the eye of censorial watchfulness disappearing, how much freedom does this lack of reproach provide? Freedmen dress in equestrians' clothing, slaves dress as nobility, captives as freeborn, country bumpkins as city folk, dandies as men of the state, civilians as soldiers. The corpse-bearer, the pimp, and the trainer of gladiators: they dress like you.[55]

Clothing, for Tertullian, is not only directly reflective of one's inner nature and an important aspect of morality but is also essential for preserving and retaining social hierarchy. Tertullian's call to police and enforce social norms and hierarchy is a call to reinforce the boundaries dividing the sexes, separating the classes, and dividing Rome from Carthage.

That Achilles serves as Tertullian's first example is significant. As we read through Tertullian's argument, Achilles' monstrous example of crossing gendered lines becomes a sign of immorality, lust, greed, and pride. Ultimately, Achilles' transgression threatens the collapse of society itself. Nonetheless, the interpretations found in the Gospel of Thomas and the writings of Clement of Alexandria, which declare manliness godliness and allow for godly women to become manly, provide much more expansive and liberating potentials for

---

54. Trans. S. Thelwall, *ANF* 3.89.
55. Trans. is my own, borrowing some phrases from (and responding to) Hunink (*Tertullian De Pallio*).

theological readings in which one "can be assimilated to Jesus in a manner that transcends bodily (sexual) and perhaps other difference."[56]

Tertullian argues, however, for the fortification of the boundaries between men and women because any violation/crossing of those boundaries is a moral wrong/failing. Tertullian's ideas did not go uncontested, both by those writing much later (Byzantine and Western Medieval hagiographies record centuries of examples of godly women who live as male monks) as well as his contemporaries.[57] In addition to our previous discussion of Rome's more lenient ideas concerning masculinity, Lucian, writing in the Roman east, provides an even more flexible conception of identity, clothing, and gender.[58] Additionally, the writings of another contemporary North African author, Apuleius, seems to confirm that the culture in and around Carthage had more concrete and less flexible ideas behind gender than other Roman territories. Apuleius's *Metamorphoses*, based upon pseudo-Lucian's *Onos*, as it depicts the *galli* (eunuch priests depicted as feminine men or even men who have become female) is a far harsher depiction than the *Onos*'s much more neutral portrayal.[59]

The questions of "What is natural?" and "Where are the boundaries between 'man' and 'woman'?" are now, and have always been, a constant point of contestation, and the answers to these questions vary greatly across cultural, ethnic, and regional boundaries. These questions have always been answered by the Other—the question becomes "what is *not* normal?" and it is answered by bodies that are deemed nonnormative. Leah DeVun convincingly demonstrated this principle in her study of how intersex and nonnormative bodies were used to create normative ideals in later Medieval literature. Tertullian's creation of a nonnormative female Achilles in *De pallio*. parallels this argument. *De Pallio* is built around the example of Achilles, built upon his (then her and then his again) experiences of gender. These experiences are labeled as nonnormative, and this labeling empowers Tertullian's entire argument against more flexible conceptions of masculinity.

Tertullian renders his Achilles into something very familiar to modern trans audiences: a monster, who lies about being a woman in direct contradiction to supposed "biological reality," and represents a clear threat to society or to (society's) children and women. Those in the so-called gender critical movement attack trans women for being a modern part of a "gender ideology" that has no historical precedent. And yet, in *De pallio* circa 200 CE, Tertullian offers the same arguments that are wielded against transgender communities today. The

---

56. Melissa Harl Sellew, "Reading the *Gospel of Thomas* from here: A Trans-Centred Hermeneutic," *JIBS* 1:2 (2020): 89.

57. E.g., Betancourt, *Byzantine Intersectionality*, ch. 3, also Alicia Spencer-Hall and Blake Gutt, ed. *Trans and Genderqueer Subjects in Medieval Hagiography* (Amsterdam: Amsterdam University Press, 2021); Rebecca Wiegel, "Reading Matrona: The Sixth Century Life of a Trans Saint" (PhD dissertation, University of Notre Dame, 2019).

58. See *De Dea Syria, Dialogues Meretrices*, pseudo-Lucian's *Onos* etc.

59. Ashley Kirsten Weed, "The Humor of Disgust: Attitudes toward Galli in Lucian's *Onos* and Apuleius' *Metamorphoses*" (Society of Classical Studies Conference, 2021).

transtemporal and transgeographical prevalence of such arguments proves that gender nonconforming people have always been a part of our societies. Efforts to police and control these populations haven't changed in thousands of years. Today we police and control gender and gender expression, just as Tertullian desired control by policing those things as being against nature.

As I consider what Tertullian terms *natura*, I am increasingly inclined to translate the word as "gender." For gender, like Tertullian's *natura*, is a set of norms and expectations that define how certain types of bodies can act in certain situations and societies—a set of expectations that, as a result, create strict hierarchies and therefore allocate bodies along a spectrum of power and oppression. As Tertullian notes at the end of *De pallio*, gendered hierarchies extend far beyond just *male* and *female* to encompass social class and ethnicity. Such hierarchies are often connected to false ideas of moral superiority. In our own society, Black femininity is provided a different set of rules than white femininity. Class and wealth provide different sets of rules for masculinities. Ethnicity, citizenship, and even age also shape how gender can be performed. Today, we too often see how white, able-bodied, skinny androgynies are treated as normative while Black and crip androgynies are treated as monstrous. *De pallio* echoes this same conservative rhetoric millennia ago: "Let males be male," "the poor be poor," "the enslaved be enslaved," and let cultural categories and the hierarchies they support stand as they are. Tertullian, and the transphobes of today, long for a world of easy legibility. In *De pallio*, Achilles' nonnormative experience of gender serves as a prime example of the illegibility they fear and mirrors how trans women today are spotlighted and attacked for their illegibility.

While Tertullian's polemic against gender crossing might be an odd place to find optimism for trans futures, Tertullian's obsession with gender policing proves that gender *needed* to be policed because it was contested and that even within Christianity there was no easily defined orthodoxy around clothing and its relationship to gender. In this contestation, I see space for more inclusive and gender expansive readings within the Christianity of today. Just as trans people have reclaimed contemporary acts of being made monstrous, in Tertullian's trans monster-making, contemporary trans Christians have the opportunity to reclaim the vast and varied modes of being that Tertullian rejects and make them once again a part of their Christianity.

Bibliography

Ackerman, Susan. *Warrior, Dancer, Seductress, Queen: Women in Judges and Biblical Israel*. New York: Doubleday, 1998.

Adams, J. N. *The Latin Sexual Vocabulary*. Baltimore: John Hopkins University Press, 1990.

Adams, Mary Alice. "Traversing the Transcape: A Brief Historical Etymology of Trans* Terminology." In *Transgender Communications Studies: Histories, Trends, and Trajectories*, edited by Leland G. Spencer and Jamie C. Capuzza, 173–86. New York: Lexington Books, 2015.

Ahmed, Sara. *Queer Phenomenology: Orientations, Objects, Others*. Durham, NC: Duke University Press, 2006.

———. *Willful Subjects*. Durham, NC: Duke University Press, 2014.

Aichele, George, and Richard Walsh. "Metamorphosis, Transfiguration, and the Body." *BibInt* 19 (2011): 253–75.

Aitken, James. "Why Is the Giraffe Kosher? Exoticism in Dietary Laws of the Second Temple Period." *BN* 164.1 (2015): 21–34.

Aizura, Aren Z., Trystan Cotton, Carsten/La Gata, Carla Balzer, Marcia Ochoa, and Salvador Vidal-Ortiz, eds. "Decolonizing the Transgender Imaginary." Special Issue. *TSQ* 1.3 (2014): 303–465.

Alliance Defending Freedom. "Alliance Defending Freedom Doctrinal Distinctives." https://www.adflegal.org/about-us/careers/statement-of-faith.

Althaus-Reid, Marcella. *Indecent Theology: Theological Perversions in Sex, Gender, and Politics*. London: Routledge, 2000.

Althaus-Reid, Marcella, and Lisa Isherwood, eds. *The Sexual Theologian: Essays on Sex, God and Politics*. Queering Theology Series. London: T&T Clark, 2004.

American Civil Liberties Union (ACLU). Mapping Attacks on LGBTQ Rights in U.S. State Legislatures in 2024. https://www.aclu.org/legislative-attacks-on-lgbtq-rights-2024.

American Psychological Association. "Criminalizing Gender Affirmative Care with Minors: Suggested Talking Points with Resources to Oppose Transgender Exclusion Bills." 2023. https://www.apa.org/topics/lgbtq/gender-affirmative-care.

Anderson, Cheryl B. *Women, Ideology, and Violence: Critical Theory and the Construction of Gender in the Book of the Covenant and the Deuteronomic Law*. London: T&T Clark, 2004.

Annus, Amar and Alan Lenzi. *Ludlul Bēl Nēmeqi: The Standard Babylonian Poem of the Righteous Sufferer*. Helsinki: Neo-Assyrian Text Corpus Project, 2010.

Arendell, Terry. "Conceiving and Investigating Motherhood: The Decade's Scholarship." *Journal of Marriage and Family* 62.4 (2000): 1192–207.

Armstrong, Amaryah. "Of Flesh and Spirit: Race, Reproduction, and Sexual Difference in the Turn to Paul." *Journal for Cultural and Religious Theory* 16.2 (2017): 126–41.

Asgeirsson, Jon Ma. "Conflicting Epic Worlds." In Asgeirsson, DeConick, and Uro, *Thomasine Traditions in Antiquity*, 155–74.

———, April D. DeConick, and Risto Uri, eds. *Thomasine Traditions in Antiquity: The Social and Cultural World of the Gospel of Thomas*. Leiden: Brill, 2006.

Ashton, John. *Understanding the Fourth Gospel*. 2nd ed. Oxford: Oxford University Press, 2007.

Assis, Elie. "'The Hand of a Woman': Deborah and Yael (Judges 4)." *The Journal of Hebrew Scriptures* 5.19 (2005): 1–12.

Bach, Alice. *Women, Seduction, and Betrayal in Biblical Narrative*. Cambridge: Cambridge University Press, 1997.

Baer, Richard A. *Philo's Use of the Categories Male and Female*. Leiden: Brill, 1970.

Bailey, Randall C. "'That's Why They Didn't Call the Book Hadassah!': The Interse(ct)/(x)ionality of Race/Ethnicity, Gender, and Sexuality in the Book of Esther." In Bailey, Liew, and Segovia, *They Were All Together in One Place?*, 227–50.

———, Tat-siong Benny Liew, and Fernando F. Segovia, eds. *They Were All Together in One Place? Toward Minority Biblical Criticism*. Atlanta: SBL Press, 2009.

Bal, Mieke. *Death and Dissymmetry: The Politics of Coherence in the Book of Judges*. Chicago: University of Chicago Press, 1988.

Baroin, C. and E. Valett-Cagnac. "S'habiller et se déshabille en Grèce et à Rome (III). Quands les Romaines s'habillaient à la grecque ou les divers usages du *pallium*." *Revue Historique* 643 (2007): 517–51.

Bassichis, Morgan, Alexander Lee, and Dean Space. "Building an Abolitionist Trans & Queer Movement with Everything We've Got." In Stanley and Smith, *Captive Genders*, 21–46.

Beal, Timothy. *The Book of Hiding: Gender, Ethnicity, Annihilation, and Esther*. London: Routledge, 1997.

Beardsley, Christina, ed. *Transfaith: A Transgender Pastoral Resource*. London: Darton Longman & Todd, 2018.

Beemyn, Genny. "A Presence in the Past: A Transgender Historiography." *Journal of Women's History* 25 (2013): 113–21.

———. "Transgender History." In *Trans Bodies, Trans Selves*, edited by Laura Erickson-Schroth, 501–36. Oxford: Oxford University Press, 2014.

Belser, Julia Watts. "Queering the Dissident Body: Race, Sex, and Disability in Rabbinic Blessings on Bodily Difference." In *Unsettling Science and Religion: Contributions and Questions from Queer Studies*, edited by Lisa Stenmark and Whitney Bauman, 161–82. New York: Lexington Books, 2018.

Bergmann, Claudia D. "Mothers of a Nation: How Motherhood and Religion Intermingle in the Hebrew Bible." *Open Theology* 6.1 (2020): 132–44.

Berkowitz, Beth. *Animals and Animality in the Babylonian Talmud*. Cambridge: Cambridge University Press, 2018.

Berlant, Lauren. *Cruel Optimism*. Durham, NC: Duke University Press, 2011.

Betancourt, Roland. *Byzantine Intersectionality: Sexuality, Gender, and Race in the Middle Ages*. Princeton, NJ: Princeton University Press, 2021.

Bey, Marquis. "Black Fugitivity Un/Gendered." *The Black Scholar: Journal of Black Studies and Research* 49.1 (2019): 55–62.

———. *Black Trans Feminism*. Durham, NC: Duke University Press, 2022.

Biale, Rachel. *Women and Jewish Law: The Essential Texts, Their History, and Their Relevance for Today*. New York: Schocken, 1984.

Bienkowski, Piotr. "Jericho Was Destroyed in the Middle Bronze Age, Not the Late Bronze Age." *BAR* 16 (1990): 45–49.
Bledstein, Adrien Janis. "Is Judges a Woman's Satire of Men who Play God?" In Brenner, *Feminist Companion to Judges*, 34–55.
Block, Daniel. "Marriage and Family in Ancient Israel." In *Marriage and Family in the Biblical World*, edited by Ken M. Campbell, 33–103. Downers Grove: InterVarsity Press, 2003.
Boer, Roland. "Yahweh as Top: A Lost Targum." In *Queer Commentary and the Hebrew Bible*, edited by Ken Stone, 75–105. Cleveland: Pilgrim Press, 2001.
Bolich, G. G. *Transgender History and Geography*. Raleigh, NC: Psyche's Press, 2007.
———. *Transgender and Religion*. Raleigh, NC: Psyche's Press, 2009.
Bornstein, Kate. *Gender Outlaw: On Men, Women, and the Rest of Us*. New York: Routledge, 1994.
Bourdieu, Pierre. *Masculine Domination*. Translated by Richard Nice. Stanford: Stanford University Press, 2001.
Bowman, Sabienna. "'Pose' Star Indya Moore's Earrings Paid Tribute to Black Transgender Women Who Were Murdered in 2019." *Bustle*. September 7, 2019. https://www.bustle.com/p/pose-star-indya-moores-earrings-paid-tribute-to-black-transgender-women-who-were-murdered-in-2019-photos-18734027.
Boyarin, Daniel. *Carnal Israel: Reading Sex in Talmudic Culture*. Berkeley: University of California Press, 1993.
———. "Gender." In *Critical Terms for Religious Studies*, edited by Mark Taylor, 117–36. Chicago: University of Chicago Press, 1998.
Boyd, Barbara Weiden. "Teaching Ovid's Love Elegy." In *A Companion to Roman Love Elegy*, edited by Barbara K. Gold, 526–40. Oxford: Blackwell, 2012.
Boydston, Jeanne. "Gender as a Question of Historical Analysis." *Gender and History* 20 (2008): 558–83.
Bradley, Keith. "Appearing for the Defense: Apuleius on Display." In Edmondson and Keith, *Roman Dress and the Fabrics of Roman Culture*, 238–56.
———. "Romanitas and the Roman Family: The Evidence of Apuleius' Apology." In *Apuleius and Antonine Rome*, 41–58. Toronto: University of Toronto Press, 2012.
Brennan, T. Corey. "Tertullian's *De Pallio* and Roman Dress in North Africa." In Edmondson and Keith, *Roman Dress and the Fabrics of Roman Culture*, 257–70.
Brenner, Athalya. ed. *A Feminist Companion to Judges*. Sheffield: Sheffield Academic Press, 1993.
———, "A Triangle and a Rhombus in Narrative Structure: A Proposed Integrative Reading of Judges 4 and 5." In Brenner, *Feminist Companion to Judges*, 98–109.
Brenner-Idan, Athalya. *Colour Terms in the Old Testament*. Sheffield: JSOT Press, 1982.
Brintnall, Kent L., Joseph A. Marchal, and Stephen D. Moore, eds. *Sexual Disorientations: Queer Temporalities, Affects, Theologies*. New York: Fordham University Press, 2017.
Brisson, Luc. *Sexual Ambivalence: Androgyny and Hermaphroditism in Graeco-Roman Antiquity*. Translated by Janet Lloyd. Berkeley: University of California Press, 2002.
Brooten, Bernadette. *Love Between Women: Early Christian Responses to Female Homoeroticism*. Chicago: University of Chicago Press, 1996.
Brown, Ian Phillip. "Where Indeed Was the Gospel of Thomas Written? Thomas in Alexandria." *JBL* 138 (2019): 451–72.
Brown, Michael Joseph. *Blackening of the Bible: The Aims of African American Biblical Scholarship*. Harrisburg, PA: Trinity Press International, 2004.
Brown, Raymond E. *The Gospel according to John I–XII*. Garden City, NJ: Doubleday, 1966.

Brownsmith, Esther. "Love and Eunuchs: Esther and Ishtar as Queer Queens." Paper presented at the SBL Annual Conference, San Antonio, November 2021.

Buch-Hansen, Gitte. *"It Is the Spirit That Gives Life": A Stoic Understanding of Pneuma in John's Gospel.* Berlin: De Gruyter, 2010.

Buell, Denise Kimber. "God's Own People: Specters of Race, Ethnicity, and Gender in Early Christian Studies." In *Prejudice and Christian Beginnings: Investigating Race, Gender, and Ethnicity in Early Christian Studies,* edited by Elisabeth Schüssler Fiorenza and Laura Nasrallah, 169–90. Minneapolis: Fortress Press, 2009.

———. "Hauntology Meets Post-Humanism: Some Payoffs for Biblical Studies." In *The Bible and Posthumanism,* edited by Jennifer L. Koosed, 29–56. Atlanta: SBL Press, 2014.

Burkert, Walter. "Towards Plato and Paul: The 'Inner' Human Being." In *Ancient and Modern Contests over the Image of the Apostle: Essays in Honor of Hans Dieter Betz,* edited by Adela Yarbo Collins, 59–82. Atlanta: Scholars Press, 1998.

Burrus, Virginia. *Begotten, Not Made: Conceiving Manhood in Late Antiquity.* Stanford: Stanford University Press, 2000.

———. *The Sex Lives of Saints: An Erotics of Ancient Hagiography.* Philadelphia: University of Pennsylvania Press, 2004.

Butler, Judith. "Against Proper Objects." *differences* 6.2–3 (1994): 1–26.

———. *Gender Trouble: Feminism and the Subversion of Identity.* London: Routledge, 1999.

———. "Melancholy Gender-Refused Identification." *Psychoanalytic Dialogues* 5 (1995): 165–80.

———. *Undoing Gender.* New York: Routledge, 2004.

Bychowski, M.W., and Dorothy Kim. "Visions of *Medieval Trans Feminism* (Special Issue)." *Medieval Feminist Forum* 55.1 (2019).

Bychowski, M. W. et al. "'Trans*historicities': A Roundtable Discussion with M. W. Bychowski, Howard Chiang, Jack Halberstam, Jacob Lau, Kathleen P. Long, Marcia Ochoa, and C. Riley Snorton." Curated by Leah DeVun and Zeb Tortorici." *TSQ* 5.4 (2018): 658–85.

Bynum, Caroline Walker. *Jesus as Mother: Studies in the Spirituality of the High Middle Ages.* Berkeley: University of California Press, 1982.

Byron, John. *Recent Research on Paul and Slavery.* Sheffield: Sheffield Phoenix Press, 2008.

Cahana, Jonathan. "Gnostically Queer: Gender Trouble in Gnosticism." *BTB* 41.1 (2011): 24–35.

Calaway, Jaeda C. *The Sabbath and the Sanctuary: Access to God in the Letter to the Hebrews and its Priestly Context.* Tübingen: Mohr Siebeck, 2013.

Callahan, Allen Dwight. "The Gospel of John." In *True to Our Native Land: An African American New Testament Commentary,* edited by Brian Blount, Cain Hope Felder, Clarice J. Martin, and Emerson B. Powery, 186–212. Minneapolis: Fortress Press, 2007.

Calvino, Italo. *Invisible Cities.* Translated by William Weaver. San Diego: Harcourt, 1974.

Campanile, Domitilla, Filippo Carlà-Uhink, and Margherita Facella, eds. *TransAntiquity: Cross-Dressing and Transgender Dynamics in the Ancient World.* London: Routledge, 2017.

Caner, Daniel. "The Practice and Prohibition of Self-Castration in Early Christianity." *VC* 51 (1997): 396–415.

Case-Winters, Anna. *Matthew.* Louisville, KY: Westminster John Knox Press, 2015.

Castelli, Elizabeth A. *Imitating Paul: A Discourse of Power.* Louisville, KY: Westminster John Knox Press, 1991.

———. "'I Will Make Mary Male': Pieties of the Body and Gender Transformation of Christian Women in Late Antiquity." In Epstein and Straub, *Body Guards*, 29–49.
Cavanagh, Sheila. "Gender, Sexuality, and Race in the Lacanian Mirror: Urinary Segregation and the Bodily Ego." In *Psychoanalytic Geographies*, edited by Paul Kingsbury and Steve Pile, 323–39. New York: Routledge, 2014.
Celoria, Francis. *The Metamorphoses of Antoninus Liberalis: A Translation with a Commentary*. London: Routledge, 1992.
Chauncey, George. *Gay New York: Gender, Urban Culture, and the Making of the Gay Male World, 1890–1940*. New York: Basic Books, 1994.
Chen, Mel Y. "Everywhere Archives: Transgendering, Trans Asians, and the Internet." In Tourmaline, Stanley, and Burton, *Trap Door*, 147–59.
Chess, Simone, Colby Gordon, and Will Fisher, eds. "Early Modern Trans Studies (Special Issue)." *Journal for Early Modern Cultural Studies* 19.4 (2019).
Chiang, Howard, ed. *Transgender China*. New York: Palgrave MacMillan, 2012.
Colebrook, Claire. "What Is It Like to Be Human." *TSQ* 2.2 (2015): 227–43.
Collins, Adela Yarbro. "New Testament Perspectives: The Gospel of John." *JSOT* (1982): 47–53.
Collins, Jack. "Appropriation and Development of Castration as a Symbol and Practice in Early Christianity." In Tracy, *Castration and Culture*, 73–86.
Concannon, Cavan. "Reading Paul Obliquely: Reading against the Grain in a Latourian Pluriverse." In Marchal, *After the Corinthian Women Prophets*, 99–122.
Conway, Colleen M. "Gender Matters in John." In *A Feminist Companion to John*, vol. 2, edited by Amy-Jill Levine with Marianne Blickenstaff, 79–103. Cleveland: Pilgrim Press, 2003.
———. *Sex and Slaughter in the Tent of Jael: A Cultural History of a Biblical Story*. Oxford: Oxford University Press, 2017.
Copeland, M. Shawn. *Enfleshing Freedom: Body, Race, and Being*. Minneapolis: Fortress Press, 2010.
Corbeill, Anthony. *Nature Embodied: Gesture in Ancient Rome*. Princeton, NJ: Princeton University Press, 2004.
Councilor, K. C. "The Specter of Trans Bodies: Public and Political Discourse about 'Bathroom Bills.'" In *The Routledge Handbook of Gender and Communication*, edited by Marnel Niles Goins, Joan Faber McAlister, and Bryant Keith Alexander, 274–88. New York: Routledge, 2020.
Crasnow, S. J. "'Becoming' Bodies: Affect Theory, Transgender Jews, and the Rejection of the Coherent Subject." *Crosscurrents* 71 (2021): 49–62.
Crawley, Ashon T. *Blackpentecostal Breath: The Aesthetics of Possibility*. New York: Fordham University Press, 2017.
———. *The Lonely Letters*. Durham, NC: Duke University Press, 2020.
Creangă, Ovidiu, ed. *Men and Masculinity in the Hebrew Bible and Beyond*. Sheffield: Sheffield Phoenix Press, 2010.
Currah, Paisley. *Sex Is as Sex Does: Governing Transgender Identity*. New York: NYU Press, 2022.
Currah, Paisley, Richard Juang, and Shannon Price Minter, eds. *Transgender Rights*. Minneapolis: University of Minnesota Press, 2006.
Cwikla, Anna. "Placeholders, Lessons, and Emasculators: The Literary Function of Women in Early Christian Texts." PhD diss., University of Toronto, 2024.
Cyrino, Monica Silveira. "Heroes in D(u)ress: Transvestism and Power in the Myths of Herakles and Achilles." *Helios* 31.2 (1998): 207–41.
Daly, Mary. *Gyn/Ecology: The Metaethics of Radical Feminism*. Boston: Beacon Press, 1978.

Darby, Erin. *Interpreting Judean Pillar Figurines: Gender and Empire in Judean Apotropaic Ritual.* Tübingen: Mohr Siebeck, 2014.

Darwin, Helana. "Navigating the Religious Gender Binary." *Sociology of Religion* 81.2 (2020): 185–205.

Davies, Stevan L. "The Christology and Protology of the Gospel of Thomas." *JBL* 111 (1992): 663–82.

Davis, Stephen J. "Crossed Texts, Crossed Sex: Intertextuality and Gender in Early Christian Legends of Holy Women Disguised as Men." *JECS* 10 (2002): 1–36.

DeConick, April D. *Seek to See Him: Ascent and Vision Mysticism in the Gospel of Thomas.* Leiden: Brill, 1996.

DeVun, Leah. *The Shape of Sex: Nonbinary Gender from Genesis to the Renaissance.* New York: Columbia University Press, 2021.

DeVun, Leah, and Zeb Tortorici. "Trans, Time, and History." *TSQ* 5.4 (2018): 518–39.

———, eds. "Trans*historicities" (Special Issue). *TSQ* 5.4 (2018).

Diamond, Ashley. *Memoirs of a Chain Gang Sissy.* See https://www.youtube.com/watch?v=YwuhEF7_-yI.

Dickson, Kwesi. *Theology in Africa.* Maryknoll, NY: Orbis Books, 1984.

Dillon, John. *The Middle Platonists, 80 B.C. to A.D. 220.* Ithaca, NY: Cornell University Press, 1996.

Dinshaw, Carolyn. *Getting Medieval: Sexualities and Communities, Pre- and Postmodern.* Durham, NC: Duke University Press, 1999.

———. *How Soon Is Now? Medieval Texts, Amateur Readers, and the Queerness of Time.* Durham, NC: Duke University Press, 2012.

DiPalma, Brian Charles. "De/Constructing Masculinity in Exodus 1–4." In Creangă, *Men and Masculinity*, 36–53.

Dolansky, Fanny. "*Togam virile sumere*: Coming of Age in the Roman World." In Edmondson and Keith, *Roman Dress and the Fabrics of Roman Culture*, 47–70.

Donahue, Jayden, and Miss Major Griffin-Gracy. "Making It Happen, Mama: A Conversation with Miss Major." In Stanley and Smith, *Captive Genders*, 301–13.

Douglas, Kelly Brown. *Resurrection Hope: A Future Where Black Lives Matter.* Maryknoll, NY: Orbis Books, 2021.

Dreger, Alice Domurat. *Hermaphrodites and the Medical Invention of Sex.* Cambridge, MA: Harvard University Press, 1998.

Dunderberg, Ismo. *The Beloved Disciple in Conflict? Revisiting the Gospels of John and Thomas.* Oxford: Oxford University Press, 2006.

Dunham, Grace. "Out of Obscurity: Trans Resistance, 1969–2016." In Tourmaline, Stanley, and Burton, *Trap Door*, 91–119.

Dunning, Benjamin. *Christ without Adam: Subjectivity and Sexual Difference in the Philosophers' Paul.* New York: Columbia University Press, 2014.

Dyer, Rebekah. "Envisioning Fire Theophanies as Gender-Neutral Expressions of Selfhood." *JIBS* 1.2 (2020): 40–60.

Eckert, Penelope, and Sally McConnell-Ginet. *Language and Gender.* Cambridge: Cambridge University Press, 2003.

Edmondson, Jonathan. "Public Dress and Social Control in Late Republican and Early Imperial Rome." In Edmondson and Keith, *Roman Dress and the Fabrics of Roman Culture*, 21–46.

Edmondson, Jonathan, and Alison Keith, eds. *Roman Dress and the Fabrics of Roman Culture.* Toronto: University of Toronto Press, 2009.

Eilberg-Schwartz, Howard. *God's Phallus and Other Problems for Men and Monotheism.* Boston: Beacon Press, 1994.

Elliot, Patricia. *Debates in Transgender, Queer, and Feminist Theory: Contested Sites.* Farnham: Ashgate Publishing, 2010.

Emergency Release Fund. https://www.emergencyrelease.org/.
Engberg-Pedersen, Troels. "Complete and Incomplete Transformation in Paul: A Philosophical Reading of Paul on Body and Spirit." In Seim and Økland, *Metamorphoses*, 123–46.
———. *Cosmology and the Self in the Apostle Paul: The Material Spirit*. Oxford: Oxford University Press, 2010.
———, ed. *From Stoicism to Platonism: The Development of Philosophy, 100 BCE–100 CE*. Cambridge: Cambridge University Press, 2017.
———. *John and Philosophy: A New Reading of the Fourth Gospel*. Oxford: Oxford University Press, 2017.
———. *Paul and the Stoics*. Louisville, KY: Westminster John Knox, 2000.
———, ed. *Paul in His Hellenistic Context*. Minneapolis: Fortress Press, 1995.
Engberg-Pedersen, Troels, and Stanley K. Stowers, eds. "The Dilemma of Paul's Physics: Features Stoic-Platonist or Platonist-Stoic?" In *From Stoicism to Platonism: The Development of Philosophy, 100 BCE–100 CE*, 231–53. Cambridge: Cambridge University Press, 2017.
Enke, Finn. "The Education of Little Cis: Cisgender and the Discipline of Opposing Bodies." In *Transfeminist Perspectives: In and beyond Transgender and Gender Studies*, edited by Enke, 60–77. Philadelphia: Temple University Press, 2012.
———. "Transgender History (And Otherwise Approaches to Queer Embodiment)." In *The Routledge History of Queer America*, edited by Don Romesburg, 224–36. New York: Routledge, 2018.
Epstein, Julia and Kristina Straub, eds. *Body Guards: The Cultural Politics of Gender Ambiguity*. New York: Routledge, 1991.
Epstein, Yakov N. *M'vo'ot l'Sifrut haTanaim: Mishnah, Tosefta, u'midrashei halachah*. Jerusalem: Magnes, 1957.
Espinoza, Roberto Che. *Activist Theology*. Minneapolis: Fortress Press, 2019.
———. *Body Becoming: A Path to Our Liberation*. Minneapolis: Broadleaf, 2022.
———. "Difference, Becoming, and Interrelatedness: A Material Resistance Becoming." *CrossCurrents* 66.2 (2016): 281–89.
Estes, Douglas. "Dualism or Paradox? A New 'Light' on the Gospel of John." *NTS* 71 (2020): 90–118.
Ettner, Randi et al., eds. *Principles of Transgender Medicine and Surgery*. 2nd ed. New York: Haworth Press, 2016.
Evans, Craig A. *Matthew*. New York: Cambridge University Press, 2012.
Exum, J. Cheryl. "'Mother in Israel': A Familiar Figure Reconsidered." In *Feminist Interpretation of the Bible*, edited by Letty M. Russell, 73–85. Philadelphia: Westminster Press, 1985.
———. "Shared Glory: Salomon de Bray's *Jael, Deborah and Barak*." In *Between the Text and the Canvas: The Bible and Art in Dialogue*, edited by Exum and Ela Nutu, 11–38. Sheffield: Sheffield Phoenix Press, 2009.
———. "Whose Interests Are Being Served?" In *Judges and Method: New Approaches in Biblical Studies*, edited by Gale A. Yee, 65–95. Minneapolis: Fortress Press, 2007.
Feinberg, Leslie. *Trans Liberation: Beyond Pink or Blue*. Boston: Beacon Press, 1998.
———. *Transgender Liberation—Digital Transgender Archive*. New York: World View Forum, 1992. https://www.digitaltransgenderarchive.net/files/3t945r069.
———. *Transgender Warriors: Making History from Joan of Arc to Dennis Rodman*. Boston: Beacon Press, 1996.
Ferguson, Roderick A. *One-Dimensional Queer*. Cambridge: Polity Press, 2019.
Fewell, Danna Nolan and David M. Gunn. "Controlling Perspectives: Women, Men, and the Authority of Violence in Judges 4 and 5." *JAAR* 58.3 (1990): 389–411.

———. *Gender, Power, and Promise: The Subject of the Bible's First Story*. Nashville: Abingdon Press, 1993.

Fonrobert, Charlotte. "Gender Duality and Its Subversions in Rabbinic Law." In *Gender in Judaism and Islam: Common Lives, Uncommon Heritage*, edited by Firoozeh Kashani-Sabet and Beth Wenger, 106–25. New York: NYU Press, 2014.

———. "Regulating the Human Body: Rabbinic Legal Discourse and the Making of Jewish Gender." In *The Cambridge Companion to the Talmud and Rabbinic Literature*, edited by Fonrobert and Martin Jaffee, 270–94. Cambridge: Cambridge University Press, 2007.

———. "The Semiotics of the Sexed Body in Early Halakhic Discourse." In *Closed and Open: Readings of Rabbinic Texts*, edited by M. A. Kraus, 69–96. Piscataway, NJ: Gorgias Press, 2006.

Forbes, Greg W. *The God of Old: The Role of the Lukan Parables in the Purpose of Luke's Gospel*. Sheffield: Sheffield Academic Press, 2000.

Foster, Paul. "Polymorphic Christology: Its Origins and Development in Early Christianity." *JTS* 58.1 (2007): 66–99.

Fox, Arminta. "Decentering Paul, Contextualizing Crimes: Reading in Light of the Imprisoned." *JFSR* 33.2 (2017): 37–54.

———. *Paul Decentered: Reading 2 Corinthians with the Corinthian Women*. Minneapolis: Lexington/Fortress Academic, 2019.

Fox, Michael V. *Character and Ideology in the Book of Esther*. 2nd edition. Eugene, OR: Wipf & Stock, 2010.

France, R. T. *The Gospel of Matthew*. Grand Rapids: Eerdmans, 2007.

Frankel, Zechariah. *Darchei HaMishnah: Chelek Rishon*. Leipzig: Sumptibus Henrici Hunger, 1859.

Fredriksen, Paula. "Mandatory Retirement: Ideas in the Study of Christian Origins Whose Time Has Come to Go." *SR* 35 (2006): 231–46.

Freeman, Elizabeth. *Time Binds: Queer Temporalities, Queer Histories*. Durham, NC: Duke University Press, 2010.

Fremi, Stella. "Aphrodite and Her Sisters." *Lancet Psychiatry* 3.2 (2016): 111–13.

Frymer-Kensky, Tikva. *In the Wake of the Goddesses: Women, Culture, and the Biblical Transformation of Pagan Myth*. New York: Free Press, 1992.

Fuchs, Esther. "The Literary Characterization of Mothers and Sexual Politics in the Hebrew Bible." In *Feminist Perspectives on Biblical Scholarship*, edited by Adela Yarbro Collins, 117–36. Chico, CA: Scholars Press, 1985.

———. *Sexual Politics in the Biblical Narrative: Reading the Hebrew Bible as a Woman*. Sheffield: Sheffield Academic Press, 2000.

Gallia, Andrew B. "The Vestal Habit." *CP* 109.3 (2014): 222–40.

Gamauf, Richard. "Culpa." In *Brill's New Pauly: The Classical Tradition*, edited by Manfred Landfester; English edition by Francis G. Gentry. Leiden: Brill, 2006.

Garland, David E. *Reading Matthew: A Literary and Theological Commentary on the First Gospel*. New York: Crossroad, 1993.

Gathercole, Simon J. *The Composition of the Gospel of Thomas: Original Language and Influences*. Cambridge: Cambridge University Press, 2012.

———. *The Gospel of Thomas: Introduction and Commentary*. Leiden: Brill, 2014.

Gaventa, Beverly Roberts. *Our Mother Saint Paul*. Louisville, KY: Westminster John Knox Press, 2007.

George, Michelle. "The Dark Side of the Toga." In Edmondson and Keith, *Roman Dress and the Fabrics of Roman Culture*, 94–113.

Gill, Christopher. *The Structured Self in Hellenistic and Roman Thought*. Oxford: Oxford University Press, 2006.

Gill-Peterson, Jules. *Histories of the Transgender Child*. Minneapolis: University of Minnesota Press, 2018.

———. *A Short History of Trans Misogyny*. London: Verso, 2024.

Gillespie, Rosemary. "When No Means No: Disbelief, Disregard and Deviance as Discourses of Voluntary Childlessness." *Women's Studies International Forum* 23.2 (2000): 223–34.

Gilmore, Ruth Wilson. *Golden Gulag: Prisons, Surplus, Crisis, and Opposition in Globalizing California*. Berkeley: University of California Press, 2007.

Glancy, Jennifer A. "Hagar as/against Bare Life." *JFSR* 37.1 (2021): 103–21.

Goss, Robert E. "Luke." In Guest et al. *The Queer Bible Commentary*, 526–47.

———. "John". In Guest et al. *The Queer Bible Commentary*, 548–65.

Goss, Robert E., and Mona West, eds. *Take Back the Word: A Queer Reading of the Bible*. Cleveland: Pilgrim Press, 2000.

Gottlieb, Freema. "Three Mothers." *Judaism: Periodicals Archive Online* 30.2 (1981): 194–203.

Grant, Jaime, Lisa Mottet, and Justin Tanis. "Injustice at Every Turn: A Report of the National Transgender Discrimination Survey." Washington, DC: National Center for Transgender Equality and National Gay and Lesbian Task Force, 2011. https://transequality.org/resources/national-transgender-discrimination-survey-full-report.

Graybill, Rhiannon. *Are We Not Men? Unstable Masculinity in the Hebrew Prophets*. New York: Oxford University Press, 2016.

———. "Masculinity, Materiality, and the Body of Moses." *BibInt* 23.4–5 (2015): 518–40.

Green, Erica, Katie Benner, and Robert Pear. "'Transgender' Could Be Defined Out of Existence under Trump Administration." *New York Times*, October 2018. https://nyti.ms/2R9W1jB.

Green, Richard. "Mythological, Historical, and Cross-Cultural Aspects of Transsexualism." In *The Transsexual Phenomenon*, edited by Harry Benjamin (New York: The Julian Press, 1966); reprinted in *Currents in Transgender Identity*, edited by Dallas Denny, 3–14. New York: Garland Publishing, 1998.

Greene, Ellen. *The Erotics of Domination: Male Desire and the Mistress in Latin Love Poetry*. Baltimore: Johns Hopkins University Press, 1998.

Greene-Hayes, Ahmad. "Street Evangelists and Transgender Saints: Sylvia Rivera, Marsha P. Johnson, and the Religions of the Afro-Americas." *QTR: A Journal of Trans and Queer Studies in Religion* 1.1 (2024): 32–52.

Gribetz, Sarit Katan, David M. Grossberg, Martha Himmelfarb, and Peter Schäfer, eds. *Genesis Rabbah in Text and Context*. Tübingen: Mohr Siebeck, 2016.

Griffin, Horace L. *Their Own Receive Them Not: African American Lesbians and Gays in Black Churches*. Cleveland: Pilgrim Press, 2006.

Griffin-Gracy, Miss Major, and CeCe MacDonald in Conversation with Toshio Meronek. "Cautious Living: Black Trans Women and the Politics of Documentation." In Tourmaline, Stanley, and Burton, *Trap Door*, 23–37.

Gross, Sally. "Intersexuality and Scripture." *Theology and Sexuality* 11 (1999): 65–74.

Grossman, Jonathan. *Esther: The Outer Narrative and the Hidden Reading*. Winona Lake, IN: Eisenbrauns, 2011.

Guest, Deryn. *Beyond Feminist Biblical Studies*. Sheffield: Sheffield Phoenix Press, 2012.

———. "From Gender Reversal to Genderfuck: Reading Jael through a Lesbian Lens." In Hornsby and Stone, *Bible Trouble*, 9–43.

———. "Modeling the Transgender Gaze: Performances of Masculinities in 2 Kings 9–10." In Hornsby and Guest, *Transgender, Intersex, and Biblical Interpretation*, 45–80.

———. *When Deborah Met Jael: Lesbian Biblical Hermeneutics*. London: SCM Press, 2005.
Guest, Deryn, Robert E. Goss, Mona West, and Thomas Bohache, eds. *The Queer Bible Commentary*. 1st ed. London: SCM Press, 2015.
Gwyther, Katherine and Jo Henderson-Merrygold. "The Disidentification of Mordecai: A Drag Interpretation of Esther 8:15." *HS* 63 (2022): 119–41.
Hackett, Jo Ann. "In the Days of Jael: Reclaiming the History of Women in Ancient Israel." In *Immaculate and Powerful: The Female in Sacred Image and Social Reality*, edited by Clarissa W. Atkinson, Constance H. Buchanan, and Margaret R. Miles, 15–39. Boston: Beacon Press, 1987.
Halberstam, Jack. *Female Masculinity*. Durham, NC: Duke University Press, 1998.
———. *In a Queer Time and Place: Transgender Bodies, Subcultural Lives*. New York: NYU Press, 2005.
———. *Trans*: A Quick and Quirky Account of Gender Variability*. Oakland: University of California Press, 2018.
Halbertal, Moshe. *The Birth of Doubt: Confronting Uncertainty in Early Rabbinic Literature*. Translated by Elli Fischer. Providence: Brown Judaic Studies, 2020.
Haritaworn, Jin, Adi Kuntsman, and Silvia Posocco, eds. *Queer Necropolitics*. New York: Routledge, 2014.
Hartke, Austen. *Transforming: The Bible and the Lives of Transgender Christians*. Louisville, KY: Westminster John Knox, 2018. 2nd ed. 2023.
Harvard Political Review. "South Africa's 'Corrective Rape Problem'." (October 2014) Online: https://harvardpolitics.com/south-africas-corrective-rape-problem/.
Harvey, A. E. "Eunuchs for the Sake of the Kingdom." *HeyJ* 48 (2007): 1–17.
Hays, Sharon. *The Cultural Contradictions of Motherhood*. New Haven, CT: Yale University Press, 1996.
Hayward, Eva. "Don't Exist." *TSQ* 4.2 (2017): 191–94.
———. "More Lessons from a Starfish: Prefixial Flesh and Transspeciated Selves." *Women's Studies Quarterly* 36.3/4 (2008): 64–85.
Henderson-Merrygold, Jo. "Gendering Sarai: Reading beyond Cisnormativity in Genesis 11:29–12:20 and 20:1–18." *Open Theology*, 6.1 (2020): 496–509.
———. *Introducing a Hermeneutics of Cispicion: Reading Sarah and Esau's Gender (Failures) beyond Cisnormativity*. London: T&T Clark, 2024.
———. "Jacob: A (Drag) King amongst Patriarchs." In *Women and Gender in the Bible: Texts, Intersections, Intertexts*, edited by Zanne Domoney-Lyttle and Sarah Nicholson, 125–40. Sheffield: Sheffield Phoenix, 2021.
———. "Viewing Sarah Cispiciously: Cisnormalisation, and the Problem of Cisnormativity." Paper presented at the SBL annual meeting. Denver, 2018.
Heslin, P. J. *The Transvestite Achilles*. Cambridge: Cambridge University Press, 2005.
Hester, J. D. "Eunuchs and the Postgender Jesus: Matthew 19.12 and Transgressive Sexualities." *JSNT* 28 (2005): 13–40.
Heyes, Cressida J. *Self-Transformations: Foucault, Ethics, and Normalized Bodies*. Oxford: Oxford University Press, 2007.
Heyward, Carter. *Our Passion for Justice: Images of Power, Sexuality, and Liberation*. New York: Pilgrim Press, 1984.
Hillman, Thea. *Intersex (for Lack of a Better Word)*. San Francisco: Manic D Press, 2008.
Hoke, Jimmy. *Feminism, Queerness, Affect, and Romans: Under God?* Atlanta: SBL Press, 2021.
———. "Unbinding Imperial Time: Chrononormativity and Paul's Letter to the Romans." In Brintnall, Marchal, and Moore, *Sexual Disorientations*, 68–83.
Holmes, Brooke. *Gender: Antiquity and Its Legacy*. Oxford: Oxford University Press, 2012.

Hornsby, Teresa J. "Gender Dualism, or the Big Lie." In Hornsby and Guest, *Transgender, Intersex, and Biblical Interpretation*, 13–20.

Hornsby, Teresa J. and Deryn Guest, *Transgender, Intersex, and Biblical Interpretation*. Atlanta: SBL Press, 2016.

Hornsby, Teresa J. and Ken Stone, eds. *Bible Trouble: Queer Reading at the Boundaries of Biblical Scholarship*. Atlanta: SBL Press, 2011.

Horowitz, Eliot. *Reckless Rites: Purim and the Legacy of Jewish Violence*. Princeton, NJ: Princeton University Press, 2006.

Horsley, Richard A., ed. *Paul and Politics: Ekklesia, Israel, Imperium, Interpretation: Essays in Honor of Krister Stendahl*. Harrisburg, PA: Trinity, 2000.

Howie, Cary. "On Transfiguration." *L'Esprit Créateur* 53.1 (2013): 158–66.

Hughes, Bettany. *Venus and Aphrodite: History of a Goddess*. London: Widenfeld and Nicolson, 2019.

Human Rights Campaign."Violence against the Transgender Community in 2019." https://www.hrc.org/resources/violence-against-the-transgender-community-in-2019.

Hunink, Vincent. *Tertullian: De Pallio: A Commentary*. Leiden: Brill, 2005.

Issue Analysts. "Transgenderism—Our Position." Focus on the Family. February 1, 2018. https://www.focusonthefamily.com/get-help/transgenderism-our-position/.

Jacobs, Andrew S. *The Life of Thecla: Apocryphal Expansion in Late Antiquity*. Eugene, OR: Cascade Books, 2024.

Jacobs, Harriet. *Incidents in the Life of a Slave Girl*, edited by L. Maria Child. Boston: Published for the Author, 1861.

James, S. E., J. L. Herman, S. Rankin, M. Keisling, L. Mottet, and M. Anafi. "The Report of the 2015 U.S. Transgender Survey." Washington, DC: National Center for Transgender Equality, 2016. https://transequality.org/sites/default/files/docs/usts/USTS%20Full%20Report%20-%20FINAL%201.6.17.pdf.

Jennings, Theodore W. *Jacob's Wound: Homoerotic Narrative in the Literature of Ancient Israel*. New York: Continuum, 2005.

Jensen, P. "Elamitische Eigennamen: Ein Beitrag zur Erklärung der elamitischen Inschriften." *WZKM* 6 (1892): 47–70.

Jensen, Robin E. "From Barren to Sterile: The Evolution of a Mixed Metaphor." *Rhetoric Society Quarterly* 45.1 (2015): 25–46.

Johnson, Scott F. *The Life and Miracles of Thecla: A Literary Study*. Cambridge, MA: Harvard University Press, 2006.

Johnson-DeBaufre, Melanie. *Jesus among her Children: Q, Eschatology, and the Construction of Christian Origins*. Cambridge, MA: Harvard University Press, 2005.

Kaalund, Jennifer T. "'You Can't See What I See': Black Bodies in Galatians." In *Stony the Road We Trod: African American Biblical Interpretation*, edited by Cain Hope Felder, Thirtieth Anniversary Expanded Edition, 324–38. Minneapolis: Fortress Press, 2021.

Kahl, Brigitte. "Gender Trouble in Galatia?: Paul and the Rethinking of Difference." In *Is There a Future for Feminist Theology?*, edited by Deborah F. Sawyer and Diane M. Collier, 57–73. Sheffield: Sheffield Academic Press, 1999.

———. "No Longer Male: Masculinity Struggles Behind Galatians 3.28?" *JSNT* 79 (1999): 37–49.

Kawashima, Robert S. "From Song to Story: The Genesis of Narrative in Judges 4 and 5." *Prooftexts* 21.2 (2001): 151–78.

Keith, Alison. *Propertius: Poet of Love and Leisure*. Bristol: Bristol Classical Press, 2008.

Kennedy, Elizabeth Lapovsky, and Madeline D. Davis. *Boots of Leather, Slippers of Gold: The History of a Lesbian Community*. New York: Routledge, 1993.

Kessler, Gwynn. "Bodies in Motion: Preliminary Notes on Queer Theory and Rabbinic Literature." In *Mapping Gender in Ancient Religious Discourse*, edited by Todd Penner and Caroline Vander Stichele, 389–409. Leiden: Brill, 2007.
———. "Let's Cross That Body When We Get to It: Gender and Ethnicity in Rabbinic Literature," *JAAR* 73.2 (2005): 329–59.
———. "Perspectives on Rabbinic Constructions of Gendered Bodies." In *The Wiley Blackwell Companion to Religion and Materiality*, edited by Vasudha Narayanan, 61–89. Hoboken, NJ: Wiley, 2020.
———. "Rabbinic Gender: Beyond Male and Female." In *A Companion to Late Ancient Jews and Judaism: Third Century BCE to Seventh Century CE*, edited by Naomi Koltun-Fromm and Kessler, 353–70. Hoboken, NJ: Wiley, 2020.
King, Helen. "Sex and Gender: The Hippocratic Case of Phaethousa and Her Beard." *EuGeSta: Gender Studies in Antiquity* 3 (n.d.): 124–42.
King, Martin Luther, Jr. "Beyond Vietnam." Speech given in New York, April 4, 1967.
———. "The Three Dimensions of a Complete Life." Sermon Delivered at the Unitarian Church of Germantown, December 11, 1960. https://kinginstitute.stanford.edu/king-papers/documents/three-dimensions-complete-life-sermon-delivered-unitarian-church-germantown.
Kittredge, Cynthia Briggs. "Rethinking Authorship in the Letters of Paul: Elisabeth Schüssler Fiorenza's Model of Pauline Theology." In *Walk in the Ways of Wisdom: Essays in Honor of Elisabeth Schüssler Fiorenza*, edited by Shelly Matthews, Kittredge, and Melanie Johnson-DeBaufre, 318–33. Harrisburg, PA: Trinity, 2003.
Klein, Lillian R. *The Triumph of Irony in the Book of Judges*. Sheffield: Sheffield Academic Press, 1988.
Knights, Chris. "Metamorphosis and Obedience: An Interpretation of Mark's Account of the Transfiguration of Jesus." *ExpTim* 121.5 (2010): 218–22.
Koama, Kapya. "Beyond Adam and Eve: Jesus, Sexual Minorities and Sexual Politics in the Church in Africa." *JTSA* 153 (2015): 7–27.
Kolakowski, Victoria. "The Concubine and the Eunuch: Queering Up the Breeder's Bible." In *Our Families, Our Values: Snapshots of Queer Kinship*, edited by Robert E. Goss and Amy A.S. Strongheart, 35–49. New York: Harrington Park Press, 1997.
———. "Throwing a Party: Patriarchy, Gender, and the Death of Jezebel." In Goss and West, *Take Back the Word*, 103–14.
Koosed, Jennifer L. "Moses, Feminism, and The Male Subject." In *The Bible and Feminism: Remapping the Field*, edited by Yvonne Sherwood, 223–39. London: Oxford University Press, 2017.
Kooten, George H. van. "The 'True Light Which Enlightens Everyone' (John 1:9): John, Genesis, the Platonic Notion of the 'True, Noetic Light' and the Allegory of the Cave in Plato's *Republic*." In *The Creation of Heaven and Earth: Re-Interpretations of Genesis 1 in the Context of Judaism, Ancient Philosophy, Christianity, and Modern Physics*, edited by van Kooten, 149–94. Leiden: Brill, 2005.
Kostenberger, Andreas J., and David W. Jones, *God, Marriage, and Family: Rebuilding the Biblical Foundation*. Wheaton, IL: Crossway, 2004.
Kotrosits, Maia. "Queer Persistence: On Death, History, and Longing for Endings." In Brintnall, Marchal, and Moore, *Sexual Disorientations*, 133–44.
Kuefler, Mathew. *The Manly Eunuch: Masculinity, Gender Ambiguity, and Christian Ideology in Late Antiquity*. Chicago: University of Chicago Press, 2001.
Kukla, Elliot. *A Created Being of Its Own*. Master's Thesis, Hebrew Union College, 2006.
Labovitz, Gail. *Marriage and Metaphor: Constructions of Gender in Rabbinic Literature*. Lanham, MD: Lexington Books, 2009.

Ladin, Joy. "In the Image of God, God Created Them: Toward a Trans Theology." *JFSR* 34.1 (2018): 53–58.
———. *The Soul of the Stranger: Reading God and Torah from a Transgender Perspective*. Waltham, MA: Brandeis University Press, 2019.
LaFleur, Greta, Masha Raskolnikov, and Anna Kłosowska. "Introduction: The Benefits of Being Trans Historical." In *Trans Historical: Gender Plurality before the Modern*, edited by LaFleur, Raskolnikov, and Klosowska, 1–24. Ithaca, NY: Cornell University Press, 2021.
Larsen, Matthew D. C., and Mark Letteny. *Ancient Mediterranean Incarceration*. Berkeley: University of California Press, 2025.
Lasine, Stuart. "Guest and Host in Judges 19: Lot's Hospitality in an Inverted World." *JSOT* 9.29 (1984): 37–59.
Layton, Bentley, and Harold W. Attridge. *Nag Hammadi Codex II, 2–7*. Vol. 1. Leiden: Brill, 1989.
Lee, Dorothy A. *Transfiguration*. New York: Continuum, 2004.
Lee, Simon S. *Jesus' Transfiguration and the Believers' Transformation: A Study of the Transfiguration and Its Development in Early Christian Writings*. Tübingen: Mohr Siebeck, 2009.
Lerner, Gerda. *The Creation of Patriarchy*. Oxford: Oxford University Press, 1986.
Letherby, Gayle. "Mother or Not, Mother or What? Problems of Definition and Identity." *Women's Studies International Forum* 17.5 (1994): 525–32.
Lev, Sarra. *And the Sages Did Not Know: Early Rabbinic Approaches to Intersex*. Philadelphia: University of Pennsylvania Press, 2024.
———. "Defying the Binary? The Androgynous in Tosefta Bikkurim." Paper presented at the AJS Annual Meeting. Washington, DC, 2011.
———. "Genital Trouble: On the Innovations of Tannaitic Thought Regarding Damaging Genitals and Eunuchs." PhD diss., New York University, 2004.
Levenson, Jon. *Esther: A Commentary*. Louisville, KY: Westminster John Knox Press, 1997.
Lewis, Abram J. "Trans History in a Moment of Danger: Organizing within and beyond 'Visibility' in the 1970s." In Tourmaline, Stanley, and Burton, *Trap Door*, 57–89.
Lieberman, Saul. *Tosefta Kifshuta*. New York: Jewish Theological Seminary Press, 2007.
Liew, Tat-siong Benny. "Queering Closets and Perverting Desires: Cross-Examining John's Engendering and Transgendering Word across Different Worlds." In Bailey, Liew, and Segovia, *They Were All Together in One Place?*, 251–88.
Litwa, M. David, *Posthuman Transformation in Ancient Mediterranean Thought: Becoming Angels and Demons*. Cambridge: Cambridge University Press, 2020.
Løland Levinson, Hannah. "Still Invisible after All These Years? Female God-Language in the Hebrew Bible: A Response to David J. A. Clines." *JBL* 141.2 (2022): 199–217.
Lopez, Davina C. *Apostle to the Conquered: Reimagining Paul's Mission*. Minneapolis: Fortress Press, 2008.
Lorde, Audre. *Sister Outsider: Essays and Speeches*. Trumansburg: Crossing Press, 1984.
MacLachlan, Bonnie. "The Ungendering of Aphrodite." In *Engendering Aphrodite: Women and Society in Ancient Cyprus*, edited by Diane Bolger and Nancy Serwint, 365–78. Boston: The American Schools of Oriental Research, 2002.
Maduro, Otto. "Once Again Liberating Theology? Towards a Latin American Liberation Theological Self-Criticism." In *Liberation Theology and Sexuality*, edited by Marcella Althaus-Reid. London: SCM Press, 2009.
Malatino, Hil. *Side Affects: On Being Trans and Feeling Bad*. Minneapolis: University of Minnesota Press, 2022.
———. *Trans Care*. Minneapolis: University of Minnesota Press, 2020.

Malherbe, Abraham J. *Paul and the Popular Philosophers*. Minneapolis: Fortress Press, 1989.

Marchal, Joseph A., ed. *After the Corinthian Women Prophets: Reimagining Rhetoric and Power*. Atlanta: SBL Press, 2021.

———. *Appalling Bodies: Queer Figures Before and After Paul's Letters*. New York: Oxford University Press, 2020.

———, ed. *Bodies on the Verge: Queering Pauline Epistles*. Atlanta: SBL Press, 2019.

———. "The Corinthian Women Prophets and Trans Activism: Rethinking Canonical Gender Claims." In Hornsby and Stone, *Bible Trouble*, 223–46.

———. "Female Masculinity in Corinth? Bodily Citations and the Drag of History." *Neot* 48.1 (2014): 93–113.

———. "How Soon Is (This Apocalypse) Now? Queer Velocities after a Corinthian Already and a Pauline Not Yet." In Brintnall, Marchal, and Moore, *Sexual Disorientations*, 45–58.

———. "'Making History' Queerly: Touches across Time through a Biblical Behind." *BibInt* 19 (2011): 373–95.

———. "Melancholic Hopes, Trans Temporalities, and Haunted Biblical Receptions: A Response." *BibInt* 28.4 (2020): 495–515.

———. *Philippians: Historical Problems, Hierarchical Visions, Hysterical Anxieties*. Sheffield: Sheffield Phoenix, 2014.

———. *The Politics of Heaven: Women, Gender, and Empire in the Study of Paul*. Minneapolis: Fortress Press, 2009.

———. "Queer Approaches: Improper Relations with Pauline Letters." In *Studying Paul's Letters: Contemporary Perspectives and Methods*, edited by Marchal, 209–27. Minneapolis: Fortress Press, 2012.

———. "Slaves as Wo/Men and Unmen: Reflecting upon Euodia, Syntyche, and Epaphroditus in Philippi." In *The People Beside Paul: The Philippian Assembly and History from Below*, edited by Marchal, 141–76. Atlanta: SBL Press, 2015.

———. "The Usefulness of an Onesimus: The Sexual Use of Slaves and Paul's Letter to Philemon." *JBL* 130. 4 (2011): 749–70.

Marcus, Joel. *Mark 1–8*. New Haven, CT: Yale University Press, 2002.

Marjanen, Antti. "Is *Thomas* a Gnostic Gospel?" In *Thomas at the Crossroads: Essays on the Gospel of Thomas*, edited by Risto Uro, 107–39. Edinburgh: T&T Clark, 2000.

Martin, Dale B. *The Corinthian Body*. New Haven, CT: Yale University Press, 1995.

Mase, J, III. "'Josephine': Reconciling My Queer Faith." *Huffington Post*. October 4, 2013. http://www.huffingtonpost.com/j-mase-iii/josephine-reconciling-my-queer-faith_b_4014580.html.

Matthews, Shelly. "Hearing Wo/men Prophets: Intersections, Silences, Publics." In Marchal, *After the Corinthian Women Prophets*, 47–68.

———. Cynthia Briggs Kittredge, and Melanie Johnson-DeBaufre, eds. *Walk in the Ways of Wisdom: Essays in Honor of Elisabeth Schüssler Fiorenza*. Harrisburg, PA: Trinity Press International, 2003.

Matthews, Victor H. and Don C. Benjamin. *Social World of Ancient Israel 1250–587*. Peabody, MA: Hendrickson Publishers, 1993.

McDonald, Cece. "'Go beyond Our Natural Selves': The Prison Letters of CeCe McDonald," edited by Omise'eke Natasha Tinsley. *TSQ* 4.2 (2017): 243–65.

McDonald, Cece, Toshio Meronek, and Miss Major Griffin-Gracy. "Cautious Living: Black Trans Women and the Politics of Documentation." In Tourmaline, Stanley, and Burton, *Trap Door*, 23–37.

McKenzie, Alyce M. *The Parables for Today*. Louisville, KY: Westminster John Knox Press, 2007.

McNeill, John. *Taking a Chance on God: Liberating Theology for Gays, Lesbians, and Their Lovers, Families, and Friends.* Boston: Beacon Press, 1988.

Merkley, Ky. "Writing Trans Histories with an Ethics of Care, While Reading Gender in Imperial Roman Literature." *Gender and History* 36.1 (2024): 14–31.

Meronek, Toshio, and Miss Major Griffin-Gracy. *Miss Major Speaks: Conversations with a Black Trans Revolutionary.* London: Verso, 2023.

Merriam-Webster.com. "'Clocking' as Realizing or Understanding." https://www.merriam-webster.com/words-at-play/clock-new-senses-verb-usage.

Meyerowitz, Joanne. *How Sex Changed: A History of Transsexuality in the United States.* Cambridge, MA: Harvard University Press, 2002.

Michaels, Samantha. "We Tracked Down the Lawyers behind the Recent Wave of Anti-Trans Bathroom Bills." *Mother Jones,* April 25, 2016, sec. Politics. https://www.motherjones.com/politics/2016/04/alliance-defending-freedom-lobbies-anti-lgbt-bathroom-bills/00.

Miller, Geoffrey P. "Verbal Feud in the Hebrew Bible: Judges 3:12–30 and 19–21." *JNES* 55.2 (1996): 105–17.

Miller, Wendell, Penny Nixon, and Randall C. Bailey. "Last Sunday after the Epiphany or Transfiguration Sunday, Year B." In *Out in Scripture: An Honest Encounter between LGBT Lives & the Bible: Epiphany, Year B.* Accessed February 28, 2023. https://hrc-prod-requests.s3-us-west-2.amazonaws.com/files/assets/resources/OutinScripture_Epiphany_YearB.pdf.

Miroshnikov, Ivan. *The Gospel of Thomas and Plato: A Study of the Impact of Platonism on the "Fifth Gospel."* Leiden: Brill, 2018.

Moilanen, Ulla, Tuija Kirkinen, Nelli-Johanna Saari, Adam B. Rohrlach, Johannes Krause, Päivi Onkamo, and Elina Salmela. "A Woman with a Sword? Weapon Grave at Suontaka Vesitorninmäki, Finland." *European Journal of Archaeology* 25.1 (2022): 42–60.

Mollenkott, Virginia Ramey. *Omnigender: A Trans-Religious Approach.* Cleveland: Pilgrim Press, 2001.

Mollenkott, Virginia Ramey, and Vanessa Sheridan, *Transgender Journeys.* Eugene, OR: Wipf & Stock, 2010.

Moore, Carey. *Esther.* Anchor Bible. New York: Doubleday, 1974.

Moore, Stephen, Kent L. Brintnall, and Joseph A. Marchal. "Introducing Queer Disorientations: Four Turns and a Twist." In Brintnall, Marchal, and Moore, *Sexual Disorientations,* 1–27.

Morland, Iain. "Afterword: Genitals Are History." *Postmedieval* 9.2 (2018): 209–15.

Moslener, Sara. *Virgin Nation: Sexual Purity and American Adolescence.* Oxford: Oxford University Press, 2015.

Moss, Candida R. *God's Ghostwriters: Enslaved Christians and the Bible.* New York: Hachette, 2024.

———. "The Transfiguration: An Exercise in Markan Accommodation." *BibInt* 12.1 (2004): 69–89.

Movement Advancement Project, GLSEN, National Center for Transgender Equality, and National Education Association. "Separation and Stigma: Transgender Youth & School Facilities." 2017. https://www.glsen.org/sites/default/files/2019-11/Separation_and_Stigma_2017.pdf.

Movement for Black Lives. "End the War on Black People," https://m4bl.org/end-the-war-on-black-people/.

———. End the War on Black, Trans, Queer, Gender Nonconforming, and Intersex People." https://m4bl.org/policy-platforms/end-the-war-trans/.

Mowat, Chris. "Don't Be a Drag, Just Be a Priest: The Clothing and Identity of the Galli of Cybele in the Roman Republic and Empire." *Gender and History* 33.2 (2021): 296–313.

Mudimbe, Valentin-Yves. *The Invention of Africa: Gnosis, Philosophy, and the Order of Knowledge*. Bloomington: Indiana University Press, 1988.

Muñoz, José Esteban. *Cruising Utopia: The Then and There of Queer Futurity*. New York: NYU Press, 2009.

Murphy, Kelly J. *Rewriting Masculinity: Gideon, Men, and Might*. Oxford: Oxford University Press, 2019.

Musa, Aysha W. "Jael Is Non-Binary; Jael Is Not a Woman." *JIBS* 1.2 (2020): 97–120.

———. "Jael's Gender Ambiguity in Judges 4 and 5." PhD diss., University of Sheffield, 2020.

Nadar, Sarojini, and van Klinken, Adriaan. "'Queering the Curriculum': Pedagogical Explorations of Gender and Sexuality in Religion and Theological Studies." *JFSR* 34.1 (2018): 101–9.

Najmabadi, Afsaneh. *Professing Selves: Transsexuality and Same-Sex Desire in Contemporary Iran*. Durham, NC: Duke University Press, 2013.

Namaste, Vivianne. *Invisible Lives: The Erasure of Transsexual and Transgendered People*. Chicago: University of Chicago Press, 2000.

Neis, Rafael Rachel. *When a Human Gives Birth to a Raven: Rabbis and the Reproduction of Species*. Oakland: University of California Press, 2023.

Nichols, Jane, and Rachel Stuart. "Transgender: A Useful Category of Biblical Analysis?" *JIBS* 1.2 (2020): 1–24.

Nicolet, Valérie. "Monstrous Bodies in Paul's Letter to the Galatians." In Marchal, *Bodies on the Verge*, 115–41.

Niditch, Susan. "The 'Sodomite' Theme in Judges 19–20: Family, Community, and Social Disintegration." *CBQ* 44.3 (1982): 365–78.

Nippel, Wilfried. *Public Order in Ancient Rome*. Cambridge, MA: Cambridge University Press, 1995.

Nissinen, Martti Keikki. "Relative Masculinities in the Hebrew Bible/Old Testament." In *Being a Man: Negotiating Ancient Constructs of Masculinity*, edited by Ilona Zsolnay, 221–47. London: Routledge, 2016.

Ngũgĩ wa Thiong'o. *Something Torn and New: An African Renaissance*. New York: Basic Civitas Books, 2009.

Nolland, John. *The Gospel of Matthew: A Commentary on the Greek Text*. Grand Rapids: Eerdmans, 2005.

N'Shea, Omar. "Royal Eunuchs and Elite Masculinity in the Neo-Assyrian Empire." *NEA* 79.3 (2016): 214–21.

Økland, Jorunn. "Genealogies of the Self: Materiality, Personal Identity, and the Body in Paul's Letters to the Corinthians." In Seim and Økland, *Metamorphoses*, 83–107.

Oliver, Mary. "Poem." In *Dream Work*. New York: Grove Atlantic, 1986.

Ormand, Kirk. "Impossible Lesbians in Ovid's *Metamorphoses*." In *Gendered Dynamics in Latin Love Poetry*, ed. by Ronnie Ancona and Ellen Greene, 79–111. Baltimore: John Hopkins University Press, 2005.

Page, Morgan M. "One from the Vaults: Gossip, Access, and Trans History-Telling." In Tourmaline, Stanley, and Burton, *Trap Door*, 135–46.

Pagels, Elaine. "Exegesis of Genesis 1 in the Gospels of Thomas and John." *JBL* 118 (1999): 477–96.

Palmer, Timothy. "Jesus Christ: Our Ancestor?" *African Journal of Evangelical Theology* 27 (2008): 65–75.

Pambazuka. "Kenya: Bishop says gays are worse than terrorists." Accessed June 1, 2022. https://www.pambazuka.org/gender-minorities/kenya-bishop-says-gays-are-worse-terrorists.

Park, Suzie. "Left-Handed Benjaminites and the Shadow of Saul." *JBL* 134.4 (2015): 701–20.

Parker, Angela N. "Feminized-Minoritized Paul? A Womanist Reading of Paul's Body in the Corinthian Context." In *Minoritized Women Reading Race and Ethnicity: Intersectional Approaches to Constructed Identity and Early Christian Texts*, edited by Mitzi J. Smith and Jin Young Choi, 71–87. Lanham, MD: Lexington, 2020.

———. "One Womanist's View of Racial Reconciliation in Galatians." *JFSR* 34.2 (2018): 23–40.

Partridge, Cameron. "'Scotch-Taped Together': Anti-'Androgyny' Rhetoric, Transmisogyny, and the Transing of Religious Studies." *JFSR* 34.1 (2018): 68–75.

Patterson, Stephen J. *The Gospel of Thomas and Christian Origins: Essays on the Fifth Gospel*. Leiden: Brill, 2013.

———. "Jesus Meets Plato: The Theology of the Gospel of Thomas and Middle Platonism." In *Das Thomasevangelium: Entstehung—Rezeption—Theologie*, edited by Jörg Frey, Enno Edzard Popkes, and Jens Schröter, 81–205. Berlin: De Gruyter, 2008.

Pellegrini, Ann, and Janet Jakobsen. *Love the Sin: Sexual Regulation and the Limits of Religious Tolerance*. Boston: Beacon Press, 2004.

Perschbacher, Wesley J. ed. *The New Analytical Greek Lexicon*. Peabody, MA: Hendrickson Publishers, 1990.

Pew Research Center. "Religious Groups' Policies on Transgender Members Vary Widely." *Pew Research Center* (blog). https://www.pewresearch.org/fact-tank/2015/12/02/religious-groups-policies-on-transgender-members-vary-widely/.

Phillips, Kathryn Leigh. "'You Are Correctly Called a Man, Because You Act Manfully': A Transgender Studies Approach to Gender-Crossing Saints in Late Antiquity." PhD diss., University of California, Riverside, 2020.

Piccin, Michela and Martin Worthington. "Schizophrenia and the Problem of Suffering in the Ludlul Hymn to Marduk." *RA* 109.1 (2015): 113–24.

Piepzna-Samarasinha, Leah Lakshmi. *Care Work: Dreaming Disability Justice*. Vancouver: Arsenal Pulp Press, 2018.

Pintabone, Diane T. "Ovid's Iphis and Ianthe: When Girls Won't Be Girls." In *Among Women: From the Homosocial to the Homoerotic in the Ancient World*, edited by Nancy Sorkin Rabinowitz and Lisa Auanger, 256–85. Austin: University of Texas Press, 2002.

Pollock, Sheldon. "Philology in Three Dimensions." *Postmedieval: A Journal of Medieval Cultural Studies* 5.4 (2014): 398–413.

Powery, Emerson. "Reading with the Enslaved: Placing Human Bondage at the Center of the Early Christian Story." In Smith, Parker, and Hill, *Bitter the Chastening Rod*, 71–90.

Prosser, Jay. *Second Skins: The Body Narratives of Transsexuality*. New York: Columbia University Press, 1998.

Puar, Jasbir K. "Bodies with New Organs: Becoming Trans, Becoming Disabled." *Social Text* 33.3 (2015): 45–73.

———. *Terrorist Assemblages: Homonationalism in Queer Times*. Durham, NC: Duke University Press, 2007.

Pumphrey, Nicholaus. "Unexpected Roles: Examining Ancient Gender Construction in the Joseph Narrative." In *Troubling Topics, Sacred Texts: Readings in Hebrew Bible, New Testament, and Qur'an*, edited by Roberta Sterman Sabbath, 71–92. Berlin: De Gruyter, 2021.

Quigley, Jennifer A. *Divine Accounting: Theo-Economics in Early Christianity*. New Haven, CT: Yale University Press, 2021.
Reay, Lewis. "Towards a Transgender Theology: Que(e)rying the Eunuchs." In *Trans/formations: Controversies in Contextual Theology*, edited by Marcella Althaus-Reid and Lisa Isherwood, 148–67. London: SCM Press, 2009.
Rebillard, Eric. *Christians and Their Many Identities in Late Antiquity: North Africa 200–450 CE*. Ithaca, NY: Cornell University Press, 2012.
Reis, Elizabeth. "Teaching Transgender History, Identity, and Politics." *Radical History Review* 88 (2004): 166–77.
Rich, Adrienne. *Of Woman Born: Motherhood as Experience and Institution*. London: W. W. Norton, 1995.
Ringe, Sharon. *Wisdom's Friends: Community and Christology in the Fourth Gospel*. Louisville, KY: Westminster John Knox Press, 1999.
Rivera, Sylvia. "'Y'all Better Quiet Down': Sylvia Rivera's Speech at the 1973 Liberation Day Rally." In *Street Transvestite Action Revolutionaries: Survival, Revolt, and Queer Antagonist Struggle*, 30–32. Untorelli Press, 2013.
Ross, Samuel. "A Transgender Gaze at Genesis 38." *JIBS* 1.2 (2020): 25–39.
Runia, David T. *Philo of Alexandria and the "Timaeus" of Plato*. Leiden: Brill, 1986.
———. *Philo of Alexandria: On the Creation of the Cosmos According to Moses*. Leiden: Brill, 2001.
Runions, Erin. *How Hysterical: Identification and Resistance in the Bible and Film*. London: Palgrave Macmillan, 2003.
———. "Mobile Theologies, Carceral Affects: Interest and Debt in Faith-Based Prison Programs." In *Religion, Emotion, Sensation: Affect Theories and Theologies*, edited by Karen Bray and Stephen D. Moore, 55–84. New York: Fordham University Press, 2020.
Ruttenberg, Danya. "(Gender)Queering Joseph." *Life Is a Sacred Text*. October 25, 2021. https://lifeisasacredtext.substack.com/p/queering-joseph.
Sabia-Tanis, Justin. "Eating the Crumbs That Fall from the Table: Trusting the Abundance of God." In Goss and West, *Take Back the Word*, 43–54.
———. *Trans-Gendered: Theology, Ministry, and Communities of Faith*. Cleveland: Pilgrim Press, 2003.
———. *Trans-Gender: Theology, Ministry, and Communities of Faith*. Eugene, OR: Wipf & Stock, 2018.
Salamon, Gayle. *The Life and Death of Latisha King: A Critical Phenomenology of Transphobia*. New York: NYU Press, 2018.
Sasson, Jack M. "'A Breeder of Two for Each Leader': On Mothers in Judges 4 and 5." In *A Critical Engagement: Essays on the Hebrew Bible in Honour of J. Cheryl Exum*, edited by David J. A. Clines and Ellen van Wolde, 333–55. Sheffield: Sheffield Phoenix Press, 2011.
Sawyer, Deborah F. "Gender Criticism: A New Discipline in Biblical Studies or Feminism in Disguise?" In *A Question of Sex? Gender and Difference in the Hebrew Bible and Beyond*, edited by Deborah W. Rooke, 2–20. Sheffield: Sheffield Phoenix Press, 2007.
———. *God, Gender, and the Bible*. London: Routledge, 2002.
Schellenberg, Paul. *Abject Joy: Paul, Prison, and the Art of Making Do*. New York: Oxford University Press, 2021.
Schneemelcher, Wilhelm, ed. *New Testament Apocrypha, Vol. 2: Writings Relating to the Apostles, Apocalypses and Related Subjects*. Translated by R. McL. Wilson. Rev. ed. Louisville, KY: Westminster John Knox Press, 1992.
Schneider, Laura C. "More Than a Feeling: A Queer Notion of Survivance." In Brintnall, Marchal, and Moore, *Sexual Disorientations*, 258–76.

Schneider, Tammi J. *Judges*. Collegeville, MN: Liturgical Press, 2000.
Scholz, Susanne. *Introducing the Women's Hebrew Bible: Feminism, Gender Justice, and the Study of the Old Testament*. London: Bloomsbury, 2017.
Schüssler Fiorenza, Elisabeth. *Bread Not Stone: The Challenge of Feminist Biblical Interpretation*. Edinburgh: T&T Clark, 1984.
———. "Paul and the Politics of Interpretation." In Horsley, *Paul and Politics*, 40–57.
Schwartz, Howard. *Tree of Souls: The Mythology of Judaism*. Annotated edition. Oxford: Oxford University Press, 2007.
Scott, Joan Wallach. "Gender: Still a Useful Category of Analysis." *Diogenes* 225 (2010): 7–14.
———. "Sexularism: On Secularism and Gender Equality." In *The Fantasy of Feminist History*, 91–116. Durham, NC: Duke University Press, 2011.
Scott, Martin. *Sophia and the Johannine Jesus*. Sheffield: Sheffield Academic Press, 1992.
Sedgwick, Eve Kosofsky. *Epistemology of the Closet*. Updated with a New Preface. Berkeley: University of California Press, 2008 [1990].
Seeman, Don. "The Watcher at the Window: Cultural Poetics of a Biblical Motif." *Prooftexts* 24.1 (2004): 1–50.
Segal, Alan F. *Paul the Convert: The Apostolate and Apostasy of Saul the Pharisee*. New Haven, CT: Yale University Press, 1990.
Segovia, Fernando F. and Mary Ann Tolbert, eds. *Reading from This Place: Social Location and Biblical Interpretation*. 2 vols. Minneapolis: Fortress Press, 1995.
Seim, Turid Karlsen, and Jorunn Økland, eds. *Metamorphoses: Resurrection, Body, and Transformative Practices in Early Christianity*. Berlin: De Gruyter, 2009.
Sellew, Melissa [née Philip] Harl. "Death, the Body, and the World in the Coptic Gospel of Thomas." *StPatr* 31 (1997): 530–34.
———. "The Gospel of Thomas and the Synoptics." In *The Oxford Handbook of the Synoptic Gospels*, edited by Stephen Ahearne-Kroll, 223–42. Oxford: Oxford University Press, 2023.
———. "Jesus and the Voice from Beyond the Grave: *Gos. Thom.* 42 in the Context of Funerary Epigraphy." In *Thomasine Traditions in Antiquity*, ed. Asgeirsson, DeConick, and Uro, 327–56.
———. "Reading Jesus in the Desert: The *Gospel of Thomas* Meets the *Apophthegmata Patrum*." In *The Nag Hammadi Codices and Late Antique Egypt*, edited by Hugo Lundhaug and Lance Jennot, 81–106. Tübingen: Mohr Siebeck, 2018.
———. "Reading the *Gospel of Thomas* from Here: A Trans-Centred Hermeneutic." *JIBS* 1.2 (2020): 61–96.
———. "Traversing the Society of Biblical Literature While Trans." In *Women and the Society of Biblical Literature*, edited by Nicole L. Tilford, 231–38. Atlanta: SBL Press, 2019.
Sellew, Melissa Harl, and Joshua Reno. "Galatians." In *The Queer Bible Commentary*, edited by Mona West and Robert E. Shore-Goss, 2nd ed., 644–62. London: SCM Press, 2022.
Severy, Beth. *Augustus and the Family at the Birth of the Roman Empire*. New York: Routledge, 2003.
Shaner, Katherine A. *Enslaved Leadership in Early Christianity*. New York: Oxford University Press, 2018.
Sharpe, A. *Transgender Jurisprudence: Dysphoric Bodies of Law*. London: Roultledge, 2002.
Shasha, Roy. "The Forms and Functions of Lists in the Mishnah." PhD diss., University of Manchester, 2006.
Shaw, Teresa M. *The Burden of the Flesh: Fasting and Sexuality in Early Christianity*. Minneapolis: Fortress Press, 1998.

Shaye, Amaryah. "Refusing to Reconcile, Part 2." https://womenintheology.org/2014/02/16/refusing-to-reconcile-part-2/.
Silverstein, Adam. "The Book of Esther and the *Enūma Elish*." *BSOAS* 69.2 (2006): 209–23.
Skidmore, Emily. *The Lives of Trans Men at the Turn of the Twentieth Century*. New York: NYU Press, 2017.
Smith, Mitzi J., Angela N. Parker, and Ericka S. Dunbar Hill, eds. *Bitter the Chastening Rod: Africana Biblical Interpretation after Stony the Road We Trod in the Age of BLM, SayHerName, and MeToo*. Lanham, MD: Lexington/Fortress Academic, 2022.
Snorton, C. Riley. *Black on Both Sides: A Racial History of Trans Identity*. Minneapolis: University of Minnesota Press, 2017.
Snorton, C. Riley, and Jin Haritaworn. "Trans Necropolitics: A Transnational Reflection on Violence, Death, and the Trans of Color Afterlife." In Stryker and Aizura, *The Transgender Studies Reader 2*, 66–76.
Songe-Møller, Vigdis. "'With What Kind of Body Will They Come?': Metamorphosis and the Concept of Change: From Platonic Thinking to Paul's Notion of the Resurrection of the Dead." In Seim and Økland, *Metamorphoses*, 109–22.
Spade, Dean. *Normal Life: Administrative Violence, Critical Trans Politics, and the Limits of Law*. Durham, NC: Duke University Press, 2015.
Spawforth, Anthony. "Hermaphroditus." In *The Oxford Classical Dictionary*, edited by Simon Hornblower, Spawforth, and Esther Eidinow. Online edition. Oxford: Oxford University Press, 2012, updated online in 2015.
Spencer-Hall, Alicia, and Blake Gutt. "Introduction." In Spencer-Hall and Gutt, *Trans and Genderqueer Subjects in Medieval Hagiography*, 11–40.
———, eds. *Trans and Genderqueer Subjects in Medieval Hagiography*. Amsterdam: Amsterdam University Press, 2021.
Stanley, Eric A. *Atmospheres of Violence: Structuring Antagonism and the Trans/Queer Ungovernable*. Durham, NC: Duke University Press, 2021.
———. "Introduction: Fugitive Flesh: Gender Self-Determination, Queer Abolition, and Trans Resistance." In Stanley and Smith, *Captive Genders*, 7–17.
Stanley, Eric A., and Nat Smith, eds. *Captive Genders: Trans Embodiment and the Prison Industrial Complex*. Expanded Ed. Chico, CA: AK Press, 2015.
Steinbock, Elizabeth. "Embodiment." In *The Sage Encyclopedia of Trans Studies*, edited by Abbie E. Goldberg and Genny Beemyn, 1:229–32. Los Angeles: Sage Reference, 2021.
Steinmetz, Devora. *Punishment and Freedom: The Rabbinic Construction of Criminal Law*. Philadelphia: University of Pennsylvania Press, 2008.
Stendahl, Krister. *Paul among Jews and Gentiles and Other Essays*. Minneapolis: Fortress Press, 1976.
Sterling, Gregory E. "Day One: Platonizing Exegetical Traditions of Genesis 1:1–5 in John and Jewish Authors" *SPhilo* 17 (2005): 18–40.
———. "Platonizing Moses: Philo and Middle Platonism." *SPhilo* A5 (1993): 96–111.
Sterman, Judy Taubes. "Themes in the Deborah Narrative (Judges 4–5)." *JBQ* 39.1 (2011): 15–24.
Stewart, Lindsey. *The Politics of Black Joy: Zora Neale Hurston and Neo-Abolitionism*. Evanston, IL: Northwestern University Press, 2021.
Stiebert, Johanna. *Fathers and Daughters in the Hebrew Bible*. Oxford: Oxford University Press, 2013.
Stiller, Brian. *Preaching Parables to Postmoderns*. Minneapolis: Fortress Press, 2005.
Stone, Ken. "The Garden of Eden and the Heterosexual Contract." In Goss and West, *Take Back the Word*, 57–70.

———. "How a Woman Unmans a King: Gender Reversal and the Woman of Thebez in Judges 9." In *From the Margins 1: Women of the Hebrew Bible and Their Afterlives*, edited by Peter S. Hawkins and Lesleigh Cushing Stahlberg, 71–85. Sheffield: Sheffield Phoenix Press, 2009.
Stone, Sandy. "The *Empire* Strikes Back: A Posttranssexual Manifesto." In Epstein and Straub, *Body Guards*, 280–304.
Stowers, Stanley K. "The Dilemma of Paul's Physics: Features Stoic-Platonist or Platonist-Stoic?" In Engberg-Pedersen, *From Stoicism to Platonism*, 231–53.
———. *A Rereading of Romans: Justice, Jews, and Gentiles*. New Haven, CT: Yale University Press, 1994.
Strassfeld, Max K. *Trans Talmud: Androgynes and Eunuchs in Rabbinic Literature*. Oakland: University of California Press, 2022.
———. "Transing Religious Studies." *JFSR* 34.1 (2018): 37–53.
Stratton, Kimberly B., and Andrea Lieber, eds. *Crossing Boundaries in Early Judaism and Christianity: Ambiguities, Complexities, and Half-Forgotten Adversaries: Essays in Honor of Alan F. Segal*. Leiden: Brill, 2016.
Stryker, Susan. ""(De)Subjugated Knowledges: An Introduction to Transgender Studies." In Stryker and Whittle, *Transgender Studies Reader*, 1–17.
———. "My Words to Victor Frankenstein Above the Village of Chamounix: Performing Transgender Rage." *GLQ* 1.3 (1994): 237–54.
———. "Transgender History, Homonormativity, and Disciplinarity." *Radical History Review* 100 (2008): 145–57.
———. *Transgender History*. Berkeley, CA: Seal Press, 2017 [2008].
———. "Transgender Studies: Queer Theory's Evil Twin." *GLQ* 10.2 (2004): 212–15.
———. "The Transgender Issue: An Introduction." *GLQ* 4.2 (1998): 145–58.
Stryker, Susan, and Aren Z. Aizura. "Introduction: Transgender Studies 2.0." In Stryker and Aizura, *Transgender Studies Reader 2*, 1–12.
Stryker, Susan, and Aren Z. Aizura, eds. *The Transgender Studies Reader 2*. New York: Routledge, 2006.
Stryker, Susan, and Paisley Currah, "Introduction." *TSQ* 1.1–2 (2014): 1–18.
Stryker, Susan, and Stephen Whittle, eds. *The Transgender Studies Reader*. New York: Routledge, 2006.
Stryker, Susan, Paisley Currah, and Lisa Jean Moore. "Introduction." *Women's Study Quarterly* 36.3–4 (2008): 11–22.
Sullivan, Kevin P. "Sexuality and Gender of Angels." In *Paradise Now: Essays on Early Jewish and Christian Mysticism*, edited by April D. DeConick, 211–28. Atlanta: SBL Press, 2006.
———. *Wrestling with Angels: A Study of the Relationship between Angels and Humans in Ancient Jewish Literature and the New Testament*. Leiden: Brill, 2004.
Surtees, Allison, and Jennifer Dyer, eds. *Exploring Gender Diversity in the Ancient World*. Edinburgh: Edinburgh University Press, 2020.
Suter, Elizabeth A., Leah M. Seurer, Stephanie Webb, Brian Grewe Jr., and Jody Koenig Kellas. "Motherhood as Contested Ideological Terrain: Essentialist and Queer Discourses of Motherhood at Play in Female–female Co-mothers' Talk." *Communication Monographs* 82/4 (2015): 458–83.
Sylvia Rivera Law Project. https://srlp.org/.
Talbott, Rick. "Imagining the Matthean Eunuch Community: Kyriarchy on the Chopping Block." *JFSR* 22 (2006): 21–43.
Tamber-Rosenau, Caryn. "The 'Mothers' Who Were Not: Motherhood Imagery and Childless Women Warriors in Early Jewish Literature." In *Mothers in the Jewish Cultural Imagination*, edited by Marjorie Lehman, Jane L. Kanarek, and Simon J. Bronner, 185–206. Liverpool: The Littman Library of Jewish Civilization, 2017.

———. *Women in Drag: Gender and Performance in the Hebrew Bible and Early Jewish Literature*. Piscataway, NJ: Gorgias Press, 2018.
Tanis. See Sabia-Tanis.
Terrell, JoAnne Marie. *Power in the Blood? The Cross in the African American Experience*. Maryknoll, NY: Orbis Books, 1998.
Thiessen, Matthew. *Contesting Conversion: Genealogy, Circumcision, and Identity in Ancient Judaism and Christianity*. Oxford: Oxford University Press, 2011.
Thiselton, Anthony C. *The First Epistle to the Corinthians: A Commentary on the Greek Text*. Grand Rapids: Eerdmans, 2000.
Thomas, Eric A. "The Futures Outside: Apocalyptic Epilogue Unveiled as Africana Queer Prologue." In Brintnall, Marchal, and Moore, *Sexual Disorientations*, 90–112.
Tigert, Leanne McCall, and Maren C. Tirabassi, eds. *Transgendering Faith: Identity, Sexuality, and Spirituality*. Cleveland: Pilgrim Press, 2004.
Tobin, Thomas H. "The Prologue of John and Hellenistic Jewish Speculation." *CBQ* 52 (1990): 252–69.
Tolbert, Mary Ann. *Sowing the Gospel: Mark's World in Literary-Historical Perspective*. Minneapolis: Fortress Press, 1996.
Tompkins, Avery. "Asterisk." *TSQ* 1.1–2 (2014): 26–27.
Toscano, Peterson. "Joseph and the Amazing Gender Non-Conforming Bible Story." Found in solo performance "Transfigurations: Transgressing Gender in the Bible." Pendle Hill DVD, 2017. Also see https://www.youtube.com/watch?v=gkikBKW8vmQ.
Tourmaline. "On Untorelli's 'New' Book." *The Spirit Was* (blog). March 13, 2013. https://thespiritwas.tumblr.com/post/45275076521/on-untorellis-new-book.
Tourmaline, Eric A. Stanley, and Johanna Burton. "Known Unknowns: An Introduction to Trap Door." In Tourmaline, Stanley, and Burton *Trap Door*, xv–xxvi.
Tourmaline, Eric A. Stanley, and Johanna Burton, ed. *Trap Door: Trans Cultural Production and the Politics of Visibility*. Cambridge, MA: MIT Press, 2017.
Towle, Evan B. and Lynn M. Morgan, "Romancing the Transgender Native: Rethinking the Use of the 'Third Gender' Concept." In Stryker and Whittle, *Transgender Studies Reader*, 666–84.
Townsley, Gillian. *The Straight Mind in Corinth: Queer Readings across 1 Corinthians 11:2–16*. Atlanta: SBL Press, 2017.
Tracy, Larissa, ed. *Castration and Culture in the Middle Ages*. Cambridge: D. S. Brewer, 2013.
———. "Introduction: A History of Calamities: The Culture of Castration." In Tracy, *Castration and Culture*, 1–28.
The Trans Youth Equality Foundation. http://www.transyouthequality.org/.
Trible, Phyllis. "Depatriarchalizing in Biblical Interpretation." *JAAR* 41.1 (1973): 30–48.
———. "Eve and Adam: Genesis 2–3 Reread." In *Womanspirit Rising: A Feminist Reader in Religion*, edited by Carol P. Christ and Judith Plaskow, 74–83. San Francisco: Harper, 1992.
———. *God and the Rhetoric of Sexuality*. Philadelphia: Fortress Press, 1978.
Trotta, Daniel. "US Republican Transgender Laws Pile Up, Setting 2024 Battle Lines." Reuters. May 18, 2023. https://www.reuters.com/world/us/us-republican-transgender-laws-pile-up-setting-2024-battle-lines-2023-05-18/.
Turman, Eboni Marshall. *Toward a Womanist Ethic of Incarnation: Black Bodies, the Black Church, and the Council of Chalcedon*. New York: Palgrave Macmillan, 2013.
Turner, David. *Matthew*. Grand Rapids: Baker Academic, 2008.
Upson-Saia, Kristi. *Early Christian Dress: Gender, Virtue, and Authority*. London: Routledge, 2011.

———, Carly Daniel-Hughes, and Alicia J. Batten, eds. *Dressing Judeans and Christians in Antiquity*. Surrey: Ashgate, 2014.
Urbano, Arturo P. "Sizing up the Philosopher's Quote: Christian Verbal and Visual Representations of the *Tribōn*." In Upson-Saia, Daniel-Hughes, and Batten, *Dressing Judeans and Christians*, 175–94.
Valantasis, Richard. *The Gospel of Thomas*. New York: Routledge, 1997.
Valentine, David. *Imagining Transgender: An Ethnography of a Category*. Durham, NC: Duke University Press, 2007.
Valentine, Katy E. "Examining Scripture in Light of Trans Women's Voices." In *The Oxford Handbook of Feminist Approaches to the Hebrew Bible*, edited by Susanne Scholz, 508–23. Oxford: Oxford University Press, 2020.
———. *For You Were Bought with a Price: Sex, Slavery, and Self-Control in a Pauline Community*. Wilmore, KY: GlossaHouse, 2017.
Van Dijk-Hemmes, Fokkelien. "Mothers and a Mediator in the Song of Debora." In Brenner, *Feminist Companion to Judges*, 110–16.
Van Wijk-Bos, Johanna W. H. *Reformed and Feminist, A Challenge to the Church*. Louisville, KY: Westminster John Knox Press, 1991.
Vearncombe, Erin K. "Adorning the Protagonist: The Use of Dress in the Book of Judith." In Upson-Saia, Daniel-Hughes, and Batten, *Dressing Judeans and Christians*, 116–37.
Wan, Sze-kar. "Collection for the Saints as Anticolonial Act: Implications of Paul's Ethnic Reconstruction." In Horsley, *Paul and Politics*, 191–215.
Wansink, Craig S. *Chained in Christ: The Experience and Rhetoric of Paul's Imprisonment*. Sheffield: Sheffield Academic, 1996.
Wasserman, Emma. *The Death of the Soul in Romans 7: Sin, Death, and the Law in Light of Hellenistic Moral Psychology*. Tübingen: Mohr Siebeck, 2008.
Wasserman, Mira. *Jews, Gentiles, and Other Animals: The Talmud after the Humanities*. Philadelphia: University of Pennsylvania Press, 2017.
Weed, Ashley Kirsten. "The Humor of Disgust: Attitudes toward Galli in Lucian's *Onos* and Apuleius' *Metamorphoses*." Paper presented at the SCS annual meeting, 2021.
Weekley, David E. "Across Generations: Becoming Grateful Allies: An Interview with Dr. Virginia Ramey Mollenkott." *JFSR* 34.1 (2018): 28–36.
———. *Retreating Forward: A Spiritual Practice with Transgender Persons*. Eugene, OR: Resource Publications, 2017.
Wegner, Judith Romney. "Tragelaphos Revisited: The Anomaly of Women in the Mishnah." *Judaism* 37.2 (1988): 160–72.
Weheliye, Alexander. *Habeas Viscus: Racializing Assemblages, Biopolitics, and Black Feminist Theories of the Human*. Durham, NC: Duke University Press, 2014.
Weismantel, Mary. "Towards a Transgender Archaeology: A Queer Rampage through Prehistory." In Stryker and Aizura, *Transgender Studies Reader 2*, 319–34.
Weiss, Shira. *Ethical Ambiguity in the Hebrew Bible: Philosophical Analysis of Scriptural Narrative*. Cambridge: Cambridge University Press, 2018.
Whittaker, John. "Platonic Philosophy in the Early Centuries of the Empire." *ANRW* 2:36.1 (1987): 81–123.
Whittle, Stephen. "Foreword." In Stryker and Whittle, *Transgender Studies Reader*, xi–xv.
Wiegel, Rebecca. "Reading Matrona: The Sixth Century Life of a Trans Saint." PhD diss., University of Notre Dame, 2019.
Wilhite, David E. *Tertullian the African: An Anthropological Reading of Tertullian's Context and Identities*. Berlin: De Gruyter, 2007.
Williams, James G. "Other Feminine Figures: The Multifaceted Israelite Feminine." In *Women Recounted: Narrative Thinking and the God of Israel*, edited by David M. Gunn, 67–95. Sheffield: The Almond Press, 1982.

Williams, Jeremy L. "'I Am a Human': Racializing Assemblages and Criminalized Egyptianness in Acts 21:31–39." In Smith, Parker, and Hill, *Bitter the Chastening Rod*, 91–107.

Wire, Antoinette Clark. *The Corinthian Women Prophets: A Reconstruction through Paul's Rhetoric*. Minneapolis: Fortress Press, 1990.

Wolf, Kristen. *The Way: A Girl Who Dared to Rise*. n.l.: Pixeltry, 2018.

Wyke, Maria. *The Roman Mistress: Ancient and Modern Representations*. Oxford: Oxford University Press, 2002.

Yee, Gale A. "By the Hand of a Woman: The Metaphor of the Woman Warrior in Judges 4." *Semeia* 61 (1993): 99–132.

Yurcaba, Jo. "As Anti-Trans Violence Surges, Advocates Demand Policy Reform." *NBC News*, March 11, 2021, https://www.nbcnews.com/feature/nbc-out/anti-trans-violence-surges-advocates-demand-policy-reform-n1260485.

Zanker, Paul. *The Power of Images in the Age of Augustus*. Translated by Alan Shapiro. Ann Arbor: University of Michigan Press, 1988.

Index of Scripture and Other Ancient Sources

HEBREW BIBLE

Genesis
1	25, 214, 218
1–3	15
1:26–27	16, 18
1:27	41, 44, 97, 161, 161n34, 182n72
2	214
2:7	206
3:16	11
4–5	130n66
6:1–4	168n2
11:30	69
13:16	83
15:3	83
18:10	70
19	92n39
21:1–8	56
21:10	69
24:67	70
25:21	69
25:22–34	53
27:1–29	53
31:33	70
37:3	20, 52n6
37:23	20
37:31–34	20
38:10	68n11
41:9–52	56
42:6–8	56
43:30–32	56

Exodus
34	129n60
34:29	118n2

Numbers
11:12	91

Deuteronomy
14:5	33n10, 44n45
20:1	79
20:3	79
21:10–11	68n10
22	25
22:5	11, 16, 28, 219, 220, 233
23:1	16
24:1–6	161n34

Joshua
11:6	79

Judges
3	94n53
3:12–30	94n53
3:15	94
3:19–21	94n53
4–5	20, 67, 71, 73, 74–75, 81
4:4–6	66
4:5	76
4:6	79
4:7	81
4:9	81
4:18	75, 77, 78, 79, 80
4:18–19	66, 70, 74
4:18–20	74
4:19	74, 78
4:20–21	78
4:21	80
5	67
5:7	66, 67, 73, 76, 81
5:7–9	80
5:12	75
5:24	75, 76
5:24–27	67
5:25	66, 70, 74
5:28	66, 67, 73, 75, 76, 79, 81
5:28–31	67
13:3	69
17	92n40
19–20	94–95n56, 94n53
20:16	94

Ruth
3:11	68n10
4:16	91

1 Samuel
28:7	68n10

2 Samuel
4	69
4:4	91
11	68n11
13:18–19	20

2 Kings
2:11	130
4:8–37	69
9	15
9–10	169
10:1	91n35
10:5	91n35
11	69

1 Chronicles
11:2	94

Esther
2:11	93
2:14	95
2:22	93
3:2	93
3:3	83n1, 97
5:1	95
6	95

Index of Scripture and Other Ancient Sources

Esther (*continued*)
10:3	83, 96

Psalms
111:9	69

Isaiah
6:1–9	171n21
49:23	91
56	105
56:3–5	16
64:1	183n77

Jeremiah
1:5–11	171n21

Ezekiel
1	171n21, 181
1:1	183n77
16:49	95n56

Daniel
12:3	181

NEW TESTAMENT

Matthew
3:16	183n77
5:38–44a	113
10:14	111
15:21–28	15
17:2	118, 118n1
19	16, 27, 105, 165
19:1–9	161
19:1–15	161, 162, 165
19:12	25, 160, 160nn30–31, 161, 162, 166
22:30	168

Mark
1:10	183n77
9:1–9	27, 117–18, 127–32
9:2	11, 117, 118
9:7	131, 132
9:8	132
10:45	128

Luke
3:21	183n77
9:29	118
9:51–56	100–101
9:54–55	101
10	111
20:27–28	168

John
1:1	11, 138
1:1–5	212
1:3	145
1:5	212
1:11	146
1:14	11, 137, 138, 144–45, 145, 145n46, 212, 213
1:15	11
1:27	145
1:29	138, 140, 145
1:36	138, 140, 145
1:51	140
3:3	214
3:5–6	212
3:13–14	140
3:16	212
3:19–21	213
4:9	213
4:11	213
4:14	212
4:15	213
5:16–18	140
5:27	140
6:27	140
6:35	140
6:38	213
6:53	140
6:62	140
6:63	212
7:30	140
7:32	140
7:33	213
7:45–49	140
8:12	140
8:28	140
8:59	140
9:5	213
9:35	140
10:1–5	140
10:9	140
10:10	135, 146, 146n50
10:11	140
10:17–37	140
10:31	140
10:39	140
11:25	140
11:45–57	140
12:23	140
12:34	140
12:35	213
13:31	140
14:6	140
14:28	213
15:5	140
15:15	146
15:21	147
16:5	213
16:16	213
16:21–22	16
18:1–5	140
19:1–5	140
19:7	140
19:12	140
19:15–16	140
19:17–37	140
20:1–31	140
20:31	206, 212

Acts
8	16, 105
9:15–17	171n21
22:14–16	171n21
26:16–17	171n21

Romans
1:26	233
5:3–11	179n59
5:12–17	18
6:1–10	173
6:3–5	210
6:4	182n72
7:4–6	209
7:6	179n59
7:14	209
7:18	209
7:22–23	209
8:5–6	210
8:9–10	210
8:10–11	179n59
8:18–25	180
8:29	182
9:23	182n72
10:9	206
12	172
12:2	11, 118, 171, 173, 175n38
13:1–7	173
13:14	180
16:4	201
16:7	201

1 Corinthians
1:1–10	171
2:2	210

2:6–3:5	180	4:17	182	4:11–12	193
2:8	182, 182n72	5:14	179n59	4:11–13	200
2:12–14	209	**Galatians**		4:17–19	200
3:1–2	185	1:16	192	4:19	182n72
3:1–3	209	2:19–20	179n59	4:21	200
3:18	182	2:19–20a	210	4:22	200
4:6	175n38	2:19–21	173	4:22–30	199
5:1–7	119	3:26–28	16	**Colossians**	
6–7	25, 27, 162, 165, 166	3:27–28	179n59	1:15	182
6:9–16	164	3:28	210	1:27	182n72
6:9–7:40	163, 164	4	173, 200	2:12–15	179n59
6:13	163	4:13–14	192	3:9	182
6:14	164n41	4:19	172, 185, 190, 192, 199	**1 Thessalonians**	
6:19–20	163	4:22–5:1	191	2:7	185
7:1–9	211	4:23	192	5:2–4	178
7:2	164	4:29	192	**1 Timothy**	
7:2–5	119	4:30	191	1:11	182n72
7:7	164	5:12	192, 199	2–3	211
7:9	164	5:13	193, 199	**Philemon**	
7:17–20	119	5:16–17	192	1:1	193
7:22	164	5:16–25	192	1:9–10	193
7:23	163	5:19–21	192	1:10	192
7:26–31	211	5:24	192	1:11	192
7:32–35	164	6:17	214	1:12	192
7:35	164	**Ephesians**		1:13	192, 193
11:2–16	119	1:17–18	182n72	1:14	192
11:5–7	129, 129n61	5:25–6:9	211	1:16	192
11:7	182, 182n72	5:30	16	1:17	192
11:13	129, 129n61	**Philippians**		1:18	192
15	27, 168, 175, 178, 179, 183	1:7	193	1:18–20	192
15:31	173	1:12	200	1:19	192
15:35–38	178	1:13–17	193	1:19–21	200
15:35–57	173	1:18	200	1:20	192
15:37–38	181	1:22–24	192, 193	1:23	193, 200
15:39	175	1:24–25	200	1:24	201
15:40–52	211	2:6	182	**Hebrews**	
15:42–49	178, 180	2:25	192	1:3	182n72
15:49	182	2:27	192, 201	**James**	
15:50	175, 208	2:28	192	2:1	182n72
15:51–52	175	2:28–29	192	**Revelation**	
15:54–55	174	2:30	192, 193, 201	4:1	183n77
2 Corinthians		3	173, 178		
3	129	3:2	192, 199	**PSEUDEPIGRAPHA**	
3:12–4:5	178	3:2–4	192	**2 Baruch**	
3:13–16	129n61	3:3	193, 199	51:10	181
3:18	118, 178, 179, 182	3:3–4	192, 193	**Jubilees**	
4:3	182	3:7–11	214	5:1–7	168n2
4:4	182, 182n72	3:10–11	172, 179n59		
4:6	182	3:21	174–75, 181, 182n72		
4:7–12	214				
4:7–14	179n59				

*Martyrdom and
Ascension of Isaiah*
3.13   120, 120n18

*Testament
of Abraham*   120
19:5   120n17

*Testament
of Solomon*   120
16:2   120n16
16:4   120n16

PHILO

On Abraham
135–137   95n56

On the Embassy to Gaius
95   119n6

On the Life of Moses
1.21   119n8
1.57   119, 119n6
2.291   119n10

*On the Origin
of the World*   214

*On the Sacrifices
of Cain and Abel*
9–10   119n9

On the Special Laws
4.147   119n6

RABBINIC LITERATURE

MISHNAH

Kiddushin   34

Kil'ayim
8:6   34n13

Nazir
2:7   38n24
5:7   38n24

TOSEFTA

Berakhot
6:3   45n48

Bikkurim   32, 33, 33n9,
              39, 40, 44, 45
2:3   35

Kil'ayim
1:9   44n45

Nazir
3:19   38n24

BABYLONIAN TALMUD

Berakhot
61a   44n46

Eruvin
18a   44nn45–46
45a   130, 130n65

Hullin
79b–80a   33n11
127a   44n45

Keritot
21a   33n11

Ketubbot
8a   44n46

Mo'ed Qatan
26a   130n65

Yevamot
64a–64b   89n21

OTHER RABBINIC WORKS

Genesis Rabbah
8   44n46
21:5   130n65
30:8   92n36

Leviticus Rabbah
14   44n46

Mishneh Torah
2.10   33n11

Pesiqta of Rab Kahana
9:76a   130n65

Seder Olam
2   130n65
17   130n65

Zohar
2:197a   130n65

NEW TESTAMENT APOCRYPHA

Acts of John
53–54   161n32

*Acts of Paul
and Thecla*   211

*Apocryphon
of John*   44n47

Gospel of Thomas
1   208
2   206
3   205, 207, 215
11   205
16   206
18   205
22   207, 217
23   207
24   212
24b   207
28   212, 213
29   206
38   213
49   205, 206, 207, 213
50   205, 207, 213
55   206
56   206
61   213
61b   205
77   205, 212, 213
79   206
80   206
85   205, 206, 211
87   206
99   206
101   206
106   205
111   205
114   205, 207, 217, 231

APOSTOLIC FATHERS

DIOGNETUS

Epistle
2:3   120, 120n14

PATRISTIC LITERATURE

AMBROSE

Letter 69   162n36

ATHENAGORAS

Legatio Pro Christians
33.24   161n32

BASIL OF ANCYRA

On Virginity
61–62   161n32

Index of Scripture and Other Ancient Sources 265

BASIL OF CAESAREA
Epistle
210.5   119n12

CLEMENT OF ALEXANDRIA
Exhortation to the Greeks
1   120, 120n15
Paedagogus
2.9   220, 233
Stromata
2.18   233–34

EUSEBIUS
Ecclesiastical History
6   161n32

JOHN CHRYSOSTOM
Commentary Chapter 5 Epistle to the Galatians
3.717   161n32

JUSTIN MARTYR
Apology
29.1–2   161n32

ORIGEN
Against Celsus
4.16   119n10
6.76   119n11
Commentarium in evangelium Matthaei
12   119n11
15.3   161n32
Dialogue with Heraclides
13.19–20   167n1

TATIAN
Oratio ad Graecos
10   119n13

TERTULLIAN
Apologeticus
21.20   225n25
25.7   225n25
31.2   225n25
50.14   225n25
De corona militis
1.5   231
De pallio   28, 220–25, 229, 231–36

2.1   232
3.6   232n50
4.1   232n50
4.2   228
4.3   229, 229n37
4.4   229, 229n39
4.8   232
5.6   230n39
5.7   230n39
265   228n36
De spectaculis
23   220n5, 233

THEOPHILUS OF ANTIOCH
To Autolycus
2.6   119n12

GRECO-ROMAN LITERATURE

ANTONINUS LIBERALIS
Metamorphoses   124, 124n35

APOLLODORUS
Fragmenta Historica
2.1.3   120n20
2.4.1   120n20
3.13.3   120n21
3.8.2   120n20

APULEIUS
Metamorphoses   235

ATHMAEUS
Deipnosophistae
8.334c=8.10   120n22

CASSIUS DIO
69.18.3   221n10

CICERO
Orationes philippicae
2.44   231

COLUMELLA
De re rustica   163
1.8.5   164
11.1.14   164

EPICTETUS
Enchiridion
27   232

EPIPHANIUS
De Fide
13.5   161n32

GAIUS JULIUS HYGINIUS
Fabulae   125, 125n38, 126n47

HIPPOCRATES
Epidemics
6   126n47
6.8.32   126, 126n47
7   126n47

HOMER
Odyssey   122–23
13.221–224   123n27
13.312–314   127n53
Homeric Hymn II
92–97   127n53
101–102   127n53
Homeric Hymn V
84–87   127n53
275–281   128n57

OVID
Metamorphoses   123–24
2.405–531   123n28
2.441–495   123n29
4.285–395   125n44
9.666–797   123n31
9.782–784   124n32
9.790–791   124n33
9.797   124n33

PLINY
Epistulae   230n43

PLUTARCH
Moralia
2.52B   120n19
Parallel Lives
22   120, 120n19

SCRIPTORES HISTORIAE AUGUSTAE
Hadrian
22.4   222n11

SENECA
Controversia
pr. 8–9   230n39

Seneca (*continued*)

Epistle
66.41   232

Statius

Achilleid
225–27
301–304   227n30
355–356   227
396   227n29
534–535   227
605   226n28
638–639   227n31
657–660   227n31

Virgil

Aeneid
1.296   221

Index of Subjects

abolition, 187–89, 200
Abraham (patriarch), 18, 83, 191
Achilleid (Statius), 224–27
Achilles, 225–28, 234–36
activism, 114–15, 129, 141, 187–88, 195–97
Adam, 206–7, 211
ADF (Alliance Defending Freedom). *See* Alliance Defending Freedom (ADF)
African Christology, 144
agency, in motherhood, 74–75
agenderism, 49. *See also* intersex; nonbinary gender
Ahmed, Sara, 170–71
Aizura, Aren Z., 8, 157
Alliance Defending Freedom (ADF), 41
allyship, 136, 144, 147–50, 195–97
Althaus-Reid, Marcella, 146
aman (to nurse), 91, 91n35, 92
Ambrose of Milan (saint), 162, 165
ancestors. *See* trancestors
ancient bodies, 6–7. *See also* gender transformations, ancient
androcentrism, 152, 162–63, 182–83
androginos (man and woman), 33
androgyne list
  coda of, 39–40
  functions in, 33, 33n9, 35–39
androgynes
  about, 125
  creation accounts and, 15
  functions of, in gender law, 35–39
  God and, 16
  as unique but unassimilable, 39–40
  See also eunuchs
angelic maleness, 168, 168n2
angelic transformations, 119, 130, 130n66

animality, 33–35
animals, hybrid, 33–35
Animals and Animality in the Babylonian Talmud (Berkowitz), 34
anti-trans legislation. *See* legislation
Aphrodite/Aphroditos, 125–26, 125n43
apostles, 191–94, 199
archaeology, transgender, 85, 85n6, 126
assembly communities, 198
assignments of gender, at birth. *See* birth assignments
Athena, 122–23, 128
Atmospheres of Violence (Stanley), 10
Attica prison rebellion, 187
aylonit, 19, 89

Bach, Alice, 69–70
Bailey, Randall, 93–94
Bal, Mieke, 79
Bantu theology, 144
baptism, 7, 16, 179, 210
baptism of Jesus, 128, 128n55, 132
barrenness, 69, 69n14. *See also* childlessness
bathrooms, policing of. *See* restroom regulations
Beal, Timothy, 92–94
Beardsley, Christina, 17–18
being/becoming, 138–39, 139n18, 144–46
Benjamin, Don, 70
Benjamin, tribe of, 94, 94n53, 94n56
Berkowitz, Beth, 34
Bey, Marquis, 10–11, 143, 149
Beyond Feminist Biblical Studies (Guest), 20
Bible, study of. *See* hermeneutics
biblical figures
  cisgender assumptions of, 50

bible figures (*continued*)
  gender identification of, 51–52, 52n7, 53
  in Good Samaritan parable (*See* Good Samaritan parable)
  identity-defining roles, 56
  nonbinary, scholarship on, 86–91
  struggles of, against gendered categories, 53–54
  trans future and, 97
biblically based resources, 17–18
bills, legislative. *See* legislation
binaries, Paul's use of, 180–81
binary categories, 48–49
binary gender, 39–40
biological sex, for legal definition, 42–43
biopolitics, 142
birth assignments, 42–43, 48, 53–54, 54n13, 55, 57–58
birth names. *See* deadnaming
Black Lives Matter movement, 10–11
Black on Both Sides: A Racial History of Trans Identity (Snorton), 5, 189
Black people
  communal care for, 136, 138, 148
  dignity for, 149
  femininity of vs. white femininity, 236
  feminist hermeneutics and, 23, 37–38, 43, 198
  joy and, 137
  objectification of, 189–90
  passing of, 59
  transitivity of, 189
  trans studies overlapped with, 5–6
  See also Black trans women; racism
Black trans women
  criminalization and imprisonment of, 188, 200
  erasure of, 43
  media representation of, 141
  restroom regulations and, 41, 41n36
  violence/murder of, 41, 102, 140–44, 197, 199–200, 216
  See also Black people
Bledstein, Adrien Janis, 78
bodies
  materiality of, 206 (*See also* bodily renewals, Gospel of Thomas and)
  replacements of, 207
  soulish vs. spiritual, 180–81
  as ungendered, 204
  worth of, 203, 214–16

bodily renewals, Gospel of Thomas and
  about, 203–4
  vs. Gospel of John, 212–14
  Gospel of Thomas, about, 207–8
  vs. Hellenistic Jewish literature, 213–15
  Jesus and, 216–18
  vs. Paul on, 209–12
  salvation and, as introspective process, 205–8
  vs. synoptic Gospels, 212
  trans liberation and, 204–5, 215–17
bodily transformations
  baptism and, 210
  biblical, 118–19
  in Hellenistic literature, 119–20
  of Jesus in Transfiguration, 118 (*See also* Transfiguration of Jesus)
  Jesus on, 217
  lights/shining at, 128, 130
  medical care for, 45, 155, 155n11
  to spiritual, 207, 211–12, 213–14
  See also bodily renewals, Gospel of Thomas and
Bornstein, Kate, 4, 12, 20
Brennan, Corey, 228, 231
Brown, Michael Joseph, 23–24, 150
Butler, Judith, 65, 139, 159, 213
"By the Hand of a Woman" (Yee), 87

call, gender as a, 171
Callahan, Allen Dwight, 144
Callisto (*Metamorphoses* character), 123
Canaanite mother, 106
Canaanite woman, 14–15
captive gender/flesh. *See* imprisonment
Captive Genders (Stanley), 10
captivity, 189. *See also* enslavement/enslaved persons; imprisonment
care, communal, 136–37, 148–50. *See also* allyship
care for others, as feminine role, 69, 72
categorization
  ancient transition between, 162
  animality and hybridity, 33–38
  gender as, 222–23
  human, 22–23, 38, 43 (*See also* androgyne list)
  nonbinary rabbinic, 32–33
  trans as analytical, 159–60
  transsexual/transgender, 154–58, 154n9
celebrities, trans, 101, 189

Index of Subjects

celibacy, 27, 160, 160n30, 211
chevruta study, 63, 63n20
childbearing, 206, 210–11
childlessness, 69, 69n14, 72, 83
children
   desire for, 68–69
   of Living Father, 205, 207
   as presexual, 161
   rearing, 206, 210–11
   trans, erasure of, 45
   See also motherhood/mothers
Christianity/Christians
   clothing of ancient, 224
   discrimination/transphobia by, 31, 31n2, 41–44, 103–4, 109–10, 149
   evangelical, 2, 31, 31n2, 41–45, 41n34, 42n39
   femaleness in early, 162–63, 166
   nonbinary obstacles in, 97
   resources from, 17–18
   sexual ethics of, 163
   Tertullian on, 231–32
   trans experience in, 102–3, 102n9
   violence and, 146–47
Christology, African, 144
chrononormativity, 176, 179
cisgender, language limitations and, 121–22
Clement of Alexandria, 120, 220, 233
Cleomachus (boxer), 229–30
clothing
   of Achilles, 225–26
   ancient Roman importance of, 221–22
   changing, 224–28, 229, 231–34
   of Cleomachus, 229–30
   enforcement of, Roman, 221, 224, 231, 232–36
   God's will and, 227–32
   of Hercules, 229
   identity and, 227–28
   inner nature and, 228–29, 228n35, 234
   of Jesus, Transfiguration and, 118, 128, 133
   Joseph's coat of many colors, 20, 52n6, 89
   pallium, 221, 223–24
   purpose of, Clement on, 233
   Transfiguration of Jesus and, 133
   transformation and, 133, 133n75
   transgender studies and, 222–23
   veils, 118, 129

coat of many colors, Joseph's, 20, 52n6, 89
colonial language, 145
colonization, of modern categories, 152, 152n4
Columella (writer), 163–64
coming out, 173n34
communities of care, 148–50. *See also* allyship
Concannon, Cavan, 180
concutio (shake violently), 225–26
conformity, Paul on, 172
conversion therapy, 171
Copeland, M. Shawn, 144
Corinthian women prophets, 167, 179, 182, 182n73
corporeal transformations. *See* bodily transformations
covenants, veils and, 118
Cox, Laverne, 43
creation accounts
   feminist readings of, 15
   first human as androgyne, 16, 18, 44
   human enfleshment in, 214
   queer readings of, 15–16
   rabbinic versions, 44n46
   transphobia and, 41
criminalization, of trans population, 187–90. *See also* imprisonment
cross-dressing, 189, 225–29. *See also* clothing
culture, trans choices and, 157–58, 157n25
cultus (culture and clothing), 229
Currah, Paisley, 8
curvy time, 175–80

danger, 137, 140, 143. *See also* murder; violence
Darwin, Helana, 96–97
deadnaming, 131, 138–39, 138n16, 145, 174
death
   fear of, 148
   proximity to, of apostles, 192
   proximity to, of inmates, 198
   proximity to, of trans people, 186–87
   salvation and, 209–10
   symbolic, 173–74, 178
   systematic, 141–42, 145–46, 150, 173n34
   See also murder

Deborah
  as active mother, 74–75
  childlessness of, 73
  Jael, comparisons to, 70–72
  as liminal figure, 87
  masculine motherhood of, 66–67, 76
  as mother of Israel, 67, 73, 76, 79–81
  warfare and, 79
DeConick, April, 168
deity. *See* God
Demeter, 128
De Pallio. (Tertullian), about, 221–22. *See also* clothing
DeVun, Leah, 13, 19, 97, 169, 177–78, 235
Diamond, Ashley, 196
Diodorus Siculus, 120
discrimination
  imprisonment and (*See* imprisonment)
  of multi-marginalized people, 142, 216 (*See also* Black trans women)
  from religious communities, 31, 31n2, 41–44, 103–4, 109–10, 149
  society's vs. God's desire for neighborliness, 108–10
  systemic, 101–2, 142, 186–87 (*See also* legislation)
  See also transphobia
disease model, of transsexuality, 156–57
divorce, 161–62, 161n34, 165
doctors, 154. *See also* medical care
domestication, 40, 44–45
domesticity, 70, 75–77
dominion of God, 108–10, 112, 115
"don't exist" mandate, 43–44, 43n44, 45
Dowd, Chris, 17–18
Dunning, Benjamin, 163, 166
dwellings, Jesus in, 146–47

Early Christian Dress: Gender, Virtue, and Authority (Upson-Saia), 220
effeminacy, 230, 233–34. *See also* femaleness
egeneto (to come into existence), 145, 145n44
Elijah, 118, 128, 130, 133
emotional concern, of motherhood, 77–79
enemies, 112–13
Enke, Finn, 121–22, 153
Enoch, 130n66
enslavement/enslaved persons
  apostles, 191–94, 199 (*See also* under Paul: as prisoner)
  flight of, 189–91, 193–94, 199, 201–2
  Hagar, 191–93
  objectification of, 34, 189–94, 201
  sexuality of, 163–64
Epaphroditus (enslaved apostle), 192–94, 199–202
Epictetus, 232
erasure
  of biblical figures, gender diverse, 50–51
  of children, trans, 45
  in Mississippi law, 43–44
  trans, by Christians (*See* under Christianity/Christians: discrimination/transphobia by)
  trans/cis binary and, 49
erotophobia, 143, 149
erchomai (to come, go, or pass), 145, 145n45
Esau, 20, 56
eschatology, 211–12. *See also* salvation
Espinoza, Roberto Che, 139, 145
Esther, 91–96
eternal life, 212
ethics, sexual, 163
Eucharist, 210
eunuchs
  as biblical gender diversity, 105–6
  importance of, 16
  Jezebel's death by, 15
  Mordecai and, 93
  as non-men, 160–61
  rabbinic approaches to, 18–19, 22–23
  transness of, 162, 165
evangelical Christianity. *See under* Christianity/Christians: evangelical
excessiveness, Roman, 230
exile logic of imprisonment, 195
experience
  centered approach, trans (*See* trans-experience-centered approach, of trans hermeneutics)
  trans, 22, 59–60, 104
  trans vs. transgender-specific, 48, 55, 58–60

faces, during metamorphosis, 118
faith, transitioning and, 137. *See also* Christianity/Christians
family life, 206, 210–11

fascism, 5
fatherhood, ancient expectations of, 66
fear, warfare and, 79–80
feeding others, as feminine role, 69–70
Feinberg, Leslie, 4, 12, 16, 21
femaleness, 162–63, 166, 229–30, 233–34
femininity, motherhood expectations of
  domestic space and, 70, 75–77
  emotional concern, 69, 72, 77–79
  nourishment, providing, 69–70
  passivity, 74–75, 79–81
  women as wives/mothers, 68–69
feminism, 13, 155, 156n18, 157, 198, 198n52
feminist hermeneutics
  Black, 23, 37–38, 43, 198
  of creation accounts, 15
  masculinity and, 20
Fewell, Danna, 77, 80
figure of the trans person, 153
first-born status, 53–54, 54n13
flesh
  captive, 189
  freedom and, 193–94
  Paul's use of, 175, 180–81, 192–93, 209
  transition to from Word, 11, 143–46
  See also bodies; bodily renewals, Gospel of Thomas and; bodily transformations
Fox, Arminta, 198, 201
"From Gender Reversal to Genderfuck: Reading Jael through a Lesbian Lens" (Guests), 20, 87
Frymer-Kensky, Tikva, 68
Fuchs, Esther, 68
fugitivity, 10–11, 189–91, 201–2

galli, 235
garments. *See* clothing
gender
  about term, 222–23
  affirming care (*See* medical care)
  ambiguity, of Jael, 65–66, 71–73, 77–78, 80
  of ancient Judaism, 19
  animality and, 33–35
  as assigned at birth, 42–43, 48, 53–55, 57–58
  biblical figures, assumptions of, 60–62
  boundaries, 234–35 (*See also* clothing)
  as a call, 171
  clothing and (*See* clothing)
  confirmation, 122, 133, 133n75
  critical movement, 235–36
  enforcement of, ancient Rome, 235–36 (*See also under* clothing: enforcement of, Roman)
  expansiveness, 86
  failure, 59
  fluidity of, over time, 86
  of God, 16, 85
  human creation as Fall, 206–7
  identification, of biblical figures, 51–53, 52n7, 53
  of Jesus (*See under* Jesus Christ: gender nonconformity of)
  laws, modern (*See* legislation)
  laws, rabbinic, 35–40
  roles (*See* femininity, motherhood expectations of; masculinity)
  sacred worth of, 106
  of spirits/souls, 205, 207
  transgression, 86
gender diversity
  ancient stories of (*See* gender transformations, ancient)
  in antiquity, 105–6 (*See also* trancestors)
  eunuchs as proof of biblical, 105–6 (*See also* eunuchs)
  trans/cis binary and, 48–50
gendered category resistance (Nichols/Stuart concept), 52–54, 53n9, 54
genderfluid. *See* nonbinary gender
gender identity
  biblical understanding of, 106
  as social construct, 157–58
"Gendering Sarai: Reading beyond Cisnormativity in Gen 11:29-12:20 and 20:1-18" (Henderson-Merrygold), 88
genderqueer, 65–66, 83–97, 129. *See also* nonbinary gender
gender transformations, ancient
  androgyne images of, 125–26
  in Greek medical literature, 126
  modern issues with, 121–22
  mythological stories of, 123–25
  in *Odyssey, The* (Homer), 122–23
genitalia
  alterations, 16, 45
  in gatekeeping tactics, 122
genre, trans as, 9

Gill-Peterson, Jules, 45
glorified bodies, 173
glorified resurrection vs. modern trans embodiments
    about, 167–70, 182
    binaries, Paul's use of, 180–81
    resurrected bodies and, 181–82
    social transitions and, 170–73
    symbolic death and, 173–74
    trans temporalities and (*See* temporalities)
glory, Paul on, 181–82
God
    clothing in accordance with, 228–32
    diversity as intended by, 106
    dominion of, 108–10, 112
    gender of, 16, 85
    image of, 16, 41, 179–80
    on Jesus as "Son," 131–32
    Moses's relationship with, 129, 129n60
    nature, living in and, 231–32
    presence of, with humans, 143–44
    relations to, male vs. female, 162–63, 166
    seeking, 109–10
Golden Rule. *See* neighborliness
Good Samaritan parable
    characters of that passed by, 113–14
    hospitality in, 112
    Jesus's message in, 100, 105, 110, 114
    Martin Luther King Jr. on, 113–14
    methodologies of reading, 105–8
    modern telling of, 99–100, 112–13
    as oppression liberation story, 103–5
    Samaritans, trans community as modern-day, 102–3
    as transcestor, 105–6, 108
    transgender woman of color reading of, 99–100, 108
Gospel of Thomas. *See* bodily renewals, Gospel of Thomas and
grace, 137, 140, 143–44, 148
Graybill, Rhiannon, 88, 129
Greatest Commandments, 100–101, 108–11, 114–15
Greek metamorphosis, 119–20
Griffin, Horace L., 146
Guest, Deryn, 19–22, 65, 68, 85, 87, 87n14, 88, 169
Gunn, David, 77, 80
Gutt, Blake, 13, 89–90, 97

Habeus Viscus (Weheliye), 37
habitus (clothing and inner nature), 228–29, 228n35, 229, 234
hafas (desires), 95
Hagar, 191–94, 199–200
halakhah (law), 35–40
Halberstam, Jack, 10, 20, 176–78
Haman, 92
Hartke, Austen, 17
Hayward, Eva, 43
Health and Human Services memo (2018), 31, 41, 42n40
heaven, 205–6, 209
Hebrew pronouns, 35n15, 39n26
Henderson-Merrygold, Jo, 19–20, 50–51, 88–89
Hercules, 229
hermaphrodites, 125–26
hermeneutics
    feminist, 15, 20, 23, 37–38, 43, 198
    lesbian, 19–21, 85, 89, 96–97
    queer, 14–16, 18–20, 22–23
    traditional interpretations, ignoring, 60–62
    trans, teaching (*See* teaching trans hermeneutics)
    trans-experience-centered approach (*See* trans-experience-centered approach, of trans hermeneutics)
    truths of as partial, 84–85
hero mindset, 195, 200
Heslin, Peter, 225–26
hetero suspicion, 19–21, 85
Heyes, Cressida J., 155–57
Heyward, Carter, 109
hierarchies, 221, 230–31, 234–36
historicism, 84
historiography, trans
    narratives, problems and, 151–54
    non-men and, 160–66
    trans as analytic category, 159–60
    transsexual and transgender narratives in, 154–58
home, adaptability of, 146
hope, 170
Hornsby, Teresa, 21
hospitality, 111–12
How Sex Changed (Meyerowitz), 154
human rights, androgyne list and, 37–38
Hunink, Vincent, 223, 226
husbands, women without, 72–73

Index of Subjects

hybrid list, 33–35, 33n9, 37–40, 39n25, 40n31
hysterēma (feminized lack), 192, 202

"I AM" statements, 139–40, 139n18, 159n27
identity-defining roles, slippage between birth assignments and, 48, 54–58
image of God, 16, 41, 179–80
imprisonment
  about, 186
  alongside Paul, 198, 200–202
  letter-writing and, 195–97
  of Paul, 193–94, 198, 198n52, 199–201
  resistance to, 187–88
  See also Miss Major Griffin-Gracy
inclusion, violence increased with, 186–87
Indecent Christology (Althaus-Reid), 146
injury laws, androgyne list and, 36–37
injustice, naming, 114–15. *See also* justice, trans hermeneutics and
inmates. *See* imprisonment
Institute for Sexual Science, 5
intelligibility, 25, 27, 153, 158–60, 162
intersex
  erasure of, through trans/cis binary, 48–49
  medical care and, 5, 45
  in Medieval literature, 234–35
  as preferred term, 125–26
  Sarah/Sarai as, 89
  studies, 43n44
Iphis (in *Metamorphoses*), 123–24, 128
Isaac, 56
Israel, mother to the children of. *See* motherhood/mothers
Is the Homosexual My Neighbor: A Positive Christian Response (Mollenkott; Scanzoni), 103

Jacob, 53–54, 56, 58, 61
Jacob's Wound (Jennings), 89
Jael (killer of Sisera)
  about, 20–21
  agency of, 74–75
  comparisons with Deborah and Sisera's mother, 70–72, 76, 79
  domestic space of, 76
  emotional concern of, 77–79
  as false mother to Sisera, 66, 81

  gender ambiguity of, 65–66, 71–73, 77–78, 80, 87–88
  as liminal figure, 87
  as mother of Israel, 72–78, 80–81
  violence by, 79–81
"Jael Is Non-binary; Jael Is Not a Woman" (Musa), 88
Jennings, Theodore, 89
Jesus Christ
  Adam and, 211–12
  allyship, as example of, 148
  Canaanite woman and, 14–15
  on flesh vs. spirits, 206
  on gender, 217–18
  gender nonconformity of, 11, 22, 24, 127–33, 135–36, 138–40, 146–47, 205n8, 217–18 (*See also* Jesus Christ, scriptural transformations of)
  glory of, 181–82
  Good Samaritan parable and (*See* Good Samaritan parable)
  in Gospel of John, 213–14
  in Gospel of Thomas, 206–8, 212, 213–15
  on hospitality, 111
  multiple forms of, 130
  on neighborliness (*See* Good Samaritan parable)
  relations to, male vs. female, 162–63, 166
  resurrection of, 128, 128n55, 132–33, 148, 210
  on self-understanding process, 214–15
  as Son of God, 131
  as transcestor, 144, 148
  Transfiguration of (*See* Transfiguration of Jesus)
  transformation by, 175
  transness of (*See under this entry:* gender nonconformance of)
  See also Jesus Christ, scriptural transformations of
Jesus Christ, scriptural transformations of
  about, 135–36, 136n7
  becoming vs. passing, 145–46
  deadnaming and, 138, 145
  implications of, 143–44
  in John vs. Synoptic Gospels, 147
  Transfiguration of (*See* Transfiguration of Jesus)
  See also Jesus Christ

Jewish traditions
  chevruta study, 63, 63n20
  on eunuchs and androgynes, 18–19
  on first human as androgyne, 39–40, 44, 44n46
  gender variation in, 18–19
  on hybridity, 33–35
  law, 35–40
  vs. modern thought, 44–45
  pshat, 60–62, 60n16, 61n18
  trans studies of vs. Christian, 26
Jezebel (wife of Ahab), 15
John, Gospel of
  vs. Gospel of Thomas, 212–14
  prologue, identity of Jesus and, 135–36
Johnson, Marsha P., 4–5, 10, 188
John the Baptist, 138, 145–46
Jonah (prophet), 106
Joseph (son of Jacob), 17, 20, 52n6, 56, 89
joy, 136–38
Judaism, transphobia in, 39
Judith, 72–73
justice, trans hermeneutics and, 103–5, 109, 114–15

Kimḥi, David (Radak), 83
King, Martin Luther Jr., 113–14, 197
kingdom of God, 108, 175, 205, 208, 213. *See also* salvation
Klinken, Adriaan van, 149
Kłosowska, Anna, 12–13
Kolakowski, Victoria, 15, 21
Koosed, Jennifer L., 129
koy, 33–35, 33nn10–11. *See also* hybrid list
Kukla, Elliot, 18–19

Ladin, Joy, 22, 106, 171
LaFleur, Greta, 12–13
lamb of God, Jesus as, 139, 145
language
  colonial impositions of, 145
  LGBTQ, 59
  Paul's for transformation, 169
  trans, 59, 121–22
  in the Word became flesh, 144–46
Latinx people, 188, 200
Lau, Jacob, 189
law
  modern (*See* legislation)
  rabbinic, 35–40

Lee, Dorothy, 128
left-handedness, 94
legislation
  2018 Health and Human Services memo, 31, 41, 42n40
  bathroom laws, 24, 31n2, 41, 41n36, 123
  Christianity and, 31, 31n2, 41–45, 110, 110n23
  genitalia obsession and, 122
  prevalence of, 101–2
  Religious Liberty Accommodations Act (MS), 41–45
lesbian hermeneutics, 19–21, 85, 89, 96–97
letter-writing, imprisonment and, 11, 192–93, 195–97
Lev, Sarra, 18
liberation, trans, 103–5, 107, 116, 143, 187–89, 204–5, 215–17
Liew, Tat-siong Benny, 24
life, abundant, 146, 149
Light, 205–7, 213
lights/shining, at corporeal transformations, 128, 130
liminal biblical figures, 87
logos, 146
Lorde, Audre, 138, 216
love, neighborly, 100–101, 108–11, 115
Ludlul Bel Nemeqi, 95

Maduro, Otto, 107–8
magazines, trans representation in, 141. *See also* media, trans representation in
Malatino, Hil, 14, 222
male, angels as, 168, 168n2
male privilege, 161–62n35
Marchal, Joseph A., 210
Marduk (Babylonian deity), 95–96, 95n57
marriage
  divorce and, 161–62, 161n34, 165
  as heterosexual and monogamous, 42
  marry vs. be married, 35–36
  Paul and Gospel of Thomas on, 206, 210–11
  salvation and, 164
Mary Magdalene, 148
masculinity
  Christian, 231
  control and, 78
  divorce as male privilege and, 161–62, 161n34

female, 20
gender failure and, 59
invisible standards of, 121–22
motherhood and, 66, 71, 74–75
natura and, 232
non-men, 160–62, 161n35, 165, 199
Roman conceptions of, 223–28, 228n35, 230–31, 233
violence and, 79
materiality. *See* bodily renewals, Gospel of Thomas and
matriarchs, 70, 76
Matthews, Shelly, 182
Matthews, Victor, 70
McDonald, CeCe, 11, 141, 187, 197–200
McNeill, John, 111–12
media, trans representation in, 141, 154, 186, 188–89
medical care
 access to, 216
 early, 5
 as erasure, 45, 110
 gender-affirming care, 155, 155n11
 Gospel of Thomas reading and, 217
 legislation and, 43, 101
medical professionals, 154
Memoirs of a Chain Gang Sissy (Diamond), 196
men
 androgynes functioning as, 35–36
 androgynes functioning as and women, 36–38
 androgynes functioning as neither men nor women, 38–39
 non-men, 160–62, 161n35, 165, 199
 power of, in antiquity, 161–65
 See also masculinity
mercy, Good Samaritan parable and, 101, 104, 109–10, 114–16
metamorphoō/metamorphosis, 118–21, 119n6, 129. *See also* gender transformations, ancient
Metamorphoses (Antonius Liberalis), 124
Metamorphoses (Ovid), 123–24
Meyerowitz, Joanne, 154, 158
Miller, Geoffrey, 94
mind, 209–10, 214
misgendering, 172
Miss Major Griffin-Gracy, 187, 196–97, 199–200
Mollenkott, Virginia, 16–17, 21, 102–5

monogamy, 164
monsterization, 231, 235–36
monstrosity, 7–9
Moore, Indya, 141
morality, clothing and, 224–25, 229–30, 233, 234–35
Mordecai
 character traits of, 96
 eunuchs and, 93
 as guardian of Esther, 91–92, 96–97
 Haman and, 92–93, 97
 queen language and, 95
 Saul and, 91–97
Morland, Iain, 45
morphosis, Paul's use of, 172, 175, 180
Moses, 88, 118–19, 128–29, 129n60, 133
Moss, Candida R., 128, 132
motherhood/mothers
 agency vs. passivity of, 74–75
 biblical and modern, connection between, 106
 biblical expectations of, 67–70
 child-rearing without, 92
 domestic spaces and, 75–77
 emotional concern and, 77–79
 framework of, for Jael narrative, 70–72
 gendered expectations of, 66–70
 Hagar and Sarah, 191 (*See also* Hagar; Sarah/Sarai)
 of Israel, 72–75
 Jael's toward Sisera as false, 66, 81
 Paul as, 16, 185, 190–92
 violence and, 79–81
murder, 36–37, 72, 79–81, 140–43, 173–74
Musa, Aysha Winstanley, 20–21, 88
mythological stories of gender transformations, 123–25

Nadar, Sarojini, 149
Nag Hammadi Codex II, 208
name changes, biblical, 17
names. *See* deadnaming
Namusias (ancient medical patient), 126
narratives
 about, 151–54
 erasure of, 153 (*See also* erasure)
 as intelligible, 25, 153, 154n10, 155, 157–60
natura/natural order, gender and, 225–26, 229, 231–34, 232n50, 236

necropolitics, 141–42, 145–46, 150, 173n34
neighborliness, 100–101, 108–11, 115
Ngũgĩ wa Thiong'o, 145
Nichols, Jane, 51–56, 61, 169
nonbinary gender
　about concept of, 84–86
　erasure, of population of, 49, 97
　Jael as, 65–66, 71–73, 77–78, 80
　as modern label, 90
　Moses as, 129
　obstacles of, religious, 97
　scholarship on biblical, 86–91 (*See also* biblical figures)
nonconforming, gender. *See* nonbinary gender
non-men, 160–62, 161n35, 165, 199. *See also* eunuchs
nourishment, as feminine role, 69–70
nursing, Mordecai and, 91–92

Odyssey, The (Homer), 122–23
offspring, of Living Father, 205
Omphale, 229
Onesimus (enslaved apostle), 191–94, 199–200
ontology, of gender in rabbinic law, 39–40
oppression, liberation from, 103–5
Our Passion for Justice (Heyward), 109
Out in Scripture (Bible study), 17

Page, Morgan M., 188
pallium (cloak), 221–24, 231. *See also* clothing
parables
　Good Samaritan (*See* Good Samaritan parable)
　in Gospel of Thomas, 207, 217
　Jesus's intention of, 108–9
parenthood, vs. motherhood, 66–67
Park, Suzie, 94
passing, come to, 144–46
passing, for preferred gender, 59
passivity, of motherhood, 74–75
past, usable, 152
Paul
　on bodily renewal, vs. Gospel of Thomas, 209–12
　conversion of, 171
　on family life, 210–11
　letter writing and, 11, 185–86, 192–93, 197–98, 201
　metamorphosis, use of, 118–19
　mother imagery of, 16, 185, 190–92
　as prisoner, 193–94, 198, 198n52, 199–201
　resocialization of, 172
　sexual ethics of, 163
　transformation language and, 169
　transness of, 190–91 (*See also under this entry:* mother imagery of)
penetration, male, 229–30
pen pal programs, 195–97
people of color. *See* Black people; Black trans women; Latinx people
Peter, 130, 217
Phaethousa (ancient medical patient), 126
Philo of Alexandria, 6, 119, 119n6, 213–14
Piepzna-Samarasinha, Leah Lakshmi, 148
Plato, 213–14
Plutarch, 120
politics, necro, 141–42, 145–46, 150, 173n34
polymorphism, 130
present, usable, 152–53, 158, 160
presentism, 84
prison, letter writing and, 11, 192–93, 195–97
procreation, 164
pronouns, 35n15, 39n26, 90, 92
property, of rabbinic householder, 34
Pseudo-Apollodorus, 120
pshat, 60–62, 60n16, 61n18, 62n19
Puar, Jasbir, 142
public facilities. *See* restroom regulations
Pumphrey, Nicholaus, 89
"putting on" Christ, 7

Queer Bible Commentary, The, 108
queer hermeneutics, 14–16, 18–20, 22–23
queer hospitality, 111–12
Queer Necropolitics (Haritaworn, Kuntsman, Posocco), 142
queer theory, figure of the trans person and, 153
queer time, 137–38, 137n13, 175–80

rabbinic traditions, 18–19, 22, 25, 32–40, 44, 96

racism, 5–6, 38, 43, 138, 186–87. *See also* Black people; Black trans women
Radak (David Kimḥi), 83
rape, 123, 144, 144n39
Raskolnikov, Masha, 12–13
Rebekah, 56
rebellion, gendered, 52–54, 53n9, 56
reclamation, lesbian hermeneutic principle of, 85, 96
reengagement, lesbian hermeneutic principle of, 85, 96–97
Reis, Elizabeth, 151–53
relationships, changed after transitioning, 172
religion, 13, 41–45, 102–3, 102n9, 137. *See also* Christianity/Christians; Jewish traditions
Religious Liberty Accommodations Act (MS), 41–45
renunciation, sexual, 160–66. *See also* celibacy
repro-time, 176, 179
resistance
  gendered categories, 52–54, 53n9, 56
  lesbian hermeneutic principle of, 85
  parable readings and, 108–9
  principle of, lesbian hermeneutics, 19–21
resonance/dissonance hermeneutics. *See* glorified resurrection vs. modern trans embodiments
resource offerings, 17–18, 140, 195–96
restroom regulations, 24, 31n2, 41, 41n36, 123
resurrection, bodily, 169, 173–74, 179, 181–82, 211–12
Rivera, Sylvia, 4–5, 10, 188, 196–97, 200
River Jordan, 10
Romanitas (Roman cultural practices), 221, 223–24
rupture, lesbian hermeneutic principle of, 85, 89

Sabia-Tanis, Justin, 14, 16–18, 21, 137, 171
salvation, 164, 204–8, 209–12, 218
Samaritans, 100–103, 108. *See also* Good Samaritan parable
Sarah/Sarai
  as gender ambiguous, 88–89
  gender assumptions and, 20
  Hagar and, 191, 200
  trans hermeneutic reading of, 61n18

as trans matriarch, 50, 50n3, 51
as *tumtum*, 18
saris, 19
Saul, 94
Schneider, Laurel C., 205
schools, discrimination and violence in, 102
science/medicine, law and, 43
seclusion, laws of, 36
secrecy, 131, 134
secured housing units (SHU). *See* SHU (secured housing units)
Segal, Alan, 170–71, 179
self-identification, biblical figures and, 51–52, 52n7
Self-Transformations (Heyes), 155–56
self-understanding, process of, 206, 214–15
self-worth, 216–17
Seneca, 232
sex
  definition of by US Department of Health and Human Services, 31
  homosexual, 229–30
sexual
  ethics, Paul's, 163
  relations, extramarital, 42
  reproduction, 206, 210–11, 213
Shaw, Teresa, 162–63, 166
Sheridan, Vanessa, 102–5
shininess, bodies and, 181–82
Shore-Goss, Robert, 108, 112
SHU (secured housing units), 195
Sibyls, 17
silence, among trans population, 9
Simon/Peter, 130, 217
Sisera, 66–67, 73–74, 76–78
Sisera's mother
  domestic space of, 76
  emotional concern of, 78–79
  motherhood theme and, 67, 70–73
  passivity of, 74–75, 81
Snorton, C. Riley, 5–6, 10–11, 189, 193, 199, 213
social
  constructs, trans, 157–59
  location, 23
  transitions, 170–73
soulish body, 180–81
Soul of the Stranger, The: Reading God and Torah from a Transgender Perspective (Ladin), 22, 47, 55

souls/spirits. *See* spirits/souls
Spade, Dean, 11, 143, 187
Spencer-Hall, Alicia, 13, 89–90, 97
spirits/souls
  as authentic self-location, 204
  vs. body, in Jewish literature, 213–14
  vs. body, in John, 213–14
  as genderless, 205, 207
  Gospel of Thomas on, 203
  Jesus on, 206
  Paul's use of, 209
spiritual body, 180–81
Stanley, Eric, 10, 186
STAR (Street Transvestite Action Revolutionaries). *See* Street Transvestite Action Revolutionaries (STAR)
statue, figure with breasts and a beard, 125
Steinbock, Eliza, 177
Sterman, Judy Taubes, 72, 77
Stewart, Lindsey, 137
Stiller, Brian, 108–9
Stone, Ken, 15
Stone, Sandy, 4, 6–7, 9, 20
Stone Butch Blues (Feinberg), 16, 21
Stonewall uprising (1969), 4–5, 187–88
Strassfeld, Max K., 19, 22–23
Street Transvestite Action Revolutionaries (STAR), 5, 188
stress, physical results of, 177
Stryker, Susan, 3–4, 7–9, 157
Stuart, Rachel, 51–56, 61, 169
subversion, of gender binary, 20, 22, 39–40
suffering, human categorization and, 37–38
suicide, 103
support networks, 195–97. *See also* allyship
surgical practices. *See* medical care

Take Back the Word (Goss; West), 14–15
Taking a Chance on God (McNeill), 111
Tanis, Justin. *See* Sabia-Tanis, Justin
tannaitic literature, 18
Tatian, 119
teaching trans hermeneutics
  challenges of, 47–48
  gendered categories approach, 52–54
  trans/cis binary approach, 48–52
  trans-experience-centered approach (*See* trans-experience-centered approach, of trans hermeneutics)

television, trans representation in, 141. *See also* media, trans representation in
temporalities
  curvy time, 175–80
  queer vs. straight, 132, 137–38, 137n13
  transformative, as momentary vs. processual, 175–80
  transformative, in Paul, 174–75, 178–80
  transgender, 6–8, 12–13
  transition types and, 176–77
tents, 70, 76, 146
terminology, trans, 3–4, 8, 156
Terrill, JoAnne Marie, 143
TGIJP (Transgender, Gender Variant, and Intersex Justice Project). *See* Transgender, Gender Variant, and Intersex Justice Project (TGIJP)
Their Own Receive Them Not: African American Lesbians and Gays in Black Churches (Griffin), 146
"Themes in the Deborah Narrative (Judges 4-5)" (Sterman), 72
theophanies, 130
This Is My Body: Hearing the Theology of Transgender Christians, 17
Tigert, Leanne McCall, 17
time
  as curvy, 175–80
  queer vs. straight, 132, 137–38, 137n13
  See also temporalities
Tirabassi, Maren C., 17
Tiresias, 124–25
togas, 221–24, 230–31
torture, animal, 37
touch across time, about, 168n4
trancestors
  about, 12, 144n42
  Good Samaritan parable and, 105–6, 108
  importance of, 128
  Jesus as, 144, 148
  Moses and Elijah as, 128–29, 133
traniflesh, 143
trans*, 135, 135n1. *See also* transgender/transgender population
Trans and Genderqueer Subjects in Medieval Hagiography (Spencer-Hall; Gutt), 13, 89
Trans Care (Malantino), 222

Index of Subjects

trans-experience-centered approach, of trans hermeneutics, 54n13
   about, 54–55
   identity-defining roles, questioning, 62–63
   introduction to, 55–57
   pshat, focusing on, 60–62, 60n16, 61n18
   trans experience, recognizing, 58–60
Transfiguration of Jesus
   in apocrypha, 130
   baptism and resurrection and, 128, 128n55, 131–33
   body of Jesus and, 127–28
   clothing and, 128, 133
   gender transformations, ancient (*See* gender transformations, ancient)
   Mark and, 131
   metamorphosis, use of in antiquity, 118–21
   Moses and Elijah at, 128–29
   secrecy of, 131, 134
   See also metamorphoō/metamorphosis
transformations
   bodily, 207, 211–12, 213–14, 217 (*See also* bodily renewals, Gospel of Thomas and)
   clothing and (*See* clothing)
   glory and, 181–82
   temporality of, 174–80
   See also transitions
Transforming (Hartke), 17
Transgender, Gender Variant, and Intersex Justice Project (TGIJP), 187, 196
Transgender, Intersex, and Biblical Interpretation (Guest; Hornsby), 21
Trans-Gendered: Theology, Ministry, and Communities of Faith (Tanis), 16
Transgendering Faith (Tigert; Tirabassi), 17
Transgender Journeys (Mollenkott; Sheridan), 102–3
Transgender Studies Reader, The (Stryker; Whittle), 6–8, 128
Transgender Studies Reader 2 (Aizura, Stryker), 157
transgender/transgender people
   experience, 22, 59–60, 104
   experience, of Jacob (*See* Jacob)
   experience vs. transgender-specific experience, 48, 55, 58–60
   faith story inclusion and, 105–7
   gaze, 21–22
   Gospel of Thomas, response to, 214–17
   hospitality by, 111–12
   language and, 59, 121–22
   legislation (*See* legislation)
   modern thought on, 1–2
   multi-marginalized, 5–6, 216–17
   narrative of vs. transsexual narrative, 154–58, 154n9–154n10
   rights, in 1990s, 4
   sacred worth of, 106
   self-understanding process and, 215–17
   studies, 4–14, 21–22 (*See also* trans-experience-centered approach, of trans hermeneutics)
   as temporal, 6–8, 12–13
   terminology, 3–4, 8, 156
   trans/cis binary and, 48–52, 58
   See also trans-experience-centered approach, of trans hermeneutics
transing, about, 9–10, 32, 32n5
transitions
   changes from, 172
   deaths in, symbolic, 173–74
   from intelligible category to non-men, 162, 165–66
   men to women, in antiquity, 165–66
   process of, 137
   social, 157–59, 170–73
   women to men, in antiquity, 162–63
   See also transformations
transitivity, 136n7, 185, 189–94, 202
transphobia
   Christian, 31, 31n2, 41–44, 103–4, 109–10, 149
   creation accounts and, 41
   impact of, 104
   in Judaism, 39
   violence/murder and, 142
   See also discrimination
transsexuality, 152n2, 154–58, 154n9
transsexual vs. transgender narratives, 154–58, 154n9
Trans Talmud: Androgynes and Eunuchs in Rabbinic Literature (Strassfeld), 19, 22, 32
Trap Door (Burton, Stanley, Tourmaline), 186
Trible, Phyllis, 60
truth, 137, 140, 143, 148
tumtum, 18–19, 89
Turman, Eboni Marshall, 144

ukuhlanganisa, 136, 138–39, 149
understanding, human, 209–10, 214
unique creation, androgynes as, 39–40, 44, 44n45
Upson-Saia, Kristi, 220

Vashti, 92–93
veils, 118, 129
violence
   activism and, 114–15
   androgyne list and, 36–37
   of Black trans women, 41, 102, 140–43, 197, 199–200, 216–17
   Christian, 147
   by Jael (*See* Jael (killer of Sisera))
   modern, 1–2
   motherly, 77, 79–82
   murder, 36–37, 72, 79–81, 140–43, 173–74
   occurrence of, 103, 140
   rape, 123, 144, 144n39
   in schools, 102
   visibility and, 141, 186–87
visibility, 10, 141, 186–87, 206, 216

warfare, motherhood and, 79–81
Weekley, David, 110
Weheliye, Alexander, 23, 37
Weismantel, Mary, 8, 126, 128–29
wet-nurse, Mordecai as, 91–92
When Debroah Met Jael (Guest), 85
white supremacy, restroom regulations and, 41, 41n36

Whittle, Stephen, 6
widows, blind, 130
wild vs. domestication, 33–35
Wire, Antoinette Clark, 179, 182–83
wives. *See under* women
womanism, 23, 198
women
   androgynes functioning of, 36–39
   of color (*See* Black trans women)
   domestication of, 34
   domestic spaces of, 75–77
   erasure of, 43–44
   as inadequate to men, in antiquity, 162–63
   invisible standards of being, 121–22
   Jael, Deborah, and Sisera's mother as, 70–72
   Paul's treatment of, 191
   police targeting of, 11
   salvation and, 168, 168n2, 231
   unmarried, 72–73
   violence against, 41, 102, 140–43, 197, 199–200, 216
   as wives, 34, 68–69, 161–62, 161n34
   See also motherhood/mothers
Word to flesh transition, 11, 143–46
world-making/world's end, 10–11

Yahweh/YHWH. *See* God
"Y'All Better Quiet Down" (Rivera), 188, 196–97
Yee, Gale, 87
Yose (Rabbi), 39–40, 44
youth, 101–2, 106, 226

www.ingramcontent.com/pod-product-compliance
Lightning Source LLC
Chambersburg PA
CBHW022039290426
44109CB00014B/911